GEORGE WEISS

ALSO BY BURTON A. BOXERMAN
AND BENITA W. BOXERMAN
AND FROM MCFARLAND

*Jews and Baseball: Volume 1, Entering the American
Mainstream, 1871–1948* (2007; softcover 2016)

*Jews and Baseball: Volume 2, The Post-Greenberg
Years, 1949–2008* (2010; softcover 2016)

*Ebbets to Veeck to Busch: Eight Owners
Who Shaped Baseball* (2003)

GEORGE WEISS
Architect of the Golden Age Yankees

Burton A. Boxerman *and*
Benita W. Boxerman

McFarland & Company, Inc., Publishers
Jefferson, North Carolina

LIBRARY OF CONGRESS CATALOGUING-IN-PUBLICATION DATA

Names: Boxerman, Burton Alan, 1933– author. | Boxerman, Benita W., co-author.
Title: George Weiss : architect of the Golden Age Yankees / Burton A. Boxerman and Benita W. Boxerman.
Description: Jefferson, North Carolina : McFarland & Company, Inc., Publishers, 2016 | Includes bibliographical references and index.
Identifiers: LCCN 2016029382 | ISBN 9780786472536 (softcover : acid free paper) ∞
Subjects: LCSH: Weiss, George Martin, 1894–1972. | Baseball managers—United States—Biography. | New York Yankees (Baseball team)—History.
Classification: LCC GV865.W42 B69 2016 | DDC 796.357092 [B]—dc23
LC record available at https://lccn.loc.gov/2016029382

BRITISH LIBRARY CATALOGUING DATA ARE AVAILABLE

ISBN (print) 978-0-7864-7253-6
ISBN (ebook) 978-1-4766-2489-1

© 2016 Burton A. Boxerman and Benita W. Boxerman. All rights reserved

No part of this book may be reproduced or transmitted in any form or by any means, electronic or mechanical, including photocopying or recording, or by any information storage and retrieval system, without permission in writing from the publisher.

Front cover: George Weiss in an undated photograph (National Baseball Hall of Fame Library, Cooperstown, N.Y.)

Printed in the United States of America

McFarland & Company, Inc., Publishers
Box 611, Jefferson, North Carolina 28640
www.mcfarlandpub.com

Acknowledgments

We are grateful to many people who provided time, knowledge, and materials as we researched, wrote, and acquired pictures for this book. Many are referenced in the notes and bibliography, but we want to give special recognition to the following:

Our many friends, associates, and family who always seemed genuinely interested in the writing and contents of the book, and patiently allowed us to bore them with tales of progress when they asked, "How's the book on George Weiss coming along?"

Many members of SABR who not only followed the progress of the book but were willing and able to supply "tidbits" of information that helped make the book both more accurate and interesting.

Librarians and archivists at the St. Louis County Library, New Haven Public Library, New Haven Historical Society, Hillhouse High School and Yale University who provided us with material on George Weiss and obtained books for us through interlibrary loan.

For help in obtaining photographs for the book we are extremely grateful to Steve Steinberg; Dwayne Labakas; Maxwell Kates; Ken Roussey, National Baseball Hall of Fame Library; Charles Brown, St. Louis Mercantile Library at the University of Missouri–St. Louis; Jack Paulishen, James Hillhouse High School in New Haven; and Dave Kaplan, Yogi Berra Museum and Learning Center.

All of these individuals aided us along the way, and the book is better because of their generosity. For any errors that remain, however, we take responsibility.

Table of Contents

Preface	1
1—The Making of a Baseball Entrepreneur	3
2—Welcome to Professional Baseball	11
3—"Among the Happiest Times of My Life"	25
4—The Yankee Farmer	33
5—The Bears and the Blues	45
6—The Interregnum	60
7—The MacPhail Years	72
8—The Weiss Era Begins	83
9—The New Dynasty	95
10—Breaking the Yankees' Color Line	120
11—The Dynasty Resumes	133
12—The End of an Era	148
13—Back in the Game	157
14—The Mets Years	169
15—Final Innings	181
Chapter Notes	189
Bibliography	211
Index	219

Preface

The New York Yankees were the most successful franchise in major league baseball from the 1920s through 1964. One of their most impressive periods was the 12 seasons from 1949 to 1960, when the team captured the American League pennant ten times and became World Champions seven times. They were so good that there were constant demands from other team owners, sports writers, and fans to "break up the Yankees" and give the other AL clubs a chance. The seemingly indestructible Yankees even inspired a novel, *The Year the Yankees Lost the Pennant,* by Douglass Wallop, which was converted into the smash Broadway musical *Damn Yankees.*

Ask the average baseball fan what made those Yankees so dominant and most will come up with names such as Joe DiMaggio, Yogi Berra, Whitey Ford, Mickey Mantle, Ed Lopat, Hank Bauer—the list of great Yankees players during those years goes on and on. Some more knowledgeable fans might insist that those were the years when Casey Stengel was managing the team and that he was the reason the Yankees were so successful. But the sports pundits then and respected sports historians today credit as the real genius behind the team its general manager, a short, portly, often taciturn, and very shy man named George Martin Weiss.

George Weiss, a native of New Haven, Connecticut, loved baseball but he knew he did not have the ability to play the game. What he did have was the savvy to run a baseball team better than virtually anyone with whom he competed. According to his boyhood friends, George Weiss recognized this capability even before he was at New Haven's Hillhouse High, where he became the student manager of the school's championship baseball team.

After graduation, Weiss began his studies at Yale but was forced to leave during his first year because his father became ill and George had to run the family store. In contrast to his later character, as a young man Weiss was outgoing and able to talk convincingly with people far older than he as well as with his contemporaries. He persuaded some of the best players from his former high school team and some of the Yale players to form a semi-pro team, promising that he would set up the games and basically manage the team.

Using publicity and promotions, Weiss was so successful that his semi-pro Colonials soon outdrew the professional Class B Eastern League team in New Haven. Recognizing that they were unlikely to survive this competition, the Eastern League team's directors offered to sell the club to Weiss. Weiss borrowed the money, and in 1919, as one of the youngest owners in the game at that time, became a part of organized baseball. And as the saying goes, "the rest is history." After 50-plus years in organized ball, Weiss was inducted into Baseball's Hall of Fame for contributing "as much to baseball as any man the game could ever know."[1]

Despite the fact that George Weiss has been the subject of countless magazine and newspaper stories, there is no in-depth biography of the man, his accomplishments and his contributions to both the New York Yankees and the New York Mets. We hope this book, *George Weiss: Architect of the Golden Age Yankees* will fill that void. We also hope that you will enjoy the book and that after reading it, you will know why he so richly deserved the many honors he received, and how he achieved his lofty standing in the game he loved so long and so deeply.

1

The Making of a Baseball Entrepreneur

One Saturday afternoon, American journalist Damon Runyon was pondering the memorable features of covering a Yale football game. After a few moments, he wrote:

New Haven—what fond memories the name conjures—
Elms
The Campus
More elms.
George Weiss.[1]

Runyon was not exaggerating. For close to 30 years, New Haven, Connecticut, native George Martin Weiss was an integral part of the success of the New York Yankees. During his 15 years as farm club director and 13 years as general manager, the Yankees won 19 American League pennants and 15 World Series.[2] Weiss learned his love of baseball and first exhibited his skill in directing the game not in New York, but in his tradition-rich hometown of New Haven.

George Weiss was the son of Conrad Weiss and Anna Kapitzke Weiss. His father was born in Bavaria, Germany, in the town of Nuremberg, on March 21, 1864, one of five sons of Jeorge and Mary Koppman Weiss. Until he was 17, Conrad clerked in his father's general store, but being an ambitious youth, he felt that America offered him greater economic opportunities. He arrived in the United States in 1882 and located at Milltown, New Jersey, where he worked in a rubber factory for two years. He spent two more years doing the same kind of work in Long Island, and in 1886, left Long Island and settled in New Haven, Connecticut.[3]

Like many cities in the eastern United States, New Haven attracted a large number of European immigrants. German immigrants first came to the United States in significant numbers during the 1840s and 1850s. A few decades later, the rise of Prussia, accompanied by wars against Austria, Denmark and France, produced conditions in central Europe which helped encourage immigration to the New World. Thus after the Civil War more Germans joined those who had already settled in New Haven two decades earlier.[4]

After working in the Candee Rubber factory for two years and clerking in a grocery store for three years, Conrad Weiss opened his own grocery and meat market in 1891 at 485 Chapel Street. On June 26, 1891, Conrad married Anna Kapitzke, a first-generation United States citizen and daughter of August Kapitzke, a native of Germany. Conrad and Anna lived at 501 Chapel Street, a few blocks from their business. Conrad became active politically and was elected an alderman from the Sixth Ward, where he had bipartisan support for his advocacy of a wharfage law, which allowed New Haven to own all of the city's wharfage rights. Conrad Weiss was also an active member of the Retail Butchers and Grocers Association.[5]

The marriage produced three children—sons George and Edwin, and a daughter, Florence.[6] George, the oldest of the three children, was born June 23, 1894.[7] He received his elementary education at Orange Street School. While attending grammar school in New Haven, George Weiss became close friends with Jacob Podoloff, and both attended Hillhouse High School. Jacob, along with his brothers Maurice and Nathan, also graduates of Hillhouse High, and their father, Abraham, created the New Haven Eagles hockey team as a charter member of the Canadian-American Hockey League.[8] In addition to serving as president of the AHL, Maurice Podoloff was later appointed president of the newly formed Basketball Association of America, which ultimately merged with the National Basketball League to become the National Basketball Association.[9] Maurice graduated from Hillhouse in 1909 and, almost 100 years later, was inducted into the Hillhouse Athletic Hall of Fame in 2008; Weiss, a 1911 Hillhouse graduate, was inducted into the Hall of Fame the following year.[10]

Over 40 years after Weiss graduated from Hillhouse, Harold Rosenthal, a columnist for the *New York Herald Tribune*, wrote Jacob Podoloff, who was still a resident of New Haven, inquiring about members of George Weiss's graduating class. Podoloff replied, explaining that while he hardly remembered the names of the 1911 graduating class, he well remembered George Weiss, as he and George not only attended the same school, they lived in the same neighborhood. Conrad Weiss's store was only two blocks from Jacob's house.

> George and I played on a basketball team in grammar school. We were both guards and we had a certain tenacity which enabled us to play that position fairly well. But even in those days, George showed that he was a born manager because in no time at all he was the manager of that basketball team, and while he and I were probably the worst players on the squad, George was a prominent figure on the team from the start and somehow the team gravitated about him. This is an interesting sideline on the man's ability from the start to recognize talent, strategy etc.; and the fact that his own athletic ability was less than those about him didn't prevent him from handling the team in an efficient manner.[11]

Podoloff informed Rosenthal that Conrad's store was an excellent vehicle, which allowed George to implement both his use of promotion and public relations. "His father's store served us well. He used to butter up some of the guys with some of that good old Holland and Swiss chocolate. In any event, I know he had no enemies on the squad and he made things go smoothly with his easy way. So, you see that talent for managing and recognizing other talent etc.; originated even earlier than Hillhouse. In fact, I think it is an inborn quality."[12]

George Weiss's alma mater, Hillhouse High School, New Haven's oldest public high school, was founded in 1859. The school adopted the nickname "The Academics" to recognize the school's very close relationship with Yale University.[13] The school changed its name from New Haven High School to Hillhouse High School to honor James Hillhouse of New Haven, who represented Connecticut in both houses of Congress.[14] During Weiss's years at Hillhouse, the school was considered excellent academically, attracting competent, college-bound students. The vast majority of its graduates attended Yale, which during the first decades of the 20th century was less cosmopolitan than at the present time.[15]

George Weiss's senior class book indicates both the scope of his activities at Hillhouse and his popularity. He was associate editor of the school's newspaper, *Focus*; a member of both the Freshman and Sophomore Debating Society; and a manager of the all-class basketball team in 1910–1911, as well as managing the senior team. In the senior class poll, Weiss was voted "Our Best Natured," a student who "would laugh at any sort of a joke." He indicated that he would enroll at Yale and declared his future occupation—journalist.[16]

Although George Weiss played basketball during his early years in both grammar and high school, he was to make his mark in another sport—baseball. Weiss admitted that he had not been much of a ball player. "My class team in high school was as far as I ever got, but in my senior year I was selected as manager of the varsity team." Weiss wryly noted that the only reason he was allowed to play on the excellent Hillhouse baseball team was that he agreed to be its manager.[17] "This position," he admitted, "proved to be the opening wedge for me."[18]

Although New Haven was never home to a major league team, baseball's popularity grew after the Civil War. The first recorded baseball game involving a New Haven team was played in 1865, nearly three decades before Weiss was born. In that game, Yale defeated Wesleyan, 39–13. As baseball's popularity grew in New Haven, the Intercollegiate Baseball Association was formed in 1880. This Association consisted of six teams: Amherst, Brown, Dartmouth, Harvard, Princeton, and Yale. Two years after the Association was formed, Yale won the Intercollegiate championship.[19]

In addition to competing against other universities, Yale began scheduling games against major league teams. Its 1884 schedule included games against the Philadelphia Athletics and New York Metropolitans of the American Association, and the Boston Beaneaters and Cleveland Blues of the National League.[20]

At the beginning of the 20th century, professional baseball came to New Haven. The Connecticut State League was formed in 1899 and later changed its name to the Connecticut League, operating as a Class D league with teams in eight cities. In 1905, the league became Class B; it existed until the end of the 1912 season. The next season, the Connecticut League became the Eastern Association due to several teams outside of the state entering the league. Also a Class B league, the Eastern Association lasted only two years. In 1915, the team called itself the New Haven Max Feds and joined the newly created Colonial League. That affiliation ended in a year and New Haven then rejoined the Eastern League as the New Haven Murlins.[21] It was in the Eastern League where George Weiss would begin his more than five-decade career in professional baseball.

Although Weiss graduated from Hillhouse in 1911, he did not enter Yale until 1913, most likely to help his father, who was in poor health, run the family grocery store. Weiss remained at Yale only until February 1914. Conrad Weiss passed away on September

23, 1915, at the age of 45. According to his obituary, "his death was not unexpected, although the end came suddenly."[22] There were rumors that prior to Conrad's death, George Weiss was seriously considering pursuing his stated goal of becoming a journalist by taking a course at the Columbia School of Journalism. Because of his father's illness, however, he had to take over the business and remain in New Haven.[23] Conrad's death left George Weiss the head of the family, supporting his mother, brother and sister. When he registered for the draft on June 5, 1917, he specifically asked to be exempted on the grounds that his family's income depended on his operating the store.[24] He never served in any branch of America's armed forces.

Although he spent only one semester at Yale, Weiss was always considered a member of the "Class of 1917." Every year until his death, he was asked to update his vita for the Alumni Records Office. On the golden anniversary of what would have been the year of his graduation, his resume was prominently featured in the class history.[25]

From the moment Weiss graduated from Hillhouse, he began to demonstrate his acumen as a baseball mogul by organizing a semi-pro team. Weiss had a brainstorm—

Barely out of his teens, George Weiss (top row, first on left) rounded up a core of players from his former high school and added others to form a semi-pro team, the New Haven Colonials. At an early age Weiss was already displaying his baseball entrepreneurial skills (National Baseball Hall of Fame Library, Cooperstown, New York).

keep his powerful high school team together, add players from the Yale baseball team, and turn it into a semi-pro barnstorming unit, the New Haven Colonials.[26] "I approached the guys," said Weiss, "and suggested that we play some semi-pro ball. I told them that if they played, I'd make the dates."[27]

The team included other college athletes like Charley Brickley and Eddie Mahan of Harvard. Brickley, a high school classmate of George's, was known for both his football and basketball skills.[28] The most outstanding Hillhouse graduate to play for Weiss, however, was "Jumping" Joe Dugan. Dugan, the captain of Hillhouse's baseball team in 1916, debuted with the Philadelphia Athletics in 1917, played 14 years in the majors, including 6½ with the New York Yankees, and retired from professional baseball with a career batting mark of .280.[29]

One of the reasons Weiss organized his team as semi-pro was that it gave him a definite financial advantage over professional baseball teams. He deliberately scheduled most of his games on Sundays, the day when baseball's Blue Law prohibited organized baseball from playing on the Sabbath. Weiss's scheduling was particularly detrimental to New Haven's professional team in the Eastern League.[30]

Weiss quickly learned that there were many other differences between semi-professional and professional baseball. In their earliest days, the Colonials had no automobiles. The players usually got to the ballparks on either their bicycles or horse-drawn grocery carts. They soon graduated to the trolley. Each player was responsible for carrying his own equipment. Weiss not only managed the team, he also served as correspondent for the local newspapers. "They were happy to pay my expenses in return for accounts of the game," confessed Weiss.[31]

The Colonials' early opponents were not exactly household names. They played the Humphrey Athletic Club, the Highwood Outlaws, the Branford Hustlers, the Woodmen of the World, and even the Asylum.[32]

Weiss obtained a lease for the Colonials at Lighthouse Point Park, an amusement park just outside New Haven. Its main attraction was that it was not regulated by the Blue Laws that prohibited games on Sundays. Weiss immediately began to schedule games with some inferior, but rather attention-getting opponents for his Colonials. They ranged from a Chinese University team to a Bloomer Girls team, and from the House of David to the traveling Cubans.[33]

As a young man, Weiss was not shy about making any contacts that he felt would benefit his team. In 1915, the first year Colonel Jacob Ruppert co-owned the New York Yankees, Weiss talked the beer baron into playing a contest in the Polo Grounds when the team returned from spring training in Florida. Weiss recalled, "It was the coldest day in the history of the world. The game drew fewer than 100 paid admissions and our share of the gate was $10.00 and change. I thought that Harry Sparrow, the Yankee business manager who gave me the game, was a veritable god, and the whole prospect of baseball promotion began to fascinate me."[34]

For a while, Weiss felt that the Colonials might defeat the Yankees. His spitball pitcher, Pie Way, held the Yankees scoreless for four innings. By the seventh inning, however, the Yankees had scored five runs and the field announcer declared that the visitors "had to catch a train." Despite the loss, Weiss was elated about the day's activities. Not only did the New Haven newspapers make it sound as if the Colonials had won the game, but Weiss had the satisfaction of knowing that no other baseball club in the area, including the Murlins, the local Eastern League team, had actually played a game in the Polo Grounds, as the Colonials had.[35]

That was the last time a semi-pro outfit played a big league team in its ballpark. "Ruppert never forgot the frost or the sales talk I gave him," Weiss stated years later. "He hired me in 1932."[36]

Pleased with the publicity the Colonials received in the New Haven press, Weiss was anxious to reward the fans by bringing top-notch talent to Lighthouse Point. Weiss scheduled a number of games for the Colonials against Yale. The Yale Elis were always a good draw and when they played the Colonials, Weiss could be assured of a large crowd. On March 31, 1917, Weiss enticed major league pitcher Chief Bender, who was completing a 16-year career in the majors, to pitch for the Colonials, but the Elis defeated the Colonials, 10–2. One of the hitting stars for Yale was first baseman Prescott Bush, who got two doubles off the future Hall of Famer. Bush went on to become a senator from Connecticut and the father of future United States president George H. W. Bush.[37]

Weiss was not bashful about raiding both the major leagues and the Eastern League in bringing players to Lighthouse Point. He held parades through the streets of New Haven, welcoming professional ball players visiting to compete with his Colonials.[38]

Weiss also used his entrepreneurial skills in bringing the highest quality of baseball to the fans of New Haven, and was able to turn the misfortune of others to his own advantage. In 1914–1915, the Federal League operated as a "third major league" in competition with the established American and National Leagues. This upstart league refused to abide by the National Agreement on player contracts employed by organized baseball. Its competitors, therefore, dubbed it "an outlaw league." This pejorative didn't bother the Federals. In fact, they used their outlaw status to recruit players from established clubs and to create baseball teams in or close to established major and minor league cities, imposing a financial hardship on teams unable to compete with them. The Federal League battle forced the New Haven White Wings, as they were now called, of the Eastern League to quit organized baseball for the 1915 season. The White Wings' misfortune left the field wide open for George Weiss and his New Haven Colonials. With no professional baseball in New Haven, Weiss began to book major league clubs for exhibition games. To meet this type of competition, however, Weiss had to build a stronger, more competitive team, and as the Colonials prospered, his reputation as a baseball entrepreneur began to spread among major league moguls.[39]

Fans in New Haven were fortunate to see many of baseball's outstanding players, including three of its greatest stars, all of whom were later elected to baseball's Hall of Fame—Ty Cobb, Walter Johnson and Babe Ruth. All three were helpful to Weiss by tipping him off to good young prospects. Walter Johnson remained a close friend of Weiss until the former Senators star died in 1946.[40]

One of the greatest thrills for New Haven fans occurred in 1916. Three days after the Boston Red Sox won the World Series, defeating the Brooklyn Robins in five games, Weiss infuriated American League President Ban Johnson by persuading the Red Sox to play an exhibition game against his Colonials. Ty Cobb played first base for the Colonials, and Babe Ruth was one of the Red Sox pitchers.[41] The game ended in a 3–3 tie.

Although Ban Johnson had been unable to prevent the game, he retaliated against the Red Sox by fining each of the participants the exact amount they had received for taking part in the game.[42] As a consequence, baseball adopted a rule forbidding more than three players from any club to appear in a "barnstorming" game.[43]

But Cobb continued making appearances at New Haven. He was a fan favorite, and when he appeared in a Colonials uniform, Weiss could always count on increasing the attendance. Whenever the Tigers had an open date at either Boston or New York, Cobb would don a Colonials uniform and play for Weiss, at first insisting on a $350 guarantee to make the trip to New Haven. When Weiss voluntarily paid him $800, Cobb was impressed and came back often—with no written guarantees.[44]

For the most part, 1918 was not a very good year for the sports scene in New Haven. Early in the year, Weiss had to build almost a completely new Colonials team overnight, because the Yale athletic authorities passed a rule barring undergraduates from playing Sunday ball. In addition, the Eastern League suspended operations in July, and soon after Yale football followed suit as many Elis athletes were drafted.[45] This did not discourage Weiss, for he immediately hustled down to Boston and signed a number of players from a Boston Navy Yard team to appear every Sunday at Lighthouse Park.

The team was run by Jack Barry, a major league shortstop/second baseman, who played for the Philadelphia Athletics and Boston Red Sox from 1908 to 1917, and returned to Boston in 1919 after spending 1918 in the armed services. It also included pitcher Ernie Shore, whose major league career spanned seven years for the Giants, Red Sox and Yankees; shortstop/second baseman Rabbit Maranville, who played in the majors for 23 years beginning in 1912; and Herb Pennock, who won 240 games in a career lasting over two decades with the Athletics, Red Sox and Yankees.[46]

Barry's players did not appear at Lighthouse Park every Sunday, since six of the players were in the United States Army in 1918. Weiss himself was not dodging his war responsibilities, for he was trying to get into the flying corps, but he failed his physical exam and was never drafted.[47]

Weiss's last major coup as owner of the New Haven Colonials was to schedule an exhibition game on July 7, 1918, between the Chicago White Sox, the 1917 World Champions, and the Colonials. The semi-pro Colonials overcame a three-run deficit in the seventh inning to stun the White Sox at Lighthouse Park, 4–3. Although the White Sox had lost their best players to the draft (no other major league team had lost as many), and several prominent Chisox players took the day off, the New Haven fans were delighted. Not only did their Colonials win the game, but among those who did play for the White Sox was future Hall of Famer Eddie Collins, considered by many baseball historians the greatest second baseman in the game's history. His 3,315 hits currently place him tenth in career hits.[48]

George Weiss finished his semi-pro managerial career in 1918. From the moment he conceived the idea of bringing major league teams to Lighthouse Park or taking his team to major league cities, Weiss would visit the newspaper offices and inform the sportswriters about coming attractions. One wrote that Weiss was adamant in not wanting to play any local teams for any city title. His only interest was the "big stuff," generally meaning that playing exhibition games "was his particular line." As one New Haven writer frequently noted, "He [Weiss] is a business man through and through and knows where the money is. The fans are strong for him and his attractions."[49]

The following year George Weiss took his entrepreneurial expertise one step higher—professional baseball. Weiss later recalled, "The New Haven club apparently decided to stop fighting us. They came to me and said, 'You want to buy the club for $5,000?' I had to borrow the $5,000, but I did."[50]

2

Welcome to Professional Baseball

In 1919, the owner of the Murlins, the New Haven professional baseball team in the Eastern League, decided to sell the franchise to George Weiss for a number of reasons. The team was virtually bankrupt. It had been forced to disband in 1915 because of the incursion of the Federal League into organized baseball. The Murlins also lacked a decent playing facility and, although its players were supposedly professionals, the team's performance on the field was hardly of professional caliber. The outbreak of World War I, which took players and cut into earnings and leisure time, caused minor league baseball to suffer greatly. Finally, the Murlins' owners admitted that they were overmatched in trying to compete with George Weiss. When he acquired the New Haven team, Weiss became a legitimate part of professional baseball. At the age of 24, Weiss was the youngest club owner in organized baseball.[1]

Weiss's purchase of the Murlins came as a mild surprise to many, even though his interest in the franchise had been mentioned frequently. He immediately announced that he intended to play most of his home games in New Haven in a new ballpark he was building that would be ready before the 1920 season began. On Sundays, however, his team would play its regular league games at Lighthouse Park, so that he could continue to bring in major league teams. "There will be a number of open dates on which major league teams can come here, but the exciting race which I expect in the Eastern League will make the regular championship games welcome and attractive for the crowd."[2]

On May 3, 1919, Weiss received formal transfer of the organization from Edward J. Dugan, the Murlins' owner for the past two years. Weiss immediately began working on improving the team.[3] He hired former New York Giants star catcher and one of the smartest men in baseball, John "Chief" Meyers, as manager of the New Haven team, now to be known as the Weissmen. Weiss announced that Meyers would not only manage the Weissmen, he would also handle the bulk of the team's catching, making him New Haven's first player-manager since Jerry Connell handled both jobs from 1912 to 1914.[4]

On May 14, 1919, George Weiss fielded his first professional baseball team.[5] The city of New Haven could now boast it had a professional baseball team with a new owner, a new manager and a new name, plus the Eastern League was elevated from Class B to Class A. The city's professional baseball team would undergo numerous name changes, but from 1919 until the end of the 1932 season, it would field a Class A minor league professional baseball team.[6]

In addition to his efforts to improve the team, Weiss continued his successful promotions to bring out the fans. A favorite promotion was exhibition games against big league stars. On two consecutive Sundays in September, Weiss scheduled games against some of the most talented and popular major leaguers of the day. The first pitted the Weissmen against an array of major leaguers including Walter Johnson, George Sisler, Harry Hooper and Baby Doll Jacobson.[7] The following week, Weiss persuaded Walter Johnson to pitch for his New Haven Weissmen against the Boston Braves, whose lineup included Rabbit Maranville, Johnny Rawlings, Hank Gowdy, and Walker Holke.[8] As a result of these two games, George Weiss and Walter Johnson became very close friends.

At the end of June, Meyers resigned as manager, and former manager Danny Murphy returned to manage for the remainder of the season. The Weissmen ended the 1919 season with a record of 47–62, finishing in seventh place in an eight-team league.[9] Still, 1919 was one of only two years that a Weiss-owned team in the Eastern League did not win a pennant or finish in the first division. In fact, many baseball statisticians argue that since Weiss did not own the Weissmen for the complete year, 1919 should not be included in this assessment.

One bright spot for Weiss was that despite the poor showing of his club, he did well financially; his promotions helped draw people to the ballpark, allowing him to sell the grocery store he had inherited from his father. He used this money to pay off all of his debts by the end of his first year in professional baseball.[10]

Demonstrating his business savvy, Weiss, as franchise owner and self-appointed president of the team, incorporated the New Haven club with a capital stock of $180,000.[11] Weiss was able to induce major league players to invest in his team. Walter Johnson purchased $5,000 worth of stock, but did not take an active part in the management of the team.[12] Ty Cobb, another friend of Weiss, who was promoted to manager of the Detroit Tigers in 1921, also became a stockholder in Weiss's New Haven team. He bought a small interest in the franchise, but the amount was never disclosed.[13]

Weiss had another method of raising money to operate his team in New Haven and show a yearly profit. Weiss was always able to find customers more than eager to purchase his key players. Clark Griffith, owner of the Washington Senators, was one of Weiss's best customers. He purchased pitcher Harry Courtney during the 1919 season. Courtney won 13 games for Weiss but only three games for Griffith.[14] Pitcher Mule Watson was sold to the Boston Braves in 1920.[15] Other teams purchased players from Weiss's New Haven teams, including the Cleveland Indians, Connie Mack's Philadelphia Athletics, and the Chicago Cubs.[16] Weiss's penchant for finding good ballplayers and eventually selling them for a profit was a talent he would employ for the remainder of his baseball career.

After the miserable finish in 1919, Weiss was determined to build a winning team for 1920 and beyond. He had made many contacts during his years in the semi-pros, and he was constantly in touch with baseball men all over the East who acted as his informal scouts. Two outstanding Cleveland Indians, outfielder Tris Speaker and pitcher "Smoky" Joe Wood, often went hunting with Weiss, and they never hesitated to recommend players with potential to him.[17] Speaker highly recommended two players who were unable to make the Indians' roster, one a Cuban pitcher and the other a southpaw who had starred on the University of Vermont nine. While neither made the New Haven roster, this demonstrates the friendships and baseball connections Weiss was making in only his second year in the Eastern League.[18]

Weiss's most important acquisition in 1920 was the hiring of Charles Albert "Chief" Bender, one of the great pitchers of the early 20th century, as the team's manager. Bender, a future Hall of Famer with a lifetime record of 212–127, had pitched from 1903 to 1917, primarily with the Philadelphia Athletics.[19]

Bender was no stranger to George Weiss or to New Haven. He had pitched for Weiss's New Haven Colonials in previous years. Weiss hired Bender not only as his manager, but indicated that he would also pitch for the Weissmen. His battery-mate would be New Haven's former manager-catcher, John "Chief" Meyers. The two men constituted the only Native American battery in the country.[20] Because of the presence of both Bender and Meyers, the New Haven Weissmen were renamed the Indians in 1920. The New Haven club would retain that name until the end of the 1922 season, even though both Bender and Meyers were no longer a part of the franchise after 1921.[21]

At the beginning of 1920, 26-year-old George Weiss had accomplished much and his future looked rosy. He owned a professional baseball team in his home town of New Haven, managed by the popular Chief Bender who could help attract players for the Indians.[22] He demonstrated his business savvy by incorporating his New Haven franchise with the financial aid of such luminaries as Ty Cobb and Walter Johnson.[23] It was now time to give the fans a ballpark they could be proud of.

Completed early in 1920, the Indians' new park, naturally named Weiss Park, was located near the Yale Bowl and was the largest in the Eastern League. The new field covered six acres and was configured to divert pedestrians from vehicular traffic. The grass infield led to the players' dugouts and, in turn, to dressing rooms for both teams. A press stand with wire facilities was located directly in back of the catcher's box. The park contained 3,000 "modern" seats, including a number of box seats.[24]

The Sporting News called Weiss Park "the largest and best equipped from every point of view in the Eastern League and will not suffer by comparison with many in the major leagues." It added that with Chief Bender leading the team and "with George Weiss, that live wire, at the helm as president of the club, New Haven is sure to be in the running all the time."[25]

Weiss loved his role as the owner of New Haven's professional baseball team and took great pride in his new ballpark as well. He could be found in his "owner's box" where he was close enough to the umpire to peer over his shoulder. When he felt the umpire's call went against the Indians, Weiss would often jump out of his seat and attempt to prove the official wrong.[26]

On one occasion, Weiss argued a large number of calls. Finally, the umpire could take no more, especially since he felt that Weiss's remarks were becoming too personal. The umpire called time and walked back to Weiss's box, informing him that if he continued his tirade, he would punch the owner in the nose. The five-foot, eight-inch Weiss rose to his feet and told the umpire he was ready to "take him on." Once the game was over and the umpire seemed to have forgotten the challenge, Weiss was quite thankful and went straight home.[27]

As a minor league owner, Weiss not only took pride in his ballpark, he also took pride in his players and often got close to them. When major league ballplayers in the 1920s traveled from city to city, they enjoyed the comfort of sleeping cars on their longer trips. In the minors, players had no such luxuries—they were forced to ride on day coaches, an uncomfortable mode of travel on long road trips.

Beginning in 1923, George Weiss thought he found a better way for his players to travel. He purchased two large touring cars for his players while he made the trips in his Packard. Weiss's players enjoyed touring the East in comparative comfort. On most trips, some of the players were able to ride with Weiss and listen to him reminisce about his family, how he had enjoyed working in his father's grocery store, and his plans for helping his younger brother and sister.

Sammy Hyman, Weiss's closest friend on the team, was one of his pitchers from 1923 to 1928, and the only player he allowed to drive his car. Hyman, who never reached the major leagues, was one of the few players with whom Weiss would share his most private thoughts and ambitions. Never during his entire career as a major league executive did George Weiss become so close to a player.[28]

Hyman was not the only New Haven player who recalled Weiss's closeness to his players. In 1926, 19-year-old rookie Joe Cronin was optioned to New Haven after four appearances for the Pittsburgh Pirates, all as a pinch runner. Weiss remembered that Cronin was a well-behaved player who was always eager and usually appeared at the ballpark early. Cronin played only the 1926 season for Weiss and hit .320 in 66 games. Although Cronin played only briefly for New Haven, Weiss admired him and remarked, "I never saw a young ball player with more ambition." He predicted that some day Cronin would be a big-league star.[29]

Cronin also had fond memories of George Weiss, recalling that the New Haven mogul drove a Cadillac, one of two cars used by the team to transport the players to New Haven's road games. The other was a Hudson which belonged to John Flynn, the manager. "On the days we won," recollected Cronin, "everybody tried to climb into the Caddy because we knew George was going to pick up the dinner checks. When we lost, everybody ran for the Hudson."[30] Weiss and Cronin would later become close friends and rivals, each man running a major league baseball team. Weiss's attitude and reputation towards his players at New Haven was in stark contrast to his later reputation as a man of silence, cold, taciturn, and unsympathetic to his players.[31]

The young George Weiss differed in other ways from the Weiss who would one day run a major league team with a strong hand and a tight fist. As a young man, Weiss was considered a visionary and idealist, a club owner determined to build his team upon sportsmanship and sentiment, rather than upon a commercial basis. He felt that the Eastern League should lead the way in promoting a sentimental value to the teams rather than a commercialized amusement enterprise so prominent in other leagues.[32] Weiss's sentimentality went only so far. After his New Haven team finished in seventh place in 1919, he was determined never again to end up in the second division, a resolution he kept with one exception, until he retired as general manager of the New York Yankees.

Weiss was also financially successful, in large part because he sold more players to the majors and higher-level minor league classifications than the rest of the Eastern

League owners combined. He also boasted that he had established, without being aware of it, a kind of private "bird-dog" organization of his own. "I knew what a kid here looked like, and what another one there might do."[33]

One of Weiss's early sales occurred in the 1921 season when he sold Enoch "Ginger" Shinault, New Haven catcher, to the Cleveland Indians. The price of $10,000 was said to be the highest ever paid for an Eastern League player.[34]

George Weiss seemed to relish the action in the minors, something he almost never did in the major leagues. Once he settled in as New Haven president, Weiss attended every game, yelling encouragement to his players and celebrating their victories while suffering with them during their losses. In addition, he also delighted in creating new ways to involve the fans and publicize his team. Youngsters who promised they would not smoke before the age of 21 were invited to join his "knothole gang" so they could attend New Haven games. He prepared a booklet which attempted to explain the game of baseball to women. He hired clowns to entertain fans before the first pitch was thrown, and he encouraged organized rooting, urging fans to bring banners to the ballpark and wave them to help motivate the players. To publicize his New Haven teams, he invited big-city sportswriters and celebrities from New York to come to New Haven, with Weiss financing their travel and lodging expenses. Much to Weiss's pleasure, the "expense" checks were often returned because the guests told Weiss, "The party itself was worth the trip."[35]

In 1920, Chief Bender took the 1919 seventh-place New Haven Weissmen to first place with a record of 79–61.[36] The major leagues kept an eye on Bender and his Weissmen; during the 1920 season, George Weiss refused the New York Yankees' offer of $25,000 for his manager.[37] Not only did the 36-year-old Bender lead the Weissmen to a first-place finish, he ended the season with a pitching record of 25–12.[38]

At the conclusion of the season, Weiss made a number of announcements. He indicated that beginning in 1921, New Haven would become a farm club of Ty Cobb's team, the Detroit Tigers.[39] He also announced that when New Haven was prepared to raise its 1920 pennant flag at Weiss Park, he would invite the Springfield team, which finished in second place, to attend the ceremonies. "I think it would be a graceful thing to do," said Weiss.[40]

Things did not go as well in 1921. The Indians trailed most of the season and ended in only fourth place. In addition, there was no streetcar service, the method most fans used to get to Weiss Park. Nonetheless, the team drew almost 15,000 attendees, making it another good financial year for Weiss.[41]

During the off-season, there was talk of reducing the number of the games in the 1922 scheduled season from 154 to 140. Weiss was adamantly opposed to that suggestion, insisting that the League keep up its present standard. He maintained that it would get easier to obtain ball players with a 154-game schedule than it would be if only 140 were played. "Don't go back to the Trolley League days," argued Weiss. "Keep the league up to the present standard. Just because a few clubs lost money due to falling off business in the latter part of the season is no reason why we should cut the schedule."[42]

During the winter of 1921, Chief Bender left the New Haven Indians to manage another Eastern League team, the Reading Phillies.[43] His departure was no surprise as it had been long rumored that Weiss didn't intend to rehire Bender for the 1922 season.[44]

On the advice of Ty Cobb, his friend and a team shareholder, Weiss hired William E. "Wild Bill" Donovan to manage the New Haven team.[45] Donovan was an experienced manager. He had piloted the New York Yankees from 1915 to 1917 and the Philadelphia Nationals in 1921.[46] Donovan was nicknamed "Wild Bill" because of the many bases on balls he had given up when he was a big league pitcher. But as a major league manager, he had the misfortune of being in the wrong place at the wrong time. He managed the Yankees after Jacob Ruppert and Cap Huston purchased the team, but before the team acquired its great players.[47] Donovan was let go after the end of the 1917 season.[48] Ruppert apologized for firing Donovan, a fan favorite. "I still think that barring injuries and hard luck Bill Donovan would have brought the Yankees their first pennant. The hardest thing I ever had to do was release him."[49]

Despite their fourth-place finish in 1921, Weiss was confident that with his new manager, the Indians could win the pennant again in 1922, and he immediately began putting together the players to accomplish that feat. He re-acquired the popular Eddie Eayrs, whom he had earlier sent to Brooklyn.[50] He then signed hurler Dominic Mulrenan from the Chicago White Sox, and Louis A. Malone, former Brooklyn Robins third baseman.

In 1920 Malone had been banished from organized baseball by Commissioner Kenesaw Landis for deserting the Robins and accepting managerial jobs with two teams in the Steel League in Pennsylvania. Commissioner Landis reinstated Malone because of his splendid war record overseas in France, where he had served with a machine gun battalion for two years.

With his reinstatement, Malone reported back to the Robins, but Charles Ebbets sold him to New Haven for what Weiss called "quite a sum of money." Weiss needed Malone to fill the opening created by the departure of third sacker Neal Ball, who left to manage the Augusta club in the Virginia League. With an infield of Malone, Elmer Bowman, Guy Lacy and Marty Shay, Weiss was confident that his Indians would once again win the pennant.[51]

The Indians finished the 1922 season with a record of 100–51, winning both the league title and the Little World Series.[52] The Little World Series consisted of a three-game set, pitting George Weiss's Indians against the pennant-winning team in the International League, the Baltimore Orioles. The third and deciding game, played in bitter cold, saw the Indians score six runs in the bottom of the ninth to win the Series, two games to one, with the deciding run driven in by Lew Malone. Newspaper accounts of the final game emphasized that when Gene Martin scored the winning run, he was almost instantly lost in a mob of hysterical "natives," George Weiss among them. "The man who hit the ball, Lew Malone, dutifully completed his jaunt, placing his foot plunk in the middle of second base, with not an umpire watching."[53]

Weiss considered his 1922 Indians one of his best teams. He had an excellent battery in Johnny Cooney pitching and Jimmy Wilson catching. Cooney won 19 and lost only three for Weiss's champs, had arm trouble when promoted to the majors, and was sent back down to the minors. He later became a top outfielder for the Braves, and later a valued coach for the White Sox. Wilson went on to star with the Phillies, Reds and Cardinals, and later managed the Phillies and Cubs.[54]

In his later years, George Weiss shunned parties and the social scene, but in 1922 he was not yet 30 years old and his team had just won the Little World Series. In January 1924 Weiss hosted a banquet at New Haven's plushest hotel, the Hotel Taft, to celebrate the victory and honor his team's manager, "Wild Bill" Donovan. The guests included a panoply of baseball giants, including President John A. Heydler of the National League, Babe Ruth and Weiss's high school classmate, Joe Dugan, of the Yankees, Frank Frisch of the Giants, Joe Wood, former Red Sox and Cleveland Indians pitcher and the current Yale University baseball coach, and a large delegation of baseball writers. Weiss's special guest of honor was Commissioner Landis. Even at this age, when Weiss was called on to speak, his face turned scarlet. He managed to "choke out one or two words" and was rescued by the toastmaster.[55]

The 1923 season was as notable for events off the field as for the action on the diamond. Weiss rehired Donovan as his manager, but he also made a number of changes. With the departure of both "Chiefs," New Haven changed the team name from the Indians to the Profs.[56] Although he was still financially sound, Weiss began to focus on conserving finances. He eliminated spring training in the South, announcing that spring training would begin at Weiss Park about April 1.[57] He also intended to make extra profit for the team by booking some exhibition games with Yale University, games which had proved quite profitable when he owned the Colonials.[58]

Weiss also continued a practice begun with the Colonials of bringing major league stars to play in exhibition games with his team, a tactic which benefited both the players and his local fan base. In the summer of 1923, Weiss offered Yankees owner Jacob Ruppert a $3,000 guarantee if he would bring his pennant-winners, including the mighty Babe Ruth, to New Haven for an exhibition game. It would be the second game of a doubleheader following a regularly scheduled Eastern League game.[59] As soon as Ruppert agreed, Weiss began publicizing the event, employing parades, posters and newspaper ads, to let every fan in Connecticut know that Ruth was coming to New Haven.

On the day of the game, Ruth was a no-show. The Yankees slugger, it seems, decided to go fishing with teammate Joe Bush. Weiss went through with the game and then informed Yankees general manager Ed Barrow that he had no intention of paying the Yankees the full $3,000 financial guarantee because of Ruth's absence. The fuming Barrow went running to Commissioner Landis, but to no avail. Weiss argued that he planned to reimburse the 10,000 fans attending the game who had come primarily to see the Bambino. Landis ruled that Weiss was obligated only to refund the difference between the price of admission charged to see a regular Eastern League game and the price charged on the assumption that Ruth would be present with his teammates.[60] The $1,000 allocated to the fans, Landis ruled, would come directly out of the Yankees' guaranteed payment.[61]

Barrow was infuriated by Landis's support of Weiss. Supposedly he did not speak to Weiss again until six months later at the 1923 party celebrating the Yankees' first World Series win, when they defeated the New York Giants. "I feel so good right now," said Barrow, "that I'll shake hands even with you."[62] While the Yankees were World Champions in 1923, Weiss and Donovan had to settle for a second-place finish for the Profs with a record of 90–63.[63]

Weiss indicated that in 1924 the fans could expect a drastic house-cleaning, especially in the pitching staff. "If I intend to give the faithful following another good brand of baseball," stated Weiss, "much work needs to be done between now and next season."[64] Weiss was never hesitant about moving his players around, acquiring some and selling others. In fact, in his first four years as a minor league club owner, Weiss sold 18 players to the big leagues, more than the rest of the Eastern League combined.[65]

Throughout the autumn and early winter of 1923, George Weiss was both preparing for spring training in 1924 and denying rumors that he and Donovan would leave New Haven, possibly for the larger city of Hartford. By December, the press was reporting that Weiss, indeed, had a legitimate offer from an unknown source for his club, but that the offers were unsatisfactory and that he, the Profs, and Bill Donovan would remain in New Haven, at least for another year.[66] Just a few days later, part of that plan would change.

On Saturday, December 8, 1923, Donovan, Weiss, and a large group of baseball officials left Grand Central Station aboard New York Central's Twentieth Century Limited, to attend the annual baseball winter meetings in Chicago. The following evening, Weiss and Donovan, who were sharing a Pullman drawing room, were discussing the team's plans for the 1924 season. Pulling a cigar from his pocket, Donovan told Weiss, "I know you don't smoke, George, so I'll mosey up to the club car and smoke this for a nightcap."[67]

They had a friendly dispute over which man would take the choice lower berth and which the upper. Donovan told Weiss that it didn't look right for the club president to be in an upper while the manager had the lower. Weiss replied that the lower berth always went to the senior citizen, and even though Weiss was the boss, he was 18 months younger than Donovan. Also, Weiss reminded Donovan, since he didn't know when his manager would be back, he felt it made more sense to occupy the upper berth while Donovan had the lower. As Donovan left the drawing room, Weiss climbed into the upper berth, saying, "I'll see you in the morning."[68]

The Twentieth Century ran in three sections, each pulled by its own steam locomotive. At 1:30 on the morning of December 9, in heavy fog and rain, the lead car slammed into an abandoned automobile at a grade crossing at Forsyth, New York, 25 miles east of Erie, Pennsylvania. The second section of the train stopped behind the first to inspect the damage and remove the burning automobile, while the lead section resumed its journey. The third section, attempting to catch up, plowed into the second section, splitting the rear car, killing Donovan and injuring Weiss, who suffered a severe back injury and a lacerated thigh.[69] The New York Central authorities gave the official casualty list as nine killed, including Donovan, and five seriously injured, including Weiss.[70]

Yankees owner Jake Ruppert heard of the accident as he was leaving on another train for Chicago. He was devastated to learn that his first manager, Bill Donovan, did not survive the crash, calling Donovan one of the greatest managers in baseball and remembering how difficult it had been for him to release Donovan. "Well, Bill died with his boots on," said Ruppert. "When he died he was on his way to a baseball meeting on business for his club. I think that is the way he would have liked to go."[71]

When he regained consciousness, Weiss had little recollection of the accident.

> There was this horrible crash that awakened me and when I looked around I realized I wasn't in any train but lying there on the tracks. I had nothing on except the neck-ring from my pajama top. There were dead and dying people all around me. I learned later Donovan was among them.[72] ... I

thought that this was a dream I was having and that the shouting and lanterns were a part of it…. The man who picked me up said that I was crawling toward the lights when they found me. I was so badly hurt that I could hardly walk.

Weiss moaned again and repeated, "Bill Donovan dead. I just don't believe it."[73]

After he was examined by hospital physicians, Weiss telephoned his mother, assuring her that although he had suffered two severe cuts in his thigh and was bruised in several spots, no bones were broken. He guaranteed his mother that he would have to remain in the hospital no more than one week.[74]

However, Weiss suffered a slight relapse before noon, and authorities immediately contacted his family. According to a hospital spokesman, Weiss's complications developed due to his back injury. By the time George's mother reached her son's bedside, he was in good spirits and his physicians reported that he had an even chance of recovery. He had a nine-inch gash across his back from which glass and cinders were ultimately removed. Physicians predicted that Weiss should be on the road to complete recovery within two or three weeks.[75]

William "Wild Bill" Donovan, a big league pitcher for 18 seasons, was one of Weiss's managers for his New Haven club. In December 1923, while traveling on the Twentieth Century Limited to Chicago for the major league meetings, Donovan died when the train was wrecked in Forsyth, New York. Earlier that evening he had swapped berths with the New Haven president, George Weiss, who suffered serious injuries but escaped death (National Baseball Hall of Fame Library, Cooperstown, New York).

Weiss was released from the hospital on January 3, 1924. During both his hospital stay and his convalescence at home, he received many notes wishing him a speedy recovery. Connie Mack, owner and manager of the Philadelphia Athletics, wrote Weiss to thank him for a new year's card and informed him that "everyone at the Chicago meeting expressed the deepest regret over the loss of Bill Donovan, as well as the injury to yourself."[76] National League President John A. Heydler expressed his pleasure that Weiss was making a recovery, adding, "You did indeed have a most miraculous escape. I look forward to meeting you in the near future."[77]

One of the more interesting notes sent to Weiss was from the Hollywood movie star, Douglas Fairbanks, Jr. Fairbanks and his mother were also on the Twentieth Century Limited, headed for Los Angeles. Weiss sent a letter to Fairbanks inquiring about his condition and asking, if possible, for more information about the accident. Fairbanks responded to Weiss's letter in February, apologizing for the delay, but explaining that the letter was held in his "fan" mailbox at the Lasky Studio and he just recently had an opportunity to read it.

Fairbanks described in detail for Weiss the events of the evening of the train wreck. "The porter of our car brought you into the men's room of our car. He had personally dug you out of the wreckage and carried you back to our car, trying to get you comfortable and warm. You were one mass of blood and dirt and I could see you were suffering terribly." Fairbanks wrote that he and his mother heard that Weiss was recovering, wished him well and were happy to have helped in some small way on the evening of the crash.[78]

Weiss spent most of January resting comfortably at home, in a huge, luxuriously cushioned chair, listening to a recently installed radio. After a second operation, Weiss was allowed to go out but had to keep physical activities to a minimum.[79]

At the end of January, Weiss once again turned his attention to running his ball club. He announced that Clyde Milan would replace Donovan as manager of New Haven. Milan spent his entire 16-year playing career with the Washington Senators. When he retired in 1922, Clark Griffith named him manager, replacing the ailing George McBride. The Senators finished with a 69–85 record and a sixth-place finish. Donie Bush replaced him the following year.[80] Baseball pundits felt Milan was the colorful manager Weiss wanted to run the Profs.

One of Weiss's first acts when back at work was to announce that the late Bill Donovan would be fittingly honored on April 20 when the New Haven Profs played an exhibition game against the Philadelphia Athletics. Prior to the game, a permanent stone memorial would be unveiled in deep center field, and the proceeds of the game were to be turned over to Donovan's family.[81]

Although still weak, Weiss was not too sick to continue selling players. In February 1924, Weiss sold Elmer Bowman to Seattle for a higher sum than ever paid for a minor league baseball player. Bowman had been New Haven's regular first baseman for two years and was sought after by at least two major league teams, but Weiss said that for the first time on record, a minor league team had outbid a major. In a separate deal, Weiss bought Larry Gallagher from the Boston Braves, and said that Gallagher would play third base for New Haven.[82]

George Weiss's sale of players and his deals with both the minor and major leagues perplexed a number of baseball fans in New Haven. Many of them could not understand why Weiss was dismantling his team year in and year out. *The Sporting News* responded to Weiss's critics with what it called "an easy answer," concluding that Weiss was not only a fan himself, but a smart businessman. The paper assured its readers that Weiss felt that a change of faces was a major factor in keeping fan interest in the team alive. Weiss was very successful in building up clubs and also had been responsible for deals which resulted in increasing his team's treasury. *The Sporting News* held that Weiss would not sell players unless he was completely satisfied that he could land replacements who had the ability to fill the slots of the departing players. "Rest assured that Weiss has begun the task of reinforcing his depleted baseball structure by sales, draft, recall, etc."[83]

To insure that the public would understand the motives behind his moves, Weiss began frequent meetings with the sports editors of New Haven, turning them into a board of baseball strategy. He and his new manager, Clyde Milan, believed that newspapers made up not only the most direct but also the strongest link between the team and the public. After two meetings, popular interest in the affairs of the club and in the sports sections of the newspapers increased. An even greater benefit was the development of a much more cordial relationship between members of the press and George Weiss.[84]

After the season, rumors persisted that Weiss intended to dispose of the Profs prior to the beginning of the 1925 season and turn his attention to other sports. Weiss vehemently denied these rumors. "Just at present," he said, " I have no plans for the future and probably will not until the first of the year."[85] Meanwhile, the Profs completed their 1924 season with a record of 75–78, finishing in fourth place.[86]

Denials aside, word soon leaked out that Weiss and his good friend Walter Johnson were attempting to buy and manage the Oakland team in the Pacific Coast League. Joe Engel, scout for the Washington Senators, was reportedly also part of the deal.[87] Walter Johnson had always wanted to run a club. When he signed his 1924 contract with Clark Griffith's Senators, he gave notice that he would soon retire as an active player in order to purchase a Pacific Coast League franchise. It seemed only logical that he and Weiss should enter the venture together.[88]

For years the sale of the Oakland franchise in the Pacific Coast League was an annual source of news for baseball writers. But not since 1912, when Cal Ewing bought the franchise, was the sale of the club so close to becoming a reality.[89] On November 18, 1924, Ewing announced that he had sold his Pacific Coast franchise for an amount estimated at $350,000 to $385,000. George Weiss gave Ewing a $5,000 goodwill deposit.[90] (One source even estimated the price to have been $450,000. The recent sale of the St. Louis Cardinals had brought $275,000).[91]

With the deal completed, Johnson went to his home in Reno, Nevada, to be with his wife, who had become ill in Los Angeles. Before he left for Reno, Johnson announced he would not be just a part-owner, he would also manage the team and take his regular turn in the pitching rotation. Immediately after signing the papers, Weiss left for New Haven, where he prepared to dispose of his Eastern League holdings, then to return to Oakland and become a permanent resident of the city.[92]

Less than a week later, the deal to purchase the Oakland Oaks fell through when Johnson and his partners were unable to raise the needed capital to purchase the team. Several Oakland backers who had promised to come to Johnson's aid financially failed to do so, and he and Weiss had to surrender their option.[93]

In late December, Weiss wired Johnson that he had obtained sufficient additional backing to enable him to offer Ewing the total in cash to purchase the Oaks. Johnson flew to Oakland but got no closer to the Oaks owner than a perfunctory phone call telling Johnson that plans for the Oaks had been completed for the coming season and that the team was no longer for sale.[94]

George Weiss began the 1925 season by assuring the city of New Haven that it would be represented in the Eastern League and that he would continue as the team head. He added that with a few additions to the roster, the club would begin the season on an equal footing with its rivals. His first order of business was to hire a new manager and some players before 1925 spring training began.[95]

In March, Weiss hired former major league infielder Neal Ball to manage the Profs in 1925. Ball had played seven seasons in the American League, from 1907 to 1913, with New York, Cleveland, and Boston. He also managed the Bridgeport Hustlers of the Eastern League in 1916 and the Augusta Tygers of the Sally League in 1922.[96]

Weiss was ever optimistic about New Haven's chances to win the pennant each year. He emphasized that pitching in 1925 was the team's main asset, and that the five pitchers he signed would equal the staff of any team in the Eastern League.[97] Even the press expected the Profs to be in the thick of the pennant race. New Haven finished the year, however, with a record of 81–73, just above .500, good for a third-place finish.[98]

The status of the Profs' manager in 1926 was an indication of the state of the Eastern League. It was assumed that Weiss would rehire Ball as manager, but the league "drafted" Ball to take control of the Pittsfield team, leaving Weiss without a manager. Weiss's only public announcement concerning his 1926 team was that the club would conduct its spring training in Suffolk, VA.[99] At the beginning of March, there was a report that outfielder Harry Hooper, recently released by the Chicago White Sox, would succeed Ball as the Profs' manager. It was no secret that Weiss had a penchant for major league drawing cards, such as Chief Bender, Bill Donovan and Clyde Milan, piloting his club.[100]

On March 18, George Weiss finally hired John Flynn, a veteran minor leaguer who had played professional baseball from 1906 to 1921, but had appeared in only 149 major league games.[101] Even though Flynn was hardly the drawing card Weiss generally preferred, he announced his delight in obtaining the 43-year-old Flynn. "He is long on experience," said Weiss, "is well acquainted with Eastern League conditions, a real fighter, and enjoys the respect of all baseball men. He will act as bench manager, although he will be available in emergency for pinch hitting or first-base duty."[102]

Reaction by New Haven's baseball fans was favorable, but at the same time skeptical. They had too often seen a baseball team with an excellent nucleus, only to watch Weiss dismantle the team, dispose of the worthwhile talent, and rebuild the team in the spring. But the feeling in New Haven was that Weiss had both the talent and the manager, and that 1926 would have a different outcome.

Early in July 1926, George Weiss sold one of his pitchers, Chet Nichols, to the Pittsburgh Pirates for $20,000, a new record for one player in the Eastern League. This transaction brought Weiss's total income of sales since he took charge of the New Haven team in 1919 to $200,000, exceeding the aggregate for the entire Eastern League. According to one newspaper, "Weiss was a master discoverer of big league material, a clever workman in ironing out the flaws in this material, and a high-class salesman in disposing of major league possibilities at figures far in excess of those secured by other Eastern League magnates."[103]

Weiss emphatically defended his actions, claiming that before a team can sell a player, it first must have players big league teams want, fully developed, with rough spots polished off. Weiss felt that his New Haven club had been quite successful in its policy of developing players. "I place the credit for our sales entirely to this policy of obtaining promising youngsters and working patiently with them until they are ripe for a trial in the major leagues," said Weiss.

Weiss insisted that he had no desire to "wreck" other ball clubs with his sales. But he vehemently maintained that business conditions—as they applied to baseball—in New Haven were forcing him to part with players after a season or two. These conditions made Weiss the master developer and the master salesman of the Eastern League.[104]

In the middle of the 1926 season, Weiss announced that manager Jack Flynn was resigning to return to his law practice, and the new manager would be the Profs' 31-year-old utility infielder, Billy Gleason.[105] In August Gleason was reunited with a former teammate, Joe Cronin. As he had often done while running the New Haven Colonials, Weiss scheduled a number of exhibition games, primarily to attract fans and increase the team's coffers, including one against the Pirates. Years later, while looking back at his days at New Haven, Cronin remembered how helpful Bill Gleason had been in nurturing the young shortstop, both in the field and at the plate.[106] Under the combined field leadership of Flynn and Gleason, the Profs posted a record of 91–60, moving up to second place, quite an improvement from their fourth-place finish the previous year.[107]

During the pre–1927 baseball season, the Eastern League was as unstable and deteriorating as it had been the previous year when George Weiss lost the services of Neal Ball. To stay viable, the Eastern League had been forced to give players to its unsound clubs in 1926 merely to keep them from going under. The 1927 season was preceded by weekly strategy meetings of Eastern League owners to decide how to keep weaker teams afloat, save the league, and begin the season on time.[108] Later in the year, the Eastern League's difficulties intensified when Albert Powell, owner of the Providence Grays, announced the sale of his team and threatened to sell players on the open market if his price was not met.[109]

In the meantime, Weiss was making news of his own when he rehired Neal Ball to guide the team in 1927. Weiss also announced that he would trade Billy Gleason to an unnamed club in a Class A league to clear the way for Ball.

During spring training, Weiss urged Ball to bear down in practice, as he was eager to make his team a contender for the 1927 pennant. To raise money, draw crowds, and provide tough competition for the Profs, Weiss continued scheduling exhibition games against major league teams. In mid–April, the New Haven Profs played a game against Connie Mack's Philadelphia Athletics, whose roster included seven future Hall of Famers: Ty Cobb, who made his Athletics debut in 1927; the great catcher Mickey Cochrane; Eddie Collins, whose career lasted almost 25 years; outfielder Al Simmons, who played 12 of his 20 seasons with the Athletics; infielder Jimmy Foxx, whose 20-year major league career ended in 1945; pitcher Lefty Grove, a 300-game winner, first with the Athletics, then the Red Sox; and Zack Wheat, who debuted with the Brooklyn Dodgers and played his final season with the Athletics in 1927.[110]

Not too many years later, George Weiss would gain the reputation of being one of the most tight-fisted executives in professional baseball, but when he operated minor league teams, this was not the case. Throughout both 1926 and 1927, when his teams played the outstanding stars in the major leagues, nearly every press report of exhibition games clearly stated that there would be no increase in ticket prices for special attractions.[111]

Weiss's exhibition games might have been successful, but his 1927 season under Ball was a bust. Ball's team struggled to 74 wins, 80 losses, and a fifth-place finish. It marked only the second time that a Weiss team finished in the second division.[112]

Many attributed the poor showing of the Profs to the mass sale of players to the major leagues. During the autumn of 1927, Weiss sold Paul Hopkins to the Washington Senators for $10,000, and there were strong probabilities that more would follow. Weiss served warning on his fellow magnates that he would retain the title of "The Master Salesman of Minor League Baseball."[113]

Determined to improve his team, Weiss purchased instead of selling players. He bought infielder Fred "Happy" Meyers and Joe Dwyer from Newark of the International League.[114] Next, Weiss named one of his outfielders, 30-year-old Eugene Martin, as player-manager. Always a minor leaguer, Martin had begun his professional career with Bridgeport in 1917, at the age of 19. His best year was 1923, when he hit .314 in 148 games.[115]

The biggest shakeup for the New Haven Profs in 1928 was the team's move to Savin Rock after the land under Weiss Park was sold for new building purposes. The Profs were given permission to play all their games on the road until their new field was ready. Yale University also gave the Profs permission to use its facility for some games.[116]

The move to Savin Rock obviously agreed with the Profs, for in 1928 the team finished in first place with a record of 92–61.[117] There were no playoffs that year; the Profs were simply champions of the Eastern League. At a gathering honoring Weiss and his championship team, the magnates went through the motions of making a formal award of the pennant to New Haven, and Weiss accepted a check for $1,000 on behalf of the New Haven club for its flag-winning performance.[118]

As always, Weiss was upbeat about the Profs' chances. "I feel that we have an excellent squad of players on the string from which to select our 1929 team," said Weiss. "We won the pennant last year in a lively race, showing that we were the class of the circuit. We are hopeful of repeating this year."[119] Returning in 1929 were two players who had had outstanding years the previous season—pitcher Dutch Kemner, who won 20 games while losing only seven, and first baseman Babe Bowman, who hit .310 and slugged 21 homers for the Profs.[120]

But all preparations were halted in February 1929, when the story broke that George Weiss was leaving New Haven and the Eastern League to become vice president and general manager of the International League Baltimore Orioles. Weiss would, however, maintain control of the Profs until final arrangements were made to sell the club.[121] In the nine years Weiss had been their exclusive president, his teams at New Haven had compiled a record 763 wins and 599 losses, finishing in the first division eight times and winning the pennant three times.[122]

During his years in the Eastern League, George Weiss established his reputation as a smart evaluator of player skills and a man who had the uncanny ability to find players with potential, develop them further with New Haven, and sell them very profitably to higher minor league clubs or the major leagues. From 1919 through 1928, Weiss had made more than $300,000 from his sales, and more than half of the players he traded or sold eventually made it to the big leagues.[123] He was now going to test his skills in a larger market.

3

"Among the Happiest Times of My Life"

In late 1928, as George Weiss was meeting with Charles H. Knapp, president of the prestigious International League's Baltimore Orioles, to discuss exhibition games. Knapp, with the approval of the stockholders, abruptly asked Weiss if he would like to become general manager of the Baltimore team. The offer might have seemed sudden, but Knapp was quite familiar with Weiss's ability to judge, acquire, and develop baseball players. He had not only made the Profs successful on the field, but his astuteness in selling players to higher leagues had kept his team solvent.[1] Weiss was intrigued and said he would consider Knapp's offer. With interest in minor league baseball in New England waning, Weiss soon reached his decision.[2]

On February 15, 1929, Knapp announced that the Orioles had signed 33-year-old George M. Weiss as the team's general manager.[3] Weiss also became Vice-President of the team in charge of business affairs, as well as part-owner. He also retained his ownership of the New Haven Profs until he was able to find an acceptable offer for that team.[4]

After Weiss accepted the job, sportswriter A. W. Grainger paid tribute to him as former GM of the New Haven Profs. "Baseball men and fans all over the circuit ... feel confident the New Haven owner will make just as much a success of his job at Baltimore as he did of his old one here with the Profs."[5]

Weiss's move came as no surprise to astute observers. According to rumors, he had been looking beyond New Haven for some time. His move to Baltimore, however, represented far more than a change of city, team, and level. In Class AA Baltimore, Weiss would no longer be sole owner, answerable only to himself, but would be responsible to others who could fire him if they were unhappy. It would set the pattern for the rest of his career.

The position of general manager of the Orioles had become vacant when Jack Dunn died on October 22, 1928. Dunn not only had owned the Orioles, he had also served as the team's general manager and field manager. The 56-year-old Dunn suffered a fatal heart attack while pursuing his off-season hobby of training hunting dogs. Knapp, Dunn's attorney, had taken over running the team until the appointment of Weiss. After he left the Orioles, Knapp became president of the International League.[6]

John Joseph "Jack" Dunn was a native of Meadville, Pennsylvania, and a former infielder and pitcher in the major leagues from 1897 to 1904, primarily for Brooklyn and New York in the National League. He finished his major league career with 64 wins and 49 losses as a pitcher and a lifetime batting average of .245.[7]

After he retired from the majors, Dunn played for the Baltimore Orioles, and in the fall of 1909, with the financial help of Philadelphia Athletics owner Connie Mack, Dunn was able to purchase the Orioles.[8] It was Dunn who, on February 14, 1914, first signed a 20-year-old pitcher named George Herman Ruth. Ruth was living in southwest Baltimore at St. Mary's Industrial School, a training facility for boys who were orphaned or wards of the state. He could not be released from St. Mary's until Dunn agreed to become his legal guardian. On July 9, however, Dunn sold Ruth to the Red Sox.[9]

Also in 1914, the organization joined the majors with a short lived Federal League as the Baltimore Terrapins. The new league proved a disaster and the Terrapins had a losing year. When the league disbanded, Dunn moved the Orioles to Richmond. Dunn returned to Baltimore in 1918 as manager and owner, and from 1919 to 1925 established one of the best minor league teams in organized baseball. He brought seven consecutive pennants to Baltimore while winning more than 100 games each year.[10]

Dunn's Orioles were stocked with the biggest stars in the minor leagues. From that era, 11 Orioles, including George Earnshaw, Lefty Grove, and Dunn himself, were selected to the International League Hall of Fame.[11] In 1923, following the death of his son, Dunn relinquished all team duties to his captain, Fritz Maisel, and did not resume his duties until early June.[12]

During Dunn's seclusion, other International League executives held a secret meeting and issued an ultimatum to the Orioles owner to "start to sell your best players to the majors or we will vote to reinstate the draft." Dunn bitterly opposed the right of the major leagues to draft players from the upper minor leagues, but Commissioner Landis, was a strong pro-draft man, who clearly stated his views on the draft. "No one should be permitted to build a brick wall around a player. In a non-draft league, a minor league club owner may hold a player to eternity. Every young ball player should get his rightful opportunity to advance to the top in baseball."[13]

Knowing he could not win against Landis, in 1927 Dunn began to sell his key players to the majors rather than having them drafted. He sold his star pitcher, Lefty Grove, to the Philadelphia Athletics for $100,600. This sale enabled Connie Mack's Athletics to win the World Series in 1929 and 1930, and to come close in 1931.[14] Despite Dunn's actions, the other International League owners voted to reinstate the major league draft. The loss of key players hurt Dunn's team, and the Orioles' record began to drop dramatically in 1927 and 1928. Dunn's death in 1928 created the opportunity for George Weiss. His mission was to reconstruct the Orioles organization beginning with the 1929 season.[15]

Weiss immediately hired as field manager former New York Yankees/Highlanders and St. Louis Browns third baseman Fritz Maisel. Maisel was originally signed by the Orioles in 1910 and spent six years in the major leagues before rejoining the Orioles as team captain in 1919. After he was dismissed as manager of the Orioles, he remained with the team in various capacities until his death in 1967 at the age of 77.[16]

Jack Dunn (left) was a major league pitcher from 1897 to 1904 who became manager and owner of the Baltimore Orioles. He held that position until his death in 1928. A few months later, Charles Knapp, Orioles president, named George Weiss the team's general manager and vice president. Dunn appears with Commissioner Landis (center) and John McGraw (National Baseball Hall of Fame Library, Cooperstown, New York).

With his field manager in place, Weiss began to assess the talent he had inherited. With all its old stars sold to the majors, the team was mediocre and unhappy. "The affairs of the Baltimore club were in general confusion when I took over," reported Weiss.

> Little had been done since Jack Dunn's death. They were standing by waiting for somebody to buy the club. Things were so bad that the team had no plans for spring training and nobody was sure whether the Dunn estate intended to field a team.[17]
>
> Even though Dunn had made a lot of money selling ball players, the club treasury was empty when I took over. So, one of the first things I did was to get some money for operations. I sold Dick Porter, the International League batting champion in 1927, to the Cleveland Indians for $40,000. I also increased the admission prices that Dunn had lowered in 1927 and 1928, after Jack had dropped from the heights. That gave us some money to work with.[18]

Ironically, one factor which helped Weiss keep his team in the black was that he opposed the draft. Shortly after Dunn's death, the International League again had voted to operate as a draft league, so Weiss generally made his sales before his Orioles players were subject to the draft. Weiss later boasted that while he won no pennants at Baltimore, he had one of the greatest slugging teams in the minors, and the "empty" treasury was in pretty healthy condition.[19] Weiss would always contend that his sales were by no means general house cleanings similar to those of both the Philadelphia Athletics and Phillies. Weiss maintained that he did not strip his club through sales, but he was merely disposing of surplus talent at very high prices.[20]

Weiss's *modus operandi* was the same as he had used at New Haven and would duplicate in New York. He would make his deals with major league clubs for cash and throw-in players. Sometimes they would play for his team for some time; other times Weiss would begin shopping the throw-in players immediately to other teams. He was usually able to get a good profit.[21]

Weiss often boasted that if he had any knack for developing young ball players, then selling them to the majors at very healthy prices quickly, it was at Baltimore where he perfected that art.[22] Other baseball pros put Weiss's manipulation of players at Baltimore a little more crudely. "He could squeeze a nickel so tightly that the ass of the buffalo had a permanent crease in it."[23]

After obtaining funds from the sale of Porter, Weiss worked diligently preparing for the 1929 season. Wherever possible, he tried to accomplish this task without a large outlay of money. He purchased veteran catcher Joe Cobb from Fort Worth of the Texas League. A former Oriole, Cobb had also played for several other teams in the International League.[24] Weiss also concluded a working agreement with the Hagerstown Hubs of the Blue Ridge League that specified that Weiss would send the Hubs surplus players not needed at Baltimore.[25]

To bolster his outfield, Weiss purchased the contract of George Loepp, who was playing for the Pittsfield Hillies, the Boston Red Sox's farm club in the Eastern League.[26] While his team was at spring training in Georgia, Weiss made a scouting trip to Florida and brought back two catchers for the 1929 season—Pat Cronin and Al Bool.[27] Before the season started, Weiss firmly declared, "I have canvassed every major league club down here looking for material. I have promises of assistance now."[28]

Weiss's Orioles finished the 1929 season with a record of 90–78, good enough for a third-place finish.[29] One bright spot on the 1929 Orioles was a Baltimore native, first baseman Johnny Neun, who played his only year in the minors for the Orioles. Appearing in 96 games, Neun hit .330 and compiled a slugging percentage of .473.[30] Before coming to Baltimore, Neun played three years for the Detroit Tigers (1925–1927) where he executed an unassisted triple play, a rare feat for a first baseman. The New York Yankees later hired him as a scout and minor league director.[31]

At the end of 1929, as the country was going into the Depression, Weiss still owned the New Haven Profs. Two major league teams, Washington and Brooklyn, had expressed interest in purchasing the club, but Weiss indicated that he wanted to sell to a New Haven group if at all possible.[32] By July 1930, the economy was getting worse and Weiss still owned the Profs, but because of his personal finances and the rapidly deteriorating Eastern League, Weiss called it quits. He pulled the Profs out of the Eastern League, leaving that league with only four teams—Allentown, Bridgeport, Springfield, and Albany—and dissolved New Haven.[33]

The situation with the Profs made Weiss even more determined to make the Orioles a successful team in 1930. Through player sales, he brought both cash and new players to his team, but stars were still needed to replace the departing players. Catcher Al Bool, a solid hitter and a fan favorite, was now the property of the Pittsburgh Pirates. George Loepp, a good defensive center fielder, became a Washington Senator. Cash and players given to Weiss in exchange for these two former Orioles helped, but Bool and Loepp would be difficult to replace. A number of teams wanted Neun, but the Boston Braves had finished in the National League cellar in 1929 and had first rights to draft him in 1930. They quickly grabbed him, paying Weiss for the privilege as specified in the Major League Baseball Rule 5 Draft.[34]

Weiss and Maisel decided to focus on pitching for the 1930 season.[35] Of the 14 pitchers on the Orioles' 1930 roster, 12 spent some time in the major leagues. The most successful of the 12 was Harry Gumbert, who pitched for four teams during his 15 years in the majors—the Giants, Cardinals, Reds, and Pirates. His lifetime record was a very respectable 143–113.[36] Two other pitchers who spent time in the majors were Stew Bolen and Luther Roy. Bolen's record with the Orioles in 1930 was 19–9 and Roy's was 18–9.[37]

Although pitching was a strong point for the Orioles in 1930, Baltimore wowed its fans with its heavy hitting. The team hit 231 homers that year, with John W. Gill smacking 34 and Vincent D. Barton, a Canadian, clobbering 32. But it was a 30-year-old first baseman let go by the Philadelphia Athletics after breaking his kneecap who put on quite a show for the Orioles' faithful. His name was Joseph W. Hauser; he had played for the Athletics from 1922 to 1924, in 1926, and once more in 1928, and for the Cleveland Indians in 1929.[38]

George Weiss purchased Hauser from Cleveland in 1930 and he spent two years with the Orioles. The Milwaukee native, called "Unser Choe" in his hometown, played 168 games in 1930. At the beginning of the season, the home-run mark for any league was Yankees slugger Babe Ruth's 60, set in 1927, in a 154-game schedule. When the 1930 season ended, the record was 63, set by a lighter, smaller Joe Hauser. Three years later, Hauser broke his own 1930 record when he clouted 69 homers for Minneapolis in the American Association.[39] In 1930 he helped the Orioles improve their record to 97–70, as the team rose from third to second place.[40]

George Weiss's goal for the 1931 season was to lure more fans into the ballpark. He announced that he was going to install lights not only for baseball games, but also for football. He was well aware that Baltimore was an avid race town, and installing lights would allow his Orioles to compete with racing enthusiasts. Weiss also noted that five of the eight clubs in the International League were playing night baseball and that three of the four surviving teams in the Eastern League had also installed lights. Weiss went so far as to encourage major league teams to consider installing lights at their ballparks.[41]

He also increased attendance by introducing Boys' Day and Ladies' Day. Twice a week, the ladies were admitted free, while he had an organization of 8,000 boys registered to promote sportsmanship and interest in baseball. These two ploys, in addition to his selling and trading of ballplayers, brought money into the club's treasury and allowed the Orioles to show a profit when he left the team.[42]

By the end of 1930, George Weiss was making a name for himself in the hierarchy of professional baseball. The issue of the major leagues drafting minor league players was still a contentious one. Major league baseball had recently adopted a resolution calling for suspension of all business relations with any minor league that did not accept the draft. President John Heydler of the National League was adamant when he stated: "We simply refuse to have another conference with the minors on the draft."[43]

At a meeting held in Montreal, the three dominant minor leagues, the American Association, the Pacific Coast League, and the International League, met to discuss demands to present to the major leagues regarding drafting of minor league players. They included a $30,000 price for Class AA League draftees, the right to prevent young players whom they had discovered from being drafted until they had had ownership of these men for four years, and no changes in the number of players who could be sent into the minors under optional agreement for purchase by the majors. George Weiss, who made his baseball reputation as one of the smartest and sharpest young men in the sport while running New Haven, was one of the three men chosen to represent the International League at the meeting.[44] This question of the major league draft of minor league players would be an ongoing problem for professional baseball.

For George Weiss, his main focus was obtaining players for the Orioles and making money by selling them. One of Weiss's most successful deals in 1931 involved a former .300 hitter with the Philadelphia Phillies, Denny Sothern, who came to Baltimore from Pittsburgh as a throw-in. As one of the Orioles' regular outfielders, he hit .327. Toward the end of the season, Wilbert "Uncle Robbie" Robinson of Brooklyn, looking for hitting, bought Sothern from Weiss, but he hit only .161 in 19 games for the 1931 Dodgers and never played in the big leagues again. In the end, Weiss had gotten his price for selling a player who had cost him nothing, but who also helped Baltimore for almost all of 1931.[45]

In one of his less successful moves, Weiss dealt Orioles outfielder Frank Rodgers to Cincinnati in exchange for catcher Johnny Gooch. Rodgers appeared to be a likely starting outfielder for Baltimore until he was traded.[46] The following month, Commissioner Landis voided the trade when Gooch voluntarily retired rather than report to the Orioles. Baltimore lost Rodgers as well when he was returned to Peoria in the Three-I League by agreement between Baltimore and Cincinnati.[47]

One Baltimore player Weiss kept for 1931 was slugging first baseman Joe Hauser. Although he seemed to be a player Weiss could easily sell to the majors, Weiss obviously wanted to keep his bat in the Orioles lineup.[48]

In addition to being the business manager of the Orioles, George Weiss was also a rabid baseball fan. He ordered a radio set up in his office at the ballpark so that he could keep in touch with each game's progress while attending to his executive duties. In the past Weiss had had to rely on the cheers or groans of the fans to tell him which way the game was going. Now he knew what those sounds meant, and whenever he heard a wild outburst of cheers, he would rush into the stands to see the end of the play.[49]

By mid–May 1931, Baltimore was leading the league and Weiss was credited with a number of player moves which helped the Orioles get there. Although Joe Hauser was out with an injury, Weiss was able to obtain Joe Kuhel from the Washington Senators on option. Kuhel greatly helped the team, but when Senators first baseman Joe Judge had an appendectomy, Kuhel returned to Clark Griffith's team. Weiss soon made a deal with Minneapolis and obtained Charles "Slug" Tolson on option. In his Orioles debut he got six hits in six at-bats, including two homers, helping sweep a doubleheader from Rochester. It was understood that when Hauser returned to the Orioles, Tolson would return to Minneapolis. Jim Stroner was performing well at third base, as were infielders Heine Sand and Don Heffner. Denny Sothern, Frank McGowan, and Ralph

Boyle patrolled the outfield, and behind the plate Weiss had Ike Danning and Bob Linton. On the mound, Weiss was receiving outstanding work from hurlers Beryl Richmond, Harry Smythe, Ken Holloway, Luther Roy, Lou Koupal, and especially Monte Weaver.[50]

Weaver was formerly on the faculty of the University of Virginia, where he taught analytic geometry. Opting for baseball rather than academia, Weaver won the first five games he started for the Orioles; his winning streak was halted through no fault of his own. In the next three games he started, his team was able to score only one earned run and he was the one who scored it.[51]

By the end of June, hampered by injuries and a lack of punch, the Orioles were no longer in first place. Weiss tried to shake the jinx by loading his team with new players. He acquired Bill Regan from the Pittsburgh Pirates, and signed Rolf "Swede" Carlston who starred at second base for the University of Pennsylvania. Although both proved adequate, it was not enough to compensate for a poor second half. In addition, the sensational Joe Hauser had an "off year" in 1931. His batting average dropped from .313 to .259, and his home run total dipped from 63 to 31.[52] Weiss told the press that Hauser had been benched because he was unable to regain his natural batting stride after being out with his injury.[53]

The Orioles finished the 1931 season with a record of 94–72, good enough for third place.[54] They ended the season six games behind Rochester, which won its fourth consecutive pennant. Weaver finished the 1931 season 21–11 and was the only 20-game winner on Weiss's roster during his entire stint as Orioles general manager.[55]

Immediately after the season ended, Weiss tried to compensate for his third-place finish and build for 1932. He began dealing his players. The first player to go was pitcher Luther Roy, who won 18 games in 1930 but only five in 1931. Next was outfielder Frank "Beauty" McGowan, who hit .336 in 1930 but slumped to .261 in 1931. Roy was traded to New Orleans and McGowan was sold outright to Minneapolis.[56] Even though Joe Hauser's 31 home runs in 1931 were enough to lead the International League, Weiss disposed of him, sending him to Minneapolis for cash and a player to be named later.[57]

Weiss had not yet won a pennant during his three years with the Baltimore Orioles, but the team was financially profitable from the onset of his management. In those three years, Weiss brought in about $240,000 through his sale of players, an amazing sum of money considering the nation was in the midst of the Great Depression and also that the players he disposed of proved quite ordinary if and when they reached the big leagues. Weiss did not exaggerate when he stated that no other minor league club owner or general manager, not even Jack Dunn, was as financially successful as he was.[58] Many of his Eastern League friends were confident that eventually George Weiss would purchase the Orioles.[59] And then he received a phone call which was to alter his life forever.

In December 1931, the minor league meetings were held at West Baden, Indiana, not far from French Lick Springs. Weiss was at West Baden attending the meetings while Colonel Jacob Ruppert, owner of the New York Yankees, was at French Lick on his annual vacation. Weiss received a phone call from Colonel Ruppert that was short and to the point. "I want to go into the chain store business and I want you to create a farm system similar to Rickey's Cardinals...."[60]

Weiss hesitated, saying "I have commitments in Baltimore. I must go back there and see Mr. Knapp. He has been very kind to me."

"Well, you see Knapp and make ready to move to New York," Ruppert concluded.

There is no doubt that Weiss was conflicted. He agreed with his friends that if he remained in Baltimore, there was an excellent possibility that some day he could become the owner of the Baltimore Orioles, a club that had always been a big money-maker.[61] On the other hand, he had always dreamed of an opportunity to be in the majors. Knapp told him, "George, I will not stand in your way. If you want to go to New York, you have my best wishes. But don't fall for that big league glamour. You stay here and you will own the Baltimore club. You will be your own boss and in time develop a rich property. However, you have my permission to accept Ruppert's bid if you so desire."[62]

Weiss also turned to someone else to whom he had become very close during his three-year stint with the Orioles. George's sister had introduced him to her friend, Hazel H. Wood,[63] who was very much the opposite of George in temperament. The petite, dark-haired, 32-year-old Hazel was an accomplished sculptress, outgoing, and she loved to sing and dance. She had been involved in what she called a "bad experience" in her previous marriage, and therefore she was cautious. Furthermore, she was not all taken with George when they first met. In fact she told George's sister that there was nothing she liked about him. She went so far as to say, "I didn't know you had such a big, fat brother."[64]

When Hazel first met Weiss, he was living in Baltimore with his mother. Despite the fact that his first encounter with Hazel was not very encouraging, the ever-persistent Weiss invited her to meet him in New York, where he took her to the city's finest places, often "double-dating" with Walter Johnson. Their relationship slowly improved, and when Colonel Ruppert asked him to work for the Yankees, George confided in Hazel, "I don't know what to do." When Hazel asked him if he wanted to be "tops in baseball," George said yes. Hazel told him, "The Yankees are the place to go." And so he went.[65] On February 11, 1932, Weiss accepted the Yankees' offer.[66]

Even though he had won no pennants, the Baltimore fans thought enough of Weiss to throw him a huge farewell party, wishing him well with the Yankees. The party was described as one of the strangest testimonial dinners on record, for the guest of honor received his plaudits *in absentia*. George Weiss, always the introvert and still a bachelor, remained home with his mother, and the two of them listened to the dinner speeches over the radio.[67]

Before he left Baltimore, Weiss told the city's baseball fans that while he certainly regretted leaving Baltimore in 1932, he could not turn down Colonel Ruppert's offer to build a farm system and develop players for the Yankees.[68] However, as he looked back on his three years in Baltimore, he freely admitted that they were "among the happiest years in my life."[69]

4

The Yankee Farmer

Jacob Ruppert, George Weiss's new boss, was born in New York City in 1867. He served as a private in the Seventh Regiment, National Guard of New York, and was appointed a colonel serving on the staff of Gov. David B. Hill. Ruppert was also elected for four terms (1899–1907) as a Democratic Congressman from New York. He retired from Congress to return to his father's brewing business and became president of the company in 1915. In 1914, he and Colonel Tillinghast L'Hommedieu Huston, a Spanish-American War hero, had bought the New York club which had changed its name from the Highlanders to the Yankees the previous year. Ruppert eventually bought out his partner, and in 1921 hired Ed Barrow, former general manager of the Boston Red Sox, as general manager of the New York Yankees.[1]

Ed Barrow was Ruppert's contemporary and a mid–Westerner. Born in Springfield, Illinois, in 1868, he was a newspaperman who never played professional baseball. He entered the game in 1894 as manager and GM at Wheeling, West Virginia, in the International League. Other than player, Barrow held nearly every position in professional baseball: scout, minor league manager, president of the Eastern League, and manager of the Boston Red Sox in 1918. The Sox sold Babe Ruth to the New York Yankees in 1920, and a year later Barrow followed the famous hitter to New York, where he became the business manager of the same team.[2]

Ever since Col. Ruppert purchased the New York Yankees, he had firmly believed that the best way to develop pennant-winning teams was through shrewd deals with other clubs. But lately, a number of factors had caused Ruppert to have second thoughts. One deal in particular continued to haunt him. The Colonel had paid $103,000 in cash to Oakland of the Pacific Coast League for infielders Lyn Lary and Jimmy Reese, two players whose skills in the American League certainly did not justify anywhere near what they had cost.[3]

A second factor that changed Ruppert's thinking was that in 1929 the major leagues adopted new rules which greatly increased the advantages of a farm system. One allowed a major league club not only to own a minor league team, but also to have full rights to all its players. Another rule permitted a parent club, which had used up its options on one of its minor league players, to return that player to another minor league team in its farm system. Previously, that player would have had to have been placed on waivers or released to an unaffiliated minor league team.[4]

Finally, and most persuasively, Branch Rickey, St. Louis Cardinals vice-president, was actually using a farm club or "chain store" system and making it work. Although other major league executives were skeptical, Ruppert, who once called the farm system "Rickey's Folly," was beginning to believe Rickey when he claimed that this system was worth the cost. The Cardinals were having as much success as the Yankees, yet Rickey was spending less on his farms than Ruppert was on his trades.[5]

In addition, Rickey was signing hundreds of kids, hoping that perhaps three or four might make it to the big leagues. He sold those who were not up to his standards to other major league teams. Not only did Rickey win a string of pennants, he made hundreds of thousands of dollars by selling his rejects. By emulating Rickey, both Ruppert and later Weiss agreed that this scheme would provide some stability to minor league franchises and also ensure a flow of revenue to the Yankees. Ruppert expected his farm club director to create a similar system for the Yankees.[6]

Although Barrow was not in favor of Ruppert's new venture, he told Ruppert that he had found the ideal man to run the system—Bob Connery, president of the St. Paul club of the American Association, a former Yankees scout, and an old friend of his. Connery was only 48 years old, but Ruppert said he wanted a younger man. It was obvious to everyone but Barrow that in addition to a farm director, Ruppert also wanted this person to understudy the 63-year-old Barrow.[7] Ruppert had another reason for bypassing Barrow's choice. He didn't like Connery because of some player transactions. Ruppert had once paid Connery approximately $300,000 for a group of players but only one—Mark Koenig—ever came close to making the big leagues.[8]

The man Ruppert had in mind for the farm job was George Weiss. Ruppert remembered how Weiss had refused to give the Yankees their guarantee when Babe Ruth did not come with the team for a game between the Yankees and Weiss's New Haven team. The Yankees owner was reported to have said to Barrow, "That man Weiss is a tough business man. Maybe we ought to have him on our side."[9]

Ruppert and Barrow arranged an interview with George Weiss, who eagerly advocated to the two Yankees moguls the merits of a strong farm system. The two men listened intently as Weiss praised Rickey, but promised even better results. "With the resources of the Yankees," said Weiss, "you can do an even better job than Rickey has done." He felt that the Yankees' scouting staff had been doing an excellent job, but that the team needed a place for these players to develop. "Would you rather have them on minor league clubs of your own, being taught by managers you have selected—or on some clubs managed by fellows you don't know much about and that might ruin a good prospect for you overnight?" Weiss convinced Ruppert and Barrow that he was the man for the job, and in 1932, George Weiss became the first New York farm director. Hiring Weiss to take charge of the club's minor league operation launched a 29-year association that many baseball observers think produced the greatest dynasty in diamond history.[10]

Weiss's first task was to identify and acquire a complete "chain" of minor league teams as the framework for the system that would turn out good players and good profits.[11] Ruppert told Weiss that he had been hired because of his years with the Eastern League and with Baltimore, where he had demonstrated the qualities needed to build up a successful "chain store" system. "You have been a consistent developer of new talent and a large number of major league stars have come from your clubs. I expect the same results with the Yankees."[12]

Ruppert, Weiss, and Barrow had agreed, even before Weiss was officially hired, that the Yankees' farm system would always try to avoid three fundamentally dangerous practices: picking up a lot of minor league franchises haphazardly simply because they were cheap or might be operated at a profit; using too many players who had major league experience but who were no longer likely to help the parent club; and rushing stars of the minor league clubs to the aid of the parent team at the height of the pennant race before they were ready.[13]

A number of baseball experts applauded Weiss's hiring. *The Sporting News* noted the remarkable job he did succeeding the late Jack Dunn, and how successfully he had handled his former teams. "He has sold more players during his 11 years at New Haven than all the seven other Eastern League clubs combined." The newspaper also noted that Weiss was a great developer of players in both New Haven and Baltimore, crediting him with building the careers of Joe Cronin, Jimmy Wilson, Horace Ford, Pinky Hargrave, and Jim Weaver.[14] Sportswriter Alan Gould called the appointment of Weiss an excellent choice. "Colonel Ruppert" wrote Gould, "has picked one of the best known minor league men in George Weiss.... He has shown himself a keen judge of player talent as well as a good organizer."[15]

Ruppert had given his new farm director a head start. Late in 1931, he had purchased the AA Newark Bears of the International League. The deal had cost him $350,000. This was just the beginning, Ruppert announced. "I will spend millions to perfect a farm system that will be as big as that of the Cardinals and Weiss will be placed in complete control of the chain," stated Ruppert.[16]

Less than two weeks after Weiss took up his new duties, he was chief negotiator for the Yankees' purchase of the Springfield club of the Class A Eastern League.[17] The Yankees also announced their interest in Class B Scranton in the New York-Pennsylvania League, as well as Cumberland in the Class C Mid-Atlantic League.[18] The press took note of Weiss's effort in bringing a workable farm system to the Yankees in so short a period of time. Sportswriter Randall Cassell said of Weiss, "That is the man who is on his way up the ladder of baseball triumphs and to great success in his chosen profession—from independent ball to New Haven in Class A to Baltimore in Class AA and now the majors."[19]

By April 1932, the Yankees' "chain" numbered five teams, including a "working agreement" with the Erie club in the Central League.[20] What made it easier for Weiss either to purchase minor league teams outright or to ink working relations with them, was that Yankees GM Ed Barrow, never a strong advocate of a farm system, had his hands full with his major league duties.[21]

Commissioner Landis also opposed farm systems. He accused the Cardinals and the Yankees of stifling competition and monopolizing younger players, but he took no action against the chains.[22]

On July 4, 1932, organized baseball's traditional mid-season, three of the Yankees' "chain stores"—Newark, Springfield and Erie—were in first place in their respective leagues. Springfield led the Eastern League by eight games, and Erie was ahead in the Central League by a half-game.[23]

Late in 1931, after Colonel Ruppert made it clear that Weiss was his man, Ed Barrow (on the left) grudgingly accepted George Weiss as the team's first farm director (National Baseball Hall of Fame Library, Cooperstown, New York).

At the conclusion of the 1932 season, Weiss could note at least two successes for his newly established farm system. There was a consistent availability of good replacement players credited for some of the Yankees' success. Second, Weiss calculated that it cost the Yankees no more to operate and assist the five clubs than it would have been to purchase outright one outstanding minor league player. Weiss was so positive he was on the right track that he predicted that within a few years, every major league organization would be able to boast several minor league affiliates. Those who opted not to have any affiliates "would be helplessly in the rear of the more progressive organizations."[24]

Soon after he became farm director, Weiss's personality began to alter. Thirty-seven years of age in 1932, he was now older than most of his players, and an employee rather than an employer. The perception of him was transforming from a quiet, player-friendly owner/manager at New Haven and Baltimore to a silent, impersonal, tough negotiator who was cold and exacting when dealing with his players.[25]

During the next four years, Weiss's acumen and Ruppert's support built the Yankees' farm system into an organization that many said equaled or outdid Rickey's system for the Cardinals. It included one or more farm teams at each of the minor league levels.[26] The number of clubs in Weiss's farm system peaked at 24. Due to the Depression, mergers and World II, the number was reduced to a more controllable seven or eight clubs.[27]

Weiss saw a definite need for providing challenging opponents for his teams. He not only brought teams into the Yankees' chain, he acted to revive the minor league system, which was feeling the effects of the Depression.[28] "What we want," said Weiss, "is a league where each hop is a bus ride."[29] Other clubs that became Yankees' farm clubs in the early and mid–1930s in addition to AA Newark included Asheville and Norfolk in the Piedmont League, and Wheeling and Washington, Pennsylvania, in the Class C Mid-Atlantic Coast League.[30]

Weiss also worked to re-establish the Eastern League, suggesting it be made up of teams in the Boston area. The Yankees would operate a team in Springfield, Massachusetts, again. His purchase of Wheeling in early 1933 was credited with restoring the Mid-Atlantic League.[31]

For the 1935 season, the chain expanded westward with clubs in Joplin, Missouri, in the Class C Western Association, and Oakland in the AA Pacific Coast League. The Oakland team remained in the Yankees' farm system for three years and produced such stars as Spud Chandler, Ernie Bonham and Joe Gordon.[32]

Late in 1935, Weiss transferred the Stogies, the Yankees' franchise at Wheeling, to Akron, Ohio. Now located in the Middle Atlantic League as a Class C farm club, the Stogies existed from 1935 until 1941.[33]

Dan Parker of the *New York Daily Mirror* reported that by 1937, Weiss had formed the most formidable chain organization in the game. Parker noted that of the 13 clubs on the Yankees' chain, four were leading their leagues, one was in second place, one in third, and two in fourth. The Yankees' farm system included teams in the International League, the Pacific Coast League, the American Association, and the New York–Pennsylvania, Piedmont, South Atlantic, Western Association, Middle Atlantic, Canadian-American, Florida State, Pennsylvania State, Coastal Plain, and Bi-State Leagues.[34]

In 1937 the Yankees won both the major league World Series and the Junior World Series, and *The Sporting News* stressed the remarkable accomplishments of George Weiss. Noting that it had taken Weiss some time to produce dividends, the paper acknowledged that Weiss had been correct when he insisted that the construction of a chain store system be done in only one way—the right and slow way. Weiss kept plugging away and, as he envisaged, the Yankees could boast that they possessed the most successful farm system in the game. "It looks very much as if Rickey will have to run second from now on, as Weiss is rated the wisest chain handler the game yet has developed."[35]

With the number of farm clubs growing and the workload increasing, Weiss needed some help. The Yankees appointed former Norfolk Tars manager Bill Skiff supervisor and co-coordinator of the Yankees' farm system. A former first baseman, Skiff's job description called for him to visit the training camps of the farm clubs and assist the managers in the selection of their players.[36]

George Weiss began his seventh year as head of the Yankees' farm system, which consisted of 13 teams. Colonel Ruppert proudly stated that the Yankees' farms were paying fast and fat dividends. Weiss had sent the Yankees some badly needed pitching help in Johnny Murphy, Jimmy DeShong, Atley Donald, Lee Stine and Joe Beggs. Others coming out of the farm system included infielder Red Rolfe and outfielder George Selkirk. George Weiss was especially enthusiastic about infielder Joe Gordon and sent him to the Yanks to replace the famous Tony Lazzeri at second base. Not all of the players were sent to the Yankees. The chain realized a hefty profit when they developed and sold two first basemen, Buddy Hassett and Johnny McCarthy, to Brooklyn.[37]

By the end of 1937, as George Weiss took a look at his chain system he was proud of his accomplishments. "With the chain set-up," said Weiss, "minor league players are sure of salaries, they are being watched closely and will be graduated as fast as they show the proper abilities. Territories have been cut down to next to nothing. Baseball marches on."[38]

By the middle of 1938, only Sam Breadon's St. Louis Cardinals, with the help of Branch Rickey, had more farm clubs (30) than the Yankees. The two organizations differed in another way. The Yankees' farm clubs would hold two or three "tryouts" each season. All promising players in the area were invited to come to the ballpark and demonstrate their skills. Those displaying ability were signed up. The Yankees' chain, unlike that of the Cardinals, did not conduct baseball "schools." The Yankees' farm clubs would merely try out prospects and train them after signing them up. They made no attempt to train them prior to the tryout.[39]

Weiss's farm system was a shining example of organization. Dr. Earl Painter, New York trainer since 1929, told *The Sporting News* that George Weiss deserved much credit for the success of the New York Yankees.

> The success of the Yankees is due, in large part, to George Weiss's genius for organizing a development system that seems to produce the most from all our rookie material. The farm system has been successful because it is progressively scaled. There is a coordinated chain organized to receive a player at the earliest evidence of his ability, and to bring him along gradually until he gets his chance in the majors. Youngsters are not rushed ahead faster than their talents warrant. Players are not taken away from minor league clubs so that they are broken up and loyalty killed.[40]

Making the results even better, the Yankees were spending less money on talent than any other team except the Cardinals, but from 1932, when Weiss began his farm system, to 1943, when the war interrupted, the Yankees won the American League pennant eight times. During that time, the Yankees purchased only five players, two of whom were Joe DiMaggio and Tommy Henrich. The players that Weiss signed and sold to other organizations earned the Yankees more than $2,000,000. Weiss had an uncanny ability to evaluate player talent; he never made a deal without knowing more about the opposition's talent than the opposition did.[41]

Helping Ruppert create a farm system was Weiss's first major task as farm director. His second was to populate his farm clubs with young players who could become Yankees or could be traded or sold to make money for the Yankees organization. For much of the needed information on these young players, Weiss depended on reliable scouts; he always considered scouts "the backbone of any baseball organization."[42] "You can have the greatest front office in the business but it won't mean a thing unless you have the scouts who bring back the ball players. That's exactly where the game begins and ends—with the scouts."[43]

Not only did Weiss have a large number of capable scouts, he also had a willing owner who could afford to pay these players once they were discovered.[44] Until 1965, young prospects were fair game on the open market, and those teams with the best scouting departments, such as the Yankees, "gobbled" up most of the talent. After 1965 the drafting of amateur prospects was implemented to provide parity.[45]

Two later Yankees stars confirmed both Weiss's ability to recognize baseball talent and his acumen in picking the right people to search for future major leaguers. Jerry Coleman, a Yankees infielder from 1949 to 1967, became director of personnel after his playing days were over. Coleman said, "Weiss hardly ever missed acquiring the best available players. He would contact both college and high school coaches to be on the lookout for upcoming talent. He was also able to hire the best players from the minor leagues, with scouts being a key to his organization."[46]

Dr. Bobby Brown, former third baseman for the Yankees from 1946 to 1953, also lauded Weiss's use of scouts to recruit future Yankees players. "His greatness," said Brown, "was very much due to the fact that he had great scouts all around the country. He kept a pipeline of talent which comprised his farm system."[47]

Weiss was fortunate that he had inherited not only the beginning of a chain system with the Newark Bears, but also three perceptive, knowledgeable men who formed the nucleus of one of the largest and most successful scouting staffs in the majors. Before 1932, these scouts—Paul Krichell, Gene McCann, and Bill Essick—provided much of the information and advice Ruppert had used in player acquisitions and trades. Now they were Weiss's eyes and ears to discover, evaluate, and obtain young players for the rosters of farm clubs at every level.

Weiss made sure that all of his scouts had considerable minor league experience and had the baseball country covered geographically. His scouts were well known throughout the baseball world and had important contacts through which they were immediately tipped off about up-and-coming youngsters.[48] He insisted on choosing his scouts with care, if possible hiring those who had previously worked with other clubs. "Then," said Weiss, "the problem becomes one of development. We have a school, and the small minors and the top farm clubs. We try to select minor league managers who know our system and who stress player versatility." Weiss always had a penchant for those players capable of playing a multitude of positions.[49]

Paul Krichell, a former catcher for the St. Louis Browns who joined the Yankees in 1921, headed the team of scouts. Krichell was born in 1882 and joined the St. Louis Browns in 1911. He started his coaching career with the Boston Red Sox in 1920. Ed

Barrow, then Yankees secretary, brought him to the Yankees the following year. He scouted the East and colleges during the spring.[50]

Krichell quickly demonstrated his talent by signing Columbia University student Lou Gehrig at a game between Columbia and Rutgers.[51] He built a two-man scouting staff to 20 and went on to sign such Yankees stars as Red Rolfe, Vic Raschi, Whitey Ford, Bill Dickey, Spud Chandler, Atley Donald, Charley Keller, and Hank Borowy.[52] Marty Appel, for many years head of public relations for the New York Yankees, wrote of Krichell, "If ever an early twentieth century figure defined the role of scout, it was Krichell, a good candidate for the Hall of Fame should they ever get around to scouts."[53]

In the summer of 1936, Krichell convinced Barrow and Weiss to organize a camp for prep stars. From this camp the Yankees landed future Hall of Fame shortstop Phil Rizzuto.[54] Krichell also supervised scouts who were responsible for geographic regions. He reasoned that by working in small groups, it was easier to check each scout's judgment.

Krichell convinced Weiss that major league scouts should be men who had previously played in the major leagues. "Scouts should be honest and have initiative. Above all, scouts should be one hundred percent organizational men. Credit for any players reaching the major leagues should be given to the team's entire scouting system."[55]

In 1953 Krichell received the coveted William Slocum Memorial Award for "outstanding service over a long period of years," awarded annually by the Baseball Writers' Association of America. Krichell scouted for the Yankees from 1921 until his death in 1957 at the age of 54, serving for most of those years as chief scout.[56]

Gene McCann became a Yankees scout in 1927. He pitched for a number of minor league organizations from 1895 to 1904, when an arm injury ended his playing career. He became a press agent, manager, and even an umpire for one day. He had a hand in recommending a number of major league stars, including Charley Keller, Buddy Rosar and Bud Metheny. He was president of two Yankees farm clubs, Binghamton and Norfolk, when, at the age of 66, he died of cancer on April 26, 1943.[57]

The third of George Weiss's inherited scouts was Illinois native Bill Essick, who was in baseball for more than 45 years, but was best known as a Yankees scout.[58] After graduating from college in 1903, Essick spent the next ten years pitching for various minor league teams, including the Portland Browns in the Pacific Coast League and the former Cincinnati Pars, and in 1911 he tossed a no-hitter for the Grand Rapids Furniture Makers in the Class B Central League.[59]

During his brief stint with the Pars, he earned the nickname "Vinegar Bill" because he hated to lose and sometimes refused to talk for hours after a defeat.[60] From 1913 to 1925, Essick was a successful manager of several minor league teams, including eight years with the Vernon (CA) Tigers in the Class AA Pacific Coast League. His sale of Bob Meusel to the New York Yankees prior to the 1919 season began a close relationship between Essick and the Yankees' management. In 1925, after a dispute with Vernon's owner, Essick joined the Yankees as a scout, concentrating on California. Interestingly, Essick was indirectly responsible for George Weiss's hiring. In 1927, Essick was the scout who recommended that Col. Ruppert purchase shortstop Lyn Lary and second baseman Jimmy Reese from Oakland, the disastrous deal that caused Ruppert to become disillusioned with this method of acquiring talent.[61] Essick remained with the Yankees for 25 years, retiring a year before his death on October 12, 1951, at the age of 69.[62]

Weiss began to expand his scouting staff soon after taking over as farm director. The men he wanted not only recognized players with skills and drive needed for success, but also had "that special something that enables him to deal with parents as well as boys." Weiss cited Bill Essick and Paul Krichell, who "practically used to live with the families of the boys they were after." Weiss also praised Joe Devine, hired in late 1932, as "one of the best."[63]

Devine was born in Oakland in 1892 and spent most of his life in northern California. World War I broke out after he had played only two games in the Pacific Coast League. During the war he worked in Seattle shipyards and managed the yard's baseball team. In the early 1920s, he became a minor league coach, a manager in Calgary and San Francisco, and a scout. He earned his reputation for being an astute judge of player talent while working the West Coast, scouting for the Pittsburgh Pirates from 1924 to 1930, where he signed brothers Paul and Lloyd Waner, Arky Vaughn and Joe Cronin. Joe Cronin, who spent most of his career as a player with the Boston Red Sox, was constantly asked why the Red Sox lagged so far behind the Yankees despite all of their high-priced young players. According to Cronin, "The Yankees have had superior scouts. One man alone—Joe Devine—picked up three players who were regulars in the Yankee infield—Gil McDougald, Jerry Coleman, and Andy Carey."[64] Weiss quickly hired Devine

The recruitment of two star Yankees outfielders, Charlie Keller (left) and Joe DiMaggio, can be attributed to three of the team's excellent scouting staff: Bill Essick, Joe Devine and Paul Krichell (National Baseball Hall of Fame Library, Cooperstown, New York).

when the Cincinnati Reds fired him after the 1932 season, assigning him as supervisor of the West Coast scouts.⁶⁵

Although the scouts had to concentrate more and more on amateurs as the Yankees increased the number of their farm clubs, they still never missed an opportunity to acquire promising minor league talent.⁶⁶ One of the best examples was the acquisition of Joe DiMaggio.

In 1933 Essick and Devine, as well as a number of other major league scouts, all wanted 18-year-old Joe DiMaggio, a speedy outfielder with an outstanding throwing arm and incredible batting skills. He was playing his rookie season with the San Francisco Seals of the Pacific Coast League. Seals owner Charley Graham wanted $75,000–$100,000 for him, an enormous sum especially during the Great Depression.⁶⁷

DiMaggio's future, once so rosy, began to look bleak, however, in May 1934, when the young outfielder suffered torn cartilage in his left knee. The original diagnosis was strained tendons, and he continued to play for two more days, which made the injury worse. The following morning, DiMaggio's leg collapsed again. As a pinch-hitter that same day, he hit a home run, but he literally had to limp around the bases.⁶⁸

Many major league clubs had been interested in DiMaggio, but they were frightened by the report of his knee injury, which they believed he suffered while playing shortstop. Devine and Essick, however, investigated further, and found that DiMaggio had hurt his knee as a result of a freakish accident. He had stepped from a taxi without realizing that his left foot was asleep. "I went down like I'd been shot," DiMaggio later said. "There was no twisting, just four sharp cracks at the knee. I couldn't straighten out my leg. The pain was terrible, like a whole set of aching teeth in my knee."⁶⁹

The two scouts were convinced that Weiss ought to make a deal for him. While Barrow was skeptical of DiMaggio's physical condition, Weiss accepted his scouts' recommendation and urged Colonel Ruppert to make an offer for DiMaggio. On the strength of Devine's and Essick's recommendations, and the report of a local doctor that DiMaggio's knee was okay, Ruppert acquiesced. The Yankees paid the Seals owner $25,000 in cash and five minor league players for DiMaggio. It was agreed that DiMaggio would play the 1935 season for the Seals, where he hit .395.⁷⁰

During his life, Jacob Ruppert, Jr., wore many hats—brewer, businessman, National Guard Colonel, and a four-term congressman from New York. He also was sole owner of the New York Yankees from 1922 until his death in 1939. One of his most important baseball decisions was to appoint George Weiss his farm director in 1932 (National Baseball Hall of Fame Library, Cooperstown, New York).

The fact that Essick and Devine contacted Weiss about acquiring DiMaggio, and not Barrow, reveals much about the relationship of the Yankees' farm director and their general manager. The two men were compatible most of the time, but on occasion they would differ on important issues. In the case of DiMaggio, Barrow simply could not see the need to spend money when the farm was supposed to provide the club with players.[71] It is also possible that in many respects they clashed because they were too much alike, or as Hazel Weiss said, they were both "German square heads."[72]

Nearly two decades after the Yankees signed DiMaggio, Joe Devine wrote Weiss, defending his acquisition of the great player. "I believe that you should get full credit for the DiMaggio deal and for this reason I am putting all this on paper as I want to go on record as being there on the spot and to give you my version of the purchase. I like to see credit go where credit is due and I wanted to get this on paper and send it to you for the future in case in the years to come you may like to have it." He made it quite clear that had it not been for Weiss, the Yankees would never have acquired DiMaggio.[73]

Joe Devine died on September 21, 1951, in a San Francisco hospital at the age of 56.[74] George Weiss was distressed that his death received so little notice in the press. "It won't be the same around here without him," Weiss said on the day the Yankees clinched the pennant. "The fans never read much about him, but he was as vital to our success as anyone in the organization. The material he got for us was only part of his contribution. To him, the Yankees were something more than just a baseball outfit; they were a deep part of his life."[75]

In 1945 Weiss hired Tom Greenwade, a former scout for the Browns and Dodgers. He is credited with signing a number of prominent major leaguers, including George Kell, Rex Barney, Bill Virdon, Pee Wee Reese, Gil Hodges, Hank Bauer, Elston Howard, Bobby Murcer, Clete Boyer, Tom Sturdivant, Ralph Terry and a 19-year-old prospect named Mickey Mantle. Few know that Greenwade was the man who suggested to Weiss that the Yankees trade for a young Kansas City Athletics outfielder named Roger Maris after the 1959 season.

He was considered one of the best judges of prospects. One time at a meeting discussing a possible player with George Weiss, Greenwade said, " Mr. Weiss, he just isn't a Yankee." The Yankees did not sign the prospect who never made it to the major leagues. Greenwade was considered the finest scout of his era by the time of his retirement in 1982. He died August 10, 1986.[76]

In the opinion of many baseball observers, Branch Rickey may have started the chain system, but Weiss perfected it.[77] He made sure that the farm club managers and coaches not only developed the professional skills of their squads, but also taught the recruits how to be Yankees, instilling Weiss's standards of how Yankees were expected to behave on and off the field. The Yankees picked their players carefully, with an eye not only to skill but also to character. On those rare occasions when a "wrong person" slipped through the net and began to make trouble, he did not last very long.[78] Most importantly, players who came through the Yankees' farm system were helped to understand their role in contributing to a winning team.[79]

In the summer of 1937, columnist Francis J. Powers, assessed the future of the Yankees under Colonel Ruppert and George Weiss. He concluded that the New York Yankees' farm system rivaled that of the Cardinals in productivity even though it had not yet been completed. Powers predicted that with Weiss's expertise and Ruppert's financial resources, the New York Yankees had such a phenomenal advantage, that some day the American League might find it necessary to take steps to break up a Yankees pennant monopoly.[80]

Ruppert responded by suggesting that the rest of baseball follow the Yankees' example. He gleefully predicted that the Yankees' farm system "would go on and on."[81]

5

The Bears and the Blues

Colonel Jacob Ruppert hired George Weiss not only as the director of the Yankees' farm system, but also as general manager of all the minor league clubs.[1] It was not surprising that Weiss would take particular interest and involve himself in the Newark Bears, the Yankees' first farm club in the chain and the only AA club for Weiss's first five years. Unlike Branch Rickey, whose sole purpose for the St. Louis Cardinals' minor league teams was to help the Cardinals win pennants, George Weiss adhered strictly to Ruppert's commitment to having his minor league clubs, especially Newark, post winning records.[2] Up to the time the Bears were owned by the Yankees, the team had never finished in first place. During George Weiss's regime, the Bears finished their season in first place in 1932, 1933 and 1934, and would repeat in 1937 and 1938.[3]

The first manager to guide the Bears to a first-place finish was Al Mamaux. Born on May 30, 1894, Mamaux was almost the identical age of Weiss, but at 6 feet and 168 pounds, a much bigger man. A right-handed pitcher with the Pirates and Brooklyn, Mamaux also spent part of the 1924 season with the Yankees. He pitched for Newark from 1927 through 1931 and had his best year in 1927 with a record of 25–10, hurling 318 innings.[4]

Mamaux had replaced Tris Speaker as manager of the Bears midway through the 1931 season. Newark finished fifth that year with an 80–88 record. The question of whether to rehire Mamaux as manager was quickly resolved when Colonel Ruppert was inundated with fan requests to retain the popular manager. Letters and petitions from organizations, public officials, and private citizens poured into Ruppert's office. Finally, on December 3, 1931, Colonel Ruppert gave in and announced that Mamaux would not only be rehired for the 1932 season, but that he would be in full charge of the Bears. Much to the delight of the Bears' fans, Ruppert added that the players the Yankees sent to Newark would remain with the Bears for at least one year, even if that might put the Yankees' chances of winning a pennant at risk.[5] When Ruppert hired Weiss in February 1932, Mamaux continued managing the Bears as well as pitching for the team.[6]

The 1932 season for the Newark Bears was the first under Yankees ownership. Although most experts expected the Bears to finish first, Weiss remained cautiously optimistic. He had always felt that it was difficult to fix a team owned by a major league squad, especially one that played its home games so close to the parent club.[7]

With the team dressing in hand-me-down, pinstriped uniforms on a bitter cold Opening Day, more than 13,000 Newark fans came out to the rainy, windswept, renamed Ruppert Stadium to watch the Bears face the Toronto Leafs. Newark entered the bottom of the ninth trailing, 5–1, but most of the diehard Newark fans stayed despite the still falling rain and a temperature that had plunged to 28 degrees. With the bases loaded, second baseman Andy Cohen tied the game with a grand slam home run, and the Bears scored the tie-breaking run in the bottom of the tenth on relief pitcher Frank Nelson's single.[8] Sitting in his box seat, Colonel Ruppert was quite pleased with his farm club's accomplishment on Opening Day. "No World Series the Yankees ever won gave me a greater thrill," he later gloated. "And they call it minor league baseball."[9]

As June wore on, the team improved its play and by mid–July the Bears were in first place. In mid–August the team widened its margin to 11½ games and were on their way to winning the pennant. Their starting pitchers, Don Brennan, Jim Weaver, and Harry Holsclaw, were all doing well, and John Murphy was excellent coming out of the bullpen. Five of the Bears regulars—Dixie Walker, Jess Hill, Forrest Jensen, Red Rolfe, and Marvin Owen—were all hitting above .300. Weiss had acquired three of these players—Owen, one of the best infielders in the league, from Toronto; Forrest Jensen from the Pittsburgh Pirates; and Johnny Murphy, sent down from the Yankees in order to bolster the pitching staff.[10] While the Yankees helped Newark by sending them players needed to win their pennant, George Weiss's farm system was lauded for supplying the Yankees with players they needed to win the American League pennant and the World Series.[11]

Newark finished the 1932 season with a remarkable record of 109 wins and only 59 losses for a .649 percentage, 15½ games ahead of the second-place team. They faced the Minneapolis Millers of the American Association in the Little World Series. With Marvin Owen hitting three home runs, the Bears won the Series in six games, claiming their first Little World Series Championship under Ruppert and Weiss.[12]

At the minor league winter meeting held in Columbus, Ohio, the International League adopted two major resolutions. First, it agreed to a salary limit for minor league baseball clubs of $39,000 a season for each club. At the same time, the International League adopted an 18-player limit. This number included a manager, in case he played, and was exclusive of the pilot if he did not. George Weiss cast the only dissenting vote on both of the questions. The action of the International League was similar to the one taken by the American Association several weeks earlier. Only the Pacific League among the AA leagues opposed the salary cap.[13]

With the success of the 1932 Bears, Weiss began to garner more attention personally. He was described at this time as genial "but quiet, even sphinx-like," meaning that he made no wild predictions. He accomplished the job of acquiring players and talked only afterwards.[14]

Despite his success in 1932 and the predictions of a strong 1933 squad, Weiss, in what would become a trademark of sorts, sent out contracts to his players with lower salary amounts or offered small raises to stars such as Johnny Neun or Red Rolfe. The exact amounts were never disclosed because Weiss's policy regarding his players' salaries was to maintain "ultimate secrecy." Weiss did not seem too concerned about any player "holdouts." He was well aware that he could always obtain new players from the parent club, if necessary. In fact, Newark had recently obtained pitcher Jim Weaver by outright purchase from the Yankees, along with outfielder George Selkirk, someone Weiss felt had the ability to become an outstanding player.[15]

Weiss not only handled player personnel for the Yankees' farm system, but he was helpful to Colonel Ruppert in other ways. Prior to spring training in 1933, the Yankees held their annual hot stove league dinner. Colonel Ruppert, who was scheduled to preside at the dinner, was confined to his home because of a severe cold. Weiss, acting in Ruppert's behalf, presented gold, engraved buckles to nine of the Newark players present, to Bears manager Al Mamaux, and to both the team's trainer and its business manager. Players living in the area were brought to the affair by the ball club. Walter Johnson, a close friend of Weiss and a former Newark manager, was at the speakers' table and received an ovation when he was introduced.[16]

The onset of the Great Depression during the 1930s threatened the economic viability of the minor leagues, whose major source of income was tied to ballpark attendance. The clubs tried many strategies to curb this loss of income. A number of them installed lights to play night games during the week, while others routinely played doubleheaders on Sundays. Unfortunately, these were only stopgap measures, since attendance kept dropping and many clubs went into bankruptcy.[17]

One man, Frank "Shag" Shaughnessy, a former outfielder who had played nine major-league games in 1905 and 1908, thought he had a solution. Shaughnessy had held various positions with minor league baseball teams before he moved his family to Montreal in 1921, where he entered the insurance business while still coaching the football and ice hockey teams at McGill University. Midway through the 1921 baseball season, he returned to manage the Syracuse Stars in the International League.[18]

In 1932 Shaughnessy became the business manager of the Montreal Royals in the International League.[19] He attempted to implement a plan which he felt would maintain the integrity of baseball, and at the same time help stabilize the finances of the clubs that were in fiscal trouble. The major problem as he saw it, was that the fans in cities whose clubs were not contending for post-season play by the beginning of July stayed away from their team's games the rest of the season. Shaughnessy, an avid hockey fan, knew that the National Hockey League was using a playoff system that qualified eight teams for a five-stage playoff process to determine the Stanley Cup champion.[20]

After Newark ran away with the pennant in 1932, Shaughnessy was able to convince the International League to rethink its winner-take-all approach to the pennant. Instead, Shaughnessy proposed the "Shaughnessy Playoffs." Rather than recognizing only the regular season winner, the top four clubs competed in a post-season playoff for the Governors' Club Trophy. Unlike hockey, the first- and second-place teams and the third- and fourth-place teams would each play best-three-of-five semi-finals. The winners of the semi-finals would face each other in a best-four-of seven series to determine the International League representative to the Junior World Series.[21] Playoffs were a hit with the fans, and a playoff soon became a permanent fixture of professional baseball.[22] Weiss never liked the plan; the only important victory he won was that the first-place team during the regular season would be recognized as the "winner of the pennant."[23]

Weiss began the 1933 season by losing two of his stars from the 1932 Bears championship team. Outfielders Dixie Walker and Woody Jensen were elevated to the majors—Walker to the Yankees and Jensen to the Pittsburgh Pirates. The biggest blow to Weiss, however, was his loss of star pitcher Don Brennan, a 25-game winner in 1932, who was also promoted to the parent club in 1933. Weiss was able to beef up the hitting when he re-acquired left-handed slugger George Selkirk from Toronto. The Yankees also sent Weiss two outfielders—right-handed hitting Myril Hoag and left-handed Dusty Cooke. Cooke not only added more .punch to the lineup, but he had great speed on the bases. Finally, the Yankees provided Weiss with two right-handed pitchers, Jimmie DeShong and Charlie Devens.[24]

Despite all of Weiss's maneuvering, by June the Bears had played inconsistently. Recognizing the need for a power hitter, Weiss made two moves which assured the Bears of a first-place finish. He acquired Vince Barton from Albany in June, and the following month he made a blockbuster deal when he sent Selkirk to Rochester for George Puccinelli, who was elated at the move. Weiss was thrilled to acquire Puccinelli, whose sobriquet was the "towering Italian." Always looking for ways to draw fans, Weiss felt Puccinelli would be a profitable gate attraction for the large number of Italian fans in Newark.

On the other hand, Selkirk was unhappy to leave many old friends and an apartment he had recently leased. Ultimately he accepted the trade and commented, "But that's baseball, and to be expected now and then." Additional changes, combined with a 22-for-46 hitting streak by Johnny Neun, put the Bears solidly in first place, and they never looked back, finishing the season 14½ games ahead of the second-place Rochester Red Wings. Other season standouts included pitcher Jim Weaver (25–11), and outstanding offense from MVP shortstop Red Rolfe (.326) and infielder Jack Saltzgaver (.305).[25] Their record in 1933 was an outstanding 102–62.[26]

In 1933, the inaugural year for the Shaughnessy playoffs, Newark faced Rochester while third-place Baltimore squared off against fourth-place Buffalo. Although Newark was favored to beat Rochester, the Red Wings, who lost the first game, came back to win the next three and eliminate the Bears from the playoffs. After the game, both Red Wings manager Specs Toporcer and Bears manager Al Mamaux expressed concern about the value of the playoff system and the future of baseball. Directing his comments to Mamaux, Toporcer said, "It's a damn shame, Al, that your fellows should lose after proving beyond doubt that you had the best team in the league. And I fear for the future of baseball if our pennant races are to be meaningless."[27]

To make matters worse, fourth-place Buffalo, which posted a losing record for the 1933 season (83–85), swept third-place Baltimore in the semi-finals, then defeated Rochester in the finals, four games to two. In the Junior World Series, the Bisons lost to American Association Columbus, but a fourth-place team with a record below .500 taking part in post-season playoffs gave fans of more teams hope. In addition, the players received playoff bonuses, which totaled a large percentage of their salaries. Most baseball executives immediately saw the possibilities of Shaughnessy's plan.[28]

Weiss, however, was furious. He was slightly placated by receiving five percent of all playoff gate receipts for finishing first, but Newark's fans were appalled that the Bears had been eliminated in the playoffs and blamed the league magnates in general, and Shaughnessy in particular, for the travesty. Weiss commented that, "It is going to be hard work to build Newark up again as a real baseball city."[29]

Weiss attempted to abolish the "Shaughnessy Plan" but he had to settle for a first vs. third and second vs. fourth semi-finals, which were expanded to a best-four-out-of-seven format. Also, because the post-season games had been played in frigid, rainy weather, it was decided to reduce the 168-game schedule, in use since 1921, to the major league standard of 154 games.[30]

In 1939 the International League adopted its final version for its playoffs, making the Shaughnessy Plan nearly a universal part of every minor league. The team with the best won-lost record squares off against the playoff eligible team with the worst record, with the other teams matched up accordingly.[31]

Weiss had other problems to resolve regarding the 1934 season. In late September, the Bears announced that they would not renew the contract of their manager, Al Mamaux. Although his teams had dominated the International League for two years, many felt that his fate was sealed by the shocking playoff loss in 1933.[32]

While the Newark fans anxiously waited the announcement of the Bears' new manager, rumors proliferated about who he might be. By the first week in November, names were still being tossed around—aging Yankees such as Herb Pennock and Joe Sewell; and Mike Kelly, former Yankees coach and most recently manager of Jersey City.[33] Then on November 23, the *Newark Evening News* ran a story that Babe Ruth had been offered the job. Colonel Ruppert would neither affirm nor deny the rumor, while Weiss called the move "far fetched." Weiss, who along with Ruppert was vacationing in French Lick, Indiana, added that there were a number of obstacles. "The Babe would have to be waived out of both the big leagues and that is hardly conceivable. Ruth has not even been approached on the matter."[34]

A month later, Ruth, in an *Associated Press* interview, stated that Ruppert had offered him the job of managing the Newark Bears. "The Colonel wanted me to go to Newark," Ruth told the sportswriter, "but I couldn't see it." This ended the "Ruth-for-Manager" speculation, and the Yankees brass still had no manager for the Bears.

A week after Ruth declined, Weiss announced that Bob Shawkey, a former major league pitching star, would succeed Al Mamaux as Newark's manager. Shawkey was no stranger to Newark fans; he had been in the International League in 1926 with Montreal, and in 1931 he was manager of the Jersey City Skeeters. His selection, however, came as a surprise to the local fans, because his name had never been mentioned in the pre-election speculation.[35]

Shawkey pitched for 15 years in the major leagues, winning 20 games four times and reaching the World Series five times. He began his major league career with the Philadelphia Athletics, hurling for Connie Mack, who traded him to the Yankees during the 1915 season. Shawkey pitched for the Yankees until he retired at the end of the 1927 season.[36]

In 1929 Shawkey rejoined the Yankees as coach, and when Miller Huggins died that September, Shawkey replaced him as manager and brought the Yankees to a third-place finish in 1930. The following season Shawkey was replaced by Joe McCarthy.[37]

In his first press conference as Bears manager, Shawkey had this to say about his new job. "I never had any rules for my ball club, unless you take this one: Keep in condition. I don't believe in curfews and all that stuff. With the Yankees I asked only that every man do his best," and added, "I have no intention of placing myself on the eligible list as a relief pitcher." He then turned his attention to the same topic George Weiss considered a priority—the overall team makeup for the 1934 season. "We have holes to fill in the Bears' outfield, infield, and pitching and catching staffs."[38]

Weiss made a genuine attempt to fill some of those holes. He acquired second baseman Roy Schalk from the parent team on option. The Yankees sent the Bears pitcher Wilcy "Cy" Moore, a 40-year-old sinkerball pitcher, and the Bears also signed pitcher Joe Olsen and shortstop Jack Hawkins.[39] In addition, Weiss announced that the Yankees had optioned former star Bears pitcher Don Brennan back to his old team, and Shawkey stated he was counting on him for the upcoming season. Weiss was also elated about his infield for the 1934 season. Johnnie Neun was scheduled to play first base, Ray Schalk second, Bob Gibson third, and Doc Farrell would replace Red Rolfe at short.[40] Although he admitted that they would be missed, Weiss was elated that three former Newark Bears were slated to play for the Yankees in 1934—Red Rolfe, Johnny Murphy and Jack Saltzgaver.[41]

The changes in the Newark club were not restricted to the field. In the front office, the Bears announced the appointment of a new road secretary, Ray L. Kennedy, replacing Wilbur C. Crelin. Kennedy was business manager at Binghamton, where, through his efforts, the club showed a nice profit.[42]

Weiss also made news concerning one of his favorite topics—players' contracts. Prior to the 1934 season, Weiss heard that there were potential holdouts on his team. He denied those rumors, but did admit that some players were slow in returning their contracts. This perplexed Weiss because he felt that the Bears had been generous in their offers and bluntly stated, "Our payroll is almost exactly the same as last year, and the league rules prevent us from going any higher."[43]

At the annual minor league winter meeting, the International League owners voted 7–1 to retain for another year the playoff system which it adopted for 1933.[44] Unfortunately, this move cost baseball the Junior World Series in 1934. The American Association refused to play any team but the first-place finisher in the International League.[45]

As the Bears left for their spring training camp at Clearwater, Florida, Weiss announced a new policy for the team. They would take to camp a number of players from lower-level Yankees farm clubs. If they showed any promise, Weiss agreed they might be promoted to the Bears' roster. To help Shawkey run the camp, Weiss sent two fan favorites to Clearwater: Bill Skiff, manager of Norfolk, and Binghamton skipper Bill Meyer.[46] Weiss realized that the Bears needed all the help they could get, having lost 12 of the 1933 players to the majors, and he would literally have to build a new team.[47]

As the 1934 season began, Shawkey optimistically declared, "The Bears will hold their own."[48] They did that and more, playing exceptional ball through April and May. The Bears moved into first place on June 8 and remained there until they clinched their third straight pennant on September 6. However, the Bears lost the first round of the playoffs to the Toronto Maple Leafs. Baseball observers thought their defeat might have been based on Weiss's failure to bring in extra players when help was needed. For example, the Bears' leading hitter, George Selkirk, whom Weiss reacquired for 1934, was injured in July. Instead of calling for replacements, the Bears opted to send Johnny Neun, a first baseman, to the outfield. Selkirk was out for over a month.[49]

Weiss still blamed the playoff system and continued to complain about how unfair it was. "It is eminently unfair to the players," said Weiss. "The club that leads for most of the season during a 154-game campaign naturally is under the strain of protecting its position. It is too much to ask these same performers to go through two brief series where anything can happen." Weiss was also infuriated that Toronto acquired help the last month of the season from Cincinnati, its parent club. "If the Yankees ever did anything like that for the Bears, there would have been a tremendous howl around the league about chain store baseball." Shawkey echoed Weiss's strong feelings. "In a seven game series, luck plays too great a part in the proceedings. The first two games which Toronto won are proof enough of that."[50]

C. M. Gibbs, writing in the *Baltimore Sun*, sympathized with Weiss's plight but defended the playoff system. He noted that the Bears did win the pennant and their players received a cut of the receipts of the Junior World Series without actually playing. "That should appeal to them, or to anybody, for that matter," wrote Gibbs. He also noted that the Bears' misfortunes were actually a benefit to the league's other clubs. "The battle to get into the playoffs helps every club in the league financially during the late months of the season," wrote Gibbs, "and if Newark hasn't what it takes to win the series, it's too bad, but there are other things of almost equal importance in the life of the league."[51]

In preparation for the 1935 season, Weiss began to make deals to strengthen his club. The first move was to sell outfielder Vince Barton and first baseman Sollie Mishkin to the Baltimore Orioles. In another deal, the Bears returned pitcher Floyd Newkirk to the parent club.[52] Weiss was making it quite clear that the policy of the Bears was that the club would not keep any individual who could not demonstrate the ability to make the grade with the Yankees.[53]

After playing coy for a couple of months, the Bears finally announced the rehiring of Bob Shawkey as manager for 1935. In making the announcement, Weiss praised Shawkey for his success in achieving Weiss's two most important criteria. "He not only won the International League pennant, but at the same time developed players valued at thousands of dollars."[54]

Weiss was not only reshuffling the Bears' roster and rehiring his manager, he was expanding the Yankees' farm system. He added Joplin, Missouri, of the Western Association to his list. Acquiring Joplin was the first move the Yankees made with a club not in Eastern territory. Baseball experts called the acquisition of Joplin an indication that the Yankees' chain would reach from the Atlantic to the Pacific.

Weiss then completed some unfinished business. He selected the five players owed to the San Francisco Seals as part of the Joe DiMaggio deal. None of them ever made it to the major leagues.[55]

By the end of 1934, George Weiss was adding to his reputation as one of the shrewdest men in baseball, one who would not part with any of his players unless he received at least an even break in return.[56] By the beginning of 1935, Weiss had expanded the Yankees' farm system to seven clubs with the addition of Oakland (AA). In the short space of five years, the Yankees had constructed a network of minor league connections, placing them virtually on a par with Rickey's St. Louis Cardinals.[57]

Colonel Ruppert did his best to help the Bears in 1935, sending Weiss first baseman George McQuinn, second baseman Ray Schalk, and catcher Willard Hershberger to

Weiss is shown doing what he did best—working the telephone to obtain the best players at the lowest prices (Steve Steinberg Collection).

bolster the Bears' chances for a fourth consecutive pennant.[58] Despite the help Weiss received from the parent club, the 1935 club was primarily a youthful team with a dash of experience. Although they won ten of their first 14 at home, they struggled on their first road trip. In spite of some personnel changes, including obtaining "Dixie" Walker for the remainder of the season, the Bears went into an appalling tailspin and ultimately finished the season in fourth place, barely making the playoffs. They again went no further than the first round, losing four straight games to the Syracuse Chiefs, a Boston Red Sox affiliate.[59] The Bears had the unenviable distinction of being the first team since the playoff system began to be eliminated in four games. The Newark fans found little consolation in the fact that the Chiefs eventually went on to defeat the Montreal Royals in seven games to capture the International League pennant.[60]

Triple Crown winner George Puccinelli was the only bright spot in an otherwise dismal season for the Bears. He led the International League in batting average (.359), home runs (53), and runs batted in (172) to win his second IL batting title in four years and become only the second Triple Crown winner in league history. There would not be another two-time Triple Crown winner in the International League until 1955.[61]

Later that fall, George Trautman, President of the American Association, announced that his league would finally end their differences with the International League and signed an agreement to resume the popular Junior World Series. The reason was simple. Almost all the other minor leagues had adopted some form of playoff system because it was popular for the fans and a money-maker for the leagues.[62]

In October 1935, the Bears announced that Sebring, Florida, would be their spring training site. Weiss decided to move to Sebring after the Dodgers announced that they were moving back to Clearwater. The Bears had no desire to compete with a major league team or even share their facilities. Since Sebring had never hosted a "big minor league club," the city eagerly awaited the arrival of the Bears.[63]

A month later, George Weiss read a brief statement to the press: "The Newark Baseball Club regrets to announce that Bob Shawkey will not return as its manager next season." Although no specific reasons were given, it was rumored that Shawkey's "interests outside of baseball" (a Canadian gold mine he owned) would not permit him to give the 100 percent attention required in his position as manager of the club.[64]

Weiss selected Oscar Vitt to replace Shawkey as Newark's manager. Vitt, a product of the sandlots of San Francisco, broke into the Pacific Coast League as a third baseman for the Seals in 1911. In the major leagues, he played with the Detroit Tigers from 1912 to 1918, and with the Boston Red Sox from 1919 to 1921.[65] In 1935 he managed the Oakland Oaks, a Yankees AA farm club. Described as being both "abrasive and motivational," Vitt managed to push the Oaks to a third-place finish his first year.[66]

Weiss felt that Vitt had the right kind of tough-minded leadership to take his Bears to a championship season. *The Sporting News* described him as "a colorful individual likely to liven up the Bears."[67] Newark's fans were enthusiastic about Vitt's tough discipline, with emphasis on physical conditioning and fundamentals. They also liked some of the new Bears players including first baseman John McCarthy, a player Weiss obtained from Brooklyn for Buddy Hassett, another first sacker, but one unlikely to replace Lou Gehrig for the position. In addition, Weiss also received $40,000 and two "throw-in" players from Brooklyn in the trade.[68] In typical Weiss fashion, he later sold these two players for $65,000, which meant he had netted $105,000 total for a player who did not figure in the Yankees' picture.[69]

In addition to good baseball, Weiss still offered a few fan promotions to build loyalty and enthusiasm. One fan recalled that he could buy tickets for seven games at Newark's Ruppert Field for a nickel.[70] Newark fans also loved what had become an annual promotion, an "old-timers" event that placed on the field former Newark greats as well as scout Paul Krichell. Weiss even brought in Olympian Jesse Owens and dancer Bill Robinson to entertain the crowd.[71]

Meanwhile the Bears were fighting four teams for the 1936 pennant: Buffalo, Rochester, Birmingham, and Toronto. The Yankees' brass was shuffling players in an attempt to help their farm team. They sent the Bears two experienced pitchers—Steve Sundra and Vito Tamulis. Unfortunately, the Yankees were forced to take the Bears' first-string catcher, Willard Hershberger, and send him to Oakland to replace the Oaks' injured receiver, Norman Kies. This left the Bears with Bill Baker as the team's only full-time receiver. Even though the Bears also suffered from mid-season injuries, they finished only one game out of second place, in a dead heat with Rochester for third place. This necessitated a single playoff game that turned out to be a disaster. Rochester scored three unearned runs in the first inning, and Newark lost, 5–2. Rochester lost in the first round of the playoffs to league-leading Buffalo.[72]

At the 1936 International League winter meetings held in Montreal this year, Frank Shaughnessy was elected successor to Warren Giles as president of the International League. George Weiss was named vice-president; both men were to serve a one-year term.[73] *The Sporting News* applauded the new officers as "efficient and progressive baseball men."[74]

Weiss waited until after the winter meetings to announce that he was renewing Vitt's contract to manage the Bears for a second season in 1937. This came as no surprise, since no one in the Bears or Yankees organization blamed Vitt for the fourth-place finish. Although Vitt had managed the Bears for only one year, he had become a favorite not only among the fans, but also among the Bears' players and local scribes. "Ossie always had a story to pass out to any typewriter puncher looking for copy," wrote *The Sporting News*. His immense fund of baseball yarns also made him in demand as a speaker.[75]

Weiss's sixth year with Newark and the Yankees' farm system would prove one of the most significant in his long and successful baseball career, and his personal life as well. The performance of the International League AA Newark Bears was certainly one of the highlights.

The year began routinely. After renewing Vitt's contract, Weiss, as was his practice, constantly used the telephone and telegraph to learn everything he could about every player and team in the Yankees' entire chain, assessing their strengths and shortcomings. He also made it a point to know as much as possible about players in his opponents' camps.[76]

One of the first tasks for Newark in 1937 was to replace players moved up to the Yankees. Weiss assumed he could obtain some players from the parent club, but he expected most from the lower farms that continued to attract high quality talent.[77] From that combination of sources, Weiss and Vitt built what all baseball authorities recognize as a great team and some call one of the best minor league clubs ever assembled.[78]

Newark got off to a great start in 1937, and by May 20 had a 3½-game lead over the rest of the field. They won 17 of their next 21 games, and their lead stretched to eight games as the team stood at 35–11. After the Bears completed a long home stand in June, the team's record stood at 46–14, 13½ games ahead of the Montreal Royals. Although they played most of July on the road, the Bears gradually increased their lead to 17 games. In August, playing mostly at home, the team jumped farther ahead, finally clinching the flag on August 23. The Bears ended the season with a record of 109–43 (.717), a gigantic 25½ games in front of Montreal. The team's overall batting average was .299; they scored 890 runs, posted 1,594 hits, and hit 292 doubles and 80 triples—all league highs.[79]

A number of Bears had outstanding years in 1937. First baseman George McQuinn hit .330 with 21 homers; third-sacker Babe Dahlgren hit .340; utility infielder Frank Kelleher, who played in only 92 games, hit .306; and Buddy Rosar, part-time catcher, batted .332. Second baseman Joe "Flash" Gordon was the Bear who ultimately had the most successful major league career. George Weiss was rightfully credited for Gordon's success. In 1936, when Tony Lazzeri, the Yankees' regular second baseman since 1927, started to "slip," it was Weiss who suggested that Oakland begin converting Gordon from a shortstop to a second baseman. He was promoted to Newark for the 1937 season, and in 1938 he became the Yankees' regular second baseman.[80]

Newark's number one catcher was the unfortunate Willard Hershberger. The 27-year-old hit. .325 for the Bears in 96 games. Hershberger was traded to the Cincinnati Reds, where he was the backup catcher to Ernie Lombardi.[81] In August 1940, Hershberger, who had grown despondent, committed suicide. Although no suicide note was found, Hershberger had told his manager, Bill McKechnie, that he was going to end his life at some future time because "my father did it and I'm going to do the same."[82]

The Bears' pitching staff dominated the opposition. Four starting pitchers—Joe Beggs, Atley Donald, Vito Tamulis, and Steve Sundra—combined for an amazing record of 73–16. Joe Beggs was the team's only 20-game winner (21–4), but Donald, with 19 wins, and Tamulis, with 18, came close. A fifth pitcher, veteran Kemp Wicker, who was with the Bears on option from late May into July, went 7–2. Five Bears hurlers accounted for 80 of Newark's 109 victories, including 12 shutouts.[83]

The outfield was exceptional even on this outstanding team. It consisted of Bob Seeds in center field, Jimmy Gleeson in left and Charlie Keller in right. Keller, only 20 years old, finished the season with a .353 average and was the youngest player to win the International League batting title.[84]

Weiss was particularly enthusiastic about Keller, predicting a future as a star Yankees' outfielder. Weiss sent him to the Yankees to answer Yankees manager Joe McCarthy's plea for additional left-handed hitting, especially to replace an aging Lou Gehrig. Weiss had signed Keller right out of the University of Maryland by offering him a Yankees contract. Keller didn't even wait for the school year to end. "He reported to the Newark club almost immediately," Weiss later recalled. "From his first time at bat, we knew we had something. Keller was a natural as a college boy."[85]

The hated playoffs, in which the Bears had lost in the first round the previous four years, provided no challenge as the 1937 Bears first defeated Syracuse and then Baltimore, each in four straight games.[86] Only the Junior World Series proved more of a contest for the Bears. Their American Association opponent was the top farm club of the St. Louis Cardinals, the Columbus Red Birds. To the numbing disappointment of the Newark fans, Columbus won the first three games, all played on the Bears' home field. The Red Birds needed only one win to clinch the title as the action moved to Columbus. There the Bears made an unbelievable comeback. Newark swept four straight games on their opponent's field to win the 1937 Junior World Championship.

As a reward, Weiss arranged a victory celebration in New York. Ruppert also promised his players that he would try to promote as many of them as possible to the major leagues, either playing for the Yankees or selling them to other major league teams if possible.[87] As it turned out, every player on the 1937 Newark roster except pitcher Jack Fallon, who injured his arm, played in the major leagues.[88]

At the victory party, Ruppert was especially effusive in his praise for Weiss. He lauded him as the man responsible for the success of the Yankees' farm system. Turning directly to the players attending the dinner, Ruppert said, "I keep tabs on him, like I keep tabs on you. I watched him in a small league and knew how capable he was before he ever knew that I was watching him. Then I decided to have a farm system. I am proud of the club; it did its job and came back a winner."[89]

It seemed fitting that the best team in the International League had played the top team in the American Association in the Junior World Series in 1937. The two teams were affiliates of the two major league teams with the best farm chains. For years, Commissioner Landis had been battling against farm systems in general and Branch Rickey, architect of the Cardinals' farm system, in particular. It was becoming evident that minor league connections were crucial for success in the major leagues. It would not be long before big league control of the minors would become complete.[90]

Another highlight of 1937 came very early in the year when Weiss announced that the Yankees had signed a working agreement with the American Association's Kansas City Blues, a second AA level team. According to Weiss, the agreement allowed the Yankees to assist the Blues with players in return for allowing the Yankees to have first call on any Kansas City star.[91]

The Kansas City owner was Johnny Kling, a former standout catcher on the winning Chicago Cubs teams of 1906–1910. Kling had returned to his hometown of Kansas City, Kansas, after his baseball career ended. He purchased the ailing Blues in 1934 and although his team finished last in the league—as it had the previous year—Kling began increasing attendance from the previous all-time season low of 53,000. In 1935 Kling brought back as manager the popular Dutch Zwilling, who pulled the Blues up to third place in both 1935 and 1936, while attendance rose to more than 200,000, second in the league.[92] However, by late July 1937, it was widely known that Kling was in poor health, and Weiss soon revealed that Kling had sold the Blues and their home stadium, Muehlebach Field, outright to the Yankees.[93]

As soon as the Yanks took over, fans were excited, looking forward to player deals for which Weiss was noted. Weiss also made administrative moves, retaining Zwilling as manager and Charles Burwell as business manager, but also bringing in Roy Hamey from the Yankees' farm team in Binghamton, as traveling secretary. Weiss tried to spark fan enthusiasm, explaining that it was too late in the season for a drastic turnaround, but that the Yankees were working to ensure that the Blues would be competitive next season.[94]

The Blues finished in fifth place in 1937. Weiss's first task was to work on the physical condition of the Blues' park, which was renamed Ruppert Stadium. He budgeted $20,000 to improve the field, erected a 12-foot fence inside the park to cut foul line distances to 350 feet and center field to 450 feet, making it more in line with other AA fields and specifically to aid KC home run production. In 1937, every home run in the Kansas City stadium, except two, was inside-the-park. Weiss also had the stadium painted and increased the lighting by 100 percent, making the park one of the best-lighted in the American Association.[95]

The year 1937 was also a very important year in Weiss's personal life. George Weiss was a loving son. Perhaps because of his father's early death, Weiss was very close to his mother, Anna Weiss, and always took care of her. When he moved from his hometown of New Haven to become the Orioles' GM, he moved his mother to Baltimore. His mother moved with him again to East Orange, New Jersey, just outside of Newark, when he accepted the job of farm director for the Yankees. While they were living in

East Orange, Anna Weiss became ill and although she lingered for quite some time, she died at their home at East Orange on June 13, 1937. Not only her son George, but also his sister Florence, who had married and was living in Dallas, and his brother, Edwin, who was living in New York City, survived her. Anna Weiss was buried in New Haven.[96]

Happier times were ahead for George. His relationship with Hazel Wood had deepened and grown closer. She had met his mother and got along well with her, often helping with her care when Weiss was out of town. In turn, Weiss and Hazel's teenage son by her first marriage, Allen Wood, who called him "Uncle George," also got along quite well. When George proposed marriage, Hazel asked Allen, who was attending prep school, for his reaction. "I think you better marry him," Allen responded, "because there are a lot of young pretty girls who would."[97]

George and Hazel were married quietly on December 18, 1937, at Trinity Lutheran Church in New York City. George was 46 years old.[98] Hazel, 37, was described by the press as "prominent in social and sports circles in Boston." For their honeymoon, the newlyweds sailed to Central America and through the Panama Canal to California.[99]

While with the Baltimore Orioles, general manager George Weiss, still a bachelor at nearly 40, met Hazel Wood, a young divorced woman, who had a teenaged son. After a long courtship and with the urging of her son, Hazel agreed to marry George in 1937. Despite his hectic schedule as a baseball executive, the couple had a happy 35-year marriage, until George's death in 1972 (Steve Steinberg Collection).

Even on his honeymoon, Weiss had baseball on his mind; he planned to spend time while in California looking over possible West Coast sites for training lower level Yankees farm players. He was also thinking about how successful his chain system was working out. "The chains have proved the salvation of baseball," he said. "Nothing will stop them. They are essential. They now are the life of the game. Minor league players are sure of salaries, they are sure of expert handling, they are sure they are being watched closely and will be graduated as fast as they show the proper abilities."[100]

Weiss had much to prepare for in 1938. The final months of 1937 found Weiss absorbed not only by personal events but also by the annual postseason activities and preparing for the following year up and down the chain, which now included two wholly owned AA clubs. In addition, Oakland of the Pacific Coast League, which had resigned its working agreement with the Yankees, also needed players.[101]

Weiss also had the task of naming new managers for both Kansas City and Newark. Weiss strategically chose

Billy Meyer, Oakland's manager, in 1937, to manage the Blues in 1938, replacing Dutch Zwilling, who replaced Meyer at Oakland.[102]

With Oakland and Kansas City settled, Weiss turned his attention back to the Bears. In a surprise move, Oscar Vitt, who had led the Bears to a victorious Junior World Series, abruptly resigned as manager of the Bears to accept the job of manager of the Cleveland Indians.[103] Weiss chose Johnny Neun, the former star infielder for the Bears from 1932 to 1934 to succeed Vitt as skipper. Neun had been managing the Norfolk Tars, a B level team in the Yankees' chain, in 1936 and 1937, when he was chosen to return to Newark.[104] This move had the full backing of not only Colonel Ruppert, but also of Yankees manager Joe McCarthy, who always worked closely with Weiss and with high-level farm club managers. McCarthy was fond of Neun and admired his leadership skill.[105] Neun was so popular in Newark that hundreds of fans had to be turned away from a large gala welcoming banquet featuring Ruppert, McCarthy and other notables including Lou Gehrig.[106]

Both Neun and Weiss had their jobs cut out for them. The Bears were going into 1938 with a team that been nearly dismantled after the 1937 season. The Bears had sent nine of their stars to the majors, including Joe Gordon, Babe Dahlgren, Steve Sundra, Spud Chandler, Tito Tamulis, and George McQuinn.[107]

During 1938 spring training in Florida, the Bears posted a long string of exhibition game wins with Charlie Keller again leading the hitters.[108] Weiss also brought to the Yankees' spring training site two rookies that he had obtained during the winter meetings. Although neither ever played for the Yankees, both had long, successful careers in the majors. Eddie Miller played for the Reds, Braves, Phillies and Cardinals from 1936 to 1950, and Eddie Joost had a 17-year career (1936–1955) with the Reds, Braves, Athletics and Red Sox.[109]

In a move that baffled even Ed Barrow, Weiss also sold one of the stars of the 1937 season, Bob Seeds, to the New York Giants for $40,000. The perplexed Barrow, who was never known for his sentimentality, asked Weiss, "George, doesn't your conscience ever bother you?" Weiss nonchalantly replied, "Why should it? I force nothing on anybody. I have my job to do as the others have theirs. The real answer is not in what's sold, but what has been kept."[110]

Once the 1938 season began, Weiss was extremely pleased with the Bears, who were again leading the International League despite not having "the pitchers that we had last year."[111] Fortunately for Newark, Weiss restocked the Bears with not only "King Kong" Keller, but also third baseman Merrill May, switch-hitting outfielder Jimmy Gleeson and first-sacker Les Scarsella.[112]

For the second year in a row, Newark outdistanced the rest of the league, winning the pennant by 18 games over second-place Syracuse. At the same time the Bears were running away with the International League pennant, Weiss was busily occupied with the Kansas City Blues, a team Weiss described "as having improved pitching, youth and speed."[113]

As a member of the Yankees' Board of Strategy, Weiss was also involved with the parent squad, which was driving toward a third straight world championship, thriving on players from the farms. In fact, knowledgeable baseball observers were giving the 44-year-old Weiss credit for developing the players who were producing these outstanding results. According to an unnamed friend of Weiss, the secret of his success was that, "He's the hardest working son-of-a-gun in the business."[114]

In round one of the 1938 playoffs, Rochester battled Newark for seven games before the Bears ultimately triumphed. Newark then defeated Buffalo in five games. One of the few spoilers of the Bears 1938 season story was actually a source of pride to Weiss. The International League pennant-winning Bears lost the Junior World Series to the Yankees' other AA farm team, the Kansas City Blues. Kansas City had finished second in the AA but won the playoffs and represented the American Association. During the series, Weiss sat 4½ innings behind each dugout.[115]

Weiss's 1938 season proved all along what many had suspected—Weiss was able to sell so much talent because he developed so much of it.[116] A look at the farm clubs' records tells the whole story. In 1938, only one club affiliated with the Yankees finished in the second division. One columnist stated simply, "Not so bad for Ed Barrow, George Weiss and their lieutenants."[117]

Weiss especially relished one aspect of the 1938 season—sometimes his Bears drew more fans than the Yankees. "I used to call Barrow every day on the phone and tell him our attendance," Weiss recalled. "And he'd blow up when we had more fans than the Yankees. One day, however, on Decoration Day, the Yankees drew 81,841 paid for a doubleheader with the Red Sox. Ed couldn't wait to get to the phone to call me in Newark with the figures."[118]

As the 1938 winter meetings approached without any announcement regarding the rehiring of Johnny Neun in Newark, Weiss reminded the press that he liked to keep as many deals going as possible to liven up the meetings, this year held in New Orleans.[119] Just prior to the winter meeting, Weiss did announce that Neun would be retained as Bears manager for a second year. Observers noted that Neun's leadership skills would be truly tested as again Newark sent key players to the Yankees and sold players to other major league teams. Those sent to the Yankees included Charlie Keller, Buddy Rosar, Les Scarsella, and Merril May. When Weiss left for New Orleans, there were only ten members of the 1938 club still on the Newark roster, but there was no assurance they would still be there when the 1939 campaign began. There was also a likelihood that additional players might be sold to other major league teams.[120]

But Weiss did not make it to the 1938 meetings in New Orleans. He came down with pneumonia and was hospitalized in the Crescent City, where he improved rapidly but was not released until Christmas. Hazel came to be with him.[121] While recuperating, Weiss had ample time to reflect on his first seven seasons as Yankees farm director, especially after a very successful 1938 season. When pressed for reasons for his success, Weiss concisely replied, "Let your managers manage, your scouts scout, your players play."[122] George Weiss was eagerly looking forward to 1939.

6

The Interregnum

In 1939 the most important event in world history was the German invasion of Poland on September 1; for George Weiss personally, the most meaningful event in 1939 happened far earlier in the year. On January 13, 1939, Weiss's boss and mentor, multi-millionaire Colonel Jake Ruppert, owner of the Yankees organization, died following a long illness. Ruppert, a leader in the brewing industry and one of the largest real property owners in New York, was stricken with a painful affliction of phlebitis, which according to the *Associated Press* he "endured with his customary cheerfulness and good nature," complaining only when unable to attend the 1938 World Series when his "beloved Yankees" won their third straight championship.[1]

A bachelor, Ruppert provided for his "favorite child" and one of his most valuable assets, the Yankees, by creating the team's governing structure to be very similar to the organization during his life. The 70-year-old Ed Barrow would run the big league club at an annual salary of $50,000. The job became his when Ruppert's younger brother, George, who represented the estate, declined the offer. Weiss, at Ruppert's explicit orders, was to continue running the farm system, which was valued at more than $3 million. Weiss was not only to continue as general manager of the entire Yankees farm system, he also assumed additional responsibilities when he was elected to Barrow's old spot as secretary of the entire organization. Some observers believed his additional duties indicated that he was likely to become General Manager whenever Barrow retired.[2]

Barrow pointed out that although he had formerly been skeptical about the value of farms, he would now strongly support the system. "I believe we have the proper minor league setup now. At present the Yankees own five minor league clubs and have working agreements with eight others. Some people have gone in over their heads on farm clubs. We won't do that. We're just about right now." He added that since the Yankees had won several pennants before branching out into farms about six years earlier, he was impressed by the success of George Weiss, who Barrow admitted "had sold him on the idea."[3]

While *The Sporting News* praised Ruppert for the success of the New York Yankees, it noted that much of the credit should be given to George Weiss.

> His ability proved itself by the success these farms have enjoyed in various pennant races and by the wealth of material which they have sent up as replacements for fading Yankees. Under the regime of Weiss and Barrow the policies of Colonel Ruppert are certain to be continued and those who may be looking for the Yankees to disintegrate because of the absence of the former guiding hand are likely to be disappointed.[4]

Jimmy Powers of the *New York Daily News* also paid tribute to Weiss's success. "It isn't money alone," wrote Powell. "Yawkey of Boston, Bradley of Cleveland, and Briggs of Detroit are millionaires. It must be brains or a combination." He noted that Weiss had the ability to spot and develop raw, gangling rookies better than anyone in baseball. "I think Weiss, der Fuehrer of the Yank farms can step right up and take a bow on this angle. He makes a minimum of boners and has to make a maximum of decisions."[5]

Just as before, Weiss continued to build his teams throughout the chain for the new season. Results were soon apparent. By August 1, eight of the clubs in the Yankees' system were in first place.[6] Newark, unfortunately, was not one of those teams. Early in the year, Weiss disposed of two veterans sent down to Newark by the parent club, saying his emphasis was on young talent. Nevertheless, the Bears got off to a miserable 1939 spring training start, losing ten games in a row,[7] a portent of things to come. Newark made the playoffs in 1939, only by defeating Syracuse in a playoff game to determine the fourth-place team. The Bears upset the Little Giants of Jersey City in the opening round of the playoffs, while the Buffalo Bisons, finishing third, lost to the Rochester Red Wings in the playoff opener. Rochester then defeated the Bears in the finals, four games to three, but in the 1939 Junior World Series, Rochester lost to Louisville in seven games.[8]

The Yankees' other major farm club, the Kansas City Blues, fared much better in their 1939 season even with a roster heavily loaded with rookies. In fact, many baseball observers claim that the 1939 Blues was one of the top all-time minor league teams.[9] Two rookie infielders, 19-year-old second baseman Gerry Priddy and 21-year-old shortstop Phil Rizzuto, garnered most of the attention. Sports writers picked both of them unanimously for the 1939 American Association All-Star team ahead of Pee Wee Reese, who had recently been bought by the Dodgers for $75,000. With the ultimate goal of making both of his young infielders into Yankees in a few years, Weiss reportedly turned down offers of $100,000 for Rizzuto, who had learned his baseball on the sandlots of New York City.[10]

Priddy, who was signed by the legendary scout, Bill Essick, played for Rogers, Arkansas, in the Class D Arkansas-Missouri League in 1937, where he hit .336. The following year he hit .323 for Norfolk (Piedmont League), both years leading all second basemen in fielding.[11] Baseball historian Bill James concluded that Priddy was one of the great defensive players in history, ranking him as the 73rd best second baseman of all time.[12] Both Rizzuto and Priddy would be promoted to the Yankees in 1941.[13]

Playing third base in his first year of pro ball was 23-year-old Billy Hitchcock. He played three years with the Blues before making it to the majors with the Detroit Tigers. After three years in the armed forces, he played eight years in the American League with several teams.[14]

Rounding out the infield was veteran first sacker Jack Saltzgaver, who lent experience to the three rookies. A veteran of 14 years in pro ball, Saltzgaver played for the Yankees from 1934 to 1937, then joined the Blues in 1938 for seven seasons. He was a player-manager for the Blues in 1944.[15]

Behind the plate was another rookie, 22-year-old Clyde McCullough, who broke into pro ball in 1935. After the 1939 season, the Chicago Cubs purchased his contract, and at the tail end of the 1940 season he was promoted to the major leagues. McCullough played primarily for the Cubs until 1956, when he retired as an active player.[16]

Thirty-three-year-old veteran Johnny Riddle who had come from the University of Georgia in 1927, handled regular catching duties. He played all or parts of seven seasons in the majors with the Senators, Boston Bees, Reds and Pirates, but spent most of his career in the American Association, 12 years with Indianapolis and three with Kansas City.[17]

The outstanding pitcher for the 1939 Blues, and the one who had the greatest major league success, was Ernie "Tiny" Bonham, a 26-year-old right-hander. He joined Kansas City from Newark in the middle of the 1938 season and pitched for the Yankees and Pirates from 1940 until his sudden death in 1949 following stomach surgery.[18]

The biggest bat in the Kansas City lineup belonged to center fielder Vince DiMaggio, the oldest of the three baseball-playing brothers. He broke in with the Tucson Lizards in 1932 and finished the year with the San Francisco Seals. He started with San Francisco in 1933, but was released early in the season and signed by Hollywood (PCL). After a successful 1936 season, the Boston Bees purchased his contract and he spent the 1937 and 1938 seasons in the major leagues.

In 1939 he was traded to the New York Yankees in a deal that brought shortstop Eddie Miller to the Bees. Vince DiMaggio never played for the Yankees. They sent him to their farm club at Kansas City, where Blues manager Bill Meyer worked with him to eliminate a pronounced hitch in his swing. In 154 games for the Blues in 1939 Vince struck out 123 times, but managed to hit 46 home runs and bat .290. Vince DiMaggio spent the next six years in the National League before finishing his career in 1946.[19]

Kansas City fans were ecstatic as the Blues won the 1939 American Association pennant with a record of 107–47, a .695 winning percentage. It was their first pennant in ten years, and *The Sporting News* named Blues manager Bill Meyer "Minor League Manager of the Year." The potential sale value of the team's players grew to an estimated half-million dollars. The pennant-winning Blues were matched up with the third-place Indianapolis Indians in the first post-season round, while the second-place Minneapolis Millers faced a weaker opponent in the Louisville Colonels. Unfortunately, the Blues' regular season magic suddenly disappeared. The Indians, with a record of 82–72, on paper seemed to be no match for the Blues. But the Blues could not handle the Indians' pitching and easily dropped the series, winning one game and losing four. They were outscored, 34–9, over the five games. Louisville went on to defeat Indianapolis, also in five games, and then won the Junior World Series from Rochester, the International League representative, four games to three.[20]

Once the playoffs were over, George Weiss attempted to complete all of Newark's business. First, he rehired Johnny Neun to manage the Bears in 1940, his third consecutive year with Newark. Weiss made it quite clear that Neun was not being blamed in any way for the team's sudden death in the final round of the 1939 playoffs. Neun was the first Newark manager to return for a third season since Colonel Ruppert assumed ownership of the team.[21]

In the majors, after the Yankees swept the Cincinnati Reds four straight games in the 1939 World Series, Weiss, Barrow, and Yankees manager Joe McCarthy began to assess the Yankees' needs for the upcoming 1940 season. It was decided that both Rizzuto

The Yankees' brain trust in a more formal setting, from left to right: Manager Joe McCarthy, General Manager Ed Barrow, and Farm Director George Weiss (Steve Steinberg Collection).

and Priddy would remain at Kansas City until they were eligible for the draft in September 1940. The Yankees admitted that they did need help at finding a replacement for the retiring Lou Gehrig, who had played only eight games for the Yankees at first base in 1939. Weiss also admitted that the Yanks desperately needed some mound help.[22]

Turning to the needs of the Kansas City Blues for the 1940 season, Weiss decided that changes would be made. He liked his infield, but knew that the outfield had to be rebuilt and also that the entire Yankees organization had to obtain pitchers. He was pleased, however, that the Blues had a better start than the previous year and they were still the team to beat in the American Association.[23]

The premier topic at the 1939 winter meetings was Commissioner Landis's plan to restrict farm systems. Always opposed to the chains, Landis hoped to weaken their ability to move players from club to club within their system, offering only unneeded players for sale or trade to other organizations. Another baseball executive, Brooklyn president Larry MacPhail, was becoming upset with the actions of the commissioner. Landis could always count on the support of Clark Griffith, who said of MacPhail and Weiss, "They wanted to amend the rules to permit them to manipulate ball players as they saw fit. And the judge wouldn't tolerate any money doodled business." Barrow laughed and replied, "We'll be doing business at the old stand.... I see no reason for cutting down on our minor league holdings as some other owners have threatened. We've never had any difficulty on this score and we expect none in the future."[24]

The Yankees brass officially began the 1940 season by holding their own annual meeting to plan for the new campaign. More and more, Weiss's input at these meetings was extremely important. He would report on the development and progress of each player in the organization. Once his input had been given, he remained at all meetings while a related major topic was discussed—players' salaries.[25]

The Yankees had no reason to change the method of operating their farm system. Weiss's astuteness in identifying baseball talent helped the Yankees not only acquire new players for the parent team, but also proved vital in trading and selling unneeded players, especially to the National League. More than 30 players formerly with the Yankees or the team's chain were playing in the senior circuit in early 1940. The Yankees' best customer was Larry MacPhail of the Dodgers along with his manager, Leo Durocher. Other teams who had an imposing list of former Yankees included the Reds, Giants, Cubs, and Pirates.[26]

The Yankees' success continued to infuriate Commissioner Landis as he attempted to hamstring the chains. He issued rulings that left the situation regarding player movements and working agreements blurred and slowed farm operations considerably. As one newspaper asked, "When such a bright young man as George Weiss, head of the far flung Yankee chains is puzzled, how does Commissioner Landis expect duller baseball men with less expert bookkeeping at their command to keep things straight?"[27] Basically, Landis's intentions were to divide the baseball world into camps—chain stores vs. independent ownership. It was Landis's contention that he should be able to determine how major league officials could and could not manipulate players in the minors. To men such as MacPhail and Weiss who spent much time, effort and money on their minor league farm clubs, "Landis frankly is opposed to chain store baseball ... in favor of independent minor league ownership."[28]

At the minor league meeting in February 1940, it was apparent that many of the teams were dependent on their major league connections, which had helped the number of players almost triple by 1939. Landis finally heeded the eloquent pleadings of minor league presidents and backed down, removing most of the offensive edicts, and allowed farm operations to proceed almost as before with few restrictions.[29]

In addition to good performances from the Blues in 1940, several events also livened up the 1940 season. In late June the New York Yankees visited Kansas City to play an exhibition game against their farm club. Weiss held a party and invited the Yankees, Kansas City players, local writers and publishers, Yankees scouts and the writers covering Yankees to the shindig. It was described as a "big feed with entertainment." The following month, Kansas Citians proudly hosted the American Association All-Star Game in Ruppert Stadium.[30]

Although the Yankees did not win their fifth consecutive pennant in 1940, finishing in only third place, both AA farm teams did well. The Bears under Johnny Neun finished second, with a record of 95–65. They swept Jersey City in the playoff opener, defeated Baltimore in a seven-game finals series, and then won the Junior World Series over Louisville, four games to two.[31] The 1940 Blues, still led by Bill Meyer, finished in first place with a record of 93–57. Nevertheless, they did not win the playoffs. These results validated predictions Weiss had made when he was a guest of honor at a gala dinner in Hollywood back in January of 1940, that he fully expected a banner year for minor league baseball (and of course, for his farms.)[32]

On January 27, 1941, the Connecticut Sportswriters Alliance, at their annual banquet, honored George Weiss, the Connecticut native, with a gold key award for distinguished service in sports. Among the celebrities who addressed the 500 attendees was Yankees manager Joe McCarthy, who optimistically forecast that the new players from Weiss's chain would be excellent replacements.[33] "We have some splendid material coming up," said Weiss, and McCarthy agreed, saying "If needed, I am sure we will get the replacements we need to make us stronger than last year."[34]

In particular, McCarthy may have had in mind Blues star second baseman Gerry Priddy, diminutive shortstop Phil Rizzuto, and first baseman John Sturm, who were all called up to the Yankees for 1941, leaving the Blues with some large holes to fill. Blues Secretary Roy Hamey, who carried out some of the GM duties for the team, also expressed confidence. "We lost a lot, but we'll be all right. By the middle of February we will have the nucleus of another good team. It may be near the end of spring training before the club is set, but I have confidence in George Weiss and in the Yankee organization," said Hamey.[35]

Whenever future Yankees were mentioned, the names of Priddy and Rizzuto invariably came up. Chief scout Paul Krichell declared that Bill Essick, the same scout who discovered Joe Gordon, spotted Priddy. Krichell discovered Rizzuto when George Weiss allowed him to conduct a school at Yankee Stadium. "Our organization receives something like 2,000 letters a year recommending that the Yankees look at prospective players. We follow up every lead, no matter where the boy is. Years ago we would have been forced to neglect virtually all of these boys because we had no place to put them. That's where the chain store system comes in. With a big chain, you need a lot of players. That makes the job of the scout more exciting," said Krichell.[36] A number of players brought to spring training from the Bears and the Blues eventually made the big leagues, including Johnny Lindell, Hank Borowy, Allen Gittel, Tommy Holmes, Mike Chartak, Johnny Murphy and Spud Chandler.[37]

Although renovated and somewhat rejuvenated late in the season by the arrival of sensational right-handed pitcher Mel Queen, the Blues were unable to repeat as AA champions, finishing in third place with a record of 83–69. The Blues again were eliminated in the playoffs, and this year Columbus represented the American Association in the Junior World Series. Columbus beat Montreal for the title, four games to two.[38]

Johnny Neun's 1941 Bears followed the 1940 playoff and Junior World Series wins with back-to-back pennants. The 1941 Bears won their pennant by ten games, with an outstanding 100–54 record. Bears stars included pitcher Johnny Lindell (23–4), league leader Frank Kelleher, with 37 home runs and 125 RBI, and Tommy Holmes, who hit .302.[39] Newark pilot Johnny Neun attributed the great play of the Bears to the deal George Weiss made with the Boston Braves in May when he acquired third baseman Hank Majeski, who replaced the weak-hitting Don Lang. As soon as the deal was made, the Bears began their climb to the pennant.[40]

In the opening round of the playoffs, Newark easily handled the Rochester Red Wings to reach the playoff finals for the fifth consecutive year. The Bears battled the Montreal Royals for seven games before Montreal finally won the Governors' Cup, but Columbus disposed of Montreal to win the Junior World Series.

The Yankees, however, won their sixth pennant since 1932 and became World Champions again, led by the bats of players Weiss had grown or acquired. Joe DiMaggio,

Charlie Keller and Tommy Henrich all hit at least 30 home runs in 1941, and Joe Gordon contributed 24.[41] Bob Consodine, sports columnist of the *New York Mirror*, noted that it was the 12th pennant since Ed Barrow was placed in charge of the Ruppert baseball empire. "Barrow was a good manager himself," wrote Consodine, "but his real genius is selecting the right man for the right job. It was he who found George Weiss and gave him the support which built up the great Yankee farm and scouting system."[42] The Yankees won the pennant in 1941 primarily employing "home grown players." In addition, with very few exceptions, Barrow and Weiss insisted that their farm hands remain in the minors for four years or more before they were considered Yankees.[43]

George and Hazel Weiss not only enjoyed the results of the 1941 season, but also relished their new home, a six-acre estate in New Jersey. The 12-room, four-bath house, with its six columns supporting the Southern mansion–style porch, kept Weiss close to Newark, where he spent most of his time.[44]

It had been the policy of the New York Yankees to keep a minor league manager only three years, and both Johnny Neun and Bill Meyer had held their posts longer than the three-year limit. The shift of managers in Kansas City and Newark came a year late. After making the change in December, Weiss explained that he waited an extra year to allow Kansas City manager Meyer to compete for a managerial post in the major leagues.[45]

Shortly after Weiss made his managerial shifts, the Yankees announced at their yearly directors' meeting that in addition to his duties as secretary, the Yankees were elevating their farm chief to the vice presidency. The press noted that Weiss's contributions to the consistent success of the Yankees had been vital. Since Ruppert and Weiss had installed the Yankees' farm system, the team had won six championships, developing these championships rather than buying them. The *Syracuse Herald Journal* noted, "Weiss' success has been too marked and consistent to have involved luck."[46]

As vice president, Weiss became the official heir-apparent to Ed Barrow as president of the Yankees. Noting his promotion, *The Sporting News* wrote, "In Weiss, the Yankees have a man whose judgment on players is uncanny; whose skill as a trader is acknowledged; whose background is unmatched for the job which will be his when Barrow retires. The New York club is to be congratulated."[47]

In the midst of preparing for the 1942 season, the official declaration of war on December 8, 1941, had a huge impact on the country and on professional baseball. Uncertain how to proceed and despite his intense dislike of Franklin Delano Roosevelt, Landis asked the White House to clarify the status of baseball during the War. Roosevelt responded, "I honestly feel it would be best for the country to keep baseball going.… These players are a definite recreational asset to their fellow citizens—and that, in my opinion, is thoroughly worthwhile."[48] Roosevelt's reply freed baseball officials to resume planning for the 1942 season.

No one lobbied Roosevelt more to continue professional baseball during wartime than Clark Griffith, owner of the Washington Senators. He was in good standing with President Roosevelt and made numerous trips to the White House to work for baseball's survival. It took little effort to lobby Roosevelt, an ardent fan of the game, for the president felt that baseball would keep more people employed and increase the nation's morale during the war. Even though Roosevelt gave his memorable "green light" decree that baseball continue during World War II, there were no illusions that it was going to be the same.[49]

And things were not the same. Throughout the 1942 season, the effects of war began to hit home at every ballpark. Spectators were asked to return foul balls hit into the stands to allow servicemen to use them at a later time. Baseball announcers were banned from talking about the weather on the air because the enemy might be listening in. Everywhere in the ballpark fans could see signage informing them where to go in case of an air raid. FDR was hoping that more night games could be played during the 1940s, but at least on the eastern seaboard, it was not going to happen. Those teams on or near the Atlantic Ocean were barred from playing at night lest the illuminated city skylines and harbors become easy targets for Nazi U-boats prowling offshore.

The war brought additional changes. Prior to each game, the *Star Spangled Banner* was played for the first time to help increase the patriotic mood of the times. America's entry into the war delayed the exodus of the St. Louis Browns by a decade. The Brownies were preparing for a move westward until the events at Pearl Harbor not only kept the team back east, but also, as it turned out, eliminated their chances of adding an American League team to Los Angeles. Finally, the war delayed for 46 years the installation of lights at Wrigley Field. The Cubs had been prepared to install lights for the 1942 season, but re-routed the necessary material to more essential, military destinations.[50]

Baseball continued during the war, but with still more changes. Road trips were more difficult, for the military had priority on trains and in hotels. Spring training camps had to be moved because of travel restrictions, and baseball equipment became extremely scarce.

World War II brought another concern to many ball clubs—the loss of talent on the field. As players entered military service, either by enlistment or the draft, who would replace the departing players? Regardless of how dominant the Yankees were on the field, they were not immune to world events. One of their first losses was the talented first baseman, Johnny Sturm, who enlisted in January 1942. Fortunately, both Barrow and Weiss were capable of adjusting to Sturm's loss. On February 5, 1942, the Yanks traded minor league outfielder Tommy Holmes to the Boston Braves for first baseman Buddy Hassett and outfielder Gene Moore. It appeared that Weiss had made an excellent deal, obtaining Hassett, a full-time first baseman, for Holmes, an outfielder who probably would not have made the Yankees' roster. However, it proved to be one of the worst trades the club ever made. While Hassett did play a full season for the Yankees in 1942, it was his last year in the major leagues.[51] On the other hand, Tommy Holmes went on to have a first-rate major league career with the Boston Braves, leading the National League in base hits in both 1945 and 1947.[52]

Even before the country was officially at war, apprehension of U.S. involvement had reduced attendance in the minor leagues—from a total paid attendance in 1940 of nearly 20,000,000 to 16,000,000 in 1941. There were 43 minor leagues in 1940—by the spring of 1942 there were 31.[53] On the eve of World War II, the Yankees' chain numbered 12—Kansas City in the American Association, and Newark in the International League; Class A Binghamton; Class B Norfolk, Virginia, and Augusta; Class C Akron, Joplin, Amsterdam and Idaho Falls; and Class D Butler, Pennsylvania, Norfolk, Nebraska, and Easton, Maryland. The Yankees owned Kansas City, Newark, Norfolk, Virginia, Binghamton, and Akron; the other clubs had working agreements with New York.[54]

Anticipating more changes war would bring to the United States and to minor league baseball in particular, in February 1942, Weiss announced that the Yankees would reduce the number of farm teams from 12 to ten, with only 250 rather than 300 players under contract. Approximately 50 players were released for military duty. Akron in the Middle Atlantic League and Norfolk, Nebraska, in the Western League were the first two clubs to be removed from the Yankees' chain. "We would have pulled out of Akron, war or no war," indicated Weiss. "We had operated the club for several years and taken some heavy losses and we made up our minds last fall to end what had proved to be an unsatisfactory arrangement." Weiss also indicated that the St. Louis Cardinals, who operated more than a score of minor league clubs, would also have to curtail their minor league affiliations.[55]

The war did not seem to distract the Bears or the Blues in 1942. Kansas City finished in first place with a record of 84–69.[56] Bill Meyer, the new Bears' manager, also led his team to a first-place finish. Apparently George Weiss was able to continue to find solid players for the Bears as the team led the International League in hitting, fielding, and home runs. Third baseman Hank Majeski hit .345 with 115 RBI; George Stirnweiss, with 73, led the league in stolen bases, and pitcher Tommy Byrne (17–4) was the league's winning percentage leader. For the second year in a row, the Bears won the pennant by ten games. Nonetheless, Newark was upset in the playoff opener by fourth-place Jersey City.[57]

Joe McCarthy's New York Yankees, led by Joe DiMaggio, also won the pennant, posting a record of 103–51, but won only the first game of the World Series. The St. Louis Cardinals swept the next four, winning the World Series.[58]

Even though the Yankees could not win the 1942 World Series, baseball observers were quick to note the general success of the Yankees, a team that had won 13 pennants in 22 seasons. George Weiss was given much of the credit for building up the farm system. "Chain store ball pays dividends," noted one newspaper. "The conclusion is obvious. A farm system isn't an absolute necessity to build a team into a pennant winner, but it is required if a club is going to be a contender season after season."[59]

After the 1942 season ended, two major league teams made important changes in the administration of their excellent farm systems. Branch Rickey, the originator of the farm system, resigned as vice-president and general manager of the St. Louis Cardinals, and GM Larry MacPhail left the Brooklyn Dodgers to become a lieutenant colonel in the United States Army.[60]

The Cardinals found a replacement for Rickey almost immediately. William Walsingham, Jr., had spent the bulk of his 30-year baseball career with the St. Louis Cardinals. He began as a ticket-taker with the Cardinals, a team his uncle Sam Breadon owned from 1920 through 1947. By the early 1940s he had become a vice president of the Redbirds and when Rickey and Breadon parted company, Walsingham became the chief of operation, although the GM title was not officially assigned to him. He was part of a management triumvirate that included Sam Breadon and the team's chief scout, Joe Mathes.[61]

The search for a successor to MacPhail was more intriguing. Immediately speculation grew concerning MacPhail's replacement in Brooklyn. Bill Corum of the *New*

York Journal American boldly predicted that George Weiss would leave the Yankees organization and succeed MacPhail at Brooklyn. "Weiss has gone as far as he can go with that organization," wrote Corum. "He is young and ambitious as well as capable, and to get the Dodgers would be to get his own show in perhaps the best town of all. The Dodgers and the National League can get George now."[62]

Weiss immediately squelched any rumors about his leaving the Yankees, declaring, "My contract with the Yankees is far from over. In fact, it still has two years to go. I doubt whether I'll be switching jobs for a while."[63] One can speculate about Weiss's motives for not pursuing the Dodgers position, which did go to Branch Rickey. Although ambitious, Weiss was always careful to maintain dignity, and perhaps he realized that Rickey was the Dodgers' choice all along. Possibly Weiss also remained with the Yankees because he felt that he would replace Ed Barrow if and when Barrow decided to give up his post of president of the Yankees.[64]

The first of the three "baseball war seasons" was 1943 and was defined by a scarcity of young players and draft/enlistment of even established players like Joe DiMaggio. The leader of the 1942 Yankees was inducted in 1943, proving that being a baseball star didn't exempt anyone from service.[65] During the 1943 season the Yankees also lost Phil Rizzuto and Red Ruffing to tours of duty.[66] As a result, the Yankees were forced to bring up a large number of players from their AA farms. For example, the Yankees took almost the entire Newark Bears first-string nine—purchasing nine players and recalling two, including George "Snuffy" Stirnweiss, southpaw Tommy Byrne, third baseman Hank Majeski, shortstop Billy Johnson, pitcher Milo Candini, and catcher Aaron Robinson. Sending Johnson to the Yankees turned out to be one of the best moves of the season. He became one of those rare players who hit consistently in both the minor and major leagues, and was a standout for the Yankees in the 1943 World Series.[67]

Having given up their best players to the parent club, it was not surprising that the Bears did not do well in 1943. They did manage to finish in second place with a record of 85–68, but they lost the first round of their playoffs. Because so many of Weiss's players moved to the Yankees during the season, only five of the 1943 Bears appeared in more than 100 games for Newark.[68]

If Weiss was disappointed about his Bears in 1943, he was devastated about the Blues. Their 1943 record was a 67–85 disaster, and the Blues finished in seventh place. The farm system in 1943 was simply "run down," and the 1943 Blues produced no future stars for the New York team. As Yankees Secretary Roy Hamey and Blues manager Johnny Neun noted, "We have to accept it as such and plow along."[69]

Meanwhile the 1943 Yankees under veteran manager Joe McCarthy, stocked with players developed in the chain, won the American League pennant by 13½ games, their eighth pennant since 1931, accomplishing this feat even without such stars as DiMaggio, Rizzuto, Henrich, and Ruffing. They received help from pitcher Spud Chandler, who went 20–4 with a 1.64 ERA. Other former players for Weiss who helped McCarthy included Johnny Lindell and Charlie Keller.[70]

Weiss was gratified that his players were having excellent performances with the Yankees, but he admitted that his job of finding players was becoming more and more difficult, causing the usually somber Weiss to joke, "I may wind up playing myself."[71] The paucity of players in Weiss's chain system drove the Yankees to cut back the number of farm teams still further, from ten to five (two Class AA clubs in Newark and Kansas City; a Class A team in Binghamton, New York; a Class B team in Norfolk, Virginia, and a Class D team in Wellsville, New York) The Yankees would retain a farm system of five clubs through the 1945 season.[72]

The one bright spot to a generally miserable season for Weiss was his re-election as vice-president of the National Association of Professional Baseball Leagues.[73] The outbreak of World War II seemed to bring Yankees manager Joe McCarthy and George Weiss closer together. One reason was that of the 28 men on the Yankees' roster at the beginning of the 1944 season, 21 were products of Weiss's farms. In fact, Jim Turner and Bill Zuber were the only pitchers on the staff who did not come up through the Yankees' minor league system. Weiss was also spending much more of his time as Yankees vice-president and assistant to president Ed Barrow.[74] When the Yankees left for spring training in 1944, there had been a few changes in the organization. In addition to cutting the farm system down to five clubs, Kansas City manager Johnny Neun went to the Yankees as a coach, and Jack Saltzgaver, former Yankees infielder, replaced him at Kansas City.[75]

George Weiss was unable to accompany the Yankees to spring training because he was recovering from a fractured left leg and hobbling around on crutches. He did, however, meet often with Joe McCarthy when the Yankees returned. Among the many issues they discussed were their problems in the outfield. With Joe DiMaggio in the service, the Yankees had only one solid outfielder—Bud Metheny. Johnny Lindell, who failed his army physical, continued to have back problems. Ed Levy, recently discharged from the army also because of back problems, had developed soreness in his right arm. Jack Phillips, under contract to the Bears, was scheduled to play center field, but he had already been accepted for service in the Navy.[76]

Weiss also became involved in an off-the-field issue involving the question of night baseball. Curbed during the war, the question arose as to whether to resume unlimited weekday night games after the war ended. Both Barrow and Weiss were vehemently opposed to night baseball. Weiss stressed that night baseball's hold on the public would be relaxed once the novelty wore off. "It is our job to see that it remains just that—a novelty."[77]

The 1944 season was unsuccessful for both AA teams. The Blues lost 110 of their 151 games and finished at the bottom of the American Association.[78] Newark, even with all the players they had given up to the parent club, finished second in the International League and got as far as the championship round before losing to Baltimore in seven games.[79]

Nineteen forty-four was unsuccessful for the Yankees, too. Unable to continue their string of three consecutive pennant wins, they finished third behind the St. Louis Browns, who won their first pennant since entering the American League in 1903. (It would be the Browns' only pennant). In true Browns style, they lost the World Series to their cross-town rivals, the St. Louis Cardinals, four games to two.[80]

By the end of 1944, war news had become more optimistic. The country cheered that the Allies were beginning to win on both the European and the Pacific fronts.[81] For baseball particularly, as preparations began for the 1945 season, the good war news meant that a few former players were being released from military duty. Red Ruffing, who was near the age limit when he was drafted two years previously, and Joe DiMaggio, in a California hospital being treated for stomach ulcers, would likely be able to report to the Yankees for the 1945 season.[82]

For the most part, however, finding players good enough for the 1945 Yankees' training camp proved more difficult for George Weiss. It is probable that at this point Weiss felt that 1945's biggest challenge was solving player shortages. He would soon learn that other changes in the Yankees' organization might test him even more.

7

The MacPhail Years

On January 27, 1945, a new set of owners announced that they had purchased the entire Yankees organization, marking the second—and far more drastic—complete change of ownership since Weiss had joined the Yankees 13 years earlier.[1] For $2.8 million, the powerful triumvirate of Larry MacPhail, Dan Topping, and Del Webb bought nearly 97 percent of the stock owned by heirs of the late Jacob Ruppert and by Yankees president Ed Barrow. George Ruppert, who had been titular head of the organization following the death of his brother, retained his stock.

The principal owners, Topping and Webb, were both wealthy and successful businessmen. One of Topping's grandfathers had been president of Republic Steel and the other had made a fortune in tin. Dan Topping owned two professional football teams in New York and spent most of his time serving on numerous corporate boards, including National Airlines and Madison Square Garden. During World War II he was a major in the Marine Corps, spending 26 months in the Pacific.[2]

Del Webb was a successful construction executive, a partner in 31 companies, and a member of the board of 43 corporations. Like Topping, Webb was an avid sports fan and had been a semi-pro pitcher in California.[3]

But it was Larry MacPhail who put the package together with his two new partners. A World War I veteran, MacPhail was hired in 1933 by the Cincinnati Reds as chief executive and general manager. In 1938 MacPhail went to the Brooklyn Dodgers, where he again served as chief executive and general manager. He was instrumental in bringing to Brooklyn sportscaster Red Barber to break New York's long-standing radio blackout of local teams' games. Barber had previously broadcast the Reds' games for MacPhail. MacPhail's other innovations included broadcasting baseball night games and televising games on a regular basis.[4]

At the outbreak of World War II, MacPhail enlisted in the army, advancing to the rank of colonel. During MacPhail's service, Branch Rickey had taken his job as Dodgers president. The newly discharged MacPhail decided to buy the New York Giants, who had collapsed into last place in 1943. Unfortunately the Giants were not for sale, so he turned his attention to the Yankees and ultimately became co-owner of the Yankees in 1945.[5]

Less than a month later, Webb, Topping and MacPhail officially took over control of the complete Yankees empire: the American League New York Yankees and their

7. The MacPhail Years

Left: Del Webb was a real estate developer and life-long baseball fan. He, Dan Topping, and Larry MacPhail purchased the Yankees in 1945 for $2.8 million. After buying out MacPhail in 1947, Webb remained with the Yankees until 1964, when he sold his shares to CBS and devoted all of his time to his construction business (National Baseball Hall of Fame Library, Cooperstown, New York). *Right:* Daniel Reed Topping was part-owner of the New York Yankees from 1945 to 1964, when he sold his controlling interest in the team to CBS. He continued as team president until 1966, when he sold his remaining stake in the Yankees (National Baseball Hall of Fame Library, Cooperstown, New York).

minor league clubs including Newark in the International League, Kansas City in the American Association, Norfolk in the Eastern League, and Binghamton in the Piedmont League. The deal also took in all Yankees properties—Yankee Stadium in the Bronx, and Ruppert Fields in Newark and Kansas City, as well as the contracts of approximately 400 major and minor league players.[6]

Although he was not officially in charge of the team until his formal retirement from the service, Colonel Larry MacPhail quickly asserted his new positions as president of the organization and general manager of the Yankees. He named the 77-year-old Ed Barrow chairman of the board, a new, undefined job with virtually no power. Although MacPhail acknowledged that the position of board chairman was not in effect under the team's current by-laws, it would be incorporated as soon as the rules could be changed.[7] MacPhail announced that the sale of the Yankees would not affect the status of Joe McCarthy or George Weiss. Colonel MacPhail indicated that his manager, McCarthy, who had two more years on his present contract, would remain as field leader, while Weiss, who had three years left on his contract as head of the club's farm system, would also remain.[8] MacPhail was especially emphatic about Weiss remaining with the Yankees. "As far as I am concerned, Weiss has a lifetime job with the organization."[9]

Although MacPhail insisted he wanted to keep the Yankees organization the same, baseball observers noted that his *modus operandi* was quite different from its former ways.[10] MacPhail contrasted with Weiss in a number of ways—their demeanors, their outlooks on promotions and even their attitudes toward the players differed. MacPhail was a successful promoter who brought with him a great deal of money, but he was not always well liked by his players.[11]

One innovation which was not always popular with MacPhail's players was his attitude toward night baseball. MacPhail had been a trailblazer of night games when he installed lights in Columbus in the American Association in 1932, two years after the first installation of lights in professional baseball by the Kansas City Monarchs of the Negro leagues in 1930. In Cincinnati, on May 24, 1935, while general manager of the Reds, he introduced night baseball in the major leagues. After that he popularized night baseball at Brooklyn's Ebbets Field. Another "first" occurred when MacPhail arranged air travel for his players to the league's western cities. The majority of his players vehemently opposed this innovation.[12]

Meanwhile, the preparations for the 1945 season continued. Newark was delighted when Weiss announced that the popular Bill Meyer would stay with the Bears for a fourth season. In another move, the Yankees announced that Casey Stengel, a native of Kansas City, would replace Jack Saltzgaver, who had managed the Blues to a last-place finish in 1944.[13]

World War II was slowly drawing to a close as the 1945 major league season progressed, and several more Yankees players returned from Europe and the Pacific. During the final two months of the season, Charlie Keller and Spud Chandler rejoined the squad. Forty-year-old Red Ruffing, who compiled a record of 7–3 and an ERA of 2.89, started 11 games for the Yankees in 1945. Most of the team's best players, however, were still serving in the military, and the Yankees found the Detroit Tigers too much of a challenge that year. Despite the excellent contributions of Nick Etten, George Stirnweiss, Bill Bevens, and Joe Page, the Yankees missed their stars—Joe DiMaggio, Tommy Henrich and Joe Gordon. For the second consecutive year, the Yankees failed to make it to the World Series, finishing in fourth place behind the Detroit Tigers, who were buoyed by the return of their first sacker, Hank Greenberg.[14]

As the 1945 season wound down, Weiss made a move that was both symbolic and practical. He transferred his office from Newark, where he had been for more than a decade, to Manhattan, where he was now spending more and more of his time working directly with the Yankees while delegating a number of his farm system duties to his assistants.[15]

He and Hazel continued to live in New Jersey, where they opened their home to Hazel's son, Allen, now a cadet at West Point, and his friends. Several of them recalled later that Weiss always made box seats available to his son and their friends.[16]

But Weiss was soon without one of his longtime associates. In mid–November 1945, Ray Kennedy, Newark's business manager for 11 years, was named to the newly created post of general manager of the Pittsburgh Pirates. Weiss was sincere in praising Kennedy and wishing him well, but the quiet Weiss, who might well have expected to succeed Barrow, would have been justified in wondering if he would ever become a major league general manager.[17]

Less than a week later, the unpredictable MacPhail announced that the entire farm system would undergo "elaborate changes which would include the goal of expanding

Tommy Henrich was a Yankee from 1937 to 1950 and was Joe DiMaggio's teammate longer than any other player. Henrich ("Old Reliable" on the left), and DiMaggio (the "Yankee Clipper"), along with Charlie Keller, formed one of baseball's most legendary outfields for the Yankees before and after World War II (National Baseball Hall of Fame Library, Cooperstown, New York).

the chain to 24 clubs by the end of 1947, and renovating all the minor league fields and arenas."[18]

MacPhail's most important change was to make George Weiss effectively one of the most powerful men in baseball. At a press conference in New York on November 15, 1945, MacPhail announced that Weiss was to be placed in command of all the players in the Yankees organization, both on the parent club as well as in the minors. He would have sole charge of signing the players to their contracts in the spring, and full authority to make any trades he might consider beneficial to the Yankees.[19] In making this announcement, MacPhail emphasized that Weiss was one of the best men in the game for this work. "I have discovered," admitted MacPhail, "that this job of running the Yankees is too much for me alone."[20]

Baseball writers were impressed with George Weiss's reputation as a shrewd trader, one of the best in the business. They recalled that as owner of New Haven for ten years, and chief executive and trader for both Baltimore and the Yankees' chain for an additional six years, Weiss had wangled deals that had brought in an incredible total of nearly $2,000,000. In 1945 he attended minor league winter meetings looking for deals not only for the chain, but also for the parent club.[21]

Fortunately, more player slots became available as former farm teams were welcomed back for the 1946 season. Joplin, for example, resumed its affiliation with the Yankees after the team had been disrupted by war.[22] By the end of January 1946, the Yankees' chain was now up to 14 teams, eight in the eastern United States—Newark, Binghamton, Augusta, Norfolk, Sunbury, Amsterdam, Wellsville and Easton—and the other six west of the Mississippi—Kansas City, Beaumont, Quincy, Twin Falls, Joplin, and Fond du Lac.[23]

MacPhail was not finished. He continued to realign the Yankees administration by assigning a number of Weiss's minor league duties to others, focusing Weiss more and more on the parent club. In a major move, MacPhail named Commander Frank Lane general manger of the Kansas City Blues. Lane had been assistant general manager for the Cincinnati Reds before his four years in the U.S. Navy during World War II.[24]

MacPhail made still more significant changes to the Yankees in 1946 as more veterans and former stars returned from the military. Making room on the Yanks' major league roster for these returning players had been a priority at the minor league meetings. Weiss's negotiating skills and talent judgment were severely tested in spring training as he dealt with the signing of some of these former stars such as George Stirnweiss. After bargaining for a month over Stirnweiss's 1946 salary, Weiss reached a compromise with the Yankees infielder, ending rumors that he might be traded.[25]

Weiss had to deal with new prospects as well as veteran players. For example, Bobby Brown, a 21-year-old pre-med student at Tulane, showed up at the Yankees' camp. Supposedly he was the most sought-after free agent in the country. Fortunately his father, Bill Brown, was a one-time second baseman for the semi-pro Meadowbrooks of Newark, and a close friend of Weiss. MacPhail, delighted with Weiss, said, "Bobby went with the Yankees after having offers from all other major league clubs, one of them better than ours." It cost exactly $35,000 to acquire the young shortstop.[26] To make room for those returning from military service, the Yankees cut ties with two veterans, Russ Derry and Tuck Stainback.[27]

Both MacPhail and Weiss realized that not all the players returning to the Yankees would come back to the team with the same skills they had before they entered the armed services. For this reason, the 1946 season was one of transition. Two star players, Joe Gordon and Joe DiMaggio, were prime examples of players who had difficulties returning to their earlier forms. DiMaggio ended the 1946 season with a batting average of .290, failing to hit over .300 in the majors for the first time in his career. Gordon had only 11 home runs, hit only .210 and drove in a disappointing 47 runs. Tommy Henrich also had a subpar year for the Yankees in 1946, hitting only .251. Charlie Keller, who had returned to the Yankees midway during the 1945 campaign, was the best Yankees player in 1946, hitting .275, smacking 30 home runs and driving in 101 runs. It was little wonder that the Yankees failed to win the American League pennant for the third consecutive year, finishing in third place, 17 games behind the Boston Red Sox.[28]

It was evident that the 1947 Yankees would have a different look than the 1946 team. Two rookie players who would play prominent roles in the future of the team were brought up at the tail end of the 1946 season—21-year-old catcher Lawrence

7. The MacPhail Years

Weiss (left), manager Joe McCarthy (center) and co-owner Larry MacPhail (right) look the team over during spring training in 1946. Two years later, only Weiss remained with the Yankees (Steve Steinberg Collection).

"Yogi" Berra, and 27-year-old, right-handed pitcher Vic Raschi. They would replace two retiring players, catcher Bill Dickey and hurler Red Ruffing, both future Hall of Famers.[29]

The relatively poor Yankees finish might have been attributed to the constant shifting of managers that occurred that year. Joe McCarthy, who was suffering from gall bladder disease and frustrated by his team's poor results from the outset, retired on May 24, 1946. McCarthy called a newspaper friend, Billy Kelly, sports editor of the *Buffalo Courier Express*, to announce his retirement, stating that his doctor had ordered him to quit as manager but that he would remain with the organization as a scout.[30]

Left unsaid was his private reason—a lack of rapport with his new boss, Larry MacPhail. Many thought McCarthy's condition was exacerbated by MacPhail's operating style, completely different from Barrow's. McCarthy was a quiet man, strict with his players, and influential in developing the Yankees' culture of always dressing and behaving like champions. Similarities in temperament might have explained how Weiss and Hazel developed a close relationship with McCarthy and his wife. In fact, Weiss was with McCarthy when he made his announcement.[31]

Upon McCarthy's resignation, Bill Dickey, former Yankees catcher and farm club manager, became the Yankees' manager. He inherited McCarthy's record of 22–13, and then managed 105 games for the Yankees. In mid–September, Dickey resigned; the Yankees refused to offer him a longer deal. With only a few games left in the season, Johnny Neun finished the uninspiring 1946 Yankees year. The team may have been uninspiring on the field, but it was a resounding success at the gate. Yankees attendance of 2,265,512 marked the first time a big-league baseball team had ever attracted more than two million fans.[32]

Wishing to get his team back on track, MacPhail announced he had hired 50-year-old Bucky Harris, former player-manager of the Washington Senators. Harris, who won pennants for his teams in 1924 and 1925, was to lead the Yankees in 1947. Known as the "Boy Wonder" of the Senators, Harris had managed 20 seasons, but with largely mediocre results.[33]

As 1946 drew to a close, major league baseball was rife with rumors. Shortly after Harris was named Yankees manager for 1947, it was rumored that George Weiss was going to sever his connections with the Yankees and Bill Meyer, for years a manager in the New York farm system, was slated for another post. Neither of these rumors proved to be true.[34]

The following month, Judge William Bramham, President of Minor League Baseball, announced his retirement. George Weiss was mentioned as a possible successor to Bramham, but Weiss firmly declared he was not interested in the job and added, "As for the qualifications of Judge Bramham's successor, he should have the same qualifications as the Judge. Those things, plus a degree of youth and experience to be gained in the office, should fill the bill."[35]

With all rumors put to rest, Weiss could now concentrate on preparing for 1947. He and Larry MacPhail finally made a trade with Bill Veeck, president of the Cleveland Indians. In Veeck's first deal, he traded pitcher Allie Reynolds to the Yankees for second baseman Joe Gordon. Although Reynolds compiled a record of 11–15 for the Indians in 1946, the hard-throwing right-hander had won 18 games for the Indians the previous year, and both Weiss and MacPhail felt he had the ability to help the Yankees in 1947. On the other half of the deal, the Yankees had George Stirnweiss waiting in the wings to take over at second for Gordon.[36]

The Yankees made some other roster moves. They signed veteran George McQuinn to play first base. The Yankees had released the 37-year-old veteran following the 1946 season but they now felt his left-handed bat and outstanding glove might help the team.[37] In addition to Bobby Brown and Yogi Berra, the Yankees added rookie pitcher Frank " Spec" Shea to their 1947 roster.[38]

Nineteen-forty-seven was literally a game-changing year for organized baseball, for the New York Yankees, and for George M. Weiss. It was the year that finally saw the beginnings of integration in major league baseball when Branch Rickey made the outstanding infielder, Jackie Robinson, a Brooklyn Dodger. In the Yankees' organization, George Weiss was operating with a newly expanded Yankees chain, a new high of 20 teams divided into three geographical regions. The Eastern Division, headed by now reclassified Class AAA Newark in the International League, had nine teams; the Mid-West Division, headed by Class AAA Kansas City in the American Association, included seven teams; and the Pacific Coast Division, headed by Class B Victoria in the Western International League, included four teams.[39]

The mercurial MacPhail decided to "re-announce or clarify" the executive duties of various of his operatives. He clarified Weiss's position—Weiss's sole job was to be the head man of the farm system. On the other hand, manager Bucky Harris was "doubling in brass." In addition to being the field manager, Harris was now in charge of all player deals, the signing of players and "responsible" for all players. Harris would quickly discover he would be dealing with several players who had already expressed dissatisfaction with their contract offers, and had requested a "chat."[40]

With the farm system his main concern again, Weiss was producing a quality AAA club in Newark as well as developing other players for Bucky Harris.[41] It was Weiss who suggested to Harris that he try Berra in the outfield, where he did an admirable job. The rookie Berra willingly accepted Weiss's idea to hone his skills at a position in addition to catcher. "Gee, it's wonderful to think I'm going to play the same outfield where Babe Ruth used to play.... I wish I could have as many homers as he did," he remarked.[42]

The 22-year-old Berra hardly looked like a ballplayer, but he was extremely gifted. With the help of former catcher Bill Dickey, Berra learned how to catch like a major leaguer. He appeared in 83 games after his discharge from the Navy, alternating behind the plate and in the outfield, and hit 11 homers that season.[43]

George Weiss was given credit for the remarkable comeback of the 1947 Yankees after failing to win the pennant the past three seasons. The only players on the pennant-winning Yankees in 1947 who were not developed in the chain were Joe DiMaggio, Tommy Henrich, Allie Reynolds and Bobo Newsom. With support from farm products, including Yogi Berra, Ralph Houk, Don Johnson, Karl Drews, and Allie Clark, the Yankees not only won the pennant in 1947, they finished 12 games ahead of the second-place Detroit Tigers.[44] Sports writer Dan Daniel was still singing the praises of Weiss when he noted, "There have been numerous changes in other farm systems but George Weiss of the Yankees goes on right through the years, the wisest operator in the business."[45]

Widely considered one of the greatest catchers in baseball history, Yogi Berra was called "my assistant manager" by Casey Stengel. Despite Yogi's reputation for malapropisms, George Weiss quickly discovered that Yogi Berra had a clear sense of his own value regardless of whether he could articulate it (Yogi Berra Museum and Learning Center).

The Yankees also received much help from unexpected sources. Veteran first baseman George McQuinn, a Weiss protégé, hit .304, second only to DiMaggio's .315. Relief pitcher Joe Page contributed by winning 14 games and saving 17 others (a statistic not yet officially recorded). Allie Reynolds, 32-year-old pitcher, who came to the Yankees in the Joe Gordon trade, was 19–8 in his first season with the Yankees. Fellow hurler Vic Raschi, 28, was called up from Portland in 1947.[46]

With the Yankees capturing the American League pennant, members of the Baseball Writers' Association of America selected Joe DiMaggio as league MVP in an extremely close race with Ted Williams. Williams, for the second time in his career, had won the American League's Triple Crown. DiMaggio also was selected to the 1947 All-Star Game for the ninth time in as many seasons. He was joined by teammates George McQuinn, Billy Johnson, Spud Chandler, Tommy Henrich, Joe Page, Eddie Robinson, Frank Shea, and Charlie Keller.[47]

7. The MacPhail Years

The Yankees might have been successful on the field in 1947, but MacPhail's relations continued to deteriorate. Many of the Yankees players were still unhappy about flying to the league's western cities. They also strongly disliked MacPhail's plan to expand the American League's schedule to 168 games to compensate owners for concessions made to the players on pension fund contributions. Only the fierce and bitter opposition of Red Sox owner Tom Yawkey crushed that plan.

MacPhail's relations with the players worsened even more when he levied fines on Keller and DiMaggio, among others, because they refused to participate in some of his promotional stunts. This incident nearly caused a player insurrection. After the team had won the pennant, their accomplishment was nearly dampened when the Yankees' team physician, Mal Stevens, resigned, declaring his revulsion with MacPhail's interference. Dr. Stevens even suggested that the owner might be very close to a nervous breakdown.[48]

Despite all these distractions, the Yankees not only won their first pennant since 1943, they defeated the newly integrated Brooklyn Dodgers. The Yankees won the first two games at home but the pesky Dodgers won games three and four, played at Ebbets Field. The Yankees ultimately went on to win the Series in seven games, thanks to the stellar pitching of Joe Page, who threw five scoreless innings, allowing only one hit in the final, 5–2 Yankees victory.[49]

When the World Series ended, Larry MacPhail should have been the happiest man in professional baseball. But he wasn't. After the victorious Game Seven, MacPhail congratulated his manager, Bucky Harris. He slapped his farm boss, George Weiss, on the back, and with tears streaming down his cheeks, exclaimed, "This is my last year and it sure is great to go out as a world champion." Referring to the Brooklyn Dodgers, MacPhail added, "I built the team that lost today." He then turned to George Weiss and said, "Here's the man who built the team that won."[50]

That evening the Yankees' owners gave an extravagant ($10,000) victory dinner at the midtown Biltmore Hotel for the winning team, the management, their families, and their friends. MacPhail, whose fondness for alcohol was well known, allegedly arrived drunk and turned ugly. He berated his partners, Topping and Webb, railed profanely against his successor in Brooklyn, Branch Rickey, and punched John McDonald, his friend and former traveling secretary, in the eye for defending Rickey. MacPhail then spotted Weiss, whom he had praised so lavishly just a few hours earlier. No one knew for sure the reason for what transpired next—theories ranged from MacPhail's general dislike of Weiss, fueled that day by an abundance of champagne, to a rumor that he wanted to replace Weiss with his son, Lee.[51]

Various dinner attendees, each of whom related the story as he or she had seen it, described the actual events differently. All versions seem to agree that when MacPhail came over to Weiss's table, he directed a tirade of several unprintable names at Weiss, concluding with an explosive, "You are fired right now. Stop by in the morning and get your check." Dan Topping, tolerating MacPhail's actions no longer, exclaimed, "I have taken enough," and carried MacPhail out a side door and downstairs. Hazel Weiss dissolved in tears while George, in a state of shock, sat inconsolable. Then he went up to his hotel room with Hazel and a sizable group of friends, including long-time associate Paul Krichell. The normally calm, unemotional Weiss cried, feeling he had been disgraced.[52]

Topping stopped by Weiss's room to reassure him that nothing would happen to him, and then he returned to the party by himself. "Don't worry about George Weiss," Topping told those who had heard about Weiss's firing. "He's going to be taken care of."

The following evening, October 7, at about 7:30 p.m., Del Webb and Dan Topping announced that they had bought out MacPhail's share in the Yankees for $2,000,000, and that MacPhail was now out of baseball. Dan Topping would take over the duties as president; Bucky Harris would remain as field manager, and George Weiss would be general manager, running the ball club and its minor league affiliates with absolute authority.[53]

8

The Weiss Era Begins

In 1947, after being employed by the New York Yankees for 15 years, George Weiss became general manager of the entire Yankees organization.[1] He finally obtained the position he obviously had been seeking for a long time, even turning down similar offers from other major league teams.[2] Most baseball pundits were not at all surprised by Weiss's promotion, for they were confident that as he had advanced up the Yankees' hierarchy, first as secretary and then as vice-president, he would one day succeed Ed Barrow.[3] In fact, Dan Topping stated as much when he and Del Webb made Weiss general manager. "In Weiss we have the greatest front office man in baseball. He should have had this job long ago, and it makes Del and myself very happy to be able to gratify his lifelong ambition."[4]

Sportswriter Stanley Frank was among those expecting Topping and Webb to select Weiss to replace Larry MacPhail. "He has established and guided the enormously efficient network of subsidiary, minor-league teams that discovers, then develops the steady stream of fresh talent which has kept the Yankees, the greatest ball club in the business, young and vibrant," wrote Frank. He added that Weiss had performed his function in a manner that few fans understood or appreciated.[5]

As the general manager of the New York Yankees, George Martin Weiss was now in charge of all baseball operations, and like Barrow and MacPhail, was now the face of the Yankees. Weiss was given the same sweeping power over player control that Ruppert had given to Barrow. Topping assumed the presidency and admitted that although he intended to report to his Yankees office on a regular basis, handling the day-to-day affairs of the team never was his "cup of tea." He therefore gave Weiss a myriad of responsibilities—the company checkbook, operation of the minor league teams, club policy and overseeing the office staff. Most importantly, Topping told Weiss that he was the absolute boss and had complete authority to hire and fire, make deals, sign players and settle all financial matters.[6]

Topping also made it clear that along with these powers went responsibility, and he and Del Webb would hold Weiss ultimately responsible for the team's successes and failures.[7] Lee MacPhail, Gene Martin, Paul Krichell and Eddie Leishman would run the farm system.[8]

Fortunately, most baseball men were happy for Weiss and predicted that he would succeed in his new role. He was particularly encouraged by a congratulatory telegram from Will Harridge, President of the American League, who wished him well and added, "Feel free at any time to contact the American League Office if we can be of service. I know you will do a grand job."[9]

As might be expected, there were those who doubted that Weiss had the ability "to go it alone." After all, Weiss had always operated the Yankees under someone else—first Ed Barrow and then Larry MacPhail. One critic complained that "George is a fine No. 2 man, but he hasn't class to be head man."[10]

But Webb and Topping knew otherwise. Weiss's experience in New Haven, Baltimore, and Newark certainly prepared him for the daunting task of running the most successful franchise in the major leagues. He knew precisely what he needed to do to ensure that the Yankees would continue their dominance in the American League. He continued his policy of hiring the most knowledgeable full-time and part-time scouts to identify and sign players for the Yankees' well-regulated farm system. He stated that his overall goal was to make sure there would be a steady stream of good players coming to the parent club. At the same time, however, he wanted to continue Ruppert's legacy of giving Yankees-affiliated minor league cities winning teams.[11]

Weiss was a realist. He was well aware that as "holder of baseball's most important job," he would find that not only would his actions be scrutinized, but also his philosophy, personality, motives, and the impact of his actions.[12] George Weiss would be closely scrutinized for a number of reasons. First, he was now the top decision maker on what was perceived as a first-class team and undoubtedly the most successful one in the New York area. Second, the players he would be dealing with were no longer unknowns, but often baseball icons recognized and admired throughout the United States. Finally, New York was the headquarters for an extremely large number of baseball writers and broadcasters, many with both local and national influence.[13]

When the 52-year-old Weiss assumed his post as the Yankee general manager, he started with a positive reaction from most of the New York based press who welcomed him "as a return to normalcy." The stocky, balding, quiet, dignified and rather shy Weiss was in marked contrast to the flamboyant MacPhail. More than 150 congratulatory telegrams credited Weiss for building the current Yankees team and hailed him as the "best baseball man in the country" and "one of the ablest men baseball has ever known."[14]

One of the nation's most respected sports writers, Grantland Rice, who knew Weiss when he was in New Haven, echoed those sentiments and added, "The combination of Weiss and Harris give the Yankees a sound, solid leadership that I don't believe any other team can match. They may have better ballplayers—but they won't have stronger or abler men at the top."[15]

Weiss also won kudos for his honesty in dealing with the press. One of Weiss's first tasks was to appoint Arthur "Red" Patterson, former *Herald-Tribune* writer, as the team's public relations director, the first full-time major league publicist ever. Weiss ordered him to "move around the newspaper offices" to try to undo the harm committed by the MacPhail administration, which had succeeded in alienating every sports editor and practically every sports columnist in New York. As one columnist wrote, "We don't want any more garrulity, but we expect information on things moving ahead. Weiss is not likely to become talkative ever, but at least he won't lie to the writers."[16]

Weiss retained Bucky Harris as his manager and announced that the "front office" would attempt to remove, or at least minimize, the manager's authority over his players. Weiss promised to give preference to former Yankees when filling coaching and managerial jobs on the Yankees and in the farm system.

Weiss was prepared to meet the tasks new to him as general manager, off the field as well as on—decisions about issues such as night baseball, radio broadcasts, and the increasingly different methods used to promote the game of baseball. Weiss would also become involved with spring training schedules, public relations, and finally, legislative problems which included the ever-changing relations between players and management. Finally, Weiss reassured the public he would remain very active when it came to player contracts and trading players.[17]

As a promoter during his early days in baseball, Weiss recognized the value of promotions that might increase attendance at Yankee Stadium. At no time did Weiss castigate MacPhail for any of his promotions or for the way he ran the Yankees. On the contrary, by the summer of 1948, one writer noted that Weiss had out–MacPhailed MacPhail. That year, those attending home games at Yankee Stadium might see tennis matches in center field, an all-around sports exhibition by Babe Didrikson Zaharias, a dog show, a national baton twirling champion, fireworks, bands and baseball clown Al Schacht in a comedy act.[18]

This undated photograph portrait shows George Weiss in a more contemplative mood (National Baseball Hall of Fame Library, Cooperstown, New York).

Weiss liked MacPhail's introduction of a Stadium Club, which he felt had great potential. MacPhail had vastly improved Yankee Stadium, paying for these improvements out of club profits. Like MacPhail, Weiss also favored limiting the number of night games. Both men believed no team should play more than 14 night games in its home park.[19]

The owners, manager Bucky Harris, the players, and the press were delighted with one change Weiss made from the MacPhail regime—the elimination of barnstorming trips to Puerto Rico and South America during spring training. Instead, Weiss kept the Yankees strictly at the 1948 spring training field in St. Petersburg.[20] "The big goal of spring training," said Weiss, " is to get into shape for the pennant season. I believe these desires are best achieved with a training session in Florida and a short Northward trip home."[21]

Weiss also announced, with manager Bucky Harris, scouts, and farm officials present, that there would be managerial changes in the Yankees' organization. Weiss selected Dick Bartell to manage the farm club in Kansas City following the resignation of Bill Meyer, who became manager of the Pittsburgh Pirates. Meyer was not the only Yankee who had left the MacPhail organization. Johnny Neun had agreed to manage the Cincinnati

Reds, and Weiss's old friend, Joe McCarthy, had accepted the post of manager of the Yankees' longtime rival, the Boston Red Sox.[22]

Having dealt with minor league leadership, Weiss's next job was to create an even better Yankees club in 1948 than the 1947 World Champions. Never willing to stand pat even with a championship club, Weiss was not only on the phone constantly discussing possible trades, he was bringing up players from his farm clubs for tryouts at spring training, pointing out that in terms of "market value," the group was worth about $750,000. This value was increased by four top farm prospects Weiss had purchased for the parent club: Joe Collins and Jim Dyck from Newark and Ed Stewart and Jerry Coleman from Kansas City.[23] He also obtained catchers Gus Niarhos and Charlie Silvera.[24]

The list of new additions included pitcher "Red" Embree, a six-year veteran obtained from the Cleveland Indians in exchange for outfielder Allie Clark, a rookie with the Yankees. Unfortunately for Weiss, Embree had a 5–3 record in his only year with the Yankees, and he ended his major league career the following year pitching for the St. Louis Browns.[25]

In an effort to keep his chain loaded with prime prospects, Weiss set up an innovative development plan where, in late December 1947, former major leaguers conducted training sessions and tryout camps throughout the country. Lefty Gomez, Yankees pitcher and the 1947 manager of the Yankees' farm club at Binghamton, assigned tryout camps throughout the East; Bert Niehoff, former major league infielder (1913–1918) and veteran minor league pilot, was asked to create similar schools throughout the South; Burleigh Grimes, a 19-year veteran pitcher, was asked to be pitching instructor for the Yankees' clubs in the lower class leagues, mainly in the Midwest; and George Selkirk, former Yankees outfielder, was assigned to the Midwest to instruct young players in other fundamentals, including sliding and batting stance.[26]

George Weiss wanted to end 1947 on a positive note—the signing of his star player, Joe DiMaggio. Not only was DiMaggio key to the Yankees' pennant hopes in 1948, he was key to getting other Yankees players in line. Although he played with a sore arm in 1947, DiMaggio was the only Yankees representative in that year's All-Star Game. In the fall of 1947, DiMaggio had undergone surgery and the prognosis was excellent for a full recovery. It was rumored that the star center fielder was asking for $60,000, or a salary close to that of Ted Williams. With Topping's support, Weiss was able to sign DiMaggio easily in early 1948 at a purported salary of somewhere between $60,000 and $70,000, compared with Williams' $75,000.[27]

Weiss made it a practice never to publicize his players' salaries, and it was clear from the outset that, as Yankees general manager, he would never confirm details of contract negotiations.[28]

Weiss still had a long list of contract talks with returning Yankees. It was actually the first occasion players had of dealing directly with Weiss, who was known to be hard-nosed and even parsimonious. Talks went smoothly, however, with most players, whose signed contracts were returned quickly. Baseball pundits credited rapid, successful discussions to Weiss's negotiating skills and his long-standing practice of continually keeping in touch by telephone with everyone. It was also thought that the owners helped Weiss by promising to provide as much cash as needed to try to match MacPhail's 1947 record of "no holdouts." Veterans such as Henrich, Stirnweiss and Page reached agreement quickly after DiMaggio came on board. Weiss happily announced that Charlie Keller was also returning for 1948 following back surgery, and that in addition, the Yankees had signed a top, hard-hitting outfield farm prospect, Cliff Mapes. Just a few days later, Weiss had 17 players signed including Ed Stewart, Bill Johnson, Bobby Brown, Steve Souchock and the Kansas City pitching prospects Bill Wight, Cuddles Marshall, and Fred Bradley—hurlers Weiss hoped would help build up the pitching staff.

Backup catchers Gus Niarhos and Ralph Houk signed a few days later. Weiss was particularly pleased when ace right-hander Vic Raschi came to terms and when he received a signed contract from pitcher Spud Chandler, who reported great progress following bone-chip removal surgery the previous fall. Yogi Berra signed in February, along with Johnny Lindell, who assured Weiss that his broken ribs from the previous year were now healed. Even pitching ace Allie Reynolds (19–8 in 1947) and promising rookie right-hander Spec Shea (14–5) eventually inked their contracts, although both held out well into February.[29]

Before the Yankees headed for Florida for their 1948 spring training, George Weiss made his first major trade as Yankees general manager. Determined to strengthen his pitching squad for the upcoming season, Weiss traded catcher Aaron Robinson, left-handed pitcher Bill Wight, and minor league right-handed pitcher Fred Bradley to the Chicago White Sox for southpaw pitcher Eddie Lopat.[30] By acquiring Lopat, the Yankees now had their first dependable left-handed starter since the prewar days of Lefty Gomez. Only Detroit Tiger Hal Newhouser was considered a better left-hander in the American League than the 29 year-old Lopat.[31]

Lopat was exactly the type of pitcher Weiss craved. Although not a great fastball hurler, he possessed the intelligence and control that Weiss admired, and more importantly, his ability to beat the Yankees was a trait which appealed to Weiss—one that was often a prerequisite when Weiss acquired a player in a trade.[32]

The Lopat trade turned out to be one of the best trades engineered by Weiss. Lopat would remain in the majors until his retirement in 1955, ending his major league career with a record of 166–112.[33] Weiss felt that catcher Aaron Robinson was expendable since he believed that Niarhos was a better catcher. Robinson played for the Chisox in 1948 and remained in the majors three more years with the Tigers and Red Sox.[34] Fred Bradley pitched in the majors only in 1948 and 1949, appearing in only nine games without being involved in a decision.[35] Bill Wight spent three years with the White Sox, winning 34 games and losing 49. He remained in the major leagues until his retirement after the 1958 season, pitching for numerous teams.[36]

The Yankees were expected to compete with the Boston Red Sox for the American League pennant in 1948, and Red Sox owner Tom Yawkey was not happy when he heard that Weiss had snared Lopat from the White Sox. Red Sox manager Joe McCarthy said, "The Yankees have landed a fine pitcher." His star outfielder Ted Williams added, "I hated to see that deal."[37]

The acquisition of a player of the caliber of Eddie Lopat was only the first of many George Weiss would make as Yankees general manager. Negotiations over Lopat's salary set the pattern that would be repeated numerous times. Weiss suggested that Lopat come to spring training and sign his contract there, but the hurler insisted that Weiss first reveal in advance how much he would be making. "I don't want to go all the way down there and not sign and then come back," he said.[38]

Lopat, who had earned $14,000 the previous year, insisted on a salary of $20,000. After several days of hard negotiating, Lopat agreed to a salary of $18,500 plus $1,500 in expenses, which Weiss felt would at least keep his base salary down. Weiss was not finished. He reminded Lopat that there were many major league pitchers not earning anywhere near that salary. Lopat told Weiss, "I don't care what they're making. I completed sixteen games last year, and was second in earned-run average." Weiss bluntly countered, "What if our other pitchers find out how much you're making?" "Sir," Lopat said, ending the conversation, "if they find out it'll be from you—not from me."[39]

For all practical purposes, the Yankees were prepared for the 1948 season. Many of their injured players were back, and their pitching staff now contained the outstanding combination of Vic Raschi, Allie Reynolds and Eddie Lopat.

The 1948 Yankees were indeed competitive as DiMaggio had his best post-war record to date despite playing the last part of the season with painful bone spurs in his right heel. Yankees pitchers compiled a team ERA of 3.75 while the "Big Three" had a combined win-loss total of 52–26.[40] At the urging of Bucky Harris, George Weiss brought up rookie pitcher Bob Porterfield from Newark, rated by scouts as the greatest young pitcher in all the minor leagues. Even the writers covering the Yankees had been shouting at Weiss to give them Porterfield. Finally Weiss acquiesced and the pitcher arrived in New York in August hailed as the pennant-winning inspiration and the pennant-winning edge.[41]

In his brief stint with the Yankees in 1948, Porterfield compiled a record of 5–3.[42] The Bombers, however, were eliminated from the pennant race in the last series of the year, finishing third behind the Red Sox and Bill Veeck's pennant-winning Indians with a record of 94–60.[43]

Even before the 1948 season ended, Yankees fans wondered if Bucky Harris would return to manage the team in 1949. Club president Dan Topping evaded the question but denied that there was any "rift" between Harris and George Weiss. Many viewed this statement as support for Harris, but others noted that Topping had failed to say that Harris would return as manager.[44]

Noted sports writer Bill Corum thought he saw the handwriting on the wall for Harris. He wrote that it was obligatory for the Yankees to begin a rebuilding program for 1949 and that both Topping and Weiss "knew it." Corum was positive that Weiss was too smart, too practical, and much too experienced a baseball man not to realize that. "Personally," wrote Corum, "I don't think Harris wants to be manager that long."[45]

Weiss decided to end rumors about the possibility of Harris not returning to the Yankees in 1949. He too denied that any rift existed between him and his manager, saying that there had never been even a cross word between them. If any differences existed between the two men, Weiss admitted, especially concerning the call-up of young players to the Yankees, they had worked together on all the problems. Everyone knew Weiss was referring to the timing on bringing players such as Bob Porterfield up to the parent club.[46]

Despite Weiss's comments to the press, on October 4, 1948, almost a year to the day when Weiss became general manager, he and Yankees president Dan Topping announced that Harris was leaving as team manager. In a brief press release, the Yankees merely announced that the decision not to renew Harris' contract was by mutual agreement.[47]

Although anticipated, the dismissal of Harris was unpopular with the press, who felt the close pennant race in 1948 and Harris's winning record earned an extension of his contract. They also resented the timing of the announcement made between a pennant-deciding playoff game and the start of the World Series. One newspaper bluntly complained that Harris's dismissal came because of his demands for players. It claimed that Weiss did accede to Harris's request that Porterfield be brought up from Newark, but then Weiss had the last say. "He helped to arrange for the dismissal of Harris," the paper claimed. "It had to be Weiss or Harris. It was Harris who hit the skids."[48]

A Massachusetts paper editorialized that general manager George Weiss simply had his own ideas about running the ball club, and that he didn't hesitate to "dish 'em out to the manager.... Bucky Harris found this out to his dismay.... It was the constant disagreements between Harris and Weiss which prompted the junking of Harris."[49]

The Yankees' players were unhappy about Harris's dismissal, chiefly because they felt loose and relaxed while working under him. Yogi Berra was one of Harris's chief boosters. "I was sad to see Bucky go," said Berra. "He was a good guy and good to me. When I was struggling behind the plate Bucky told me not to worry. He wanted my bat in the lineup."[50] Not all the players echoed Yogi's opinion. Tommy Henrich admitted he never did like the Harris style of managing. He felt Harris was too soft. "I wanted someone I respected more," said Henrich.[51]

Weiss, too, thought Harris's "too-relaxed attitude" had much to do with the Yankees coming up short for the pennant. Harris's mindset was apparent as far back as spring training when he frequently joined his players at their nightly visit to the dog track instead of keeping them occupied with more practice sessions. During the season, Harris overlooked late-night partying for a number of his players, which Weiss felt made him responsible for the disappointing pitching records of such 1947 standouts as Joe Page (known to be a heavy drinker) and Spec Shea. Weiss even hired private investigators to follow the suspected "playboys" and report to Harris, but the manager ignored the detectives' findings and refused to fine or even confront the curfew violators.[52] Harris also frustrated Weiss, a confirmed workaholic, by being a "four-hour" manager. Harris would come to the park, manage the game, and then go home where he had an unlisted phone number, unknown even to the Yankees' front office.[53]

The more knowledgeable columnists suspected that the most important reason Harris was fired was that George Weiss considered Harris MacPhail's man, and Weiss wanted his own manager. In late 1946, when MacPhail brought Harris into the organization without specific duties, Weiss got the feeling that his 14-year career with the Yankees was in jeopardy. The Yankees' third-place finish in 1948, a year when Weiss felt the team should have won, gave him the perfect justification for firing Harris.[54]

Most members of the press were incredulous when on October 12, 1948, the Yankees announced their new manager—58-year-old Charles Dillon "Casey" Stengel. Just as Weiss had been MacPhail's opposite in so many ways, Stengel was in marked contrast to his predecessor, Harris. Harris was often described as genial and soft-spoken; Stengel, widely known as a practical jokester, was always ready to argue with umpires. He was also notorious for "Stengelese," his tortuous way of speaking. For example, he often began practice sessions by telling players to "line up by size, alphabetically."[55]

Stengel was definitely Weiss's man and had been his friend for many years. Weiss knew that behind Stengel's clownish exterior was a demanding perfectionist, a man with incredible baseball knowledge, the ability to work with young players, and a good understanding of the business side of the game.[56]

Weiss first met Stengel in 1916 in New Haven when Weiss organized an exhibition game pitting the "Ty Cobb All Stars," which included two members of the Dodgers, Zack Wheat and Stengel, against the Boston Red Sox.[57] Almost a decade later, in 1925, Weiss and Stengel were both active in the Eastern League, Weiss as owner of the New Haven team and Stengel as a player-manager in Worcester, Massachusetts.[58] Although dissimilar in personality, "Lonesome George" (a much-disliked name used frequently by the press to describe George Weiss and purportedly given him by sportswriter Jimmy Cannon)[59] and the "Old Perfesser" became friendly.[60]

In 1926 Stengel's mentor, John McGraw, helped him become manager of the Toledo Club of the American Association, a position he held for six years. Stengel learned much about every facet of the game from McGraw. Stengel and Weiss continued their friendship, meeting whenever possible. It was through this association that Weiss began to realize that Stengel was a perceptive baseball man, and more importantly, an even shrewder money manager, both traits Weiss appreciated.[61]

In 1932 George Weiss went to New York to run the Yankees' minor league operations and Casey Stengel's reputation took him to Brooklyn as a coach for the Dodgers, a position he held for three years. In 1934 he succeeded Max Carey as manager, but he was fired in 1937 after a mediocre three-year record of 208–251. A year later he signed on with the Boston Bees in his second major league managerial job, but was let go by a new owner in 1943.[62]

In 1944 Stengel was hired as the manager of the minor league Milwaukee Brewers over the vigorous objections of owner Bill Veeck, who was serving in the South Pacific at the time. Stengel led the Brewers to the American Association pennant that year, but declared that he would not return as manager "under any circumstances."[63]

After that year with the Brewers, Stengel fully expected to stay out of baseball in 1945, but attended the major league meetings during the winter of 1944 "for old times' sake." He had the "misfortune" to run into his old friend, George Weiss, at the meeting. Weiss badgered Stengel to take the managerial job of the Blues in his native Kansas City. Weiss wore Stengel down, and he ultimately accepted his friend's offer, but he was as unsuccessful at Kansas City as he had been successful the previous year at Milwaukee, finishing seventh. Weiss admitted that the Blues' roster contained some of the worst farmhands in many years.[64]

Despite Stengel's resolve to stay out of baseball, he accepted the manager job with the Oakland Oaks, another Yankees affiliate. Since Stengel was living in the Los Angeles area, the job allowed him to spend more time with his wife as they traveled up and down the Pacific Coast together.[65]

Stengel managed the Oaks for three years, finishing second in 1946 and dropping to fourth place in 1947. They made the playoffs both years, but lost to Los Angeles and

San Francisco respectively. In 1948, Stengel led the Oaks to first place in both the regular season and the playoffs, Oakland's first pennant since 1927.[66]

When Weiss offered Stengel the Yankees' managerial post, he had to convince the owners and the rest of the front office to go along with his selection. The front office had never challenged Weiss publicly, but they questioned his move privately. Lee MacPhail, son of the former co-owner of the Yankees and now in the Yankees' farm department, told Weiss that the general consensus was that Stengel simply did not fit in with the Yankees. "Everybody knows Casey Stengel," said MacPhail. "He talks a lot, is loud and drinks publicly."[67] Weiss's reply to MacPhail was brief: "Casey will win with the club and he'll make money."[68]

Webb opposed the move, also calling Stengel a "clown" and stating that the Yankees were serious business. Weiss apparently won Webb over by listing Stengel's virtues, explaining how Stengel was a successful teacher of baseball, how he worked well with young players, and reassuring Webb that Stengel was definitely not a clown—he was a great baseball man. "Casey never makes a move without knowing why he does it," said Weiss."[69]

What really impressed Webb was Stengel's overwhelming love for the game. Webb recalled that one evening while on the way to an appointment, his cab drove past a vacant lot and Webb noticed a bunch of kinds with bats and gloves gathered around an "old gaffer" giving the kids some instructions. "That 'old gaffer,' said Webb, "was Casey. I thought to myself then that if he cared that much about baseball he must be a terrific manager."[70]

Webb was persuaded and Topping also agreed. Stengel was the choice.[71] Years later, Webb freely admitted, "My sole contribution to the Yankees was signing Casey Stengel as manager."[72]

The Yankees signed Stengel to a two-year contract at a purported salary of $25,000 per year.[73] As the excited but nervous Stengel headed east from his home in Los Angeles, Grantland Rice commented, "His previous managerial experience had been slightly on the melancholy side. I wonder how things will be next season."[74]

Most of the New York "beat writers" knew Stengel from his tenure in Brooklyn and liked him personally. They did not think, however, that he was the right man for the job. Most of them were sure that Weiss chose Stengel as a "pleasant caretaker" who would keep the managerial seat warm until Weiss rebuilt the Yankees, and then he would hire a "real manager." Weiss, however, who never thought much of the press and once said that they could be bought "with a five-dollar steak," cared little what the press thought of Stengel. Weiss was aware that well-informed baseball personnel recognized that Stengel possessed a vast reservoir of baseball knowledge, an unorthodox but effective ability at handling men, and the highest confidence in his own judgment.[75]

At one of his first press conferences as the new Yankees manager, one of the scribes informed Stengel that nobody was picking the Yankees to finish better than third. Stengel's reaction was: "Third? That's pretty good. I've never finished that high before."[76] Another writer brazenly told Stengel that the Yankees had hired him because Weiss wanted to have a friend. Stengel retorted, "This is a five-million dollar business. They don't hand out jobs because you're a friend."[77]

After Weiss named Stengel manager, the two men assembled a new group of coaches to replace all of MacPhail's appointees. Frank Crosetti, longtime Yankees shortstop, was released from his player contract and hired as a coach in place of the last MacPhail man, Charlie Dressen.[78] Dressen, ironically, signed for Stengel's old job, manager of the Oakland Oaks club of the Pacific Coast League.[79]

Weiss's other replacement coaches included Jim Turner, who had pitched for Stengel in Boston, and Bill Dickey, the Yankees catcher who briefly had been the team's manager. Turner was no stranger to the Yankees, having pitched for them during the war. Weiss made a cunning move in hiring Turner as one of his coaches, for he also provided a backup manager to replace Stengel should the need arise. In Dickey and Crosetti, Weiss had two shrewd, longtime favorites who provided a strong link to Yankees tradition that both Turner and Stengel lacked.[80] Rounding out the coaching staff was another Yankee from the past, Johnny Neun, rejoining the team as a "player-contact man."[81]

Weiss always focused on his pitching staff, which he felt had cost the Yankees the pennant in 1948. In preparation for the 1949 season, Weiss, accompanied by Casey Stengel, was determined to get more pitching but ended up making one of his least successful deals. In his one major trade at the winter meetings, he gave the St. Louis Browns $100,000 and a few lesser players for starting pitcher Fred Sanford. Sanford would pitch for the Yankees through early 1951, compiling an unimpressive record of 12–10.[82] Although the Yankees had been unsuccessful in drafting players in the past, Weiss even went to the 1948 draft meeting, but again was unable to acquire any of his targeted players.[83]

Weiss went to his farm system to acquire players for the 1949 season with much better results. One of the most outstanding was outfielder Gene Woodling, whom Weiss had purchased from the San Francisco Seals. Woodling, the Pacific Coast League batting champ in 1948, came from the same team that had produced both Frank Crosetti and Joe DiMaggio.[84] Woodling remained with the Yankees until he was traded to the Baltimore Orioles in 1955.[85] Playing alongside DiMaggio and Mantle, Woodling was among eight players who appeared in every victorious Yankees World Series from 1949 to 1953.[86]

Dismissing the needling from his perennial gadfly, Bill Veeck, who was already predicting a repeat pennant for his Indians, Weiss was upbeat about the 1949 Yankees. He cited his new manager, Casey Stengel, his team's various medical procedures over the winter with every player getting a thorough physical, coach Bill Dickey's ability to work with Yogi Berra and other catchers, and the Yankees' superior depth in proven players. He also took pride in his regular outfield of DiMaggio, Keller and Henrich, and backups Johnny Lindell, Gene Woodling and newcomer Hank Bauer, who had debuted with the Yankees in September 1948.[87]

Player signings went well although Weiss instituted a new policy for players beginning in 1949, mailing out contracts with base salaries trimmed but with the ability for the player to bring his pay back to 1948 levels with World Series bonuses. Joe DiMaggio, however, was not mailed a contract, but was invited to meet with Weiss and the owners, where he signed for a record $100,000, the first player to reach that mark.[88]

At spring training in St. Petersburg, Stengel soon proved to be the type of manager Weiss wanted. He enforced Weiss's more rigid training rules, limited his players' attendance at the dog track to once a week, imposed a late curfew, and left open the possibility of having players followed by private detectives if their behavior warranted.[89]

Despite all the medical precautions, the Yankees suffered through 71 separate injuries during the 1949 season.[90] DiMaggio missed the first 65 games; backup sluggers Henrich, Keller and Berra were hobbled. Seven men played first base at one time or another. Playing third was Bobby Brown, a part-time medical student. Berra, a catcher, played the outfield, and Johnny Lindell, a pitcher, was also made an outfielder.[91]

To compensate for all of the injuries, Stengel was forced to use players he had inherited and those Weiss traded for or purchased. In August, Weiss realized he needed more power in the lineup and through the complex waiver system, he was able to obtain Johnny Mize, a future Hall of Famer, from the New York Giants.[92] Weiss now had the left-handed power hitter to complement the right-handed Joe DiMaggio. The purchase also allowed Tommy Henrich to return to his natural position in right field.[93] Before the season ended, Weiss was able to fill other positions by obtaining both first baseman Dick Kryhoski and catcher Sherman Lollar.[94]

Despite all of Weiss's pre-season worries, it was Yankees pitching that helped win

Johnny Mize debuted with the St. Louis Cardinals in 1936, but he spent his final five seasons (1949–1953) with the New York Yankees, mostly as a part-time player. The Yankees, however, considered him a valuable contributor to their winning five consecutive World Series titles (National Baseball Hall of Fame Library, Cooperstown, New York).

the American League pennant in 1949. Led by the foursome of Vic Raschi, Allie Reynolds, Ed Lopat, and Tommy Byrne, the Yankees clinched the pennant by winning a thrilling series against the Red Sox, led by former Yankees manager Joe McCarthy. In a jubilant clubhouse, Del Webb, Dan Topping, and George Weiss all agreed that the 1949 Yankees were the greatest team they had ever seen.[95]

After four closely contested games, all determined by no more than two runs, the Yankees defeated the Dodgers in the fifth World Series game, 10–6, to capture their 12th world championship.

George Weiss, Yankees general manager, was able to push his way through the throng to shake Stengel's hand.[96] No one was laughing now at George Weiss for bringing Casey Stengel to New York to manage the Yankees. Most baseball scribes, however, were sure this would be their last win under the regime of Weiss and Stengel. The team was aging and their roster was filled with fragile veterans. The consensus was the Yankees, if lucky, might finish the 1950 season in third place. Stengel, however, felt very optimistic about another first-place finish and the creation of a Yankees dynasty. What George Weiss was doing made Stengel scoff at the pessimistic attitude of the local press. He and Weiss eagerly looked forward to next year's roster that would include four exciting additions: a teenage shortstop playing with Independence of the Kansas-Oklahoma-Missouri League named Mantle; a promising southpaw having great success with Binghamton of the Eastern League named Whitey Ford; and two players the Yankees had recently purchased from Oakland—Stengel's protégé Billy Martin and a young outfield prospect, Jackie Jensen. With all of the players Weiss had assembled, Stengel knew it was his job to produce a winning team. As he told veteran baseball scribe Fred Lieb, "I've got to win some more before I convince some people that I'm a real manager."[97]

9

The New Dynasty

During the 1920s, the Yankees twice put together a string of three consecutive pennants. From 1936 through 1943, under general manager Ed Barrow and manager Joe McCarthy, the team won the American League flag seven out of eight seasons.[1]

After his first World Series victory in 1949, George Weiss received many congratulatory letters, even one from his team's frequent adversary, Branch Rickey. Rickey called Weiss's Yankees team "a great club" comprised of high-class individuals. He concluded by praising Weiss for being responsible for much of his team's success.[2]

Obviously with only one pennant under his belt in 1949, George Weiss may have dreamed "dynasty," but he was occupied with more immediate topics, including the rules for baseball as a whole, maintaining a top-notch farm system, and building a winning Yankees team in 1950.

Representing the Yankees at both the major and minor league winter meetings in late 1949, Weiss was now more confident in pushing his views on a number of key issues. None was more important to the Yankees than repealing the 1947 Bonus Rule aimed at keeping clubs with chain systems from assigning so-called "bonus babies" to a farm club, requiring them instead to keep the player on the major league squad for two full years. Although Weiss and other clubs with extensive farms instructed all their minor league heads to vote against keeping the rule, the opposition won the vote. Weiss continued speaking out about the unfairness of the rule throughout the 1950 season. The owners did ultimately repeal it at the December 1950 winter meetings.[3]

Near the end of 1949, Weiss also initiated a policy of greater specialization in developing players for the Yankees. The organization reduced the number of farm teams from 20 to 15 while increasing the staffs of scouts and supervisors. The Newark Bears, which had suffered a decline in attendance due to television and its proximity to New York, was sold to the Chicago Cubs, leaving Kansas City as the only AAA team in the Yankees organization. The Yankees also dropped four lower level teams.[4]

The newly expanded staff of scouts and supervisors included skilled baseball operatives Johnny Neun, Burleigh Grimes, Spud Chandler, Jim Turner, Frank Crosetti, and the new Kansas City manager for 1950, Joe Kuhel, a former manager of the Washington Senators.[5] Weiss encouraged Stengel, along with his coaches and scouting staff, to begin an instructional school prior to spring training for players at every level who needed special instruction or more grounding in the basics. This school ultimately gave

Weiss and Stengel a number of advantages. Weiss noted, "These advance camps give the entire organization one pattern, one system, one way of doing things. And that's my way."[6]

It did not take George Weiss very long to become more secure in his new role as general manager, and sportswriters and the public began to learn more about him as an individual. Most saw him as a tireless, careful, somewhat introverted person, obsessed with perfection in every detail of the entire organization, who usually got his way. His concern ranged from player uniforms and equipment through what positions each player was slated to play, down to the quality of paper towels in the stadium restrooms. On one occasion, Hazel, who enjoyed teasing her husband, asked him if he found the toilet paper all right. Weiss's usual response would be either to glare at Hazel or to politely tell her to hush up.[7]

While Weiss might have been perceived as a person obsessed with perfection in every detail, his detractors simply considered him a "control freak" who was a hired hand running the Yankees as a business and with a vested interest in maximizing the profit.[8] Once he visited his farm club in Norfolk during an afternoon practice. While the outfielders were shagging flies, Weiss noticed that the players failed to pick up the practice balls but allowed them to "lie around the outfield." Weiss gave Mayo Smith, Norfolk's manager, a stern lecture on the cost of baseballs, and for the remainder of Smith's tenure as one of Weiss's minor league managers, he would chastise his players for not retrieving any balls left lying around.[9]

Weiss would inspect every one of his minor league ballparks, and his minor league managers took great pains to make sure their boss was satisfied. When Weiss made a visit to Kansas City to inspect the facility, Frank Lane, Blues general manager, told Mrs. Weiss that he had dared her husband to find one thing wrong. Hazel, who knew her husband much better than Lane did, bet him ten dollars that he was mistaken. Lane took the bet, as George inspected the grass, the dugouts, the stands, the bathrooms, all to his satisfaction. Confident he was going to win his bet, Lane and Weiss returned to the main office, where Weiss noticed a row of six telephone booths. He immediately barked to Lane, "How many years ago were the windows of those telephone booths washed last?" Hazel smiled at Lane and said, "Gimme my ten dollars."[10]

Although Weiss organized many promotions at Yankee Stadium, at times he seemed oblivious to other kinds of baseball marketing. One of his aides suggested that the Yankees sponsor a "Cap Day" at Yankee Stadium. Weiss became livid merely thinking about the idea of actually giving away free merchandise. "Do you think I want every kid in this city walking around with a Yankee cap?" he asked.[11]

By 1951 George and his wife, Hazel, lived in Greenwich, Connecticut. Weiss, who worked every day, often 24 hours a day, usually rented an apartment in town to save time commuting to his home. Years later, in explaining the success of the Yankees, Weiss, ever the workaholic, said, "Some club officials turn the key in the door and go fishing at the end of the season. We don't. We work 12 months a year."[12] Many who worked with and for Weiss feared him. One group was the sportswriters who were beholden to management, which bought their meals and paid for their hotel rooms and train rides. The sportswriters loved the game of baseball, but they loved their jobs more and were loath "to make waves." New York sportswriters were careful when writing stories about George Weiss, and there was an unwritten agreement among them that certain stories were to be avoided.[13]

From the moment he had entered professional baseball, Weiss never hesitated to trade his players if he felt it would benefit his own team. After Weiss completed a major trade in 1950, one sportswriter dubbed him "Trader George," a sobriquet that never seriously irked him.[14]

When Jimmy Cannon, however, began referring to Weiss as "Lonesome George" in print, the Yankees' general manager, unusually sensitive to begin with, was extremely upset.[15] While it is true that Weiss could be very aloof and unfriendly, according to his closest acquaintances, he was extremely shy. At Lou Gehrig's funeral and other public functions, Weiss made sure his wife was at his side, fearing that if he were left alone, he might have to strike up a conversation with a stranger. The thought of making a public speech terrified him, and he would spend many days prior to the event rewriting his speech numerous times. In the end, he always kept his remarks short and to the point. He was so formal that he would never speak in the first person, even among friends.[16]

Weiss, as he was prone to do, began building his Yankees team for the following year just days after the World Series ended. He could never resist adding a "typical" warning, cautioning the Yankees against "soft living" during the winter. He was convinced that this was the reason that the Yankees had lost the pennant in 1948.[17]

Weiss expressed great confidence in his 1950 roster and saw little need for any major changes. This roster included Hank Bauer and the "Player of the Year" for 1949, Phil Rizzuto. Weiss announced that all his coaches and, of course, Casey Stengel had been rehired for 1950. The press, satisfied with the 1949 squad, made no demands on Weiss for a "big deal" as they had done the previous year, and raised little flak when Weiss made Charlie Keller, one of his rare player friends, a free agent before the start of the season. Weiss had promised Keller a job with the Yankees when there was an appropriate opening, but Keller was let go without a job offer; Weiss and the Yankees did honor him with a lavish retirement dinner a few months later.[18]

It was now time to concentrate on 1950 player contracts. Weiss had a relatively easy time signing his players simply because both Webb and Topping were willing to provide funding for the $650,000 club payroll, highest in baseball history up to that time. Their instructions were to not "be tough on the boys."[19]

Joe DiMaggio was always afforded the opportunity to meet personally with the Yankees' top brass, and as expected, he topped the team's salary list. Coming off a productive year, "Joltin' Joe" signed another $100,000 contract to start proceedings, and hurler Joe Page, whose comeback performance led the league with 27 saves, received the $30,000 he wanted.[20]

Although Weiss, as always, refused to confirm individual salary numbers, Tommy Henrich was reputed to have received a raise to $47,000. Henrich commented happily, "I had no trouble at all with General Manager George Weiss." Among the more prominent Yankees, Phil Rizzuto, Allie Reynolds, George Stirnweiss, and up-and-coming hurler Bob Porterfield all received raises. Following back surgery over the winter, slugger Johnny Mize not only accepted a rumored salary cut, but also wrote Weiss that he was determined to compete for a regular slot.[21] By mid–February, Weiss announced that 27

Yankees had signed, but that there were still some holdouts. As a negotiating tool as well as a general concern for finances, Weiss also warned that Yankees' expenses were "beyond belief" and he cautioned against "skyrocketing salaries."[22]

At their Florida training camp in early March, Weiss had a heated discussion with Yogi Berra over his contract, and he was also attempting to sign Vic Raschi. Weiss, "never one to stand on pride" when trying to get something done, called Stengel into the next salary sessions with these two players and both quickly inked their contracts.[23]

One seemingly minor signing was carried on for months and eventually involved a number of teams and Commissioner Happy Chandler. Weiss had obtained outfielder Dick Wakefield in a trade with the Detroit Tigers, but Wakefield refused to sign a reduced contract with the Yankees. Wakefield, a hot prospect, originally signed with the Tigers in 1941 as the first of the "Bonus Babies." He was paid more than the entire starting lineup of many major league teams.[24]

When he reached the Yankees, Weiss, a no-nonsense general manager, gave Wakefield an ultimatum: sign the Yankees contract or be traded to the Washington Senators. Wakefield signed and reported to spring training. By May, however, it was evident that Wakefield was not going to win a spot on the Yankees' roster, and Weiss tried to trade him to the Chicago White Sox. Wakefield refused to go and Frank Lane, Chicago general manager, never a fan of Weiss, attempted to negate the trade. Commissioner Chandler ruled in favor of the White Sox, thus voiding the trade and leaving Wakefield Yankees property.[25]

Weiss vowed that Wakefield would never play for the Yankees and sold him to the Oakland Oaks. After first refusing to report there, Wakefield contacted Chandler again, and the next day he agreed to report to the Oaks. Weiss was finally rid of the former Bonus Baby.[26]

While Weiss did not oppose the bonus rule, calling it a fundamentally sound proposition, he felt it did not work out the way it was intended.

> The first financial pinch will supply the remedy, unless the bonus rule is killed this summer. Too much money now is going out of baseball into the hands of youngsters who possibly do not thrive on that sort of financial situation. I shudder to think of the time when we might be seeing minor leagues blow, week after week, and we might be wailing over the vast sums which had been presented to youngsters to sign contracts.[27]

Weiss still looked out for strategic changes and additions, particularly as the seasons went on and the farms were unable to fill specific needs. In the fall of 1949 Weiss had purchased two players from the Oaks for $80,000 and obtained four players in trades. Twenty-two-year-old Jackie Jensen was one of Weiss's bonus players, and he was used primarily in the outfield.

Talented, but quick-tempered infielder Billy Martin, one of Stengel's favorites and soon a hit with the New York fans, started with the Yankees but was sent down to Kansas City in May. Martin, unhappy about his demotion, was advised by Stengel to see Weiss, but the general manager got into a shouting match with him and from that day on, Weiss was perceived as "having it in" for Billy Martin. Martin was recalled to the big club in June.[28]

After recovering from a 9–0 deficit to win the season's opener in Boston, the Yankees went into and out of first place during the remainder of the season, but finally eked out a second consecutive American League pennant, this time with a three-game margin over the Detroit Tigers. DiMaggio came through for his final productive year, and Rizzuto led the team with a .324 batting average. In June, Page seemed to lose effectiveness, so to buoy up the pitching staff, Weiss made an extremely controversial trade, sending the popular Snuffy Stirnweiss, outfielder Jim Delsing and pitchers Duane Pillette and Don Johnson to the St. Louis Browns for two minor league pitchers and two major league hurlers, southpaw Joe Ostrowski and right hander Tom Ferrick.[29]

There were rumors of a deep split over the deal between Weiss and Stengel, with the press taking Stengel's side and castigating Weiss. Actually Ferrick was a key to the Yankees' edging past the Tigers to win the American League pennant. In games against Detroit, he held them scoreless over ten innings and was called by Stengel "our most important individual performer in our drive to the top."[30]

Weiss's best acquisition in 1950 was 21-year-old pitcher Edward Charles "Whitey" Ford, who came to the Yankees not in a trade, but from their AAA farm club in Kansas

Native New Yorker Whitey Ford and George Weiss were constantly squabbling over Ford's night-time activities and constant salary demands. But there was no denying Ford's contributions to the Yankees—a lifetime 236–106 record, a 2.75 earned run average, and 1,956 strikeouts (courtesy Dwayne Labakas).

City. A native of New York City, Ford broke into the big leagues on July 1, 1950, and appeared in 20 games that season, compiling a record of 9–1 with an ERA of 2.81.[31] Ford would spend the 1951 and 1952 seasons in the military before rejoining the team in 1953 at the age of 24.[32]

The Yankees needed all the help they could acquire in 1950. Two of their star players, first basemen Tommy Henrich and Johnnie Mize, were both playing with injuries. Needing backup insurance at first base, Weiss turned once again to the National League and this year picked up Johnny Hopp from the Pittsburgh Pirates after he amazingly cleared waivers. Hopp not only helped during the season, he replaced the injured Henrich on the World Series roster.[33] Weiss indicated that Hopp was not acquired merely as a stopgap or as insurance. "I hope to get a couple of more years out of the 34-year-old Nebraskan while a young outfielder or two and a first baseman are being developed."[34]

In a move that might have been viewed as very considerate but was necessary to the team's success in the World Series, Weiss called Henrich at his home to ask him if he would allow himself to be ruled ineligible for the Series because of his injuries. This would allow the healthy, but very new Yankee, Hopp, to replace him on the roster. Shaken by the request, Henrich agreed only because Weiss said his action would help Stengel and the team. Henrich's name was removed from the World Series roster.[35]

In the 1950 World Series, the experienced Yankees went up against the Philadelphia Phillies' "Whiz Kids," who were no match for the New Yorkers; they defeated the Phils in four straight games. Rookie pitcher Whitey Ford won the fourth and final game, which was saved by Allie Reynolds.[36] Baseball observers described the 1950 Yankees as a team that knew how to make the most of what they had or, in Henrich's words, had replaced the power of the old "Murderer's Row" with hustle.[37] Phillies manager Eddie Sawyer gave the Yankees credit for their sweep in the World Series, but in reflecting on the outcome he reached a simple conclusion. Scoring only three earned runs in the four games, Sawyer lamented, "We just didn't hit. Of course, we were facing four guys named Raschi, Reynolds, Lopat and Ford."[38]

The victory party after the fourth game reflected Dan Topping's high-living style. Yankees broadcaster Mel Allen was the emcee; 500 guests danced to the music of Guy Lombardo and his orchestra, and Milton Berle performed his nightclub act. Of course, there were speeches. When he took the microphone, Weiss, as always when speaking, dampened the crowd's enthusiasm by announcing that the team should expect no salary raises for 1951 because the owners had made very little profit on the short-game Series. The players laughed, but Weiss was serious, since the Yankees were forced to refund some $364,000 for unused tickets for a possible fifth game.[39]

Weiss may not have been a polished speaker, but as the "unseen hand behind the successes," *The Sporting News* selected him as the "Major League Executive of the Year" for 1950. In his many years working in the minors, Weiss had won the award for minor league executive a number of times, but to be selected after just his third year in the majors was extremely satisfying.[40]

Nevertheless, Weiss faced a number of issues during the weeks following the 1950 World Series. He was concerned about the effect the military action in Korea might have on the makeup of his 1951 team. He removed another concern from his list when

On April 17, 1951, American League President Will Harridge(left) presents *The Sporting News Executive of the Year Award* to George Weiss for his success during the 1950 baseball season (Steve Steinberg Collection).

the Yankees signed Casey Stengel to manage the Yankees for 1951–1952 at a rumored record annual salary of $65,000.[41]

Weiss resolved still another issue when he welcomed back Roy Hamey to the Yankees organization to act as his assistant and, in particular, to help manage the farm system. Hamey had spent the previous year as general manager of the Pittsburgh Pirates. He told the press that he felt bad about leaving the Pirates, but he could not pass up the opportunity of returning home after his many years of association with the Yankees.[42]

Weiss turned his attention to his on-the-field concerns. He had to compensate for the loss of key players. Handicapped by an ailing knee, Tommy Henrich fought to remain on the active roster for 1951, refusing to accept Weiss's offer to manage the Kansas City Blues. At Weiss's insistence, Henrich consulted a doctor at Johns Hopkins, who completely obliterated Henrich's hopes. In December, Henrich finally allowed the Yankees to announce his retirement as a player to become one of Stengel's coaches and help with spring training for 1951. But Henrich's interest in a beer distributorship made him reluctant to work outside Manhattan, and the Yankees ultimately dropped him from the payroll. When he died in 2009 at the age of 96, Henrich was the oldest living Yankee and the last survivor of their teams of the 1930s.[43]

Weiss and Hamey began working on player contracts, as some Yankees seemed to prefer signing early. Phil Rizzuto was the first player Weiss got on board for 1951. Rizzuto entered negotiations asking for twice his 1950 salary of $35,000. Weiss originally offered him $40,000, but after consulting with Topping, he upped the offer to $45,000. When Rizzuto told Weiss that he was as valuable as DiMaggio, Weiss responded, "People come to the ball park to see him hit homers. They don't come to see you bunt."[44] They compromised at a supposed $50,000, obviously pleasing Rizzuto, who commented, "I'm very happy about my contract. I had no trouble getting together with the club on salary. After all, I did get a raise, didn't I?"[45] Sports writer John Drebinger called Scooter "Perhaps the most important contract signer for the 1951 campaign."[46]

For negotiating with most of his players, however, Weiss used the four-game World Series to justify contracts with very small raises or even cuts. In addition to reminding the players that the short Series meant virtually no profit for the club, he used the players' bonus money as an incentive. Repeating the refrain, "It pays to be a Yankee," Weiss demonstrated with what he felt was indisputable logic that over the years, Yankees players had earned an annual World Series bonus of almost $3,000. Therefore, he explained, the players should consider this bonus part of their contracts.[47]

Weiss also argued that he had to watch his payroll based on the previous year's revenues that might not hold up if more players were drafted or television cut into night game attendance.[48] Of course, Weiss failed to mention that the Yankees made more than $600,000 from radio and TV and that their more than 12 million home attendees over the past six seasons exceeded that of any other team.[49]

Regardless of Weiss's laments and appeals, by the end of January 1951, only two regulars, Rizzuto and Mize, had signed their contracts. Weiss, however, was confident that DiMaggio would sign his third $100,000 contract soon.[50] As for the others, Weiss told the press that the Yankees had offered raises of ten percent, and he was shocked that the players were demanding more. Nonetheless, he concluded, he really expected no serious problems with the rest of his regulars.[51]

Weiss was almost correct. By the third week in February, 22 Yankees had been signed, including 21-game winner Vic Raschi. Raschi, after a short meeting with Roy Hamey, accepted a contract for $30,000, a "satisfactory raise" of 20 percent over his 1950 salary.[52] At the end of each of his seasons, Raschi had to battle Weiss for a salary raise. Weiss would say, "Didn't you get your World Series money? Didn't I have something to do with our winning when I brought so-and-so up from the minors?" And Raschi would not mention how many strikeouts he had or what his earned run average was or even the number of games he won. "I always spoke of my value to the club," stated Raschi.[53]

When he talked about his confrontations with Weiss, Raschi insisted that Weiss was tough to deal with and never looked at a player during negotiations. "You always got the impression," he said, "that he was thinking, 'What's this guy want and how can I get rid of him in a hurry?'"[54]

By the end of February, first-string catcher Yogi Berra was still holding out. The Yankees had offered him $25,000, or as Weiss presented it, "five times his starting sal-

Pitcher Vic Raschi (right) shares a jovial moment with a very young Billy Martin (National Baseball Hall of Fame Library, Cooperstown, New York).

ary in 1947," but the prolific hitter was asking $30,000, or more than 50 percent more than he earned in 1950. As spring training began, Weiss finally gave in and signed the supposedly slow-thinking Berra for the $30,000 he wanted, making him the highest paid catcher in the history of the club.[55] As far as Berra was concerned, the raise was justified. If the Yankees weren't willing to pay him big money after he hit .322 and drove in 124 runs, when *would* they pay him?[56]

Two weeks before the 1951 spring training began, Weiss had Stengel repeat his highly successful pre-training coaching school. He and Stengel selected 28 players from throughout the farms, including nine on the Yankees' roster, who needed some particular corrective help.[57] The school and the Yankees' 1951 training were not held in Florida due to perhaps the most unusual trade the club made that year—swapping spring training camps with the Giants, which put the Bronx Bombers into Phoenix while the Giants played in St. Petersburg. Owner Del Webb orchestrated the deal with Giants owner Horace Stoneham, but Weiss was all for it, realizing the lucrative advantages of a new audience for the World Series champs.[58]

For spring training, Weiss brought in a number of farm players to get a trial with the team, emphasizing that more than one-third of the Yankees' 40-man roster would be made up of players who were reared in their farm system for all or most of the 1950 season.[59]

Unlike other years, the sports media spent less time on DiMaggio and focused more on two rookies—infielder Gil McDougald, and especially young Mickey Mantle, one of the most promising and most powerful rookies anyone could recall. He had been playing shortstop, but was being groomed to play center field as DiMaggio's eventual replacement.[60]

Despite his physical prowess, Mantle was safe from the draft, having been classified 4F for chronic osteomyelitis, a bone infection aggravated by high school football injuries.[61] Mantle began the 1951 season with the Yankees and immediately bonded with Stengel. In fact, the 19-year-old began to look on Stengel as a father figure. Unfortunately, Stengel was a permissive parent who did nothing to hold down Mantle's late-night carousing in the company of some of his teammates.[62] When Mantle began to flounder at mid-season, Weiss insisted—over Stengel's protests—that Mantle needed more seasoning and sent him down to Kansas City.[63]

Even though there were still a number of question marks, Weiss predicted that the Yankees would place a very competitive team on the field in 1951 and would win a third straight American League pennant.[64] "We placed no fewer than 60 players out of a total of something like 240 on the all-star teams of the minors in 1950," said Weiss. "Just how many of these fine prospects will remain for us in 1951 competition after the service gets through with our minor league rosters, I do not know."[65]

By the time the 1951 season opened, Weiss was beginning to field a viable team although there were still some holes to fill. He was grooming three of his "phenoms" in the minor leagues—pitcher Tom Morgan, Mickey Mantle and Gil McDougald.[66] Whitey Ford was in the service, Bobby Brown was scheduled to be called to active duty, the team had an ineffective bullpen and there was no regular first baseman. In addition, Joe DiMaggio's career was in doubt.

With Brown a question mark, Weiss called up Gil McDougald as both a reserve infielder and a player to battle Billy Johnson for third base. McDougald, who was the Texas League Rookie of the Year in 1950, was so impressive that Weiss traded Johnson to the Cardinals.[67] When Brown discovered that he would not have to serve in the military in 1951, McDougald was platooned between third and second. Rizzuto played solely at short, and the Yankees employed a committee of three to play first base—Joe Collins, Johnny Mize and Johnny Hopp. Mantle played 96 games in the outfield before being shipped to the minors. DiMaggio, Hank Bauer, and Gene Woodling played the outfield in most of the games for the Yankees in 1951.[68]

The big success story of the Yankees in 1951 was their pitching. Weiss acquired Stubby Overmire from the Browns in exchange for Tommy Byrne and cash. Weiss also traded pitchers Bob Porterfield, Tom Ferrick and the disappointing Fred Sanford to the Washington Senators for southpaw Bob Kuzava. Weiss saw Kuzava as a long reliever but also a pitcher who was capable of being the team's fifth starter.[69]

George Weiss provided his team with pitching insurance when on August 29, he sent pitching prospect Lew Burdette and $50,000 to the Boston Braves for veteran pitcher Johnny Sain. Sain proved an invaluable asset to the Yankees, augmenting the pitching staff led by their three valuable starters—Eddie Lopat, Vic Raschi and Allie Reynolds, who combined to win 59 games for the Yankees in 1951.[70] (It was the third consecutive year that Weiss acquired a veteran National League player named "Johnny" late in the season.)

The Giants, elated by winning the National League pennant on Bobby Thomson's dramatic home run, confidently faced the Yankees in the 1951 World Series. The Yankees were behind two games to one in the Series when DiMaggio led his team to victory in

Pitcher Eddie Lopat (center) and infielders Joe Collins (left) and Gil McDougald (right) all contributed greatly to the Yankees' success in the early 1950s (National Baseball Hall of Fame Library, Cooperstown, New York).

Game Four. The Yankees swept the next two games to secure their third consecutive championship.[71]

Yogi Berra, the anchor of the Yanks, was voted the American League's "Most Valuable Player" for 1951. Despite all the attention on Mantle, it was Yankees infielder Gil McDougald who was voted 1951 "Rookie of the Year" in the American League. And for the second consecutive year, George Weiss was named the *Sporting News* "Major League Executive of the Year." In giving Weiss the award, *The Sporting News* stated that it was not because the Yankees had won the American League pennant and World Series again, but because of "the wisdom with which [Weiss] operates the farm system ... with a ready replacement to fill a hole ... and the facility for coming up with a deal if the farms should fail. He is the unseen hand responsible for much of the success of the Yankees."[72]

At the 1951 victory party, Weiss banned speeches. Remembering the reaction to his remarks about World Series revenues the previous year, Weiss ruled that the 1951 celebration would consist only of eating, drinking, dancing and entertainment.[73]

In truth, the 1951 World Series victory was bittersweet. After the final game, 36-year-old Joe DiMaggio, who had fallen short of his usual production, sat in front of his locker and quietly stated that he had played his final game.[74] On December 11 he made his resignation official, turning down another $100,000 Yankees contract by simply admitting, "I no longer have it." He realized his recurrent heel spur injury would cause him to play at less than the top of his game, and in fairness to the fans and his own pride, he walked away.[75]

The 1951 Series also affected DiMaggio's designated successor, although few recognized it at the time. Mickey Mantle stepped or fell on an open drain playing the outfield at Yankee Stadium during the second game of the World Series. The injuries to his knee from that incident would plague him the rest of his career.[76]

As always, the end of the 1951 World Series signaled Weiss's full-time concentration on the next season, but with a major change in his top-notch scouting staff and another that affected the farm teams. Joe Devine, chief scout covering the West Coast, died in September 1951. His duties were assigned to John Cottrell, his assistant. Paul Krichell remained head of the entire scouting operation, but now he reported directly to Lee MacPhail, filling Weiss's old slot as head of the farm system. Weiss had looked past his history with Lee's father, Larry, and had kept Lee with the Yankees, moving him to increasingly responsible roles.[77]

In the closing days of 1951, Weiss made only one significant trade, swapping hot-headed rookie catcher Clint Courtney to the Browns for St. Louis's second-best pitcher, Jim McDonald. The 24-year-old right-hander had won only four games with the last-place Browns in 1951, but two of them came against the Yankees. Courtney left the Yankees with bitterness, proclaiming that George Weiss never paid him what he thought he was worth and that Weiss had a "cheap outfit."[78] Billy Johnson, another disgruntled ex–Yankee who had become the Cardinals' everyday third baseman after being traded to St. Louis, compared Weiss, who never said more than "hello" to him, with the Cardinals' boss, Fred Saigh, who was always friendly and personable.[79]

Although George Weiss had one more year remaining on his contract, Dan Topping announced that his general manager and vice president would be given a five-year extension on his present contract and would continue in both jobs for the Yankees. Topping emphasized that Weiss did not ask for the new deal. "It was done at my suggestion," said Topping. "In recognition of George's excellent work, I proposed the new contract to our board of directors at a meeting during the world series." Although terms were not announced, the five-year deal included renewal options and a yearly salary of $60,000, an increase of $10,000.[80]

Despite the personal rancor of some players, Weiss's trading acumen was one of the many factors in his winning still another significant award, a gold medal from his hometown's Advertising Club for "distinguished achievement." In his remarks at the New Haven awards banquet, Weiss noted that he was the first sports figure ever to receive this honor and that his greatest thrill was that baseball was "now in the high estate ... [of] ... the arts, industry, education and science." More than 600 attendees heard Commissioner Ford Frick state, "Baseball is fully deserving of this honor and you have made an excellent choice in George Weiss."[81]

Salary negotiations for 1952 began slowly with Weiss signing only two first-string Yankees by mid–January. As usual, Johnny Mize signed quickly and Ed Lopat, who posted an outstanding 21–9 record in 1951, was also an early signer.[82]

Weiss delegated to Roy Hamey the job of handling his first salary talks, but veterans like Berra could still request a meeting with Weiss. For some reason, Berra usually had no trouble talking with the GM, and he once described what was going on during a typical salary meeting. "You sit down in front of Weiss at his desk and he starts telling you how bad you were the last season. Then he shuts his eyes and starts pulling at his right eyebrow. This means the conference is getting hot. But George is okay."[83]

9. *The New Dynasty*   107

In addition to help from Roy Hamey, the absence of high-salaried players and coaches (e.g., DiMaggio, Page and Henrich) freed up extra money for Weiss and Hamey to negotiate. It was almost no surprise that by January 30, Hamey had signed MVP Berra, Rookie of the Year McDougald, first baseman Joe Collins and second baseman Jerry Coleman.[84]

The remaining holdouts included World Series MVP Phil Rizzuto and New York Sports Writers' Player of the Year Allie Reynolds, who originally had requested a $10,000 raise over his previous year's salary of $22,500. Reynolds had compiled a record of 17–8

Ed Lopat (left) and Allie Reynolds were mainstays of the Yankees' pitching staff from 1947 to 1955. Yet each year both pitchers were involved in contentious salary discussions with general manager George Weiss (National Baseball Hall of Fame Library, Cooperstown, New York).

and led the majors with seven shutouts.[85] Weiss had instructed Hamey to "not be niggardly" in his talks with these key players, and within a week the Yankees had raised Reynolds to a generous $35,000 contract. Rizzuto had made it a goal to take for himself a significant amount of the $100,000 left from DiMaggio, and although he and others had expected Weiss to fight to save it, Weiss offered the "Scooter" $45,000, the highest salary ever paid a shortstop. Rizzuto was elated.[86]

Spring training and the instructional school returned to Florida in the spring of 1952, producing good exhibition game attendance figures. With both the bottom line and the welfare of the players in mind, Weiss announced that he had eliminated long barnstorming trips, making stops only in Atlanta, Charlotte, and a few other cities en route back to New York for the beginning of the 1952 season. "I have concluded," said Weiss, "that long jaunts are not good for the club."[87]

The Yankees were hoping to tie the record of four straight World Series titles they had set back in 1939, but the team would have to adjust to a number of challenges and changes. They were still without Whitey Ford, who had one more year left on his military service. In addition, the Marine Air Corps called up Jerry Coleman shortly after the season opened. Billy Martin lived up to Stengel's faith in him by capably filling Coleman's post. Nineteen fifty-two was also the first season without DiMaggio, and the now 20-year-old Mickey Mantle did his best to try to fill the large hole left by the "Yankee Clipper."[88]

Still handicapped by his injury from the World Series, Mantle was not ready to play center field, so Weiss engineered a deal with the Senators to trade outfielder Jackie Jensen (who was hitting only .105), pitcher Spec Shea and two others for experienced center fielder Irv Noren and infielder Tommy Upton. In some respects, this turned out to be an expensive deal. After the trade, Jensen suddenly became one of the league's best players and Shea had a resurgence, winning a total of 23 games in 1952 and 1953.[89] Noren, however, provided that extra flexibility which enabled Stengel to move players around and eventually get Mantle playing center permanently.[90]

As the 1952 season wound down and the Yankees were fighting with the Indians for the pennant, Weiss made another National League acquisition. This year he claimed Dodgers pitcher Johnny Schmitz on waivers to help patch together the pitching staff, which had suffered some additional problems. Tom Morgan had left for Army duty and Ed Lopat was nursing a sore shoulder.[91]

But Weiss had acquired Schmitz only as a way to get the pitcher he really wanted. A few weeks after the Schmitz deal was finalized, Weiss traded him and three minor league farm players to the Cincinnati Reds for 30-year-old right-handed pitcher Ewell Blackwell. Weiss was quite pleased to obtain the once-excellent pitcher for the Yankees, but he was even more pleased to have beaten out rival general managers Frank Lane and Hank Greenberg for the prize.[92]

Buoyed by a pitching staff headlined by Raschi, Lopat and Reynolds, as well as contributions from Sain, the Yankees won 15 of their last 18 games, beating the Indians by two games for their fourth consecutive pennant. Berra's 30 homers—a new American League record for a catcher—and Mantle's .311 batting average were among the highlights of the team's balanced offense.[93]

The World Series opponents for the Yankees in 1952 were their Brooklyn neighbors who fought hard to prevent the Yanks' fourth consecutive championship. The Series swung back and forth as the Dodgers prevailed in Games 1, 3, and 5, with the Yankees coming right back each time to capture Games 2, 4, and 6. The seventh and deciding game belonged to the Yankees as Mantle's sixth inning homer put the Bombers ahead to stay, while Bob Kuzava came out of the bullpen to retire the final eight Dodgers batters to preserve the Yankees' 4–2 victory.[94]

New York sportswriter Joe Williams identified the key to the Yankees' success when he declared that there might have been better teams than the 1952 Bombers, but none with more determination. He cited particularly the final two games of the Series won by the Yankees at Ebbets Field.

> In these two games, a new Yankee hero emerged to take his place alongside illustrious heroes of the past.... As Ruth goes and a Joe DiMaggio takes his place, a DiMaggio goes and along comes a Mantle.... The Yankees simply make it a business to go out and get the best—and this is more a matter of expert operation than of money. They have the best front office organization in baseball and in George Weiss the most competent man in his field.[95]

As a mark of his increasing success, Weiss was given two important tributes: the Slocum Award, the top honor given by the New York Baseball Writers' Association, as well as the *Sporting News*' "Major League Executive of the Year" for the third straight year.[96] In summarizing the reasons for naming Weiss the winner of the Slocum Award, the NYBWA noted,

> The attainments of the general manager of the New York club are not just recent accomplishments, not merely current fireworks. For decades, many close observers have recognized him as a shrewd, capable operator.... The Yankee administrative chief has not merely helped his own club. He has exerted a powerful influence for good on all baseball, with outstanding contributions to the health, wealth, and happiness of the entire American League in particular, and the professional game in general.[97]

As soon as the traditionally exuberant team victory celebration was over, Weiss and his staff began dealing with issues for the upcoming season—issues that affected all of baseball as well as the Yankees and their farms. Weiss was upbeat as he looked over his "young team" and reflected on the success of his 1952 Champions, calling them a "transitional" team, not yet reaching full potential. Many sportswriters agreed that ever since 1947, Weiss had been clearing out older, post–World War II players, and creating this current team (average age 27), which had now won four straight pennants. As always, Weiss credited the farm system for "feeding us the good players [that] actually won the pennants for us." As he told *The Sporting News,* a team built pennant-winning clubs by developing players in their farm systems and not by trades.[98]

With the Yankees' and Weiss's sustained records of success in front of them, organized baseball began a series of actions with the goal of bringing down the Yankees. The first move concerned inter-league trading. Other baseball bosses, particularly the Indians' general manager, Hank Greenberg, felt that Weiss's pattern of acquiring National Leaguers on waivers late in the season—Mize, Hopp, Sain and Blackwell—tipped the balance in the Yankees' pennant wins. Weiss bristled when he was accused of running a team of NL castoffs and rightly contended that the Yankees had adhered strictly to the current rule which provided that a National League club sell its player to the highest American League bidder once the player had passed waivers from all NL teams. Under the new rule proposed by Ford Frick and targeted directly at the Yankees, any AL team could block the transfer of an NL player to the "league-leading team" by claiming him at the $10,000 waiver price. To become official, the proposed rule had to win a majority of each league's management.[99]

Weiss led a spirited fight against the passage of the rule, aiming most of his fire at Greenberg, whose team had finished only two games behind New York. According to Weiss, the Indians had had an opportunity to obtain Blackwell from the Reds, but the Yankees simply outbid the Tribe. Piling it on, Weiss claimed that the Indians couldn't even take advantage of intra-league trades, pointing out that in the past August, the Indians had the first chance to get Red Sox hurler Ray Scarborough, but allowed the Yankees to acquire him. Scarborough won five games for the Yankees in 1952.[100]

Despite Weiss's opposition, the two-league waiver rule was approved and would begin in the 1953 season, affecting all inter-league trades after June 15. Weiss reiterated that the Yankees would continue to operate under whatever rule was current.[101]

Yet another restriction was aimed primarily at the Yankees but controlled all organizations with active chain systems. Since 1950, when Weiss had been successful in getting the bonus rule repealed, there were no limits on where a "bonus baby" could be assigned. But at the 1952 winter meeting, the heads of organized baseball adopted a new bonus rule that mandated, among other things, that any amateur player signed for $5,000 or more by a major league club had to remain with that club for at least two years, or else that player could be lost through the draft. Weiss tried to marshal support for a more flexible bonus policy, but owners without well-developed farm systems, such as Horace Stoneham's New York Giants, favored the rule as proposed.[102]

One of the final issues addressed by Weiss and other executives was each team's policy regarding television and its effect on the bottom line. Television seemed to hold down attendance. For example, Yankee Stadium crowds dropped from 1.95 million in 1951 to a little over 1.6 million in 1952.[103] But all the clubs were paid fairly well for their TV rights and most felt that they could charge more from this source. After much high-level discussion, Weiss, who several years earlier had considered TV a passing fad, announced that in 1953 the Yankees would stay with a schedule of televising 14 home games, but might increase televised road games to 20. He also indicated that another year would be required before the Yankees could decide the television issue. In the meantime, he noted that the reduced gate and high expenses were likely to affect salary negotiations for the 1953 season.[104]

Casey Stengel was one Yankee whose salary would not be affected by economic conditions. The press reported that his new two-year contract called for him to receive "near $100,000" annually. Weiss and Stengel used the occasion of Stengel's signing to quash rumors of conflict between the two, declaring that they "had always been in agreement on major trades."[105]

Player negotiations would not be so easy, or in some cases, so amiable. It was assumed that the eight players who were with the Yankees on each of the championship teams—pitchers Allie Reynolds, Vic Raschi, and Ed Lopat, outfielders Hank Bauer and Gene Woodling, catcher Yogi Berra, shortstop Phil Rizzuto and pinch-hitter Johnny Mize—would be asking for raises totaling about $70,000.[106] As Dan Daniel wrote, "The players who won the championship insist on taking 100 percent of the credit. The front office, which organized the winning combination, insists on its own share of the credit, and thus is born a long sequence of salary disputes."[107]

It was not merely veteran players or those who had exceptional seasons in 1952 who expected a raise from George Weiss. Sophomore pitcher Bill Miller, whose record in 1952 had been 4–3, sent his contract back to Weiss stating, "You tell me to live like a Yankee, dress like a Yankee, act like a Yankee—so pay me like a Yankee."[108] Despite the spate of unsigned Yankees contracts, Weiss was neither pleased nor disturbed by newspaper headlines, which had him fighting a big holdout movement. "I am sure that when the main squad starts work on March 1 in St. Petersburg, we will have a 100 percent attendance," he stated.[109]

Although Weiss instructed Roy Hamey to begin contract discussion with his players, most of the regulars ended up talking with Weiss, who called the slow rate of signings "just an old Yankee custom." In fact Sain and McDougald both signed for a reported $40,000 soon after meeting with Weiss. But by late February, the list of unsigned players included top pitchers Lopat, Raschi, and Reynolds, as well as Rizzuto, Woodling, Bauer, Collins, Martin, and Mantle. Even the usually quick-signing Johnny Mize was still holding out, and Weiss had changed his public stance. "You don't realize what a problem it is to sign up a ball club that has won four straight world championships," a nervous George Weiss told the press.[110]

One of Weiss's most contentious negotiations was with Allie Reynolds, the Yankees' pitcher with the best record in 1952 (20–8) and an ERA of 2.06, leading the American League in earned run average, strikeouts (160), and shutouts (6).[111] This was the only year Reynolds won 20 games.[112]

After three heated conferences with Weiss, Reynolds left spring training camp in Florida and returned home. This time, Stengel refused to intercede, and Topping rejected by phone Reynolds's demand for a two-year contract at $25,000 per year.[113] Weiss asked Hamey to step in and deal with Reynolds, and Hamey finally signed the recalcitrant hurler. Bauer, Mantle and Collins quickly signed their contracts, and even Lopat, who had a less attractive contract, signed soon after. The Yankees had offered him a provisional contract below his old salary, but with an incentive clause. He could make his former $25,000–$28,000 if he could perform as he had prior to his 1952 injury. Eventually, with the prodding of Weiss and Hamey, all the players inked their contracts.[114] During the season, Lopat proved he was worth every penny of his 1952 salary.

Whitey Ford had returned from the military in the fall of 1952 and started the 1953 season with the Yankees. With Ford added to the pitching staff and essentially the same lineup as in 1952, the Yankees began a strong march toward the 1953 pennant. By mid–June, following an 18-game win streak that ended on June 14, sportswriters were conceding the pennant to the Yankees.[115] Even more impressive than the win streak was the fact that the Yankees were accomplishing this feat despite being the only baseball team to have the rules changed because of their success. Sportswriters commented tongue-in-cheek that the way to really bring down the Bombers would be to legislate out of existence general manager George Weiss, whose unmatched trading savvy and operation of the Yankees' farm system was the real reason for the team's achievements.[116]

At the beginning of September, the Yanks were ahead by five games and were aided by the return of Jerry Coleman from the military to his former second base position.

Manager Casey Stengel watches batting practice intensely as his team strives to win their fifth consecutive World Championship (from the Collections of the St. Louis Mercantile Library at the University of Missouri–St. Louis).

By September 15, the Yankees had clinched their fifth consecutive pennant, finishing the season 8½ games ahead of Greenberg's Cleveland Indians.[117]

Their pennant success was due in large part to their pitching. Whitey Ford compiled a record of 18–6; Ed Lopat finished at 16–4; Vic Raschi also posted 16 wins, and spot starters Allie Reynolds and Johnny Sain won 13 and 14 games respectively. Second baseman Billy Martin had his finest offensive season, hitting 15 home runs and driving in 75 runs. Third baseman Gil McDougald batted .285; leadoff hitter Hank Bauer batted .304, Gene Woodling led the team with a batting average of .306, Mantle finished third in the league with 105 runs scored, and Yogi Berra led the team with 27 home runs and 108 runs batted in, en route to earning a second-place finish to Cleveland's Al Rosen in the AL MVP voting.[118]

Once the pennant race ended, Stengel happily announced that he would fulfill the second year of his contract and his goal would be to win consecutive pennant number six. Fred Down, *United Press* writer, attributed a great deal of Stengel's success to George Weiss, who had hired him despite Stengel's reputation as baseball's funny man. Down admitted that Weiss was right on the mark when he told the press, "We knew he was one of the finest baseball men in the country. He is 100 percent baseball. He lives it day and night."[119]

In the 1953 World Series, the Yankees squared off against the Dodgers for the second year in a row, with Brooklyn asserting that this was the "wait-till-next-year" year Dodgers fans had been promised.[120] The Yankees captured the first two games at home, but the Dodgers came from behind and won the next two games at Ebbets Field, tying the Series. Game Five was the Yankees' turn to come back as they overpowered the Dodgers, 11–7, with homers by Mantle, Woodling, Martin, and McDougald. The Yankees wrapped it up in Game Six on an RBI single by Martin in the bottom of the ninth, winning the game and the Series and establishing the new record of five consecutive World Championships, and their 16th World Championship in their 50-year history. Casey Stengel said, "Everybody contributed."[121]

The Yankees organization and their fans were elated by the team's continued success, but not so the rest of the baseball world. Negative comments about the inevitability of the Yankees' repeat spoiling attendance for other American League teams had been prevalent before, during and after the season. Resentment against the Yankees' success began to appear regularly in feature articles and editorials. After the Yankees won their fifth consecutive World Championship in 1953, one journalist editorialized, "We honestly feel it would be better for baseball if the Yankees lost once in a while."[122]

Yankees players were well aware of this widespread resentment against their team coming especially from the two teams, the Giants and the Dodgers, who had to compete with the Yankees for fan loyalty. Second baseman Jerry Coleman felt this resentment first-hand. "People watched the Yankees and admired the pride of the Yankees, but unfortunately, the Yankees became so successful, people hated them for their success."[123]

According to baseball pundits, the average fan wasn't angry at the players or at Casey Stengel, but at the "arrogance of the front office," personified by George Weiss, who, they claimed, "didn't understand and love baseball" and who was a snob with no public relations skills, a humorless, emotionless man who saw all players as only price tags.[124]

George Weiss was immune to criticism of his team's successes. He shrugged his shoulders at his detractors and stated that he looked forward to an indefinite continuance of Yankees success.[125] He attributed his team's success to "visualizing the team's weaknesses," building up a strong farm system, and hiring Casey Stengel as manager in 1949 because "we knew he could handle ball players, young and old."[126]

Finally, Weiss credited his team's success to players acquired both by trades and waivers. Weiss noted that seven players acquired from other clubs were instrumental in the success of the Yankees—Johnny Mize, Irv Noren, Allie Reynolds, Ed Lopat, Johnny Sain, Bob Kuzava, and Tom Ferrick. Sain and Mize were both acquired in waiver deals, as were Johnny Hopp and Ewell Blackwell. In defending his waiver acquisitions, Weiss lashed out at his critics. "Our deals were perfectly legitimate. It was another example of a 'Hate the Yankees' campaign, which really distressed us. We simply cannot understand why we received so much criticism when we were merely trying our best to win and were operating within the laws of the game."[127]

Weiss's responses to his detractors probably did more harm than good, and he especially evaded the charges that he was both condescending and insensitive. He did conclude his remarks by adding that the Yankees' success was due, in part at least, to the dedication of Yankees management, which didn't go off golfing during the winter months. In December, however, Weiss and his wife took a well-earned vacation in Hawaii.[128]

Weiss was unfazed about the resentment factor when he pulled off a trade that surprised much of the baseball world by its size and the benefits it brought the Yankees. Because of the anti–Yankees change in inter-league trading rules, Weiss in 1953 had not brought in the traditional National League star toward the end of the season. Now in the off-season, he had several priorities: filling in his aging pitching staff and finding another experienced first baseman to replace Johnny Mize, who had retired immediately after the World Series.[129] Looking toward his own league, Weiss negotiated a player swap that was "perfect from the Yankees' point of view." The transaction sent eight promising Yankees minor leaguers, who did not fit into Weiss's plans, and cash, for two established players from the A's: young right-handed pitcher Harry Byrd and hard-hitting first baseman Eddie Robinson, who had driven in 100 or more runs each of the past three seasons.[130]

It was now time to tackle Yankees salaries for the 1954 season. The plan was, as before, that assistant general manager Hamey conduct routine meetings and for Weiss to tackle the more difficult cases. Negotiations were expected to be rough with many players who had contributed to all five pennant and world championships, and who knew that the owners had done quite well earning revenue from all sources, including television.[131]

Weiss, of course, was prepared with his arguments that the Yankees' payroll for 1953 was the "highest in history." He also reminded his players that programs to keep the Yankees winning and earning bonuses, such as the preliminary Florida training camp for returning military and others needing special help, didn't come cheap.[132]

Weiss mailed the majority of the contracts in early January, but few were returned. Meetings were begun with those players who refused to sign, including virtually all of the team's stars. One of the first players Weiss signed for 1954 was his All-Star catcher, Yogi Berra. Weiss respected Berra and the two had developed an interesting form of negotiation over the years that usually left both feeling good about the outcome. According to Weiss, Berra "never raved, ranted, pleaded, or raised his voice. He just listened until I had exhausted my words and then said, 'You're right, George, but I still want $30,000.' He got $37,000 last season and one can almost hear him say, 'Make it forty,

George.'"[133] In fact, Berra supposedly received $42,000, a $5,000 raise from 1953. When contract talks were concluded, Berra told the press, "It was so easy, maybe I should have asked for more."[134]

Throughout the month of February, Hamey met with unsigned players at Weiss's request, but as the month drew to a close, a number of stars, including Ford, Reynolds, and Raschi, were still unsigned.[135]

The touchiest negotiations were with pitcher Vic Raschi, who was almost always a holdout and was even described by a high Yankees official—not Weiss—as the "meanest holdout in baseball."[136] Raschi came to deeply dislike his general manager, who would tell him after an exceptionally successful season, "Prove to me why you deserve a raise."[137]

From 1948 through 1953, Raschi won 111 games while losing only 48 for the Yankees.[138] These figures did not impress Weiss, who was concerned that after five consecutive world championships, his payroll was beginning to swell beyond his extremely stingy budget. When Raschi received his 1954 contract, it called for a 25 percent pay cut. Raschi quickly rejected the offer and showed up at spring training to continue negotiations. It was there that he learned from a newspaperman that Weiss had sold him to the St. Louis Cardinals for $75,000 and two minor league players.[139] Raschi went to see Weiss and said simply, "Mr. Weiss, you have a very short memory."[140] The sale of Raschi created a furor among his teammates, but it had one effect Weiss desired. It sufficiently scared the other holdouts so that they quickly fell into line and signed their contracts.[141]

In explaining the sale of Raschi, Weiss told the press, "I don't want to make Raschi the whipping boy, but there is an attitude of complacency on the club. Some of the players have become independently wealthy through the winning of five straight championships. Some of the players acted as if they were the employers and the club the employee."[142] Weiss also defended the sale of Raschi by indicating that although it no doubt triggered much bad publicity, it was simply a part of his pitching staff strategy that would rely on younger arms in order to keep rebuilding the team.[143]

Most sportswriters did not agree with Weiss's rationale. Many felt Raschi became the scapegoat because he was the most expendable of the club's high-salaried veterans and also because he had been a constant thorn in Weiss's hide every spring since he had joined the club. They noted that since 1951, when he had last won 20 or more games, Raschi persistently refused to have his salary reduced from the $40,000 bracket even though he was losing velocity on his fastball.[144]

On the other hand, Weiss did have his defenders. The *Canandaigua Daily Messenger* argued that Weiss, one of baseball's smartest men, did indeed have valid reasons for ridding his roster of Vic Raschi. It argued that Weiss, realizing that Raschi was "about washed up," reasoned that he should receive something in return for his pitcher. Second, Weiss did not want his players to become overly cocky, "getting too sure of themselves and their greatness." Third, with a dozen players unsigned, the paper felt that a blow like trading a star pitcher would send the remaining holdouts a message that he might take additional action if they did not send their contracts to the front office. Finally, the Yankees saved $40,000 in salary and collected at least $75,000 from the Cardinals in addition to several rookies who might help the Yankees in the future.[145]

Without Raschi, the pitching staff was now one of Weiss's biggest challenges. Ewell

Blackwell was unable to pitch again, even after sitting out the entire 1953 season recovering from numerous major operations. Looking to the farms, Weiss brought up several prospects including Bob Grim, recently returning after two years with the military.[146]

On the field, Mantle's ability to rejoin the team was questionable. He had reinjured his bad knee in the 1953 All-Star Game, and had surgery on it in the fall to remove a cyst. Yankees orthopedists felt that he would be unable to play until May.[147] The list of temporary replacements from the chain system included the talented Bob Cerv, who had been unable to find a spot on the Yankees previously, and one of Stengel's favorites, speedy Bill Virdon.[148] And in an interesting turnaround, Jerry Coleman had returned from the military just in time to reclaim his second base position from Billy Martin, who was departing to serve his two-year duty. Martin had picked up Coleman's job when he left.[149]

The defending five-time champions managed to win only eight of 24 spring training games. Fans and baseball observers, eager to figure out why, speculated that a "take charge" player like DiMaggio was no longer with the club. Mantle was beginning to fill that role, but he was not quite ready to return to the lineup.[150] To add depth to the outfield, power at the plate, and hopefully boost morale, right before the season began, Weiss made what *New York Times* sportswriter Joseph F. Sheehan called "another of those inter-league trades." In exchange for a failed pitching prospect and three minor leaguers to be named later, the Yankees got from the St. Louis Cardinals Enos "Country" Slaughter.[151] This was the sixth time in six years that the Yankees had strategically acquired a player from the National League. The new rule requiring players to pass waivers with both leagues did not go into effect until July 15.[152]

Rumors had it that this trade was a "thank you" for the Raschi deal, as the Cardinals supposedly tipped off the Yankees that Slaughter was available. Slaughter, stunned by the trade, was bitter but got ready to join his new team. Known for his "never-give-up attitude," Slaughter told reporters, "I'll be there for the opening game and I'll give Casey Stengel 100 percent just as I've given every ball club I've played for."[153] The trade set off criticism of waivers and even questions about the strength of the Yankees' farm system, but no one questioned the value Slaughter added to the Yankees thanks to Weiss's shrewdness.[154]

In addition to changes on the field for the Yankees in 1954, there were also changes in the front office. Topping and Weiss hired William O. DeWitt to serve as assistant to general manager Weiss, replacing Roy Hamey, who had become general manager of the Philadelphia Phillies. Like Weiss, DeWitt, the former owner of the St. Louis Browns, was considered an astute baseball man.[155]

In hiring DeWitt, the Yankees made it clear that he was going to have a definite role to play in the organization. His duties included negotiation of player contracts, liaison service between Weiss and Casey Stengel, and general troubleshooter in the farm system. Co-owner Dan Topping stated, "DeWitt is not only George's assistant, but he is the man to whom we would look if something happened to Weiss. If George were hit by a truck, Bill would take over."[156] Shirley Povich wrote that the Yankees made a wise move in hiring DeWitt. "DeWitt is a shrewd baseball operator who knows how to deal with ball players, scouts, and farm clubs."[157]

Later in the year, the Yankees made another change in their front office. Arthur

"Red" Patterson resigned as public relations director because of what he called "a clash of personalities with General Manager George Weiss." Patterson had originally joined the Yankees in 1946 as traveling secretary.[158] It was commonly known that Patterson and Weiss did not always see eye to eye, and the relationship became more strained when Weiss did not choose Patterson to replace Hamey, as he had expected. In fact, Patterson expected to move up in the organization even before Hamey was hired.[159]

Patterson had a number of disputes with Weiss, and his time came to a close allegedly over free tickets for an elevator operator. According to Patterson, Weiss reprimanded him for giving a couple of tickets to the game to an elevator operator in the building in which the club offices were located. Patterson felt the scolding was uncalled for and he "let Weiss have it." On July 26, Patterson informed the press association that he had moved out of the job. He eventually became National League publicity director under Ford Frick.[160]

Weiss chose Bob Fishel, former publicist with the St. Louis Browns, as Patterson's replacement. Fishel was highly regarded by baseball writers in both Cleveland and St. Louis, where he had had public relations and promotional jobs. He worked for Bill Veeck in Cleveland and moved to St. Louis when Veeck bought the Browns. In becoming affiliated with the Yankees, Fishel rejoined Bill DeWitt, Weiss's new assistant.[161]

Fishel remained with the Yankees until he became the American League's chief publicist. His replacement was Marty Appel, who originally was hired by Fishel to answer Mickey Mantle's mail. Fishel once confessed to Appel that he felt Weiss had chosen Fishel as Patterson's successor because "we had a lot of Jewish writers covering the team, and Weiss thought it would be good to have a Jewish PR director."[162]

The Yankees began the 1954 season feeling good about their chances of winning their sixth consecutive pennant. Mantle's return in April increased their confidence on achieving their goal.[163] Even the loss of a veteran infielder worked out well. Third baseman Dr. Bobby Brown retired on June 30 to do his internship; he eventually became a cardiologist in Texas.[164] Brown's replacement, rookie Andy Carey, a $60,000 bonus baby, was so good at the hot corner that *The Sporting News* called him "a bargain."[165]

Carey was one of the few Yankees who consistently had kind words to say about George Weiss. "He liked me, kept me there, and treated me well. If I had any problems, he would take care of them. Every year I held out. He would take over the negotiations from a subordinate and asked 'what do you want, Andy?' I would tell him and I would get it."[166]

Even though the Yankees won 103 games in 1954, their best year under Stengel, and Berra was again the MVP, they finished in second place, eight games behind the Indians.[167] Led by Early Wynn and Bob Lemon, who each won 23 games, and Bobby Avila, Larry Doby and Al Rosen at the plate, the Indians took over first place on June 12 and never gave it up, capturing the pennant with an impressive 111 wins.[168] The World Series championship would remain in New York, however, as the seemingly unbeatable Indians lost four straight games to the Giants.[169]

Despite the 103 wins, Weiss was disappointed that his team dropped to second place. He was a proud man who hated to lose. Once Hazel embroidered throw pillows for a charity contest. Among the thousands of entries of beautifully embroidered pillows, hers were awarded second place, an accomplishment as far as she was concerned. But

George didn't see it that way, responding, "There's no such thing as second place. Either you're first or you're nothing."[170]

Perhaps because the Yankees had put on such a strong showing, even though they lost the pennant, Weiss and the team escaped much blame. A *Sporting News* editorial felt the end of the Yankees' run was actually beneficial to baseball. "An oft-repeating champion isn't good for the game. Interest falters when one club is the class of its league for too many seasons."[171] Most writers concentrated on Weiss's tasks for the future, suggesting that he replace aging veteran players with talented, younger men, and make a concerted effort to improve the team's pitching staff.[172]

Despite the apparent "end of a dynasty" Weiss seemed as positive as ever about the Yankees as he began executing a rebuilding program emphasizing young players and especially pitchers. He conferred with Stengel to decide which veterans might be traded to obtain new players..[173]

The Yankees had good reason to be concerned about their pitching, especially with the unexpected absence of Allie Reynolds, the highest paid pitcher on the club. While on an elk and deer hunting expedition in Colorado, Reynolds had a mishap in a glass-enclosed shower in his Colorado Springs hotel. He fell when the mat slipped beneath him and he suffered an 18-stitch cut on the index finger of his pitching hand as well as lacerations in his back.[174] Reynolds announced his retirement shortly after his accident.

Weiss's pitching needs were so serious that despite the animosity between him and White Sox general manager Frank Lane, Weiss offered the Chisox GM a package of Yanks for top hurler Billy Pierce. Lane turned him down, so he turned to the Baltimore Orioles, and on November 17, 1954, Weiss and Paul Richards, Orioles GM, negotiated a record 17-player trade. Weiss secured a number of young players and two outstanding right-handed pitchers, 24-year-old Bob Turley and 25-year-old Don Larsen.[175] "Getting Turley and Larsen," said Weiss, "helped plug the major weakness of the Yankee club—pitching. They are two of the finest and fastest young right-handers in the game. Both figure to get better and they are young."[176]

Along with pitching, Weiss also had been seeking a shortstop, realizing that Phil Rizzuto, who had hit only .195 in 1954, was nearing the end of his career. Rebuffed in his efforts to acquire White Sox shortstop Chico Carrasquel, Weiss had acquired 26-year-old Billy Hunter, a former Dodgers farmhand, who had been the Browns/Orioles shortstop the past two seasons.[177]

The Yankees were elated with the trade. Baseball pundits agreed that Weiss got the better of the deal. He was called the "student of Machiavelli." According to sportswriters, Weiss not only obtained players for his team, he "ruined the market for both the Indians and the Chisox."[178] Shirley Povich viewed the deal as one more example of the Yankees and Weiss proving "they were the shrewdest traders in baseball." The Yankees' Bill DeWitt frankly stated, "The Turley deal puts the flag in the bag for the Yankees."[179]

One more event changed the picture of the upcoming season. In 1953 Chicago businessman Arnold Johnson bought the Kansas City Blues, but he maintained a very close relationship with the Yankees. He also bought not only the Blues' home park but also Yankee Stadium, leasing the New York field back to the Yankees.[180] The following year, Johnson purchased the Philadelphia Athletics from Connie Mack and moved the team to Kansas City.[181]

The league owners were happy to approve the club's sale and relocation, while Johnson rewarded the Yankees and Weiss handsomely for their efforts. Between 1955 and 1960, the period when Johnson owned the A's, the Yankees and Athletics completed 16 trades involving 58 players. In most cases, the result was that the Yankees acquired prospects while the A's were left with over-the-hill stars.[182]

Once Kansas City had a major league club, the Yankees moved their American Association franchise in Kansas City to Denver—the Denver Bears became the Yankees' AAA club and would have the same relationship to the Yankees as the Kansas City Blues had had.[183]

For the first time in many years, neither Weiss nor Stengel attended the winter meetings, probably because the team did not have much to trade any more.[184] In any event, Weiss had his focus elsewhere as he made plans for the next season when the Yankees would try once again to regain their top position and would finally add their first black player to the roster.

10
Breaking the Yankees' Color Line

Eight years after Jackie Robinson began playing for the Brooklyn Dodgers, and six years after Monte Irvin broke the Giants' color line, the Yankees finally added a Negro player to their roster. The American League's first Negro player, Larry Doby, became a Cleveland Indian shortly after Robinson debuted in 1947, and in that same year, the St. Louis Browns, headquartered in the Southern-most city in the majors, briefly played Willard Brown. It was particularly ironic that the Yankees waited so long to include a black player on their major league roster because the Yankees had the inside track for dealing with several Negro Leagues teams. In both Kansas City and Newark, the Yankees rented their ballparks to Negro Leagues teams. Both teams offered the Yankees first pick of their best talent—including both Doby and Irvin—but the Yankees failed to take advantage of their unique position. Instead, they became a symbol of intransigence.[1]

This was a time when black soldiers were returning from service in Korea and multiple civil rights groups were becoming active. They directed much of their action against the Yankees as the only "holdout" in one of the country's most inclusive cities. What's more, although the law was seldom cited, discrimination was illegal in the state of New York.[2]

The very success of the team was one of the major reasons why the Yankees waited so long to integrate. From 1949 through 1953, the Yankees won five pennants and five world championships without any of the highly talented black players who were appearing on the rosters of other teams. Weiss and his farm director, Lee MacPhail, were able to continue supplying new Yankees like Mickey Mantle and Whitey Ford to help them do it. Weiss also believed that he still had the ability to obtain needed talent the way he had always acquired his players—trade or purchase.[3]

Weiss was certainly entitled to his opinion, but many sports writers and baseball observers felt that Weiss's refusal to integrate his roster earlier had allowed other teams to build up their systems with emerging Negro stars, leaving the Yankees lagging behind. According to baseball pundits, "Weiss relied on the cynical excuse that the Yankees were a winning ball club *without* the contribution of black men. That was a lame excuse for such inaction, especially when so many black stars had begun to dominate every department of major league play."[4]

One of the reasons why the Yankees were not adding black prospects to their system was that the scouts, on whom Weiss relied heavily, were not identifying talented

Negroes as possible future Yankees. A number of baseball writers, especially those who felt Weiss was a racist, claimed Weiss told his scouts that he was unequivocally not interested in signing Negroes. It was rumored that he had given this edict to Tom Greenwade, who had scouted Jackie Robinson for the Dodgers. Greenwade had the reputation of being unmatched in his knowledge of black prospects in the Midwest and South.[5]

There were also instances where Yankees scouts deliberately misled Weiss. An unsigned 1947 scouting report called two black players, Artie Wilson and Piper Davis, good players, but also said,

> There isn't an outstanding Negro player that anybody could recommend to step into the big leagues and hold down a regular job.... I know of not one that would stick. If they come up with certain players please advise me and I will give you the low down on them.... I am aware of how these committees apply pressure on the big leagues to hire one or perhaps two players. If you hire one or two, they will want you to hire another one.[6]

The most blatant example of Yankees scouting involved the way the team scouted Willie Mays. In 1949 Weiss sent road secretary and sometimes scout Bill McCorry to Birmingham to check out Mays. McCorry, an outspoken bigot, recommended that the Yankees not sign him, reporting that Mays could run and field "a little" but couldn't hit curve balls. Of course, virtually no player just out of high school could. Although allegations were made, there was no evidence that Weiss purposely chose McCorry in order to get a negative report.[7]

The attitude of management was another factor. Weiss, as general manager, had a great deal of autonomy in running the Yankees' organization, but he still needed to operate in line with the wishes of Del Webb and Dan Topping. Even baseball observers who called Weiss a bigot and blamed him for the delay in integrating admitted that the ownership of the Yankees was decidedly "racist."

While both men vehemently denied this assertion, it was noted that Webb's construction firm had built one of the Japanese internment camps during World War II, and that Topping came from a white, wealthy social world that still believed in negative stereotypes of Negroes. Yet, surprisingly, when Topping owned the football Dodgers, the team played Buddy Young, the first black in the All-American Conference. Whenever Topping was called a racist, he referred to his hiring of Buddy Young and angrily asked, "How can anybody accuse any organization of which I am the head of Jim Crowism?"[8] In the meantime, George Weiss repeatedly denied any racism on his part. "We have been looking for a Negro player for some years," he maintained. "We will have a Negro player as soon as we are able to find a Negro player among the availables."[9]

Beliefs aside, both Weiss and the owners were concerned not only with the performance success of the Yankees, but also with financial success. They were not interested in driving the Negro Leagues out of business because of the rent they paid to use Yankees ballparks when the home teams were on the road.[10]

Of far more importance to the Yankees' bottom line was the gate at Yankees home games. There was no question that the Yankees' fan base was far different from those of the other New York teams, especially the Dodgers fans. According to Yankees star Ed Lopat, "They [Yankees fans] were refined people for the most part. You'd hear the cheering, but they were kind of sedate, generally people with character. The fans were controlled and there was control in the ball park."[11]

Weiss thought Yankees fans wouldn't pay to see black players, but some baseball writers felt Weiss just did not want "white rabble" or Negroes sitting next to his "best" supporters, upper-middle class residents from the wealthier all-white parts of the Bronx and the Connecticut suburbs. "I will never allow a black man to wear a Yankee uniform. Box holders from Westchester don't want that sort of crowd. They would be offended to have to sit with niggers," Weiss is alleged to have said.[12] Ironically, the Yankees felt they had no economic incentive to integrate, as the club was immensely popular with both white and black fans. In fact, the Yankees retained loyal and devoted fan support in Harlem.[13]

Even though the delay in integrating the Yankees was likely a combination of factors including financial success, outstanding performance, unproductive scouts and possibly the owners' bias against Negroes, it was Weiss, the chief decision maker in the system, who was held responsible for the lack of a black Yankee. Did deep personal bigotry drive his decisions to delay integrating the Yankees as long as he could? Writers such as Roger Kahn and David Halberstam called him vicious and unable to empathize with any players, especially Negroes.

It seemed a much more probable scenario that Weiss's true reason for the delay in hiring black players was pretty much what he repeatedly declared when asked point-blank why there were no black Yankees; namely that he was determined to choose a black player who would fit the "Yankee mold."[14] The "Yankee mold" or model—the image that differentiated a Yankee—was as important to the club as their logo and pinstripes. Loosely defined, it implied a player with superior playing skills, giving an all-out effort, and looking and behaving like a gentleman. Yankees fans believed "their" players were not just winners, but that they possessed the character and appearance that epitomized "class." As Weiss repeatedly stated, it was expected that every player in the Yankees' organization, regardless of color, would exemplify this image. Less biased baseball writers admitted that the Yankees at that time did use the same standards for white and black players.[15]

What many professional observers and fans often overlooked was the importance of the Yankee model to the players themselves. By insisting that the first Negro should be a "real" Yankee, Weiss was supporting their efforts to guarantee that everyone lived up to these criteria. As an example, Yogi Berra was a young catcher when he chose to sit out the second game of a doubleheader on a very hot day. As the veterans came back into the locker room victorious at the end of the day, DiMaggio jumped all over the showered and rested youngster. "What are you so happy about?" Joe asked Yogi. "You're 21 years old and you can't catch a double header." Then the others picked up the theme. According to Ed Lopat, "That was part of the Yankee way [that] they tried to instill in the young fellows coming up…. If there's something wrong with you, you don't play, but if you do play, you give it 105 percent." Lopat continued, "After I was traded here, I understood that this emphasis on quality was what made the Yankees tick."[16] As for the players' feelings towards a Negro teammate, Tommy Henrich stated that any one who could help the team would be welcome.[17]

Yankees star Mickey Mantle, who was in high school when Jackie Robinson broke the color line, echoed Henrich's feelings. "I don't think Webb and Topping, who owned the club, or George Weiss, the general manager, were bigots. But the Yankees were winning, and Casey felt no pressure to seek out the gifted players who became available as the Negro Leagues began to fade away."[18]

Weiss encountered the issue of black players long before he became part of the Yankees' organization, and no major problems ever arose. Even before he became owner of a professional baseball team in New Haven, his semi-pro team was scheduled to play another semi-pro team from Putnam, Connecticut. On the mound for Putnam was one of the best black pitchers in the country, Cannonball Dick Redding, who had been hired to pitch specifically against Weiss's team. Weiss's team also included a black player, a former high school classmate. In addition, Weiss's team had faced many clubs with black players on their rosters, so he gave little thought in having his team oppose a black pitcher. Unfortunately, Weiss realized that he had hired Ty Cobb to play first base for his team, and when the "Georgia Peach" discovered that a "colored pitcher" was going to start the game, Cobb balked. "I don't play with a nigger on the field," he roared.

Weiss was in a quandary. Most of the fans had come to see Cobb play, and if Weiss kept him out of the lineup, they would demand their money back. Weiss always refunded the ticket money if an advertised star did not appear. On the other hand, many fans attended the game specifically to see Redding pitch, and Weiss realized that if Redding did not pitch, the local fans would cause an uproar. Weiss and the Putnam manager reached a compromise. Cobb would play the first half of the game and Redding would pitch the second half. Both Cobb and Redding begrudgingly agreed to the compromise. Cobb went hitless during his half of the game, but Redding awed the crowd. He struck out 11 of the 12 batters he faced, and he had a bloop double and scored the run that won the game for Putnam.

Many years later Weiss recalled that game, admitting that Dick Redding, "if he were pitching today, would be on his way to the Hall of Fame." In addition, Weiss always wondered, "What would Cobb have done with those screaming fastballs?"[19]

Weiss did made some efforts to sign black ballplayers after Robinson had signed his contract with the Brooklyn Dodgers. He claimed that in 1948 he had sent scouts to Cuba, Panama, and Puerto Rico "to look over Negro prospects." In that respect he was one of the first teams to follow the Dodgers' example in making an effort to recruit blacks.[20]

In 1949 the Yankees made their first serious attempts at working Negro players into their system. Weiss signed two outfielders, Bob Thurman and Puerto Rican Luis Marquez, from the Kansas City Monarchs and sent them to the AAA Newark Bears. Neither played an inning in the majors for the Yankees. Marquez played briefly for the Braves, Cubs and Pirates (1951–1954) and Thurman, at the age of 38, ultimately made it to the majors with the Cincinnati Reds. After playing 334 games, Thurman retired from professional baseball at the age of 42.[21]

That same year, based on an earlier scouting report, the Yankees attempted to purchase the contract of Artie Wilson. Wilson, a pesky, slap-hitting shortstop, played his way into the Negro Leagues with the Birmingham Barons in 1942 and led the Negro American League twice in batting. He also became a mentor and friend of his teenage teammate, Willie Mays.

After the 1949 season, Wilson was playing winter ball and managing in Puerto Rico when both the Yankees and the Cleveland Indians claimed to have purchased his contract from the Barons. Wilson preferred to play for Cleveland, whose owner, Bill Veeck, flew down to Puerto Rico to bring him back to the United States. The Yankees, however, claimed possession of Wilson because of an earlier commitment to their team via a telegram sent by Wilson. Wilson was playing for the Indians' top farm club, the San Diego Padres, when Commissioner A. B. Chandler ruled that Wilson was Yankees property. The Yankees immediately unloaded him, selling him to the Oakland Oaks, an unaffiliated club in the Pacific Coast League, where his roommate was Billy Martin.[22] The Yankees-Indians fight over Wilson was merely another incident in the continuing feud between George Weiss and Bill Veeck.[23] Chandler also ruled that the Yankees were obligated to send Luis Marquez, who was playing for Newark, to the Indians.[24]

By opening the door to black players, Branch Rickey was actually setting a "trend" for other major league executives to follow. In all fairness, attempting to follow this trend became difficult even for an experienced baseball man like George Weiss. Weiss's attempts to sign both Artie Wilson and Luis Marquez resulted in another bitter confrontation with Bill Veeck. Veeck, a baseball maverick, was not satisfied with following a trend—he was going to lead it. By also claiming Wilson and Marquez, Veeck was frustrating the Yankees' general manager. Not only did Weiss scout Wilson and Marquez, he also tried to sign slugging Negro first baseman, Luke Easter. Allegedly, Easter had agreed to sign a $3,000 minor league contract to play in the Yankees' farm system. Weiss was required, however, to conclude the purchase with both the player and the Negro Leagues team claiming ownership of the player. This was not a problem when the prospect played for only one team, but in Easter's case, there were at least two teams that claimed ownership of him, and both wanted to be compensated for his services. After failing in his attempt to sign Wilson and Marquez, Weiss gave up his attempt to go through the tedious process of signing Easter, who eventually signed with the Cleveland Indians.[25]

In what some claimed as an effort to deflect potential criticism or described as "tokenism," the Yankees began signing younger Negro Leagues players rather than focusing on aging stars. Weiss signed two black players from the Kansas City Monarchs, 24-year-old pitcher Frank Barnes and 21-year-old outfielder Elston Howard. From the Provincial League in Canada, the Yankees signed two Puerto Ricans, another outfielder, 22-year-old Vic Power, and another pitcher, 21-year-old Ruben Gomez.[26] The Yankees soon traded Barnes and released Gomez, both of whom later became very good pitchers for the Giants. Howard and Power were assigned to the Yankees' farm club in the Class A Central League.[27] Other than Howard and Power, no other African American or Latino player would rise through the Yankees' system until the 1960s.[28]

In 1952 the so-called American Labor Party picketed Yankee Stadium. Some accused the pickets, primarily whites, of being Communists. They were protesting that the Yankees were the "only lily-white team remaining in New York." These pickets would be present at every Yankees home game until the team finally signed a black player.[29]

That same year Vic Power became the first black player on the Kansas City Blues.[30] Although Power turned in a stellar performance at AAA, batting .331 and driving in 109 runs, Weiss quickly dismissed the idea he would "automatically" be invited to spring training in 1953, voicing his determination that a black player would be added to the roster strictly on merit, not because of pickets and outside pressures. The press agreed that even Negro fans wanted the Yankees to add an outstanding player like Jackie Robinson or Larry Doby.[31]

At the winter meeting late in 1952, Jackie Robinson, on television, publicly labeled the New York Yankees "prejudiced" for failing to sign a black player in the five years that baseball had been integrated. The Yankees vehemently denied Robinson's allegations, pointing to players in the farm system. Weiss again reasserted that a black player must be "Yankee" in every way, particularly in ability. Once again, vigorously denying any prejudice against Negroes, Weiss said, "The facts do not support Robinson's charges. We have had numerous Negroes in our farm system, and we are constantly trying to find a good one to bring up."[32]

Weiss also blasted back at Robinson by stating, "Rest assured that we have our scouts on the job, but we will not bring up such a player for exploitation purposes. When we find a Negro player he will be a Yankee in every respect and will have more than an even chance of staying up in the majors."[33]

Robinson claimed that Weiss had blown his comment out of proportion and added he could have named other teams as well. He did not rescind his opinion of the Yankees, however, or of George Weiss.[34]

For once, a number of writers and baseball moguls came to George Weiss's defense. Ford Frick, commissioner of baseball, asked Robinson to "avoid the issue of racism and justice in the future."[35] Columnist Wendell Smith wrote, "Everyone should be very careful in these days and times about making such charges."[36] *The Sporting News*, very conservative in its editorials, supported Weiss's position and pointed out the unfairness of Robinson in not naming other teams without Negro players anywhere in their systems. Finally, the publication chided Robinson for belittling the Yankees' organization, strongly urging Robinson "to be a player not a crusader."[37]

Blacks were undaunted by such arguments. Early in the 1953 season, circulars began appearing at Yankee Stadium urging the Yankees to "Strike out against Discrimination." One such circular bluntly asked the question, "Why can't the Yankees provide a democratic atmosphere?... More democracy by the hiring of Negro ballplayers will ensure better quality of baseball."[38]

In early 1953, the Yankees did make an effort to offset the negative publicity and to sharpen Yankees' insight for evaluating Negro prospects by hiring a new scout, former Negro Leagues pitcher Dizzy Dismukes. Weiss also announced that there were ten black players in the Yankees' system.[39] Sportswriter Milton Gross noted the signing of Dismukes, but he could not help noting that there were still a number of doubters who were amazed that an organization "so successful in its scouting of white players neglected to come across black talent capable of reaching the major leagues."[40]

In August 1953, the Yankees brought up four minor league players to bolster the team for the final pennant run. They included southpaw Bill Kraly from Binghamton, left-hander Bill Miller from Kansas City, first baseman–catcher Gus Triandos from Birmingham, and infielder Jim Bridewiser from Syracuse. The question on almost everyone's mind, with the statistics he had posted, was "Why didn't the Yankees bring up Vic Power?" After all, he was hitting around .360 for Kansas City. According to Yankees management, it was "unclear where to play him at the major league level." The Yankees also argued that they had not called up either Bill Skowron or Bob Cerv, both of whom were hitting well.⁴¹ Webb and Topping downplayed Power's baseball abilities and achievements, stating instead that Power's flashy fielding and flamboyant personality did not fit the Yankees' style.⁴²

Vic Power came from Puerto Rico, where racial mixing was the norm. He had never experienced racial discrimination before coming to the United States, and he was known to use his fists whenever he encountered prejudice or when opposing pitchers threw at him. He was also known for driving around Kansas City in his Cadillac convertible with the top down, and most damaging of all, he was often seen with a white woman in the front seat. He enjoyed being a "flashy" fielder, making astonishing catches, and then playing to the crowd for his feats.⁴³

Only two months later, on October 13, 1953, Roy Hamey made a groundbreaking announcement on behalf of vacationing George Weiss. The Yankees had purchased the contracts of Power and Howard from Kansas City and planned to take both to spring training.⁴⁴

Dan Daniel, who covered the Yankees for both the *New York Times* and *The Sporting News,* and was often a cheerleader for the team, felt that the announcement should silence critics, particularly as Negro players competed for roster spots along with white players such as Irv Noren, Bill Virdon and Joe Collins. He listed six other blacks in the Yankees' system (although at very low levels), and pointed out that there were still four teams without a black player on their major league roster—the Boston Red Sox, Detroit Tigers, Philadelphia Phillies and St. Louis Cardinals.⁴⁵

Although the Yankees claimed they had no spot appropriate for Power, other teams knew exactly where he could play on their squads and were very interested in acquiring him.⁴⁶ It did not take Weiss very long to act on their interest. Shortly before Christmas 1953, the Yankees made a trade with the Philadelphia Athletics, giving up Power, outfielder Bill Renna, first baseman Don Bollweg, pitcher John Gray, catcher Jim Robertson, third baseman Jim Finigan, two players to be announced, and an undisclosed amount of cash. In return, the Yankees obtained right-handed pitcher Harry Byrd, hard-hitting first baseman Eddie Robinson and three left-handed hitters to be sent to the Yankees' AAA affiliate, the Kansas City Blues.⁴⁷

Immediately after the deal was completed, the press implied that Power had been traded because he was black, an accusation which Weiss vehemently denied. He insisted that the Yankees did not want to trade Power, but there would have been no transaction unless the Yankees sent Power to Philadelphia. "His race had no bearing on the trade," insisted Weiss. "We're not going to keep anybody just because he's a Negro. That wouldn't be fair to the white players. I can't see why a Negro should be separated from a white man in a deal or anything else. And besides, we still have Elston Howard."⁴⁸ Power, however, did not agree with Weiss's assertions. He argued, "They were just looking for excuses…. What did they want me to do? Mow the lawn in the outfield after the game was over?"⁴⁹

At least one sportswriter agreed with Weiss. Joe Williams of the *New York World Tribune & Sun* commented, "no reasonable mind" would quarrel with this view of equality. Weiss had been "badgered by pressure groups" for some time, but "he is not a social worker but a baseball man, his job is to win pennants. And his record, five in a row, says he does it pretty good."⁵⁰ Veteran player Tommy Henrich also defended Weiss, noting that the Yankees did want a black player, but "not *that* black player.... He was considered a trouble maker and a showboat."[51]

Seven years after the Power deal, Weiss was still defending the trade and the criticism that the team was one of the last to integrate.

> We may have been slow in coming around, but there never was any question of bias. We never believed in bringing up a Negro for the purpose of exploitation or to pep up attendance.... We sought to get men like Luke Easter and Artie Wilson but ran into rhubarbs with the Negro leagues or other big league teams. With the exception of Power, none of them had what it takes until Elston Howard came along.[52]

Howard reported to Florida as announced and began training with the Yankees in March 1954. As a Negro, Howard was not permitted to stay at the team's hotel, but had to board with a local black family. But neither the housing arrangements nor the fact that the Yankees had him attend advance camp with coach and former catcher Bill Dickey in order to turn the young outfielder into a catcher were problems for Howard. "Al" or "Ellie," which his teammates called him, said he had dreamed all winter about wearing a Yankees uniform. "I prefer to play the outfield," Howard stated, "but the main thing is to make good and to stick, and if Mr. Stengel and Mr. Dickey believe I can do a better job for the club, and for myself, as a catcher—well I'll be a catcher."[53]

There were no "personality" issues with Howard, a 25-year-old native of St. Louis, where traces of Jim Crow could still be found. Howard was raised by his mother and stepfather, and was engaged to be married.[54] Both Stengel and Dickey were enthusiastic about his baseball skills, and just as importantly, about his spirit, his behavior on and off the field, and the way he fit in with the rest of the other players. "He's no showboat and he made himself one of the gang right from the start," they agreed.[55]

Howard had commented that he wouldn't like it, but that he would understand if the Yankees sent him back to the minors to hone his catching skills, and at the end of spring training, that is exactly what Weiss did. Howard and seven others, including Mel Wright, Gus Triandos and Bill Virdon, were reassigned to the minors, leaving the Yankees still without a Negro on the 1954 major league roster.[56] In the long run, however, converting Howard to catcher heightened his chances of making the team, since he was not speedy enough to win an outfield post.[57]

Sending Howard back to the minors displeased many who felt the Yankees were merely trying to postpone integrating the team by demanding a Yankees "superhero." According to one fan, the Yankees converted Howard into a catcher just to create a reason for another year in the minors.[58]

But Weiss was firm in his resolve to add Howard, the 1954 International League MVP, to the Yankees in 1955. He purchased Howard's contract and announced that the 6'2" Negro player would definitely be with the team in 1955. Eager to regain the Yankees' winning ways, Weiss also declared that the acquisition of Howard, in addition to pitchers Ed Cereghino and Tom Sturdivant, and third baseman Leon "Buddy" Carter, was "the big step in strengthening the Yankees for the 1955 American League pennant chase."[59]

The Yankees immediately signed Howard to a large contract, announcing that he "has big league talent and character," and reiterated, "That's the only yardstick the Yankees ever used in fielding a team." Most observers were forced to agree that Weiss did

Elston Howard was the first African American player on the Yankees' roster, playing for the team 13 of his 14 years in the majors. In 1963 he became the first black player in American League history to win the league's Most Valuable Player Award (courtesy Dwayne Labakas).

apply the same standards to white players. The Yankees sent Howard to play winter ball in San Juan along with Bob Cerv.[60]

The Yankees certainly liked Howard for his baseball prowess. In 1954, Howard tore up Toronto in the International League. His offense—a batting average of .330, 22 home runs and 109 runs batted in—and his winning the MVP certainly caught the eye of the Baltimore Orioles' Paul Richards, who offered Weiss $100,000 and a number one prospect for Howard's contract.[61] Weiss was tempted by Richards' offer, but turned him down; Howard's performance almost assured that he would be brought up to the major leagues in 1955. At the beginning of spring training, scout Paul Krichell approached Howard to welcome him. When Howard politely stated that he had heard much about the scout, Krichell reported back to his boss Weiss, "I like that young man. Even though he's black, he has manners."[62]

During 1955 spring training, the Yankees once more found housing an issue for Howard, but they faced a new situation—exhibition games on their way back to New

York. The team had scheduled a game in Birmingham, Alabama, where the Yankees had a working agreement. The city, however, had banned Negro players. The Yankees decided they would send Howard on ahead rather than create ill will in Alabama by canceling the game against a team in their own system. The Yankees argued that only one player would be involved and he had yet to make the team.[63]

Weiss and Howard also found housing problems in certain cities during the 1955 season. Rather than looking for alternate housing for Howard, the Yankees brought pressure against hotels in Chicago and Kansas City to accept Howard as a guest or, it was implied, the rest of the team would go elsewhere to stay together. Howard, in turn, accepted certain facts of life including Stengel's often offensive speech, realizing that it was fairly common for the time, based on life-long habits, and that Stengel was not anti–Negro. Howard even took abuse as an "Uncle Tom" for defending Stengel for remarks such as "When I finally get a nigger, I get the only one who can't run." Stengel, in fact, liked Howard, praised him, and included him on four All-Star teams. According to *The Sporting News*, in addition to his player skills, his "relations with fans, with his fellow players, with rival players, and with the press are perfect."[64]

In 1955 Elston Howard became the first and only black player on the Yankees' roster during Weiss's tenure with the Yankees. As late as 1964, four years after Weiss's departure from the team, only two other blacks, Al Downing and Hector Lopez, had joined Howard.[65] Leonard Koppett, a highly respected sports writer and author who covered the Yankees for many years for the *New York Post*, felt deeply that Weiss's failure to sign black players was one of the most egregious errors he had ever made. Weiss's apparent racism, whether the result of snobbery or ignorance, simply caused him to feel that white players did not care to play with black players, that black players were not as good as white ones and that his Yankees fans, the upper-middle class suburbanites, would not sit in the stands with black fans.[66]

Paradoxically, ever since Jacob Ruppert hired Weiss as farm director, the Yankees general manager had been seeking prototypical Yankees players—hungry, driven by a desire to win, those who not only wanted to reach the big leagues, but once there, expected to surpass goals they had set. Among those accomplishing this feat were players such as Tommy Henrich, Hank Bauer, Joe DiMaggio, Tony Kubek, Mickey Mantle, and Billy Martin. They were clutch players, a group of tough kids called "red asses," or colloquially RAs.

Koppett claimed that young black players entered the big leagues with the same mental and spiritual toughness that Weiss and the Yankees had demanded of their players. Unfortunately, according to Koppett, George Weiss could not or would not understand that these young men possessed the same anger and determination to succeed.[67]

As the Yankees' first and, for the remainder of Weiss's tenure with the team, the only black player, Howard was welcomed by his teammates. Skowron and Carey had been his teammates in Kansas City, and a number of Yankees who were acquired in trades from other teams had played with blacks in their organizations. Other players accepted him because he was a teammate or just because that was their nature. Phil Rizzuto went out of his way to welcome Howard, making sure he was included in activities away from Yankee Stadium. "He made everything he did look so easy," said Rizzuto. "You could see right away he'd be around for a long, long time."[68] Said infielder Jerry

Coleman, "Elston was a lot better Yankee the day he joined the club than guys that were around for years." "Everybody could see he was a good ballplayer," said Whitey Ford, the All-Star pitcher.[69]

The more Howard contributed to the team, the more the players accepted him. They realized that their World Series checks depended on any player with talent, and although not everyone might have altruistic motives for accepting Howard, the result was the same.[70] Howard recalled that his biggest ball game was a game-winning triple in the bottom of the ninth. "I came into the locker room after an interview and they had towels lined up from the door to my locker. Joe Collins, Mickey Mantle—they lined the towels up. It was like a red carpet. Laid out for me. I was surprised. And when they did that, I figured I was accepted just like everyone else."[71]

George Weiss was pleased with the now integrated status of the 1955 Yankees roster. Always a hard loser, he was focused on coming back from the disappointing finish in 1954 and in creating a new string of pennant-winning teams. His strategy was apparent—the Yankees were becoming a team of younger men balanced by veterans who would not only provide stability, but who could also teach and demonstrate. One area where the trend was most apparent was the pitching staff, as ten new pitchers were on the spring training roster. Vic Raschi was gone; Allie Reynolds, who won 131 games during his eight years with the Yankees and hurt his back in a bus accident the Yankees were involved in, retired following the end of the 1954 season.[72]

It was also questionable how much longer 38-year-old Johnnie Sain and 36-year-old Ed Lopat would continue pitching. But Weiss's trade with Baltimore had brought in youngsters Bob Turley and Don Larsen to supplement 27-year-old Whitey Ford and 1954's "Rookie of the Year," 25-year-old Bob Grim. In addition, the Yankees added 22-year-old John Kucks, who was a "graduate of Casey's instructional camp." Although inexperienced, Kucks threw a fastball and a sinker with great control and was able to handle the transition to "the big show." Critics applauded Weiss's moves and felt the Yankees were indeed set for a comeback.[73]

As far as Weiss was concerned, one advantage coming from the previous year's second-place finish and a drop in attendance of 100,000 was in salary negotiations. This was one year when he not only omitted bonuses in his contract offers to the majority of returning players, but he felt justified in cutting or freezing 1954 salaries.

Phil Rizzuto, now 38 years old and the Yankees' shortstop since 1941, accepted a contract offer of $35,000, reflecting a 12½ percent pay cut. After signing, Rizzuto became very loquacious with reporters, talking about details of his contract negotiations and generally breaking the time-honored Yankees tradition of not discussing club matters publicly. It's very likely that Weiss kept this event in mind for future dealings with his veteran shortstop.[74] There were exceptions of course, including MVP Yogi Berra, who reportedly signed for $48,000, again making him the highest-paid catcher in baseball history.[75]

Baseball pundits continued to laud Weiss for what he was accomplishing with the Yankees and for having something "extra." According to *The Sporting News,* "The Yankees possess class on the field and although Weiss prefers to work behind the scenes, anyone who knows him and his methods know they also have class in the front office. Weiss is part of the spirit known as the Pride of the Yankees."[76]

Knowledgeable baseball critics considered Weiss baseball's top executive, and the 1955 season justified their choice. Operating out of three offices—in the Yankees' corporate headquarters on Fifth Avenue, Yankee Stadium, and the study of his 200-year-old home in Greenwich, Connecticut—the always-working Weiss was never far from a desk or his telephone. In 1955 Weiss had orchestrated major changes to re-structure the roster and to build an even deeper backlog of talent that would provide replacements as various injuries and problems threatened the Yankees' pennant comeback.[77]

Many on the revamped pitching staff delivered. Whitey Ford led the American League with 18 wins. Bob Turley was right behind him with 17. Tommy Byrne finished with a record of 16–5 and was named "Comeback Player of the Year." Relief pitcher Jim Konstanty once again became a reliable winner.[78]

In contrast, Weiss, without displaying any emotion, removed both new and old pitchers who did not live up to his expectations. He optioned Don Larsen to AAA Denver. Weiss felt that Larsen was not only performing poorly, he was displaying a decidedly "non–Yankee" attitude.[79] Weiss was still interested in deals for pitching help, but shortly before the trading deadline, smarting from trades where they always came out losers, the other American League teams closed ranks and refused to deal with Weiss.[80] All the American League teams but one.

After the 1954 season, Connie Mack's sons sold the Philadelphia Athletics to Arnold Johnson, a Chicago real estate man and a close friend of both Dan Topping and George Weiss. It was Weiss who had suggested that Johnson buy the Athletics from Connie Mack when the team was still located in Philadelphia. After Johnson moved the Athletics to Kansas City in 1955, Weiss found a willing trading "buddy." Johnson was making money in Kansas City, and he was very accommodating when he was the only American League executive who would do business with Weiss. For example, Weiss was able to deal Johnny Sain and Enos Slaughter to the Athletics, much as he would have traded them to the Kansas City Blues. Most of the American League's owners and executives complained vocally, but neither the American League president nor baseball's commissioner took any action. Cleveland Indians general manager Hank Greenberg complained, but to no avail. "It sure must be great to have your own farm team right in your own league," he quipped.[81]

Thanks to his roster moves and trades with the Athletics, Weiss not only put together good pitching in 1955, but the Yankees' bats were intimidating and productive. Yogi Berra drove in 108 runs, helping him win his second consecutive Most Valuable Player Award. Mickey Mantle finally had a good season, posting 99 RBI, a .306 batting average and a league-leading 37 home runs. First baseman Moose Skowron finished with a .319 batting average. Moreover, the bench was deep, accounting for 44 of the team's 175 home runs. One Yankee who more than lived up to expectations and contributed greatly to the team was rookie Elston Howard. The black Yankee caught only nine games for the team, but he played 75 in the outfield, hitting a commendable .290 and handling both the positive and negative attention with great poise—as a Yankee should. Whitey Ford, Bob Turley, and Tommy Byrne accounted for 51 of the 96 Yankees victories in 1955.[82]

By September 1, four teams—the White Sox, Red Sox, Indians, and Yankees—were engaged in a nip-and-tuck battle for the American League pennant. Fired up by the return of Billy Martin and Don Larsen, the Yankees won nine out of ten games to finish at the top of the league. They faced the Dodgers in the World Series for the fifth time in nine years, having won the previous four. This time, however, the Dodgers prevailed, defeating the Bronx Bombers in seven games, even though the Yankees took a three-games-to-two lead in the Series. The Dodgers won the final game thanks to an eight-hit shutout thrown by Johnny Podres. A highlight for the Yankees was Elston Howard's home run his first time at bat in the World Series, making him only the second Yankee to accomplish that feat.[83]

The Yankees may have been able to console themselves at least partially with the upcoming tour in Japan that Weiss had agreed to. Uncharacteristically it seemed, he had committed to a project that provided no profit to the Yankees, but it was requested by the U.S. State Department with the approval of the Japanese government. Most importantly, the Mainichi chain of newspapers completely underwrote and promoted the six-week tour of Hawaii, several U.S. military bases and Japan. A few players opted out, but most of the team, along with their wives, as well as George and Hazel Weiss, Casey and Edna Stengel, Del Webb and Commissioner and Mrs. Ford Frick, made up the group of 65 that left shortly after the end of the World Series.[84]

The trip was a huge success, drawing large crowds everywhere. Even though it didn't add to the Yankees' bottom line, Weiss was able to turn it to the team's advantage. As *The Sporting News* noted, Weiss was so impressed with the caliber of baseball in the Far East that he named Harry Tadashi Wakabayashi as a scout to look for Yankees prospects in Japan. Weiss and Stengel also used the trip as pre-spring training to try out Billy Martin at shortstop as backup for the aging Phil Rizzuto (who did not go to Japan).[85] Weiss returned to New York in mid–November, pleased with the season but fully aware of what he needed to accomplish to make the 1956 Yankees the World Champions again and to fully restore what the press was likely to call "a return to the Yankee dynasty."[86]

11
The Dynasty Resumes

While George Weiss and his team were on their goodwill tour of the Philippines and Japan, assistant general manager William DeWitt, Sr., remained in New York "to plug the holes" which had prevented the Bombers from winning the World Series in 1955. Prior to his leaving, Weiss reminded DeWitt that he was only a phone call away and that he was putting the shortstop position at the top of his list of concerns, but he hoped that Billy Martin would solve that problem.[1]

The Japanese tour did convince Weiss that Andy Carey should be the Yankees' permanent third baseman and that for the upcoming season Elston Howard deserved more playing time.[2] Weiss also indicated that his "wish list" included another outfielder and more pitching, and that he was open to dealing, especially for a pitcher.[3]

At the December 1955 winter meetings, Weiss tried numerous times to acquire that pitcher. Yet after all the talks, Weiss stated that the Yankees would probably not make any trades. With the strongest American League club "on paper," Weiss noted that the Yankees' young players would help the team much more than anyone he might get in a trade. It was now time for Weiss and DeWitt to talk contracts with the players.

Coming off a pennant-winning year, naturally the players would expect raises. Weiss decided it was time to draw the line. "Our salaries have been going up and up," he stated. "This year we have to stop the trend."[4] Weiss moved slowly to sign Mickey Mantle, Irv Noren, and Billy Hunter, all returning from injuries with encouraging reports. Yogi Berra, the league's MVP for the third time in five years, wanted $50,000, and Weiss had not yet had talks with Gil McDougald or Whitey Ford. He preferred, instead, to tie down Rizzuto for probably his last year as a player.[5] "Scooter," at 38 the second-oldest Yankee on the roster, soon confirmed that he and Weiss had agreed on a $30,000 contract, which represented a significant cut from 1955.[6] Tommy Byrne signed quickly after Rizzuto[7]; Mantle inked his contract at "the raise I had counted on"[8]; and Yogi Berra came on board a day later at "close enough" to $50,000 to make him happy. Weiss, commenting on the fact that Berra had never taken a pay cut, uncharacteristically bantered with the press. After he and Berra had agreed to terms, Weiss said, "How can I beat Yogi down when you gentlemen [the press] keep voting him the Most Valuable Player?" Yogi chirped, "You guys keep voting me the MVP."[9]

One contract Weiss was not worried about was his own, which had not been set to expire until the end of 1956. In late 1955, however, Webb and Topping, perhaps reacting to rumors that Baltimore was trying to lure Weiss back, but more likely in recognition of his outstanding results, extended his term five more years at $75,000 annually.[10]

As spring training approached, Weiss announced that the Yankees were willing to deal for another pitcher, and in February, in one of his less successful moves, Weiss acquired southpaw Mickey McDermott from the Washington Senators. McDermott, who had played most of his career with the Red Sox and never had a losing season in Boston, compiled a 2–6 season in 1956, the only year he spent with the Yankees.[11]

The shortstop situation was still unresolved, but by the time the Yankees reached their training camp in St. Petersburg, they discovered they had some excellent candidates, including Billy Martin, Billy Hunter, Jerry Lumpe, Jerry Coleman, and 20-year-old Tony Kubek, another of Stengel's favorites. But it was Gil McDougald—primarily through his standout work on the Japanese tour—who won the coveted role, and at Weiss's insistence, Kubek was sent to Denver for another year of seasoning.[12] As Weiss finalized the roster, baseball observers marveled at the depth of talent the Yankees possessed and predicted how successful the Yankees would be in the upcoming season.[13]

The Yankees, indeed, did have an excellent season, taking over first place in May and holding it throughout the remainder of the season, finishing nine games ahead of second-place Cleveland. A wide variety of players contributed to the Yankees' victory. Berra clouted 30 homers and drove in 105 runs; Skowron established himself by hitting .308 with 90 RBI; and McDougald, after taking over for Rizzuto at short, batted .311 and scored 79 runs. Yankees pitchers were outstanding. Whitey Ford completed 17 of his 19 winning starts. Second-year pitcher Johnny Kucks won 18 games, and Tom Sturdivant, who came up from the farm system in 1955, won 16 games with a 3.30 ERA before being traded to Kansas City in 1959; he retired after the 1964 season with a 59–51 career record.[14]

But the 1956 season was impressive largely due to the achievements of Mickey Mantle, who was finally living up to his potential. With a batting average of .353, 130 RBI and 52 homers, he won baseball's Triple Crown and the MVP Award. He also led the American League in OBP and runs scored.[15] In addition, he was the *Sporting News* "Major League Player of the Year," and the *Associated Press* "Male Athlete of the Year." He also received the Hickok Belt, awarded to the top professional athlete of the year, as well as the first-ever Babe Ruth Sultan of Swat crown as the major leagues' top slugger.[16]

Noting the bargain the Yankees had in Mantle's $30,000 contract, many expected a mid-season salary raise for him. Weiss replied that the Yankees had a firm tradition of not re-negotiating salaries in the middle of the season. Said Weiss, "We negotiate a contract at the beginning of the season and that's the one the player goes by for the rest of the season."[17]

One jarring note in 1956 was the release of the popular Phil Rizzuto. Earlier, Rizzuto had intimated that this was to be his final season, but Weiss had other plans. Toward the end of August, Weiss faced a dilemma. To fortify his bench, he wanted to reacquire Enos Slaughter from Kansas City, but in order to do that, he needed an empty slot on the Yankees' roster.[18]

On Old Timers' Day, one of the Yankees' few, but well-liked promotions, Weiss summoned Rizzuto into Stengel's office in the clubhouse. When the unsuspecting Rizzuto entered Stengel's office, he was told that the addition of Slaughter to the roster necessitated cutting a player to make room for him. Weiss asked Rizzuto to look over the team's roster to suggest which player should be dropped to create a spot for Slaughter. The shortstop complied and made numerous suggestions to Weiss and manager Casey Stengel, but they vetoed each of them. After the three men went over the roster numerous times, Rizzuto finally realized that Weiss and Stengel wanted to release him. Weiss assured Rizzuto that he would be reactivated after September 1, although he would not be eligible for the World Series. The stunned Rizzuto got dressed and left the stadium, ending his career as an active player for the New York Yankees.[19] The particular day that Rizzuto was released, and the manner in which he learned of it, reinforced the belief that in the eyes of many baseball people, Weiss was a cold and unfeeling individual.[20]

According to Whitey Ford, Rizzuto was in tears as he left the clubhouse. "He was hurt and insulted," said Ford. "He felt the Yankees hadn't treated him right after all the years he had spent with the team. And it was humiliating to get the news on Old-Timers' Day in front of Joe DiMaggio and all his old teammates."[21]

Although Rizzuto's career as a Yankees player ended in 1956, the following year he began a second career in the broadcasting booth, which lasted for 40 years. Ballantine Beer and Station WPIX hired Rizzuto to work with Mel Allen and Red Barber as the Yankees' radio color announcer, forcing long-time announcer Jim Woods out of the booth. Rizzuto eventually became senior broadcaster and helped turn generations of baseball fans into Yankees fans.[22]

The 1956 World Series was a dramatic conclusion to the Yankees' memorable season. The Yankees faced the team that had beaten them the previous year, the Brooklyn Dodgers. Just as they had done the year before, the Yankees lost the first two games of the Series.[23] Back at Yankee Stadium, the Yankees won all three games. In Game Five, Don Larsen pitched the only perfect game in World Series history. Mantle was a deciding factor in that game, hitting a solo home run off Dodgers mainstay Sal Maglie and making a running catch in deep center field to preserve the perfect game. The Yankees were shut out in Game Six, but won the World Championship by taking Game Seven, 9–0.[24]

The latest victories again brought out criticisms that the Yankees were ruining baseball by repeated wins, but most knowledgeable baseball commentators supported the team. And many credited hard work and baseball wisdom, particularly by Yankees general manager George Weiss. Joe Williams praised the work of Weiss: "He (Weiss) has proceeded to enlarge the scope and introduce ideas of his own. The essentials are enterprise, industry and baseball astuteness."[25] Even Weiss's rival Frank Lane, Cardinals general manager at the time, credited Weiss and his team: "The Yankees have a great scouting system. They got a good start and they are fighting like the deuce to maintain their position and it will be a long time before they finish anywhere but in the top three spots."[26]

Dan Daniel added, "Pennant or no pennant, Casey Stengel and George Weiss agree that to rest on your laurels leads to stagnation, and down that street lies fatal failure."[27] Columnist Red Smith noted that George Weiss expected his team to win the pennant every year not out of greed for victory, but for a sounder reason—"Every baseball man's job is to play the game better than anybody else. If you lost the game that meant something was wrong. Better find out what was wrong, and remedy it."[28] *The Sporting News*

Phil Rizzuto spent his entire playing career (1941–1956) as a New York Yankee. On Old-Timers' Day in 1956, Weiss abruptly released Rizzuto to re-sign Enos Slaughter in time to place him on the upcoming post-season roster. Rizzuto returned to the Yankees the next year in the radio booth and remained there for 40 years (National Baseball Hall of Fame Library, Cooperstown, New York).

noted that the Yankees "win because they absolutely refuse to take any foe for granted." They have a relentless pursuit of perfection. The paper pointed out that the Yankees' victory in 1956 should be a warning to other American League team owners that they had to find a way to bring their teams to a reasonably competitive position or at least "to divide more equitably the talent pool from which the champions seem to draw a disproportionate number of the good ones."[29]

True to this description and despite the huge success in 1956, Weiss knew better than to "stand pat" and was ready to start working on the 1957 season as soon as the World Series was once again in the Yankees' possession. Among his first chores was the signing of Stengel to another five-year contract. Already on record as reluctant to sign "bonus babies" except when "ready" for the big leagues, Weiss concentrated on his veterans and his farm teams.[30]

Unfortunately, almost all of the minor league clubs were having trouble staying afloat financially. Recognizing the need to keep the minors viable, the major league owners appointed George Weiss as one of a six-member committee of experienced baseball men to oversee a half-million dollar fund to support and restructure the minor leagues. The Yankees ended up contributing more than the other clubs as Weiss's assistant, Bill DeWitt, left the organization, with Weiss's blessing, to become administrator of the minor league support fund. Weiss increased Lee MacPhail's responsibilities, giving him the newly created title of Director of Player Personnel and assigning him DeWitt's duties.[31]

Although many sportswriters expected Weiss to have trouble negotiating salaries with his super-achievers, signings went well. At the start of 1957, Weiss, despite the usual bemoaning of higher expenses, announced that former MVP Berra had signed for another new high—an estimated $58,000—and pitching ace Whitey Ford for "about $35,000."[32]

As anticipated, many of the Yankees returned their contracts unsigned, but presumably accepted the "many good raises" Weiss had promised. In particular, the most important unsigned player, MVP Mickey Mantle, also came to an agreement a month before spring training. Weiss had supposedly offered his star outfielder $50,000, and while Mantle had asked for $65,000–$75,000, he reportedly signed for an estimated $60,000, about the same as Berra.[33] There were, of course, always some players who were reluctant to accept Weiss's first offer. Don Larsen, for example, was holding out for $27,500, threatening to end up "tending bar." The unperturbed Weiss responded nonchalantly to Larsen's threat. "Don will get every consideration in his new contract for having pitched his masterpiece. However, we have an entire season to think of, too," he replied.[34]

But Weiss had no plans to stick just with his 1956 roster. He brought back 21-year-old, versatile infielder Tony Kubek, feeling he was now ready after the additional year of seasoning Weiss had ordered in 1956, over Stengel's objections. In February 1957, Weiss announced the largest player swap since his 1954 deal with Baltimore.[35] The Yankees began a 13-player exchange with their favorite trading partner, the Kansas City Athletics. The Yankees gave up outfielder Irv Noren, right-handed pitcher Tom Morgan, southpaws Rip Coleman and Mickey McDermott, shortstop Billy Hunter, minor league second baseman Milt Graff, and a player to be named later. In return, the A's sent the Yanks right-handed pitcher Art Ditmar, southpaws Bobby Shantz and Jack McMahon, first baseman Wayne Belardi, and two players to be named later. In early April, the Yankees completed their end of the bargain, sending Jack Urban to Kansas City. The Athletics had just sent Curt Roberts to the Yankees but did not send their final player, third baseman Clete Boyer, until June 4.[36]

George Weiss called Art Ditmar "the ace in the deal." Although he had lost 22 games in 1956 for the last-place Athletics, he had won 24 games for a poor team in 1955 and

1956.[37] Shantz had won a Most Valuable Player Award for the A's in 1952 when he won 24 games. He spent eight years with the A's prior to the 1957 trade, winning 69 games while losing 65.[38] "We figure him as a relief man and he should do well in the Stadium," said Weiss.[39]

Baltimore manager Paul Richards, when asked for his opinion of the 13-player swap, bluntly stated that Kansas City got the worst of it. "You gotta be careful when you trade with George Weiss. We're the only club that ever beat the Yankees in a deal. We got Gus Triandos and Willy Miranda and Hal Smith from them and, through Smith, in a trade with Kansas City, we got Al Pilarcik, who I think can help us."[40]

Warren Brown, writing in the *Chicago American*, echoed Richards' assessment of the trade. "The Yankees in consummating the trade," he wrote, "gave away nothing they'll miss, and got in return Art Ditmar and Bobby Shantz, who may be quite useful in the run for another championship." Brown noted that Weiss would never have been able to conclude the deal if he did not have "poor relations standing by ready to do what they are told and actually put up a show of being grateful for the Yankees largess." Brown was referring, of course, to the Kansas City Athletics.[41]

Kansas City did have its defenders. John McHale, Detroit Tigers general manager, noted, "There is nothing illegal or unethical about the trading between the Yankees and Athletics. Arnold Johnson is doing a fine job for Kansas City. He took a ball club that had nothing and made it into a ball club that is tough to beat." Paul Richards added, "In Arnold Johnson's position, you have to get ballplayers. The most logical source is the team that has the most, and that is the Yankees…. In Johnson's position he can't afford not to make a deal for players who might help him. I don't buy those stories about collusion at all."[42]

The vast majority of Yankees players certainly never loved Weiss, who often hired detectives to catch the most egregious nightlife devotees, but their dislike of him and of the general atmosphere of the club as set by the front office was becoming deeper.[43] In particular, some of the players who had been traded to Kansas City, including Irv Noren, Billy Hunter, and Rip Coleman, griped publicly about the low morale in the Yankees clubhouse. Speaking personally about the way the Yankees had treated him Coleman said, "My salary and the World Series check totaled $17,000 with the Yankees last year. But if I made $77,000, I couldn't have been more miserable. I'll make a lot less money with the A's, but at least they'll treat me like a human being."[44]

Irv Noren was as outspoken as Coleman. He indicated that Weiss had told him that the club would not pay his latest doctor bill and that the Yankees had already spent enough money on him. "That's typical of the Yankees," noted Coleman. "They always think they're doing you a favor to have you around. It's a lot different with the A's. They make you feel like they're tickled to have you." Billy Hunter echoed his teammate's sentiments, feeling that the Yankees had short-changed him into signing for the money he did. Ironically, Hunter wistfully added, "The Yankee front office isn't the most considerate one in baseball. But I still like the club and I'd go back tomorrow if they'd want me."[45]

When the 1957 season began, Weiss's newest acquisitions, Shantz and Ditmar, seemed to regain the pitching ability that had made them winners in earlier years and made the Yankees GM look omniscient in evaluating players on their baseball ability.[46] But the perception of Weiss as a person (as well as Stengel's managerial skills) suffered even more as the result of an after-hours incident that became known as the Copa Affair. Billy Martin and Mickey Mantle were close friends off the field, frequently going out together after games. A number of the other players often joined them in visits to bars and clubs, where they downed a lot of alcohol and sometimes stayed out until the wee hours. Weiss wanted to stop the hijinks without destroying the team. According to some observers, he blamed Martin for the rowdy lifestyle and thought him a "bad influence" on the Yankees' young, still somewhat impressionable MVP, Mantle. Martin had always been one of Stengel's favorite "boys"; a skillful infielder and a feisty player, he could be counted on to start a fight when the Yankees needed a diversion on the field.[47] Weiss, on the other hand, never liked Martin's fights on the field and also disliked his demeanor, his swagger, his conceit and his love of bars, drinking, and women.[48]

Depending on the source, the details of the Copa Affair varied somewhat, but most agreed on this scenario. On the evening of May 15, 1957, Mantle, Ford, Kucks, Bauer, Berra and their wives went out to celebrate Billy Martin's birthday. At a table next to the Yankees at the Copacabana nightclub in Manhattan, a group of men on a neighborhood bowling team, allegedly drunk, were making lewd racial remarks directed at the Copa's headliner, Sammy Davis, Jr. Supposedly, Bauer argued with and tried to quiet the drunk, who was later found in the men's room unconscious. Bauer claimed he never touched him, but the following day, the police charged Bauer with felonious assault and the entire incident landed on the front pages of the New York tabloids.[49]

The affair also produced a $1 million lawsuit against the team and a grand jury investigation. Weiss was furious about the negative publicity and fined five of the players $1,000 each for their "un–Yankee-like" behavior. Kucks, who earned far less than the other five players, was fined $500. According to some sportswriters, the public thought the fines were excessive and added to their view of Weiss as a hard-nosed boss.[50] Weiss did not rescind the fines even though the players testified before a grand jury and the district attorney threw out the case for insufficient evidence.[51] Yogi Berra's testimony seemed to sum up the event best when he remarked, "Nobody did nothin' to nobody."[52]

One sports historian claimed that under normal circumstances, the press would not have spent much time covering the occurrence at the Copa. At the time of the incident, however, there was a newspaper "war" among the New York City papers, and a new cohort of sports writers was emerging, ever concerned about the rise of a new method of communication—television. In order to help sell newspapers, these journalists had to report more than merely the details of the game of baseball. They were forced to inform their readers about off-field incidents and skullduggery, conspiracy and intrigue.[53]

Three years after the incident at the Copa, George Weiss called Martin's birthday party a "watershed event." He, too, was becoming aware of the onset of a growing legion of irreverent and impudent young sportswriters. He realized they were bent on questioning the authority of an older generation. In an interview with *The Saturday Evening Post*, Weiss confessed that a national TV network was considering using the New York Yankees as a model for an inspirational show built around institutions similar to West Point and Annapolis. "This might have steered some good prospects to us," said Weiss, "and the players could have made some extra money appearing on the program, but the project was shelved after the Copa Affair."[54]

The Copa brouhaha had, of course, an immediate effect. While the jury failed to

From 1949 to 1958, the Yankees won the American League pennant nine times. Only three men participated in every championship—manager Casey Stengel, catcher Yogi Berra and outfielder Hank Bauer. Bauer finished his professional career after the 1959 season in Kansas City, the same city in which he began (courtesy Dwayne Labakas).

hand down an indictment against the six Yankees players involved, it afforded George Weiss the opportunity to get rid of Martin even though it appeared he actually had no direct part in the fight. Exactly a month to the day after the Copa incident, Billy Martin was traded to Kansas City. According to Whitey Ford, it was no coincidence.[55]

Now that Bobby Richardson, who was hitting .337, appeared ready to handle second base, the Yankees had a valid excuse to let Martin go. In addition, the Yankees sent pitcher Bill Terry and minor league outfielders Woodie Held and Bob Martyn to the Athletics for outfielder Harry Simpson, minor league reliever Ryne Duren and outfielder Jim Pisoni.[56]

Martin was heartbroken to leave New York and furious with Weiss for trading him and with Stengel for not protecting him.[57] "Sure, I was a bad influence on the Yankees; I hung out with Mickey Mantle and he wins the Triple Crown batting title. I hung out with Whitey Ford and he's the club's biggest winner last year. I hung out with Don Larsen the night before his second World Series start, and he pitches a perfect game."[58] The trade also cemented the public perception that Weiss, not Stengel, had the upper hand when it came to player moves. Martin had been like a son to Stengel, and he was convinced that the trade was directed as much at Stengel as it was at the players.[59]

Weiss hardly expected his most recent trade with the A's to make an impact. It was intended to demonstrate that any additional off-field activities would not be tolerated, especially if the guilty parties were not super-stars. Weiss seldom, if ever, disciplined players like Mantle or Ford. But by trading one of his manager's "pet players," who happened to be one of Mantle's close friends, Weiss hoped to send a clear message to his other players.[60]

Once trading was completed, the team settled down and played like World Champions. The quiet Richardson, with a wider range than Martin or Coleman, did an excellent job at second base, and rookie Kubek, another proof of the Yankees' farm, handled any position with skill.[61] The Yankees entered September with a comfortable lead, bolstered by the addition of pitcher Sal Maglie, acquired from the Dodgers. Maglie helped nail down the pennant but was ineligible for the World Series. The pennant, Weiss's eighth in the last nine years, was a fitting mark of his 25th year with the Yankees. According to *Newsweek*, the Yankees organization that Weiss built was "so efficient that it promises to perpetuate itself in the foreseeable future."[62]

The Yankees were the favorites to win the World Series as they faced the Milwaukee Braves in the 1957 classic, but injuries such as Mantle's sore legs and Skowron's bad back were of concern. With Lew Burdette winning three games for Milwaukee, the Braves took the Series in seven games, even though the Yankees probably played better than the Braves.[63]

Unlike 1955, baseball critics came down hard on the Yankees, primarily blaming Stengel for the loss of the championship and Weiss and the owners for keeping him on as manager. They also blasted Simpson as the "goat" of the Series for having only one safety in 12 at-bats and hitting into five double plays.[64] Lew Johnson reminded his readers that it was Weiss who had acquired Simpson in exchange for the proven talents of Billy Martin.[65]

Despite the negative comments, the pundits gave two of the most prized awards for 1957 to two Yankees: Tony Kubek was voted the American League's "Rookie of the Year" based on his hitting and fielding in all five positions he played during the season; and Mantle received his second consecutive MVP Award, edging out Ted Williams in a controversial decision.[66]

In addition to coming back from the Series defeat, Weiss and the Yankees, the only major league club in New York in 1958, felt they could attract the National League fans without special efforts as long as the Bombers were an exciting and winning club. The Phillies, however, seizing the opportunity to increase their TV audience and perhaps add some new fans, broadcast 77 games into the New York area. The Pirates and the Cardinals telecast to New York all home games with the Dodgers and Giants. Weiss admitted that legally there was nothing he could do to stop them.[67]

Despite the usual speculation from baseball critics regarding players Weiss would cut or trade from the 1957 club and the players he might deal for, these same critics noted that the 1958 roster was primarily a collection of 1957 veterans, minus retirees Jerry Coleman, Tommy Byrne and Joe Collins, but plus another excellent crop of rookies from the farm. In fact, Weiss expected that the farm players who made it through spring training—particularly Ryne Duren, Norm Siebern, and Marv Throneberry—would provide a boost to the club.[68]

While recuperating at home from a bout of pneumonia at the start of the 1958 season, Weiss made sure to tie down working agreements with ten minor league teams in the Yankees' unmatched farm system. In addition, he added Andy Cohen, former Giants player, as manager of the successful Denver AAA franchise, replacing Ralph Houk, who had been named Yankees first base coach at Weiss's suggestion. Topping had felt that the Yankees' loss of the 1957 Series was due in large part to Stengel's mismanagement, and he wanted to oust Stengel and hire Houk as Yankees manager. Weiss disagreed, arguing that Houk wasn't ready; he convinced the owner that Houk needed to be groomed as Stengel's successor by serving as Yankees coach for at least a year.[69]

Weiss expressed confidence in his players, but he also felt that he had the advantage negotiating salaries with many of them because of their reduced stats and the loss of the previous World Series. Several of those targeted for cuts or no raises held out prior to the start of spring training and eventually received salaries close to what they had sought. Weiss, of course, gave voice to his annual complaint that *this* year's Yankees payroll would be the highest in baseball history, warning that this outlay might result in an increase in the price of game tickets—not exactly a way to draw present or prospective fans to Yankee Stadium.[70]

Weiss was even more incensed over a charity game staged by the Major League Baseball Players Association in which some of his unsigned players, without benefit of spring training conditioning, participated. The irate Weiss stated, "Charity is a fine thing. But no player should ruin an arm or a leg no matter how worthy the cause. He must remember that he makes his living on physical condition." Speaking to a press conference in the club office, Weiss continued. "We gave permission for the game when we met at Colorado Springs. However, I certainly did not believe that, fresh out of the Mayo Clinic, Mantle and Ford would risk new injury and Turley would pitch two innings."[71] In the 1958 spring meetings, the owners, led by Weiss, barred similarly timed exhibition games in the future.[72]

When the 1958 season began, fans saw a few new faces, including Siebern in left field and Ryne Duren in the bullpen. They also saw Elston Howard taking over as catcher more frequently while Berra, whose hitting had fallen off in 1957, was given more outfield time. Even with an injured Skowron, and Berra still in a hitting slump, the Yankees got off to such a good start that baseball writers in late May were speculating how early New York could wrap up the American League pennant. The same critics ridiculed the other American League teams for ongoing calls to "break up the Yankees," predicting instead that Weiss's organization, with its emphasis on youth, "will keep the stars a-coming for many a year when the time of retirement comes to General Manager George Weiss, 63, and Casey Stengel, 67."[73]

In 1958, at long last Weiss was satisfied with his pitching staff. Acquired in Weiss's large deal with Baltimore four years earlier, both Turley and Larsen were turning in outstanding performances, as were Ford and Duren.[74]

There were concerns, however. Having built such a big lead, baseball observers more often were mentioning Stengel's increasingly detached or "push-button" management style. Weiss also felt that the team was growing complacent and playing without much enthusiasm. He blamed it on the players' continued excessive nightlife and hired private detectives to follow players during the evenings. Mantle, Ford, and Duren, who had a severe alcohol problem, were particular targets, but almost all the players were followed at one time or another, and most were offended and angry with Weiss.[75]

Nonetheless, thanks to their earlier lead, the Yankees clinched the 1958 American League flag on September 14 despite playing only .500 ball during August and September. They finished the season with 92 wins, ten games ahead of the Chicago White Sox, and were set to face Milwaukee again, this time focused on avenging their loss the previous year. The confident Braves jumped to a 3–1 lead in the Series, only one game from taking it all, when the Yankees roared back to win the championship, only the second team in baseball history to accomplish that feat. New York analysts and fans praised the Yankees for their ability to fight back. Jimmy Cannon even compared them favorably with the former lovable Dodgers. To top things off, Stengel was named "Manager of the Year."[76]

Webb, Topping, and Weiss, who now supported the owners' concerns about Stengel, knew they had no choice but to sign Stengel to another two-year contract. Webb, however, was still unhappy about the extension and ordered the closing of Stengel's beloved instructional school for 1959. Stengel, too, seemed reluctant to agree to the contract, waiting until the day before spring training began to ink his signature.[77]

Unlike most previous years, Weiss and the Yankees felt that the 1958 club required only a few changes to compete successfully in 1959, although some baseball mavens noted that the Yankees had signed few of the Hispanic or African American players who were building up many National League teams. Nonetheless, Weiss began fixing the issues he saw. In August 1958, Duren's doctor told Weiss that his pitcher would require knee surgery later in the year. A few weeks after the 1958 Series ended, and Duren had some time off, Weiss ordered him back to New York for the surgery, giving him the maximum recovery time before spring training—an incident which *The Sporting News* cited as an example of Weiss's efficiency.[78]

Weiss also made a few changes in the Yankees' farm system for 1959. The Yankees did not renew their working agreement with Denver and instead bought outright the Richmond club of the AAA International League, where they had had a working agreement.[79] Weiss named former Yankees star pitcher Ed Lopat, who had been managing at Richmond, farm system coach, hoping he could solve the riddle of why the farm system was so successful in developing players at every position except pitcher.[80]

Weiss also needed to select a replacement for director of player personnel Lee MacPhail, who had accepted the position of Baltimore's general manager. Most observers had speculated that Weiss had been grooming MacPhail as his eventual successor. After evaluating the small pool of senior management able to handle salary negotiations, Webb, Topping and Weiss brought back Roy Hamey as assistant GM.[81]

Late in 1958, the office of President of the American League became vacant, and the selection committee to fill that vacancy told Weiss that if he accepted the post he would receive the unanimous vote of the American League owners. Although flattered, Weiss quickly and politely turned down the offer, opting to stay with the Yankees, where he already possessed great authority and a salary commensurate with that of a league president. The fallback candidate, Weiss's one-time player, Joe Cronin, jumped at the offer.[82]

For Weiss and Yankees management, one negative about winning "all the marbles" was that a number of players wanted higher salaries for 1959 based on their 1958 performance. Siebern had batted .300 and won a Gold Glove Award; Howard had led the team with a .314 batting average; Mantle had produced 42 home runs and scored 127 runs; and Turley had won the Cy Young Award. Even so, Weiss sent out contracts with lower increases than the players felt they were worth, and even pay cuts to certain unnamed players.[83]

Just as Joe DiMaggio set the Yankees' salary structure during his playing days, Mantle, the American League's biggest drawing card at home and on the road, was the most important player that Weiss needed to sign. Despite the fact that his fielding had often been poor and his batting average had dropped from .367 in 1957 to .304 in 1958, Mantle was rumored to be demanding $85,000 to $90,000. Instead he was first offered a contract with a pay cut, which he promptly returned unsigned. Negotiations began. Finally, on February 27, after an hour-and-a-half meeting in St. Petersburg, Weiss gave Mantle an $80,000 contract, making him the second-highest paid Yankee in club history.[84]

Whitey Ford, who also did not accept his contract until late February, finally signed with a small raise. Ford complained that unlike Mantle, he was never able to see Weiss, much less negotiate with him. Interestingly, Ford's contract contained more than just a salary figure. He had missed a goodly number of games over the past two seasons for what doctors diagnosed as "high uric acid." They had advised that his condition could be controlled through diet, but Ford had often ignored this advice in 1958. Weiss made sure that to protect Ford's health (and the Yankees' investment), he was given a contract that included his medically prescribed diet.[85]

Weiss also maintained that a few of the players were offered lower salaries as a way to penalize them for breaking discipline and training rules during the 1958 World Series. Not surprisingly, those known for "good behavior" such as Berra, Turley, Skowron, and McDougald, as well as a number of other key players, held out in protest, generating much negative publicity for the team. They finally accepted contracts negotiated primarily with Hamey. Having to deal with Hamey became a "sore" spot for many Yankee players. A number of players noticed that Weiss, the general manager, was becoming more and more a sort of phantom. As one Yankee bluntly stated, "It's tougher to get to George than to see the top guy in the Kremlin."[86]

As the opening of the season neared, it became apparent that the 1959 Yankees were in for some serious competition for the American League flag. In fact, 1959 was a great year for Yankees-haters including not only fans and baseball critics, but also players on opposing teams.[87] As of May 5, the Yankees had won only seven games while losing 12, wasting occasional good pitching by not hitting. To remedy the situation, Weiss attempted to make deals, but unfortunately for the Bombers, no other American

League team, not even the A's, was willing to help him. To make matters worse, their once-productive farm system had become surprisingly unproductive. *The Sporting News* noted that Weiss's farm system had failed to turn up a single imposing pitcher since 1955.[88]

Even as the slump continued, the Yankees' brass insisted that there was no reason to panic. But the pitching staff was faltering, with former stars like Turley, Larsen, and Duren on their way to losing seasons. On May 20, the Yankees fell into the American League cellar for the first time since 1940; by the end of the month they had climbed into sixth place, but were still four games under .500.[89]

Weiss, Topping, Webb and Stengel met on a number of occasions to discuss the situation, but the brass officially announced there would be no changes in the way the club was operating. They explicitly insisted that they were going to "stand pat, go with the slumping regulars and let them swing their way out of it."[90]

Following the meeting, however, Weiss began trading again—with Kansas City. Weiss wanted to deal for the club's best hitter, Roger Maris, but since Maris was out of the lineup for an appendectomy and Weiss was looking for immediate help, he took instead slugger Hector Lopez, a good hitter but poor fielder, and former Yankee Ralph Terry. In return, the A's received infielder Jerry Lumpe, pitchers Tom Sturdivant and Johnny Kucks and a player to be determined later. (Of course the trade with Kansas City riled the other owners, but they were helpless to block the deal.) Weiss also returned to his farm teams and began to bring up prospects who could either hit or pitch.[91]

The Yanks' play began to improve, and by mid–June the team had moved up to fifth place with a 28–29 record.[92] By mid–August, the Yankees were being discussed as long shots to regain their title.[93] But it was not to be. The Yankees were officially eliminated from the pennant race on September 9 and finished third, behind the pennant-winning White Sox and the Cleveland Indians. They ended the season with a record of 79–75, 15 games behind the White Sox.[94]

It galled Weiss to lose to the White Sox, a team that had not won a pennant since 1919. He felt that his team, unlike the Chisox, was not hungry enough and perhaps the players had too many outside interests on their minds. He even stated that his key players, with their high salaries and their World Series shares, gave so much attention to their personal activities that they were unable to concentrate on baseball."[95]

It seemed as if every baseball writer, critic, and fan had an opinion as to what happened to the Yankees, and many of them blamed Weiss for things he either had or had not done. In trading, for example, Weiss was called "cold" and accused of trading players not in his mold.[96] Or Weiss traded away too many players who were originally signed by the Yankees, such as Jensen and Cerv, who were now making great contributions to new teams. Or Weiss traded for immediate results, getting veterans like Slaughter while sending away younger, long-term players.[97]

Critics also cited the farm system, emphasizing that having fewer farm teams was cutting Weiss's ability to grow players. During the first part of the 1959 season, Weiss had been unable to bring up any rookies from the farms. The critics also noted that at the same time, the Yankees' rivals were improving their personnel.[98]

Others pointed to a lack of leadership among the players, blaming both Weiss, who traded away Billy Martin, a "real take-charge guy," and Mantle, who they said needed to step forward and assume a leadership role.[99] Weiss called Mantle an "enigma" who had been the topic of much discussion in the Yankees' front office. "Our entire organization has tried to discover why Mantle hasn't capitalized on his enormous potential, and we haven't found the answer," said Weiss.[100]

Mostly, critics noted that virtually none of the players had a good year in 1959. Some problems could be related to injuries; at one time, Mantle was out with a chipped finger bone, and Skowron missed the final two months of the season because of a broken wrist. Even though the pitching staff remained mostly healthy, several writers felt they were the key to the disappointing season.[101] There was common agreement among the writers that there was no dissension in the Yankees' clubhouse.[102]

There were rumors that Webb was displeased with Weiss's leadership but that Topping still gave Weiss his complete support. Webb denied these reports, but there were even more persistent tales that all three men would be pleased if Stengel decided to retire.[103]

Once the season was finally over, Stengel organized a fall training school for 14 top prospects from the farms while Weiss dealt with a proposed third major league and served on the committee to explore possible expansion of the American League.[104] But Weiss's primary focus was on getting the players needed to rebuild the Yankees and restock the farm teams. For the first time in a long time, Weiss would need to contemplate catcher prospects, following the voluntary but emotional retirement of Yogi Berra. Since the West Coast was proving to be a vital source for prospects, Weiss hired former Dodger Dolph Camilli as the fifth West Coast scout.[105] As the fall of 1959 progressed, it became clear that to be back on top in 1960, Weiss was willing to consider trading almost any of his veterans (except Mantle) to obtain reliable hitters and good pitchers (preferably a left-handed-hitting left fielder and a southpaw hurler). He also brought up eight players from the farm—six of them pitchers.[106]

There was a new, waiver-less inter-league trading period in effect for the first time that fall. Weiss had opposed it, but he tried to take advantage of this period by relentlessly phoning and meeting with any team willing to discuss a deal. Unfortunately, he was no more successful in dealing with the National League than he had been with the majority of the American League teams, particularly the White Sox and Indians, led by his old adversaries, Frank Lane and Bill Veeck respectively.[107]

Weiss now turned back to the Athletics, his one reliable trading partner, and by giving Kansas City four Yankees—veteran Hank Bauer, former outstanding hurler Don Larsen, talented young Norm Siebern, and ever-promising Marv Throneberry, he finally acquired Roger Maris, the player he had wanted all season, as well as shortstop Joe DeMaestri and first baseman Kent Hadley. This was the 15th deal between the Yankees and the Athletics since 1955 and brought the total number of players involved between the two teams to 59. Weiss hated to part with Bauer and Larsen, but felt he had in Maris a young outfielder who should develop into a fine player.[108] Weiss fully expected that Maris, a pull-hitting outfielder with power, would take full advantage of Yankee Stadium's short right-field porch.[109]

The deal for Maris would turn out to be Weiss's last major trade for the Yankees and his last great coup as general manager. Many baseball observers claim that after the Yankees had acquired Maris, they would make no real beneficial trade until 1972,

CBS's last year as the team owner, when the Yankees acquired Sparky Lyle from the Red Sox and Graig Nettles from the Cleveland Indians.[110]

Now that Weiss had the player he had most wanted, the real question facing him as the 1960 season approached was whether it was the final piece needed to restore the Yankees to championship form.

12

The End of an Era

George Weiss was pleased with his roster as he intensified preparation for the 1960 season. He was delighted that Roger Maris was available to help bolster a weak offense. Weiss was especially elated to learn that first baseman Moose Skowron, who missed the last two months of the 1959 season due to an injury, was fully recovered. His absence from the lineup was a major factor in the team's disappointing third-place finish.[1]

Weiss understood that he would be negotiating several salary cuts due to the below-par performances of some of his key players, among them his star outfielder, Mickey Mantle. With Mantle's batting average below .300, along with only 75 RBI, Weiss proposed cutting his $75,000 salary by the maximum 20 percent for a 1960 salary of $60,000. Ryne Duren, with a record of three victories and six losses, was also offered a contract with a 20 percent cut. Both players opted to hold out.[2]

Roger Maris, Hector Lopez, and rookie Kent Hadley, acquired from Kansas City in the Maris trade, were also holdouts, but with Stengel's help, all three signed prior to the start of spring training. With those three exceptions, Stengel decided to allow Weiss and his assistant, Roy Hamey, to handle the 1960 holdouts without his interference. "I have enough worries without becoming a mediator," said Stengel.[3]

Duren reached a compromise with Weiss when he received a slight raise. (Stengel wanted to give Duren maximum time to recover from a broken wrist the previous season.)[4] Weiss, however, was losing his patience with Mantle and the other still unsigned players, calling them "ungrateful and unreasonable," and he insisted that the Yankees would make no overtures "begging Mantle or any other player to take our money." But Mantle still refused to come to Florida to negotiate, and the two sides remained far apart. This was the second time he had rejected Weiss's telephone plea to travel to St. Petersburg for further talks.[5]

The Mantle-Weiss dispute soon became reminiscent of earlier salary fights with DiMaggio and Raschi.[6] Raschi's holdout eventually ended in his being traded, but no one felt that Weiss had any intention of dealing Mantle. For one thing, Mantle was only 28, and for another, the Yankees desperately needed his power in the lineup. Even though Mantle's batting average had slipped in 1959, he still clouted 31 home runs.[7]

Weiss absolutely did not intend to trade Mantle, but he felt that his center fielder was being obstinate and irrational. He indicated that Mantle was the first player who had ever refused to negotiate in person with him and added, "I've signed some pretty big players, including Joe DiMaggio. Apparently we've got some pretty rich players who can afford to hold out all year. Well, they'll miss those big fat pay checks in the summer months."[8] Weiss' advice to Mantle was to "grow up," and become more aware of his baseball responsibilities. As for trading Mantle, Weiss scoffed: "How silly can a guy get?"[9]

A short time later Mantle, to everyone's surprise, showed up in Florida and quickly signed his 1960 contract, purportedly calling for a cut to only $50,000–$60,000. The press was quick to note that Mantle's action satisfied both parties—Mantle had come to Florida as Weiss had demanded, and he had been able to retain most of his salary. The two men conferred briefly, after which Weiss expressed hope that Mantle would have a great year in 1960 and regain his popularity with the Yankees fans. "It wouldn't take too much for the public to like him again," said Weiss. Mantle, who did not appear very happy at his signing, retorted that he had never felt that he was ever popular. "I had a couple of pretty good years and it didn't help me much," he said.[10]

Although Weiss was primarily involved with salary negotiations, he was also changing some administration posts. Former all-star catcher Bill Dickey was hired to coach/teach and Johnny Neun, a member of the corporate Yankees for many years, was named the new head of the farm system.[11]

The Yankees returned home from spring training with the worst record in the American League—11–21. Most experts predicted that the Chicago White Sox would repeat as AL champions. To make matters worse, Stengel began the 1960 season with only two reliable starting pitchers—Whitey Ford and Bob Turley—and as the season progressed, Ford would have arm problems so severe at times that he was unable to throw his usually dependable curve ball.[12]

Fortunately for the Yankees, their offense kept them in contention until Weiss could improve his pitching staff. Mantle, Maris, Berra and Skowron all got off to excellent starts, and by May 8, Maris was hitting .458, topping both leagues, and the Yankees were behind only last year's champions, the Chisox, by one game.[13] Mantle was keeping his mouth shut, thanks to the stern admonition Weiss gave him after he complained to the media about the size of his contract. Weiss constantly reminded him that Yankees players kept such thoughts to themselves, a lesson Maris quickly learned.[14]

At the end of May, Stengel was hospitalized by a viral infection, and coach Ralph Houk replaced him for 13 games, with the Yankees winning seven of them.[15] The Yankees continued to flip in and out of the league lead through August despite Weiss's almost continual roster changes. In May he released veteran outfielder Elmer Valo. and the next day he completed his 16th deal with Kansas City, sending the A's Andy Carey in exchange for former Yankee Bob Cerv. Weiss felt Cerv would provide the Yanks with additional power and a veteran presence in the outfield. In addition, adding Cerv allowed Stengel to return Yogi Berra to his catching duties, giving Elston Howard a much-needed rest.[16]

In a separate deal, Weiss also traded the now-mediocre pitcher Johnny Kucks and disappointing infielder Jerry Lumpe to Kansas City in return for outfielder Hector Lopez and hurler Ralph Terry, two players the Yankees had previously sent over in the Billy Martin trade. The rest of the American League howled in protest, but the trade stood.[17] In July Weiss optioned pitcher John Gabler to Richmond to make room for southpaw Luis Arroyo from Jersey City.[18] Even in late August, Weiss was still shuffling players as

Mickey Mantle (left) had been a Yankee for eight years when George Weiss acquired Roger Maris (right) in 1959 in the last of many trades he negotiated with the Kansas City Athletics. Mantle would help Maris make the change from an Athletic to a Yankee and the two men, known as the "M & M Boys," played well together for seven years (courtesy Dwayne Labakas).

he sent Hadley to AAA Richmond and obtained first baseman Dale Long on waivers from the Giants.[19]

At the end of the season, the Yankees stormed to a 15-game winning streak that brought them from a tie with Baltimore to another American League pennant. They finished with a record of 97–57, eight games in front of the Orioles, clinching their 25th pennant since 1921 on September 25, 1960.

The two men most responsible for the Yankees' success in 1960 were Mantle and Maris. Mantle hit only .275, but drove in 94 runs and led the American League with 40 home runs. Maris hit. 283, led the league with 112 runs batted in, and had a .581

slugging percentage. He finished second to Mantle with 39 home runs. Maris earned the American League's MVP honors, and Mantle was a close second.[20]

In the 1960 World Series, the Yankees faced a young Pittsburgh Pirates crew that was expected to be easy fodder for them. After a 33-year hiatus, the Pirates once again returned to the World Series to face an opponent who had appeared in eight of the last ten fall classics and had had to wait only one year to return to the "big show."

The Yankees lost the opening game, 6–4, at Forbes Field. Yankees power prevailed in Game 2 as the Yankees pushed 16 runs across the plate while Bob Turley held the Pirates to three runs. In Game 3, back in Yankee Stadium, Whitey Ford shut out the Buccaneers, while the Yankees, with Bob Cerv playing a key role, scored ten runs.[21]

Vern Law started Game 4 for the Pirates, and with the aid of some problematic fielding by the Yankees, led the Bucs to a 3–2 win, tying the Series. Elroy Face saved the game for Law, and Bill Virdon's single in the fifth inning drove in two of the Pirates' three runs.[22] Stengel started Ditmar in Game 5, but the Pirates got to him for three runs in the fifth, and the Yankees, continuing their run of fielding mistakes, lost the game, 5–2, giving the Pirates a 3–2 lead heading back to Pittsburgh.[23]

Back in Forbes Field for Game 6 and facing elimination, Stengel chose Whitey Ford to take the mound for the Yankees. With three days' rest, Whitey again kept the Pirates scoreless, while the Yankees' bats powered home 12 runs, shutting out the Pirates 12–0 and tying the Series at three games each. It also set up one of the most exciting World Series finishing games.[24]

A well-rested Turley started the final game for the Yankees, but the Pirates got off to an early 4–0 lead. Turley was relieved by a succession of pitchers including Stafford, Shantz, Coates and Terry. The lead seesawed back and forth and the game finally went into the bottom of the ninth, tied at 9–9. On Terry's second pitch, leadoff Pirates second baseman Bill Mazeroski lofted a home run over the left field wall—the first Series-ending home run ever. Despite being outscored 55–27 in the Series, Pittsburgh was the 1960 World Champion, surprising most of the baseball world, especially the Yankees' organization.[25]

It was a bitter loss for the Yankees. They outhit the Pirates with a batting average of .338 compared with Pittsburgh's .256. The Yankees outscored them 55–27, out-homered them 10–4, and out-pitched them with an ERA of 3.54 compared with the Pirates' 7.11. The Bombers still lost the Series in seven games because they wasted runs in lopsided 16–3, 10–0, and 12–0 wins. The Series all came down to a bad hop into Tony Kubek's throat and a game-winning home run by Bill Mazeroski in the bottom of the ninth.[26]

The Yankees were stunned in defeat. Mantle was devastated and wept openly. Years later he was quoted as saying that losing the 1960 World Series was the biggest disappointment of his career.[27] When a teammate tried to console him by pointing out the bad break on the double-play ball that hit Kubek in the throat, Mantle retorted, "From now on, all they'll know is that we lost."[28]

Even before the Series began, rumors had circulated that there would be a shake-up in the upper echelon of the Yankees' ball club, and that neither Stengel nor Weiss would be with the team in 1961. Dan Topping informed the press that he had not discussed Weiss' future with his GM, and Weiss quickly stated, "If there is to be any change,

I'm not a party to it."[29] Despite Weiss' statement, the rumors persisted. One newspaper predicted, "They're finally going to break up the Yankees."[30]

As late as mid–October, speculation on the future of both Weiss and Stengel persisted. Many observers felt that Stengel had caused the loss of the World Series because he managed his pitchers so poorly. They further noted that he was no longer able to work well with the younger players, having become "a grumpy old man ... when he wasn't dozing on the bench." In addition, Topping acknowledged that the club had established a 65-year-old retirement rule, putting 70-year-old Stengel and 66-year-old Weiss on the wrong side of the dividing line. But columnist Dan Daniel stated that neither man wanted to leave.[31]

The loss of the World Series, however, gave the Yankees' owners the opportunity to oust Stengel as manager. Ralph Houk had been waiting to move up, and Webb and Topping were afraid that they would lose him to another club if they didn't appoint him soon. At a hastily called press conference on October 18, just five days after the Series ended, the usually "hands off" owners announced that Stengel was "retiring." By calling the popular Stengel's "advanced age" the reason he was leaving, rather than their need to keep Houk, they came across as mean and cold-hearted. Stengel added to this perception by telling a sympathetic press that he wasn't retiring, he had been fired. "I'll never make the mistake of being 70 again," he proclaimed. Houk was named manager the following day.[32]

Weiss's future was not specifically determined at the press conference, but three days later, Topping announced, "He won't remain the general manager, but he won't become a mere figurehead, either.... Weiss' contract still has five years to go and we are not buying up his contract."[33] A clause in his contract prevented him from holding the title of "general manager" for any other club for five years.[34]

Weiss's official end as general manager of the Yankees came on November 2, 1960. In a one-sentence statement for the press, Weiss announced that he would remain an advisor at half-salary through 1965. He was "retiring" as of December 31, 1960.[35] He took his firing with style, and he stated at his press conference, "I'm not here to indulge in recriminations."[36] The Yankees almost immediately named Weiss's long-time assistant, 58-year-old Roy Hamey, as the new GM. Still outwardly loyal, "the introverted armchair genius" kept insisting he was "not fired," but he didn't fool the media, who reported that he was "prompted to step aside because of his age." In fact he was crushed. He knew that he would seldom be "consulted" and that he had effectively been ousted from baseball, his life since a teenager.[37]

Not many baseball observers sympathized with this man who was generally considered cold, unfeeling and ruthless. But almost all recognized his accomplishments: the man most responsible for bringing the Yankees ten pennants in his 13 years as GM. They added that he was "the greatest administrator the game has ever known."[38] Baseball historian Robert Creamer wrote, "The minor league teams Weiss put together for the Yankees were some of the best in history, and the constant flow of talent to the parent club was testimony to his skill in finding and developing players."[39]

In later years, baseball historians would produce in-depth analyses of Weiss's accomplishments and shortcomings, many of them posthumously. Much of the press coverage immediately following Weiss' retirement announcement, however, simply reviewed his

29-year career with the Yankees. Articles were written showcasing his trading prowess, his ability to evaluate players, and how he had won so much respect for his baseball shrewdness.[40] A number of journalists interviewed Weiss, but they tended to focus on his reminiscences, such as his best memories, what he thought was his "greatest deal" (Joe DiMaggio), or which players he most regretted getting away (Lew Burdette and Jackie Jensen).[41]

Weiss proudly displays two of the many trophies he had won while general manager of the New York Yankees (National Baseball Hall of Fame Library, Cooperstown, New York).

There were, however, some well-respected voices that went behind the facts, arguing that Weiss was not only "baseball's most consistently successful general manager" but also "its most misunderstood one." *New York Times* reporter Arthur Daley showed genuine affection when he described Weiss's demeanor at his farewell press conference. He called Weiss's retirement from the Yankees "an end of an era."[42] In a glowing editorial tribute to Weiss, *The Sporting News* noted,

> All of baseball perhaps obtained a better insight into this man, George Weiss, in the few moments when he quietly retired than they ever had before. He slipped out gracefully and left an immortal line behind him—"I have just one regret; I am growing old and there isn't a thing I can do about it." In retirement, Weiss emerged as high in personal stature as the teams he built for the Yankees always have emerged on the field.[43]

A number of critics reproached the Yankees for ousting Weiss. Harry Grayson, sports editor of the Newspaper Enterprise Association from 1934 to 1963, wrote, "If there were any lingering doubt about the Yankees pursuing the policy of penalizing success, it was removed along with the most successful front office man in baseball.... No other general manager enjoyed Weiss' success dealing with players. He made hundreds of successful trades in 29 years with the Yanks."[44]

New York World Telegraph & Sun sports writer Joe Williams was present at Weiss's "resignation," and described Weiss "still in a state of semi-shock, fighting hard to keep his emotions under control." Williams wrote that Weiss retained his gentility, his evenness of speech, his unruffled manner and his smiling façade. "Here was a picture of class—class personified," wrote Williams. He called Weiss a champion who never looked more like a champion even in a painful and disheartening hour. "Not that any of us should have been surprised. George Weiss was born a champion."[45]

Porter Wittich of the *Joplin Globe* chastised the Yankees' organization for "firing" both Stengel and Weiss.[46] He noted that Weiss was possibly the most successful baseball man to sit in any front office. "Success apparently means nothing to the Yankee brass who might even fire the bat boy for efficient services—or maybe move him up in the organization like a deserving relative."[47]

Red Smith hailed Weiss as one of the best general managers baseball had ever known and challenged Topping, who wanted to be more involved in day-to-day operations, to be as successful. "But nothing," he wrote, "could be an improvement on the organization he dismantled ... the Yankees had the best. They may not find his equal."[48] Smith noted that the Yankees were never the richest club nor the wildest spenders. "They were a championship organization because men like Ed Barrow and George Weiss did their jobs better than anyone else."[49]

It was not merely the papers that lauded Weiss and indicated that he would be sorely missed. Baseball great Ted Williams insisted, "During Weiss' regime, the Yankees were the most successful team in baseball. His guidance will be missed."[50]

Just in case Topping and Webb didn't get the point, a short time after Weiss made his graceful exit, *The Sporting News* named him "Major League Executive of the Year" for the fourth time in his career, a record number of awards still unmatched today. The paper stated that it was a tribute to Weiss that he was able to take the 1959, third-place Yankees and turn them into still another AL winner. Others added that his acquisition of Roger Maris alone should have won him the award.[51]

In 1961, New York sportswriter Dick Young (right) presented George Weiss *The Sporting News Executive of the Year Award*. The 1960 award marked the fourth time Weiss received the honor, a record that still stands (Steve Steinberg Collection).

At the time Weiss received the award, the Yankees neither lauded nor belittled the honor bestowed on their former general manager. However, a few months later, a sports magazine proposed to Topping and Webb that the award given Weiss in 1960 be mentioned in the Yankees' season-opening ceremonies. The two men brushed off the suggestion, indicating their break with Weiss was final and complete.[52]

On January 1, 1961, George M. Weiss began his retirement from baseball. Although

Weiss was a genius who had built the Yankees' dynasty, few shed any tears when he said his goodbyes. After 29 years with the Yankees, he cleared his desk and departed. Almost nobody said a word, but Weiss had some departing words. He predicted that the Yankees had five more good seasons left.[53] Weiss knew his business. At the end of the predicted five-year period, the Yankees finished a dismal sixth.[54]

13

Back in the Game

Retirement did not sit well with George Weiss even though it gave him more time to be with Hazel and to enjoy the 200-year-old Greenwich estate where they had resided since the early 1950s. The den of the rambling colonial house was a showcase for his huge collection of lovingly gathered baseball memorabilia—World Series rings, autographed baseballs, team photos, Hazel's antiques and even Joe DiMaggio's first signed $100,000 contract.[1]

But Weiss was not a man to relish retirement. He became restless and unhappy. He missed working, he missed some of his baseball associates, and he quickly grew tired of looking through his old baseball scrapbooks, even those from the Newark Bears or "the good old days" as Weiss referred to them. He developed ulcers and became ill. He moped around the house, a man unable to develop any hobby or interest.[2] The patient but spirited Hazel wasn't used to having him around the house all day. As she laughingly complained to their close friend, Red Smith, "I married George for better or worse but not for lunch."[3]

After they left the Yankees, both Casey Stengel and George Weiss received calls inquiring about their interest in remaining active in professional baseball. Stengel had opportunities to manage elsewhere, but he considered none of them compelling. He opted to return to his bank while working on his autobiography. Like Stengel, numerous teams called Weiss, offering him the opportunity to run a ball club, but he decided to wait until spring to make a decision. Weiss was also financially well off, and since he was receiving deferred payments from the Yankees, he felt no urgency to make a commitment.[4] He would continue to "mope" or have an occasional lunch downtown, watching the great changes in major league baseball—changes that would soon bring him out of retirement and to the forefront of a new era in the game he had loved since his youth.

Shortly after the departure of the Dodgers and Giants to the West Coast became official, New York Mayor Robert Wagner appointed a four-member commission to look into the possibilities of acquiring another National League team for the area. The commission included Jim Farley, former Postmaster General and adviser to the late President Franklin Delano Roosevelt; Bernard Gimbel, head of Gimbel's Department Store and representative of the retail industry; and real-estate mogul Clint Blume. Mayor Wagner appointed Bill Shea, a young attorney, prominent Democrat, and minor league promoter known for his organizational skills, to chair the commission. In actuality, Shea pretty much operated on his own.[5]

In 1958, Shea approached three teams—the Cincinnati Reds, the Pittsburgh Pirates, and the Philadelphia Phillies—about the possibility of moving their franchises to New York. He quickly abandoned the idea of luring an existing National League franchise, however, realizing he would be "stealing" a team from another city exactly the way the Giants and Dodgers had been "stolen" from New York.[6]

He began to work instead for expanding the two-league structure of 16 teams, an arrangement locked in place since the American League was formed in 1901. Shea and his new ally, Branch Rickey, now semi-retired as adviser to the Pittsburgh Pirates, worked throughout 1958 to add a third major league to the mix. The two men called their proposed league the Continental League, because it would include cities in Canada.[7] It would contain teams from New York, Minneapolis-St. Paul, and a changing list of six other municipalities. It would differ from the failed Federal League of 1914–1915 because unlike the Federal League, the other two leagues would accept this new league.[8]

But not everybody, especially the management of the New York Yankees, was willing to accept a third league in professional baseball. While Topping, Webb and Weiss welcomed a National League team in New York, they questioned the wisdom of adding a third major league. Weiss argued that there were not enough good ballplayers to stock the present 16 clubs, and he blasted Shea's committee and its recommendations.[9]

Weiss was also perturbed by the proposal that should a Continental League be formed and include a team in New York, the new team would benefit by the construction of a multi-million dollar, municipally owned stadium. The committee that proposed placing New York in the new league planned for the team to play its home games in Flushing Meadows, Queens. The infuriated Weiss charged, "The city won't lift a finger to give us the parking space we need desperately at Yankee Stadium, but it's ready to pour money down the drain to accommodate the Continental League."[10]

Weiss also had to contend with Senator Estes Kevauver (D, Tennessee), chairman of the Senate monopoly subcommittee, who had read with interest of the Yankees' opposition to a third major league. He warned the Yankees that Congress and his investigating subcommittee would watch very

One year after the New York Giants left for San Francisco, Mayor Robert Wagner appointed attorney William Shea to lead a committee to bring an existing franchise to New York. When he was unsuccessful, Shea proposed a third major league, the Continental League, with a team located in New York. The fear of a new rival league forced Major League Baseball to expand, and when the National League was granted two additional teams to begin play in 1962, one was awarded to New York. The team's new stadium was called Shea Stadium (National Baseball Hall of Fame Library, Cooperstown, New York).

closely the attempt to add a third major league to professional baseball. "How the two big leagues conduct themselves toward the newcomer," warned Kefauver, "ought to shed some light on whether organized baseball had achieved monopoly powers."[11]

During 1959, the owners of the existing major league teams laid down a number of exacting conditions the new league would have to meet. Shea was unperturbed as the Continental League formally announced on July 27, 1959, that it would begin play in 1961, and that New York would be home to one of the new teams. Ownership of the new team would include Donald Grant and Mrs. Charles Shipman Payson (nee Joan Whitney).[12] Grant and Mrs. Payson were among the few Giants stockholders to vote against the team's move to San Francisco. Mrs. Payson, who had a lifelong association with sports through her family's Whitney Stables, was especially upset that the move would take away Willie Mays, "her favorite athlete with two legs."[13]

Alarmed by the speed and success of the Continentals, the majors tentatively approached expansion, a concept also favored by the larger minor league teams.[14] In October 1959, the American League proposed adding Minneapolis–St. Paul if the National League would also expand to nine teams by adding New York and interleague play. The National League turned down this offer. Nevertheless, the two leagues discussed and negotiated throughout the winter and spring of 1960, finally voting in July 1960 to expand to ten teams each. The two established leagues then asked the Continentals to abandon their own efforts to form a third league.

Joan Payson, a member of the prominent Whitney family, was the co-founder and majority owner of the New York Mets. She was also the first woman to own a major league team in North America without inheriting it. She served as the team's president from 1968 to 1975 (National Baseball Hall of Fame Library, Cooperstown, New York).

The Continentals agreed for two reasons. First, for the Continental League to become a reality, Congress would have to pass a law repealing baseball's anti-trust status. There was no chance this would happen, and this would certainly end the hopes of a third league. Second, the proponents of the Continental League were certain that to avoid a judicial hearing on the anti-trust issue, the major leagues would agree to offer expansion franchises to four Continental cities and their ownership groups. In August 1960, the Continental League agreed to abandon its fight for a third league and dissolved.[15]

Most students of the game acknowledge that although the Continental League failed, it was one of the key reasons for the great expansion of major league baseball in 1961 and 1962.[16] Los Angeles and Minnesota were granted franchises in the American League for the 1961 season, and Houston and New York would have new teams in the National League beginning with the 1962 season.[17]

The original board of directors of one of the two soon-to-be expansion teams in the National League consisted of at least two of the most prominent members of the Continental League team: M. Donald Grant (Chairman of the Board) and Mrs. Joan Payson (Vice-President). Others in the ownership group included G. Herbert Walker (Executive Vice-President), Mrs. Dorothy Killiam, Dwight Davis, Jr., and William Simpson. Joan Payson became the team's majority stockholder.[18]

With less than a year before the 1962 season, the owners were hard pressed to be ready to field a team, but the first thing they needed was an official name. A newspaper contest brought in thousands of entries with name suggestions. "Mets" was the top choice of 61 voters—more than any other name. It was also the second or third choice of many other voters, and given the many variations on it that had been suggested, 287 people generally liked it.[19] The official announcement that the team's nickname would be the "Mets" was made on May 8, 1961. It was a natural shortening of the corporate name, "New York Metropolitan Baseball Club, Inc."[20]

Mrs. Payson herself preferred a name that was not even on the list—the Meadowlarks. She favored that name especially because the team's new stadium was going up in Flushing Meadows. But it seemed everyone was calling the team "Mets" already. Mrs. Payson acquiesced and later admitted that she liked "Mets." It had a nice ring to it, it was short, it captured the feeling of the town, and it could be written cheaply on the players' uniforms.[21]

Donald Grant, an investment broker by trade, was one of two members of the board of the New York Giants Baseball Team to oppose their move to San Francisco. When the National League expanded to ten teams, Grant became chairman of the board and a minority owner of the New York Mets. He was instrumental in hiring George Weiss as the team president (National Baseball Hall of Fame Library, Cooperstown, New York).

While Mrs. Payson and Grant were dealing with the team name, the New York State Assembly vetoed plans to build a stadium on Long Island for the newly named team. With backing from Mayor Wagner and the powerful Parks Commissioner, Robert Moses, Bill Shea buttonholed every assembly member he could locate. Shea talked, showed plans, and argued for the benefits the new municipal stadium would produce. Two days later, the state legislature reversed itself and approved financing a new stadium for the New York Mets' home park. It was to be called Shea Stadium, and the team would play in the Polo Grounds until it was ready.[22]

At the same time, the owners needed someone to run the day-to-day operations of the team—in other words, a general manager. Since Branch Rickey had been involved with the Continental League, he seemed the natural choice. But he not only wanted to call all the shots, he wanted several million dollars to build the player base, something Mrs. Payson was not about to give him.[23]

Grant now pursued the very best executive he could think of—George Weiss—the man who had made the Yankees into the powerhouse team they had become in the '50s. Now, unbelievably, he was available. The Yanks had cut him loose because he was "too old." Although Grant knew Weiss only slightly, he invited him to lunch. Weiss accepted the invitation, but when Grant offered him the Mets job, Weiss hesitated. Six other teams had already asked him to run their clubs, but he would have had to move from his beloved home in the New York area, and he turned them down. In addition, Weiss reminded Grant he could only collect his "advisory" fee from the Yankees if he did not become general manager of any other baseball team. But the Mets' offer tempted Weiss, and when he discussed it with Hazel, she strongly urged him to accept it. He would be back in baseball, she argued, working and using the skills for which he was noted. Of course, she probably failed to mention that her life would be easier as he would resume his old schedule of being away from home all day.[24]

Weiss flew to Florida for the winter meetings even though he knew the Yankees would probably not use his advice, but old habits are difficult to break. In Florida he met with Grant and Mrs. Payson, and on March 14, 1961, he signed a three-year contract with the Mets with a two-year option. In keeping with his agreement with the Yankees, he was not hired as general manager—he was named president.[25] As he signed his contract with the Mets, Weiss told the press, "I'm delighted at the chance to serve the new club. I wanted to remain active in baseball, and this enables me to stay in New York, where I have my roots."[26]

Weiss accepted his new position with the full approval of Dan Topping, president of the Yankees. Topping's only caveat was that if a "conflict of interests" arose between Weiss and the Yankees, Commissioner Ford Frick would have to make the final decision because Weiss was still receiving salary from the Yankees on a carry-over contract, which had five more years to run.[27]

Topping and Webb had good reason not to oppose Weiss's new position with the Mets. The Yankees had held their spring training in St. Petersburg for many years, but were moving to a new spring training stadium at Fort Lauderdale in 1962. They could not leave their old base without penalty unless another big league team could be found to take over their St. Petersburg site in 1962. Weiss afforded the Yankees' owners a satisfying solution: the Mets could replace the Yankees in St. Petersburg in 1962, while the Yankees would be free to go to Fort Lauderdale before their contract with St. Petersburg had expired.[28]

When asked whether he could, under baseball law, receive an income from two major league clubs, Weiss stated, "I see no reason

George Weiss beams broadly after he is announced as the new President of the New York Mets on March 14, 1961 (Steve Steinberg Collection).

why not as long as one is not dependent on the other and there is no conflict of interest. Actually my income from the Yankees is at a reduced scale and represents deferred compensation. It is money I earned the previous year. That income will be further adjusted now that I am with another club."[29]

Ford Frick ultimately ruled that there was no conflict of interest because his new contract with the New York National League Club specifically provided that if he took another job, the Yankees would not present any matters to him for advice. "Therefore, there cannot be any conflict," stated Frick. Frick further ruled, "During 1961 Weiss cannot act as a general manager with any other major league club, but may accept employment in any other capacity, just so his services will not conflict."[30]

When the Mets hired Weiss, the team technically had a general manager. Charlie Hurth, a Rickey protégé, was left over from the time the Mets were part of the plans for the Continental League. When Weiss made it clear he would do everything a general manager did and more, Hurth was soon superfluous and was gone.[31] Weiss reiterated that he had no intention of serving as Hurth's replacement. He made it clear that he had every legal right to become the Mets' president, quoting from his agreement, "...may accept employment in any office or capacity other than full-time general manager with another baseball club."[32]

Although Weiss had the title of president, it was obvious to most baseball observers that he had been hired to do what general managers did—run the new baseball franchise.[33]

The Sporting News congratulated Weiss on his new undertaking, noting, "no one knows the business and directional end of baseball better than George Weiss.... If Weiss' health holds up, this is the best move the fledgling National League New Yorkers could make."[34]

Since Weiss's appointment was not finalized until March, the new president of the Mets had to move at a "rapid clip." He visited each of the other six National League clubs training in Florida and planned to complete the rounds by visiting the camps in Arizona. He also announced that one of the most pressing needs was to build a farm system—from ten to 20 teams—and began negotiations with three minor league clubs, Mobile in the Class AA Southern Association, Raleigh in the Class B Carolina League, and Lexington in the Class D Western Carolina League.[35]

Weiss then began to build a major league team from scratch. He hired a staff for the Mets' office at 680 5th Avenue that included as traveling secretary Lou Niss, a former editor in Brooklyn and the Continentals' publicity man. He also selected Tom Meany, a long-time baseball writer in New York, to handle publicity. In addition, Weiss named ex-Yankee Gene Mauch team trainer.[36]

One of Weiss's problems was solved when he learned that New York was following through on its promise and building an $18,000,000 stadium in Flushing Meadows, Queens, for the Mets. Ground was officially broken on October 29, 1961. The club signed a 30-year lease to play in the stadium. While waiting for his new ballpark to be completed, Weiss planned that the Mets would play their home games in the Polo Grounds, former home of the New York Giants.[37]

Weiss consulted with Grant about everything they would need to make the old, dilapidated Polo Grounds playable. To handle this enormous task, he recruited James "Big Jim" Thomson, former stadium manager for both the Dodgers and the Yankees.

Thomson knew how to work with the unions and the construction industry, and he knew how to get things done, a necessity if the ballpark was to be ready for the 1962 season in less than ten months.[38]

One of the final, but most important, administrative tasks Weiss completed in 1961 was to assemble the announcers who would be the voices of the Mets on radio and TV. (WOR-TV-Channel 9 in New York had gained the rights to televise Mets games.) Weiss carefully chose three men who could promote the team and the sponsor's products, yet maintain enough objectivity to be credible. Ralph Kiner, the color man, had been an All-Star slugger for the Pittsburgh Pirates; he would not only add a knowledgeable perspective, but he often was quietly available to offer batting advice to the players. Bob Murphy was an experienced broadcaster for both the Red Sox and the Orioles; and Lindsey Nelson, although primarily known as a football announcer, had worked on the broadcast "Game of the Day" and was well educated and well spoken. In addition, Nelson loved colorful sports jackets and ties, perfect for color TV.[39]

From the beginning, Weiss was completely involved with the huge task of finding the best players he could get. Although his minor league system was important, he always believed that the core of a successful team was its scouting system. Weiss needed the best scouting staff he could hire to help him find and evaluate players who would make the Mets a viable competitor. "If you have good scouts," stated Weiss, "you get good players." Therefore, one of his most critical projects was to surround himself with a top scouting crew.[40]

Most scouts were recognizable former players, including Babe Herman, Red Ruffing, Rogers Hornsby, Cookie Lavagetto, Solly Hemus, Johnny Murphy, and Gil McDougald.[41] Murphy, a great relief pitcher for the Yankees, had been with the Boston Red Sox for nearly 20 years. His original title with the Mets was scouting supervisor of the New York-New England area. By 1962 he was the number two man in the Mets organization, and in 1968 he would become the team's general manager.[42]

McDougald, who had played for Weiss for ten years, was assigned to scout the New Jersey area for the Mets, concentrating on high schools and colleges.[43] George Weiss signed hitting star Rogers Hornsby to a scouting contract with a tongue-in-cheek order to "go out and find us a .400 hitter like you were."[44] Hornsby, who was assigned to scout the Chicago area for the Mets, was never one to joke too much. He had experience scouting both leagues, and he predicted the Mets would come up with a team better than Los Angeles and Washington, the two expansion teams in the American League. "We hope to do better than those two teams," said Hornsby. "I can't reveal any names, but when I turn in my reports I indicate which players will be a bigger help to us in the Polo Grounds. That's where we'll start playing our games."[45]

With his scouts' input, Weiss began signing free agents. Most importantly, he closely studied the rosters of the established National League teams. In October 1961, these teams would place players into a pool from which the Mets and the other NL expansion team, the Houston Colt .45s, would draft their rosters.[46] The Mets had scouts like Hornsby in nearly all the major league cities scouting all the established teams. Once their reports were turned in, Weiss would use them to help decide which players were worth taking once the other clubs in the league disclosed which players they were willing to part with.[47]

The Mets still needed a manager, and they wanted him on board prior to the draft. In particular, Weiss wanted Casey Stengel, who had 50 years of baseball experience, was popular with the New York press, and possessed the innate ability to keep himself (and his team) in the limelight.[48] Stengel, however, was independently wealthy and had retired to California; he was not at all sure he wanted to re-enter major league baseball. Throughout the summer of 1961, while Mantle and Maris were fighting it out for the honor of breaking Babe Ruth 's home-run record, Weiss pursued Stengel, even flying to the West Coast twice, but he came away empty each time. The best he could do was to get Stengel to promise "he'd think it over."[49] Not even a call from Donald Grant changed Stengel's mind. Weiss finally got the idea of having Mrs. Payson call Stengel directly, feeling that she would be able to win him over with her grace and charm. Weiss was correct—Stengel could not turn her down, and he also liked the idea of trying to get even with the Yankees. On September 26, 1961, just weeks before the player draft, the Mets officially signed Casey Stengel as their first manager.[50]

Weiss was positive Stengel was the right man to manage the Mets. "Casey is the ideal man to handle the type of team we will inherit," he said. "There are bound to be older men on the way out. You don't expect to get too many budding Mantles in this grab bag. You have to have a fellow they can respect and look up to."[51]

Arthur Daley lauded Weiss's choice of Stengel to guide the Mets. "As talent appraisers, the Weiss-Stengel combination long ago proved its perspicacity. The pair can be expected to choose wisely in the draft of National League players to stock the new Houston and New York clubs in the expanded ten-team league. Weiss, a master trader, will be likely to improve on what the Mets get originally, always striving for what Casey calls 'players which can execute.'"[52]

Weiss rolled out Mets publicity by hosting a press conference to announce Stengel's hiring in the exact hotel, the Savoy Hilton, where the Yankees had forcibly "retired" him the previous year. Ever since that fiasco, the public had considered Stengel, and to some extent, Weiss, martyrs. By reflection, their new team would be perceived as "the good guys"—a factor that should increase the Mets' box office appeal. In addition, Weiss's study of the National League rosters had convinced him that he would be choosing his team from a list of rejects and unproven rookies who would not attract fans for their baseball skills. Stengel, however, would help take the focus off the team and onto his entertaining self.[53]

In June 1961 the National League adopted a "liberalized" plan to provide major league talent for its newest members—the Houston Colt .45s and the New York Mets. The National League had learned much about what not to do from the American League expansion draft held the previous year. During the 1960 season, the junior circuit had frozen the rosters of the existing American League teams, preventing American League owners from shielding promising minor leaguers. There were no similar restrictions in the National League. Management of the National League teams had juggled their rosters to hide the best of the minor leaguers and to ensure that the unprotected players in their minor league clubs were either past their prime, mediocre, injury-prone, or difficult to manage. Knowing Weiss's reputation, the owners who would be competing against him were not about to make it easy for him.[54]

Under the plan, each club had to make available, after the World Series, 15 players from their August 31, 1961, roster. Of these 15 players, seven had to be from the active list and the other eight from each team's major league roster of 40. The two new clubs were each required to take 16 players at $75,000 a player, with the caveat that each established team could lose no more than four. Next the Colts and Mets each had a choice of selecting one player from every club at a price of $50,000. Finally, each established club was required to make available two additional active "premium" players, and from this list the Mets and Colts were each required to select one for $125,000. Under the entire plan, the two new teams, which had each agreed to spend $1.8 million in the draft, were required to select 20 players, but could go as high as 28 if they selected eight $50,000 players. In the end, each existing club could lose a maximum of seven active players.[55]

In 1962, George Weiss hired Casey Stengel again, this time to manage the expansion New York Mets. After 95 games in 1965, Stengel was forced to retire from baseball because of a broken hip. Weiss retired the following year (from the Collections of the St. Louis Mercantile Library at the University of Missouri–St. Louis).

The National League draft process began on October 10, 1961, when the Mets and Colts saw the official list of players the National League had made available and the cost of each one. Weiss, even with his low expectations, was appalled by the lack of talent presented. Nevertheless, with close to $2 million already committed, Weiss had to make up the bulk of the new Mets by selecting from the list. Unlike Houston, which concentrated on the younger players ("the ones who hadn't failed yet," according to Stengel), Weiss went for the veterans, especially those who had been Giants or Dodgers. He wanted players who would bring a "major league" image to the new squad. Weiss also theorized that these National Leaguers would help attract the NL fans that had felt deserted since 1958. "The fans remember players like Gil Hodges, Don Zimmer, Roger Craig, and Gus Bell," Weiss explained to reporters covering the draft. "We have to give them some people they know."[56]

When Weiss was general manager of the Yankees, winning the World Series became a habit, and he attributed his success to using big stars. He reasoned that the New York Mets fans felt the same way and that if they intended to back their team, they at least wanted to see some "big names."[57]

Weiss augmented the veterans with younger players who he felt had at least some potential. He also kept in mind that the Mets' temporary home field, the Polo Grounds, was a hitters' park, so Weiss tended to choose power hitters, even if they were no longer able to run well. In four hours at the Netherland-Hilton Hotel in Cincinnati, the Colts and Mets made their choices.[58]

Weiss's first pick in the draft was San Francisco catcher Hobie Landrith, a left-handed-hitting catcher from the Giants. Landrith was a weak hitter with a propensity for singles. Stengel's explanation for the selection of Landrith was simple—"You've gotta have a catcher, otherwise you'll have a lot of passed balls."[59]

After the selection of Landrith, Weiss began to put together his team piece by piece. His $125,000 selections included pitchers Jay Hook and Bob Miller, infielder Don Zimmer and outfielder Lee Walls.[60] For $75,000 Weiss acquired pitchers Roger Craig, Al Jackson, Craig Anderson and Ray Daviaut. In addition to Landrith, Weiss drafted two other catchers—Chris Cannizzaro from the Cardinals and Clarence "Choo Choo" Coleman from the Philadelphia Phillies. His infielders included Gil Hodges, Ed Bouchee,

Hobie Landrith was a well-traveled second- or third-string catcher, having played for four teams from 1950 to 1962. He is perhaps best known as George Weiss's first pick in the 1962 expansion draft. He played briefly for Weiss, who sent him to the Orioles in June 1962 (courtesy Dwayne Labakas).

Elio Chacon, Felix Mantilla and Sammy Drake. He selected outfielders Gus Bell, Joe Christopher, Bobby Gene Smith, and Johnny DeMerit.[61] He picked Chacon from the Reds because Mrs. Payson was impressed by his play against the Yankees in the 1961 World Series, her one and only remark concerning players during the draft.[62] At the more accommodating price of $50,000, the Mets selected two players: pitcher Sherman Jones and outfielder Jim Hickman.[63]

At the end of the draft, Weiss had spent the Mets' $1.8 million for 22 ballplayers; a collection of players few would dare call an All-Star team. Baseball "mavens" agreed that of the 22 selections, there were only three "name" players—37-year-old Gil Hodges, 33-year-old Gus Bell (whose best years were behind him), and Roger Craig, who was once one of the more formidable starters in the game, but who had suffered a broken shoulder in 1960 and had a mediocre record of 5–6 in 1961.[64]

The combined records of the players acquired were less than impressive or they would not have been made available. The top batter chosen by the Mets was Lee Walls, who had hit .280 in 1961. Don Zimmer hit the most home runs—13; Craig, with a record of 5–6, was the biggest winner among the New York Mets' hurlers. Collectively, the Mets' selections hit 53 home runs and their pitchers as a group had a mark of 13–16.[65] In the end, Weiss managed to acquire two-thirds of the choices he wanted. "We have no alibis," he declared.[66]

Weiss, needing every ounce of his baseball expertise for ferreting out talent, wasted no time in acquiring additional players. Unlike his days with the Yankees, Weiss had little talent to trade, and in almost an embarrassed manner, he approached people who had come to him in years past. Of necessity, he had to be much freer with his checkbook than during his Yankees days. He hoped to acquire enough veteran players to give his new team some semblance of "big leagues." Weiss informed the press that his draft choices were made on ability rather than position.[67]

In Hodges, Craig and Zimmer, the Mets brought a "tint" of Brooklyn familiarity to his club. Soon after the draft, he swapped Lee Walls for another former Dodger, Charlie Neal. Before the end of the year, Weiss got Richie Ashburn from the Cubs for the ubiquitous player-to-be-named-later. He purchased outfielder Frank Thomas from Milwaukee. Finally, to augment his pitching staff, Weiss bought relievers Ken MacKenzie from the Braves and former Dodgers standout Billy Loes from the San Francisco Giants.[68]

Weiss knew he would be criticized for not going for younger players as Houston had done, and he was. He defended his selections by stating that there were not many good players available, young or old, and he felt he had to come up with familiar faces. Even Casey Stengel, who had disagreed with Weiss on a number of occasions, always defended Weiss's role in the expansion draft. "I want to thank all those generous club owners," he said, "for making these fine players available to New York and to my Amazing Mets."[69]

Weiss had enough baseball savvy to realize that it would take years for the Mets to be able to rival the Yankees on the field. He did understand, however, that the city of New York had a large number of National League fans which the Yankees never could capture. Weiss counted on those fans, who were still loyal to the Dodgers and Giants, to transfer that loyalty to the newest National League team in New York—the Mets. He was very much aware that the year after the Giants and Dodgers departed New York for the West Coast, Yankees attendance had dropped from 1,497,134 to 1,428,438. Weiss was sure that these National League fans would support the Mets at the box office. "The latent interest," said Weiss, "in the National League after the Dodgers and Giants left, and the energies and personalities of people like Casey Stengel and Joan Payson, will prove me right."[70]

Weiss soon added a third asset to that list—Shea Stadium. The Mets played their first two years at the Polo Grounds before moving into their new stadium. While the fans waited to watch their new team in their brand new venue, Mets officials announced that the team had sold more season box seats (1,000) for the 1962 season than the 912 seats the old New York Giants had sold in their heyday—the 1952 season following the Giants' come-from-behind pennant win on Bobby Thomson's momentous home run in the third playoff game against the Brooklyn Dodgers.

The Mets created a contest to award $1,000 for the prize-winning emblem for the new club. Cartoonist Ray Gotto, creator of comic-strip character Ozark Ike and numerous *Sporting News* cartoons, won with the prize-winning emblem among the more than 500 submitted. The Mets' emblem showed a baseball depicting the New York City skyline in the background, including a bank, the Woolworth Tower, the Empire State Building and the United Nations. All the buildings were colored former Brooklyn Dodgers blue and the orange-colored "N.Y." was the same as those on the caps of the Giants. The word "Mets," also in orange, ran through the skyline, and the Brooklyn Bridge, in white, ran across the bottom of the skyline.[71]

Despite the Yankees' opinion of anyone over the age of 65, it was obvious that Weiss was still at the top of his game. In less than a year, he had initiated and kept his usual close eye on the myriad of details that would launch his team in 1962. He also had the vision of a Mets team that could equitably compete in the National League and he would soon begin the first steps to achieve that vision. But as 1962 began, his focus and that of almost everyone in the organization was on the Mets' first spring training.

14

The Mets Years

The Mets' first spring training was conducted in the Yankees' former St. Petersburg facility and was familiar territory to Weiss. The facility accommodated the main training camp as well as sufficient room for three farm clubs.[1] Also familiar was the subject of integration. The onset of spring training forced Weiss to confront a problem he had faced while with the Yankees—housing for black players. This problem was far more significant for the Mets, and helped reveal Weiss's updated attitude toward the thorny issue. As Yankees boss, Weiss had been accused of bigotry, while he maintained that he was only carrying out what he perceived to be the wishes of the Yankees' brass and the "higher class" Yankees' fan base. More importantly, Weiss stated that when he was involved with the task of player selection, he wanted only men with superlative talent and the temperament of a "true" Yankee. For many years, Elston Howard was the only black player who met these criteria.

In contrast, for the inaugural New York Mets team, Weiss chose from the draft Sherman Jones, Clarence "Choo Choo" Coleman, Sammy Drake, and Alvin Jackson, and following the draft, he traded a premium-priced player and $100,000 for Charlie Neal. All five were African American. As Mets president, Weiss sought affordable talent with as much fan recognition as possible. As far as he was concerned, these black players met his current criteria.[2]

A number of Florida hotels, including the Sorrento Hotel where the Yankees usually stayed, did not accept blacks as guests. Lou Niss, Weiss's traveling secretary, resourcefully tracked down some former New Yorkers who owned a beautiful beachfront hotel in St. Petersburg Beach. They were eager to accept all the Mets players, a huge improvement over years past, allowing both black and white Mets players to stay together in the upscale Colonial Inn. As pitcher Alvin Jackson, the first black Met who reported for training, told sportswriter Milton Gross, "You don't know how good this is unless you know how bad it used to be. I've been in pro baseball since 1955. I know."[3]

By mid–March 1962, almost exactly one year since Weiss signed on with the Mets, he had created a major league team with working agreements with four minor league clubs: AAA Syracuse (International League); Santa Barbara (Class C); Auburn (Class D); and Quincy (Class D). The Mets even began the exhibition season with a winning record of 2–1.[4] Unfortunately, this trend was not an omen of the future.[5]

As spring training kicked into high gear, it became clear that Weiss needed to improve his pitching staff. He signed former Dodgers ace Clem Labine for the express purpose of late-inning relief, as he continued to search for additional prospects during spring training. Near the end of March, it seemed that Weiss had his five starting pitchers set—former Dodger Roger Craig, former Cardinals Craig Anderson and Bob Miller, former Reds pitcher Jay Hook, and former Pirates hurler, Al Jackson.[6]

Both Weiss and Stengel seemed satisfied that "quality" name players covered the other eight positions. In addition, hitting coach Rogers Hornsby was turning out to be a real asset, helping not only the inexperienced but even coaching the stance of Gil Hodges and encouraging former home run standouts like Frank Thomas and Gus Bell to try to pull more long balls in the hitter-friendly Polo Grounds. Hornsby had been elated to join the Mets, praising both Weiss and Stengel for maintaining baseball's integrity.[7] Even Mrs. Payton's selection, Elio Chacon, was performing well. Many sports writers, however, were less than enthusiastic about the Mets' chances given the makeup of the roster.[8]

Nineteen hundred sixty-two marked the opening of not only the Mets and the Colt .45s, but of major league baseball with 20 teams.[9] The Mets experienced bad luck even before the season began. At their last exhibition match of the spring, "Roadblock" Jones, the scheduled starter for the second game of the season, was lighting a cigarette when a part of the match head hit his right eye, blurring his vision and requiring a patch.[10]

The Mets' scheduled season opener on Monday, April 10, in St. Louis, was rained out, but on Tuesday night, Mets "ace" Roger Craig took the hill. He balked in a run in the first inning. The Mets lost, 11–4, despite a home run by Gil Hodges. Even a ticker tape parade up lower Broadway to the Polo Grounds, where the Mets played their home opener, did not help. The Pirates defeated Weiss's new team by a score of 4–3, and the Mets soon tied a record by losing nine consecutive games to open the season.[11] The sportswriters' negative predictions for the Mets seemed to be prophetic.

Before the end of April, Weiss began "shaking things up" by purchasing catcher Harry Chiti from the Cleveland Indians and pitcher Harry Davis from the Cincinnati Reds. To make room for his recent acquisitions, Weiss released newly acquired free agents, pitcher Clem Labine and catcher Joe Ginsburg. Weiss next dealt outfielder Bobby Gene Smith to the Cubs for still another catcher, Sammy Taylor.[12]

Weiss was not alone in feeling confident that the Mets would turn things around. *The Sporting News* noted that other teams besides the Mets were having poor starts to the 1962 season—namely the Braves and Cubs. The paper editorialized that Weiss certainly realized that it took time to develop a new club, noting, "Within the next few days, other players would become available as clubs reached the cut down date. Weiss will go after some of these players, and the strengthening procedure of the Mets would commence anew."[13]

As *The Sporting News* predicted, Weiss made more roster moves. To prop up the pitching staff, he sent first baseman Jim Marshall to Pittsburgh for colorful left-hander Vinegar Bend Mizell, and traded third baseman Don Zimmer to Cincinnati for third baseman Cliff Cook and southpaw Bob J. Miller.[14] Weiss now had two pitchers named Bob Miller, and he handled the matter of differentiating between the two pitchers by referring to one as Bob "Righty" Miller, the Mets' original pick, and the other as Bob "Lefty" Miller. Fortunately, the left-hander spent a good part of the season with AAA Syracuse.[15]

One of the original 1962 New York Mets, Gil Hodges hit the first home run in the franchise's history. After playing 11 games in 1963, Hodges was traded to the Washington Senators, where he replaced Mickey Vernon as manager. In 1968 he returned to the Mets as their manager, and the following year he led the "Miracle Mets" to the World Championship (courtesy Dwayne Labakas).

The Sporting News may have seen a silver lining in Weiss's trades, but other papers were not convinced that he was heading in the right direction. The *Lima News* maintained that Weiss had overloaded his team with "a lot of old stiffs." The paper argued, "George overlooked the fact that the genuine fans who know baseball would go along with young wheels showing some promise."[16]

Weiss may have acquired mostly veterans from the players' pool, but it did not mean that he was not looking at new talent. And even with his less-than-stellar group of experienced players, just as during the Yankees years, he always tried to mix these veterans with the younger players who showed the most promise and potential. His best new acquisition for the Mets in 1962 was Ed Kranepool, just 17 years old. Weiss had personally scouted and signed him for $90,000, winning him away from a number of interested clubs.[17]

Infielder Rod Kanehl was also a younger player new to the majors. Weiss disagreed with Stengel's plan to bring Kanehl up from AAA Syracuse in 1962, but Kanehl's enthusiasm and "all out abandon on the field" earned the 28-year-old a place on the roster.[18]

Not every trade was outstanding, but one in particular was memorable. In May, Weiss acquired the legendary Marv Throneberry, giving Hobie Landrith to Baltimore in exchange. Throneberry, who had been a good-hitting minor leaguer for the Yankees in the mid–'50s, became the default first baseman when Hodges needed knee surgery. Throneberry's unique brand of ineptitude was frequently cited as a symbol of the team as a whole.[19]

Despite Weiss's many attempts to improve the squad, the "amazing Mets," as they were called derisively, continued to lose in spectacular fashion. The season high spot was a brief climb out of the cellar in May, followed by another losing streak—this one for 17 games—that lasted into June and mired them solidly in tenth place for the rest of the season. The 11-game losing streak following the All-Star break didn't help either. One area where the Mets were not losers was their fan support. By mid–August, the Mets had 50,000 more paid admissions than the 1957 Giants, including both new fans and revived Dodgers and Giants fans. Some had come to see the Mets' opponents, but many were there to support the New Yorkers. Newspaper headlines told it all—"Know Mets will lose, but how; be entertained!"[20]

Chants of "Let's Go Mets" were loud and frequent, and the fans were noted less for their numbers than for their passion and energy. Primarily young and uninhibited, despite the fact that the Mets would generally lose, they optimistically displayed their signs and banners urging their team on to victory.[21] The messages generally were doodled on bed sheets, which regularly appeared below Coogan's Bluff. Such messages as "To err is human, to forgive is a Mets fan" and "We love Throneberry" were regularly seen at the Polo Grounds, as well as one of the most common and simple—"Pray."[22]

When he ran the Yankees, Weiss considered such displays and processions mere nonsense, and he reacted negatively to the fans' actions. He thought banners unbecoming in such a holy place as a ballpark and ordered the guards to remove the banners on the grounds that they obstructed fans' vision. The more Weiss made a fuss about fan behavior, the more the banners appeared at the games. Eventually Weiss acquiesced and instructed the stadium guards to stop the confiscation. As one writer commented, "The era of the banner was upon us."[23] Within a year, the Mets would be holding a Banner Day with the blessing of M. Donald Grant and George Weiss.[24]

The Mets finished the 1962 season in tenth place with the embarrassing record of 40–120, 24 games behind the eighth-place Colt .45s at 64–96.[25] The Mets finished the year with a team batting average of .240, last in the league, but hit 139 home runs, better than four other clubs. The "friendly" fences of the Polo Grounds helped, as 93 of the 139 home runs were hit at home. The team's pitching and defense were horrible. The Mets' ERA of 5.04 was half a run higher than the next worse team, and their fielding average was the lowest in the National League.[26]

The Mets, however, drew 922,530 fans, the second highest total in baseball history for a last-place team.[27] Baseball commentators stridently attacked Weiss's strategy of choosing veterans over youth in order to compete with the Yankees at the gate, and the contrast between the records of the Mets and Houston, the other NL expansion team,

"Marvelous Marv" Throneberry began his major league career playing for George Weiss's New York Yankees in 1955 and again in 1958 and 1959. He ended his career playing for Weiss's Mets in 1962 and 1963. Throneberry is best remembered as the starting first baseman for the 1962 Mets, a team which set the modern record for most losses in a single season with 120 (courtesy Dwayne Labakas).

seemed to prove the critics right.[28] After all the criticism, Weiss, in an unusually candid interview, defended his strategy, explaining why it was the right choice for New York, a city that was no stranger to major league baseball. He concluded, "I had no idea of competing with the Yankees as some have inferred. The main idea was to select good, established National League names, so far as available, who would be familiar to the many National League fans in New York."[29]

But now it was time to begin rebuilding for 1963. Weiss first put his on-field crew in place, rehiring Stengel as manager and coaches Cookie Lavagetto and Solly Hemus.[30] Weiss also continued to build the Mets' minor league farm system. Syracuse had decided to partner with another team, but Weiss soon lined up a working agreement with Buffalo, also in the AAA International League.[31] At the end of 1962, the Mets organization included four clubs, in addition to Buffalo: the Santa Barbara Rancheros, Quincy Jets, Auburn Mets and Salisbury Braves.[32]

Weiss was determined to overhaul the Mets, and he spent virtually the entire fall and winter buying, selling and trading players. For the 1963 season, Weiss offered to trade some of his name players, usually trying to obtain two or three promising younger players in return.[33] He also participated in a minor league draft, which he had shunned when with the Yankees, and in the inter-league trading period, which he had originally opposed. In addition, the Mets president still had an amply stuffed wallet, courtesy of Mrs. Payson. He obtained six players from the minors, including a second baseman from the Texas League, Ron Hunt. Hunt would become a Stengel favorite and would be with the Mets for a number of years.[34] Weiss also obtained pitcher Galen Cisco and catcher Norman Sherry from the Dodgers, and sent Felix Mantilla to the Red Sox in return for pitcher Tracy Stallard and infielders Al Moran and Pumpsie Green, the first black player to don a Red Sox uniform.[35]

From the beginning, the Mets and the city of New York had planned on the new stadium being ready for the 1963 season. Throughout 1962, all reports of progress on the stadium indicated that the timetable for the new field was being met.[36] Whether it was the opportunity to be among the first spectators in the new stadium or merely the general enthusiasm of a young fan base for a new team, 1963 season ticket orders were huge. Virtually all box seats were renewed, and new orders and letters of support kept coming in.[37] This was amazing since it became clear as the 1962 season ended that the new Mets stadium would not be ready until August 1963.[38]

As the 1963 season approached, Weiss, as usual, became busy with contracts, but with the Mets, he did not have to negotiate with "stars." Although other clubs were eager to sound out some of the Mets' better players, especially pitchers Craig and Jackson, Weiss was confident he would be able to sign those he wanted. He felt he had made huge strides in putting together a "new" Mets team, pointing out that at the beginning of 1963, 25 of the 40 players on the Mets' reserve list had not been on the club the previous spring.[39] Furthermore, he asserted that the 1963 Mets were the speedsters that Stengel liked, for the average age of the club was only 26.[40]

Among the few players who did hold out was Marv Throneberry. Although four other first basemen were competing for his position, Throneberry knew he had the support of the "New Breed"—the large group of feverishly devoted Mets fans. In fact, he emphasized to Johnny Murphy, Weiss's assistant, that he had been presented the "Good Guy" award at a recent New York baseball writers' dinner. Neither Murphy nor Weiss was impressed. "We've offered a slight raise," responded Weiss, "but Throneberry must think his Good Guy prize is equivalent to a Most Valuable Player Award."[41] Throneberry eventually settled for a $2,000 raise, but early in the season he was sent to the minors and never came back.[42]

While Weiss had long claimed he was no longer interested in signing "big name" players ("We had a lot of big names last year and we didn't win"),[43] all winter there were rumors that he had half-heartedly attempted to purchase Duke Snider, the great Dodgers favorite. When these rumors became public, they generated a deluge of fan mail all urging Weiss to bring back "the Dook of Flatbush." Weiss's immediate reaction to these demands was, "It seems to me you're making a big fuss over an old ball player."[44] However,

Weiss began to warm to the idea that a combination of Snider and Gil Hodges on the Mets would be a great attraction and would add to a team that badly needed power. Weiss purchased Snider, who was running a bowling alley in California at the time, for $40,000. Snider considered his sale to the lowly Mets the ultimate humiliation.[45]

Despite all of Weiss's player changes, baseball pundits predicted another tenth-place finish for the Mets.[46] The 1963 season began like a replay of 1962 although this year they lost only their first eight games before notching their first win. In the next week they stunned the baseball world by sweeping four games from the Milwaukee Braves and two from the Chicago Cubs.[47] Finally Weiss was given credit for building up his team—examples: Al Moran, Weiss's throw-in in the Stallard and Green deal with the Boston Red Sox, was praised; also the pitching staff was doing well. Primarily a lack of hitting caused a number of losing streaks—one for 15 games, a record-setter of 22 consecutive road games, and 18 consecutive losses for "ace" pitcher, Roger Craig.[48]

With a record of 51–111, the team won 11 more games and lost nine fewer than the previous year, but finished the 1963 season firmly entrenched in tenth place. The amazing part of the year was that the attendance rose past the one million mark.[49] Another bright spot was the pitching of Carl Willey, obtained from Milwaukee in May. Although his record in 1963 was 9–14, he pitched four shutouts and finished the year with a creditable 3.14 E.R.A. Unfortunately he broke his jaw the following spring and never was the same.[50] Finally, Ron Hunt finished second only to Pete Rose in the voting for the 1963 "Rookie of the Year" Award. The following year he would be the only Met elected to a starting berth in the All-Star Game.[51]

In addition to his team woes, Weiss was forced to deal with happenings off the field. The New Breed, the Mets' young, loud, banner-making fans, was perceived as uncontrollable and rowdy. They were pelting opposing team players with rubbish, beer and cans. They spat on players as they passed through the dressing room doors in deep center field during the games. League President Warren Giles stated, "We do not intend to stifle fan enthusiasm, but visiting players and the home team's players, too, are entitled to the protection of this office."[52]

Another note of disappointment was the stadium situation. As late as May 1963, Weiss had expressed confidence that it would open in early August, although it wouldn't be completely finished.[53] But the date was not met and the Mets finished the season in the Polo Grounds, now believing that the team would be in its new home beginning with the first pitch of the 1964 season.[54]

Meanwhile, Houston general manager Paul Richards, whose team had finished eighth and ninth respectively in its first two major league seasons, demanded help from other National League executives to make up for the poor quality of the expansion draft. Weiss joined the effort, emphasizing increased revenues for the other National League teams playing against stronger clubs. Surprisingly, the NL owners responded positively to Richards' request, and after much discussion and negotiation, the owners agreed to set up a pool of 32 players—four from each established team. The Mets and the Colts could purchase one player from each team for the set price of $30,000 each, but unlike 1961, they were not required to buy any if they didn't find any they wanted.[55]

Before the draft began, Weiss commented, "We didn't expect much." And that was what he found in the National League plan. The Mets selected Bill Haas, a 20-year-old rookie with no major league experience who never made it to the majors, and right-handed relief pitcher Jack Fisher from the Giants, who had numerous arm and weight problems but stayed with the Mets from 1964 to 1967.[56]

With little fanfare, Weiss rehired Stengel as his field manager of what some reporters were now calling the "miserable Mets." Although Weiss kept Stengel, he swept out the old coaching staff of Hemus, Lavagetto, and Ernie White, who would remain in the Mets' organization. The new group Weiss hired included Mel Harder, a former Cleveland Indians coach, as the Mets pitching coach, and Wes Westrum, former catcher and coach with the Giants.[57]

Of course, Weiss worked to fill positions on his wish list: more hitting and, as always, pitching. Weiss stated, "We'll trade anybody, assuming we can get value in return."[58] Living up to his promise, he dealt starting pitcher Roger Craig to the St. Louis Cardinals for outfielder/slugger George Altman. He also got a "throw-in," 22-year-old pitcher Bill Wakefield, continuing Weiss's old pattern of the additional player that he could possibly use in future dealing. (It didn't work out in Wakefield's case.)[59]

Spring training for 1964 introduced a practice that Weiss and Stengel had used with great success with the Yankees: an early instructional camp designed for young players not quite ready for the major league team but whose development could be accelerated. "After two years," said Weiss, "we have enough players including promising young ball players to make an early camp worthwhile."[60] Stengel had pushed for the camps two years earlier, but Weiss wanted to ensure that there were enough high-quality candidates before he agreed. The Mets invited 34 players to the "rookie camp," including Ron Swoboda, Derrell "Bud" Harrelson, Cleon Jones and Ed Kranepool, all of whom would distinguish themselves as part of the 1969 World Champion Mets. Weiss again emphasized the youth movement of the team by calling attention to the Mets' average age: 25 in 1964, as compared with 26 the previous year and 29 in 1962 when the roster was heavy with draft picks. These numbers were boosted by Weiss getting rid of older players, even Duke Snider. Snider had been asking to be traded and Weiss obliged, selling him to San Francisco right before the opening of the season.[61]

While Stengel worked to prepare the team for what would hopefully be a higher finish this year, landscapers, concessionaires and other contractors were moving at feverish speed to prepare for the timely opening of the $20 million ballpark named Shea Stadium.[62] The new stadium, located near just one subway line, but with 20,000 parking spots and no bleachers, was providing Weiss and the Mets not only a better place to play, but also an opportunity to attract the huge middle-class pool of residents immediately to the east on Long Island.[63]

The stadium's seating capacity was 55,300 for baseball and 60,000 for the New York Jets football team. The Mets were the principal tenants, a fact that greatly concerned the Jets in later years. By the terms of the lease, the Jets could not utilize the stadium while the Mets were still playing baseball. In 1969 and in 1973, when the Mets were involved in the World Series, the Jets, much to their chagrin, were forced to play some of their home games on the road.[64]

Remarkably, advance sales for the twice-tenth-place Mets were rising, thanks in part to the fans who had sustained their enthusiasm despite a little disillusionment, but also because of the all-out promotional work of Weiss and his staff. In huge demand for local meetings was a 27-minute film titled "Let's Go, Mets." Groups vied with each other to get as a speaker one of five player-spokesmen trained by the team. Behind the scenes, Weiss began using current employee Jim Murray, a veteran promoter for the Dodgers, to organize social and other groups, particularly on Long Island. In addition, Betty King, Weiss's long-time secretary with the Yankees, was now involved with promotions, concentrating on women's groups for whom she organized lunches and dinners when they attended games. Furthermore, Weiss began to court the press, many of whom were young and sometimes as enthusiastic as the fans.[65]

The new, luxurious stadium itself was a drawing card, as was the proximity of the 1964 World's Fair where Weiss, working with *The Sporting News* and Baseball's Hall of Fame, had built a display to baseball. Baseball observers universally predicted that the Mets in 1964 would outdraw the World Champion Yankees at the box office, even if they couldn't beat many other teams on the field.[66]

On April 17, 1964, Mr. Met, whose image debuted in 1963, became Major League Baseball's first live-action mascot. On Opening Day 2000, he also became the first Major League mascot to entertain fans overseas as the Mets played their first regular season game in Japan's Tokyo Dome. Still active at Citi Field, Mr. Met is a member of the Mascot Hall of Fame.[67]

The Mets started the 1964 season on the road and, as always, lost the first game, but the opening losing streak this year was a mere four games. On April 17, 1964, the Mets played their first home game in beautiful Shea Stadium before 50,000 enthusiastic fans who were not discouraged by the strangling traffic jam around the park or the loss that day. Even the continued losses often involved interesting baseball. In a Sunday doubleheader on May 31 against the Giants before a crowd of more than 57,000 fans, the Mets lost the first game, 5–3, to Juan Marichal.

In the second game, the Giants took an early 6–1 lead, but the Mets fought back to tie the game 6–6 in the seventh inning. That was still the score after 22 innings. At one stage in the game, Willie Mays played shortstop before going back to center field. Jim Davenport triggered the winning rally in the 23rd inning by tripling off Mets hurler Galen Cisco with two out. After an intentional pass, Del Crandall pinch-hit for pitcher Gaylord Perry and hit a ground-rule double to break the tie. Jay Alou's infield single brought in another run. The game finally ended when Giants relief pitcher Bob Hendley retired all three Mets he faced.[68]

There were some surprises in June also. On Father's Day, June 21, Philadelphia hurler Jim Bunning threw a perfect game, only the eighth perfect game in history, in the first game of a doubleheader.[69]

The games might have been interesting but the Mets continued to lose. Players came and other players went. Frank Thomas was traded to the Phillies. Frank Lary was purchased from the Tigers, pitched 13 games and was shipped to the Braves. In May, Weiss traded pitcher Jay Hook, minor league outfielder Adrian Garrett and $65,000 to Milwaukee for shortstop Roy McMillan, who was the regular Mets shortstop for 1964 and half of 1965 before his protégée, Bud Harrelson, became the everyday Mets shortstop. Perhaps his best trade was late in the year when Weiss traded a player to be named later (pitcher Tom Parsons) and cash to Houston for catcher Jerry Grote, who became one of baseball's best catchers over the next ten years.[70]

The Mets' long-suffering fans were more disappointed and less charmed than in previous years. Many wondered if Stengel was to blame for the team's failure on the field, but he still had Weiss's confidence and was rehired for 1965.[71] At the same time, Weiss knew he had to give these fans a better team. He began with a shakeup of corporate management and brought in some expert help. The Cardinals, despite winning the 1964 World Series, had fired Bing Devine, the general manager. Although he was the man most responsible for the talented team, he was dismissed because of a disagreement with owner Gussie Busch.[72] Weiss lost no time in hiring Devine as his special assistant.[73] Weiss also named former Cardinals farm system boss Eddie Stanky Director of Mets Player Development, a job for which he was well suited.[74]

The Cardinals weren't the only team to make management moves after the World Series. After the Cardinals defeated the Yankees in the 1964 World Series, Yankees manager Yogi Berra was quickly fired. Weiss persuaded him to sign on as a player-coach who would also function as an aide to Casey Stengel.[75] Weiss personally signed another player-coach, veteran southpaw Warren Spahn. During salary negotiations, the 44-year-old Spahn supposedly promised to win 20 games if used as a Mets starter.[76]

Weiss also had the pleasure of seeing his strategy of developing the younger players beginning to work. As the 1965 spring training season began, 47 players with an average age of 24 reported to St. Petersburg; only four were with the original Mets of 1962—Chris Cannizzaro, Joe Christopher, Jim Hickman and Al Jackson.[77] In the minors during the winter of 1964–1965 were Ron Swoboda, Dick Selma, Frank "Tug" McGraw, Kevin Collins, and someone who had not yet thrown a ball professionally. He was in the army at Fort Bliss, Texas. His name was Jerry Koosman.[78] Many of these players were there because of the acuity of Weiss's scouts and a gem found in their own organization, Joe McDonald, who had acted as statistician for the broadcasters and then moved into the front office. He was indispensable in the minor league department and worked very closely with Bing Devine.[79]

By the time the 1965 season opened, some of these young players had moved up to the parent club and even appeared in the starting lineup, helping to make the Mets' Opening Day roster the youngest in the majors.[80]

Beyond all reason, but happily for Weiss and the Mets, the fans kept pouring through the gates, hoping for and getting entertaining games and even occasional wins. The young players contributed. After the Mets began the season with their traditional loser, in only the third game, 19-year-old reliever Jim Bethke got the first win of the season by beating the Astros in Shea Stadium. On June 14, both the Reds and the Mets pitchers held the opposition scoreless through the first 10 innings. In fact, Reds hurler Jim Maloney had a no-hitter until the top of the 11th when Mets outfielder Johnny Lewis homered for a 1–0 win. Unfortunately, it was the only Met victory during a 16-game stretch.[81]

Once again, Stengel was the brunt of most of the criticism and many began to call for his resignation. Both he and Weiss, however, stood firm.[82] On May 10, 1965, just about the time the Mets fell back into their familiar tenth-place spot again, Stengel slipped at an exhibition game at West Point and broke his wrist. With his arm in a sling, he managed the game the following night.[83]

Rumors that Stengel would retire at the end of the season were rampant, but Stengel firmly stressed that when he made a decision, he would talk with his long-time supporter, Weiss, first.[84] Almost going unnoticed amongst the discussion of Stengel's managerial status was the announcement that the Mets had decided to release their 44-year-old southpaw, Warren Spahn. Spahn had won only four games and lost 12 for the 1965 Mets. Spahn's salary was $75,000, and Weiss emphasized to the press, "This was not a move born of economy. It was Casey's decision to make. I hope he catches on with another club."[85] As a matter of fact, the San Francisco Giants signed Spahn once he was released, and he had a 3–4 record for the Giants. He retired at the end of the 1965 season with a career record of 363–245.[86]

The question of Stengel's retirement became a moot point on July 25, five days prior to his 75th birthday. There are a number of accounts of the events that follow, but the version given here is from Stengel's official biographer. Sometime after midnight after celebrating at an old-timers party at Toots Shor's restaurant, Stengel lost his balance, fell and hurt his left hip. The club's comptroller, Joseph DiGregorio, decided to take Casey to stay at his house, just a short drive from Shea Stadium, rather than to Stengel's hotel. X-rays taken the next day confirmed a broken hip and an artificial hip joint was installed. Weiss went along with Stengel's selection of Wes Westrum as temporary manager pending his return.[87] Five weeks later, Weiss arranged a news conference where Stengel announced that he was retiring effective the end of the season. There was none of the bitterness that accompanied his leaving the Yankees five years earlier.[88]

No sooner had Stengel made his resignation official than the sports pundits began asking Weiss if he was also leaving. Approximately five weeks later, during a press conference at Shea Stadium, Weiss, who had resisted sharing duties with Devine, announced that 1966 would be his last year as President of the Mets. He added that he would move into an "advisory capacity through 1971."[89] The Mets claimed that they would not name a successor until Weiss left, but according to the team, Bing Devine "will move into the home office to work more closely with Mr. Weiss."[90]

Now it was up to Weiss, along with the owners, to decide on a permanent successor to Stengel to manage the club during Weiss's final year. A number of names were mentioned, including Westrum, Stanky, Berra, and Hodges.[91] Under Stengel and Westrum, the Mets had finished 1965 with a record of 50–112, slightly worse than in 1964.[92] Although the team actually had a lower winning percentage during Westrum's weeks, Weiss and Grant chose him to manage for 1966, signing him to a one-year contract on November 11, 1965.[93]

Determined to field a team that would not finish tenth again, Weiss began dealing. In October he picked up former MVP Ken Boyer from the Cardinals, giving the Redbirds third baseman Charlie Smith and pitcher Al Jackson, the Mets' winningest pitcher.[94] Still looking for a better fielding and hitting shortstop, the following month Weiss traded Joe Christopher to the Red Sox for Ed Bressoud, an original member of the renamed Houston Astros.[95]

To help discover new players, Weiss, along with Devine and Westrum, relied on their staff of 20 full-time scouts.[96] One of the best new players, pitcher Tom Seaver, was discovered by scout Nelson Burbrink, who encouraged the Mets to try for the highly valued hurler. The Braves had signed him, but lost him by violating signing rules, and the Indians and Phillies also wanted to acquire the USC right-hander. The short-termed

Commissioner, William Eckert, put the three team names in a hat, drew one, and awarded Seaver to the Mets. He was Weiss's last significant young acquisition, but one critical to the club for many years to come.[97]

Together with the veterans, one of the youngest pitching staffs in the National League and great optimism, the Mets began 1966 spring training. The media predicted another last-place finish.[98] The Mets won their second and third games of the season, the first time the team was over .500. But Weiss was going all-out to give Westrum the tools to keep the team out of the cellar. In June Weiss acquired Giants pitcher Bob Shaw, who was unpopular in San Francisco. Shaw won his first four starts for the Mets.[99] Cleon Jones, much improved since 1963, also played a big part. One teammate felt that the dental work Weiss had the team pay for made the difference in Jones' attitude and performance.[100] In addition, Weiss gave Westrum's player development program his complete support, and it was felt that this helped make the team respectable.[101]

In 1966 the Mets were never in tenth place during the season. They finished ninth with a record of 66–95, losing fewer than 100 games for the first time in their existence and in Weiss's final season as Mets president.[102] With more than 1.9 million spectators for the year, the Mets were hailed as "the most prosperous National League team New York has ever seen." Grant, as chairman of the Mets board, presided at a ceremony in Shea Stadium where Westrum was formally rehired for the 1967 season. There, Weiss proclaimed that the team would soon finish in the first division.[103] Perhaps to Weiss, as satisfying as the Mets' accomplishments were, was the realization of an earlier forecast. The five good years he predicted for the New York Yankees in 1960 were over. The once indestructible Yankees finished tenth in the American League in 1966. Moreover, their attendance slipped to the lowest in 21 years, some 800,000 fans below the Mets.[104]

On November 14, 1966, as he had promised one year earlier, 72-year-old George Weiss stepped to the podium and, with uncharacteristic public emotion, resigned as President of the New York Mets, ending more than 50 years of one of the most successful careers in baseball history.[105]

15

Final Innings

On Monday, November 14, 1966, on behalf of George Weiss, the Public Relations Department of the New York Mets issued the following statement: "As provided in my contract I am exercising my right to retire from the Mets in an executive capacity. This has already been extended one year beyond my original executive term. I plan to continue in an advisory capacity until December 31, 1971, and I have been asked to remain as a Director of the Club which I am pleased to accept with my thanks and sincere good wishes for the future."[1]

The Mets accepted Weiss's retirement and thanked him for his work as the team's president. They noted that his executive career spanned nearly half a century, dating back to 1917, when, as a resourceful high school senior, he organized the New Haven Colonials semi-pro club.[2]

With his brief statement, Weiss retired for a second time, but this time he added, "This culminates a lifetime of the happiest kind of work I could ever indulge in. This time I go out with the right kind of taste in my mouth."[3] If this statement was a criticism of how the Yankees had let him go, it would mark the first time Weiss had shown any bitterness towards his former team, for in his heart he had always remained a Yankee. As the reporters nodded their agreement, Weiss continued, "I would have to say that the thing I am most proud of was hiring Casey Stengel twice."

Despite Weiss's praise for the Yankees, the Mets' owners had been very considerate of Weiss. They had kept his chosen successor Bing Devine, waiting an extra year to allow Weiss to leave on his own schedule.[4] Furthermore, the Mets announced that Weiss's policies, strategies, and outlook would continue unchanged. Weiss, with five percent ownership but no power, was to serve on the Mets' Board until 1971. Although Devine had stated that he would seek Weiss's advice, he began running the organization as he saw fit.[5]

Mrs. Payson and the Mets continued to show their appreciation of Weiss. In April 1967, at one of the poshest locations in Clearwater, Florida, they gave a surprise party honoring Weiss for all of his contributions. Mrs. Payson's words were inspiring and poignant. "It's been a wonderful time, George. I'm not discouraged and I've never been disappointed. I've never had so much fun in my life with anything, ever," she said.[6] In response to her words and tributes from others, Weiss, who for the most part of his career avoided delivering unprepared remarks, said with perhaps some truth, "I'll probably never again have the opportunity to speak."[7]

And the honors continued. In July of 1967, the Mets continued a tradition that Weiss had initiated back in the minor leagues—Old-Timers Day. To recognize Weiss, the Mets not only invited members of the original 1962 team, Weiss's first Mets club, they also invited members of the 1960 Yankees, Weiss's last Yankees team. Despite Weiss's alleged coldness toward players, other Yankees greats thought enough of him to come, too. Many, including DiMaggio, Berra, Allie Reynolds, Tommy Henrich, and Frank Shea, attended and participated in a two-inning game. At a party following the game, most of the guests stayed until 4 a.m., talking and reminiscing with their former general manager.[8]

At the end of 1967, frustrated partly by how strong Weiss's influence remained, Bing Devine left the New York Mets. When the Mets hired Gil Hodges away from the Washington Senators as manager in October, supposedly despite the protest of Devine, those close to him realized that his days were numbered in New York. Devine resigned his post as Mets general manager, and two days later, the St. Louis Cardinals re-hired him as their general manager to succeed Stan Musial.[9]

To replace Devine, the Mets appointed vice-president Johnny Murphy, former Yankees pitcher, as interim general manager. Murphy had been instrumental in the acquisition of Gil Hodges as the team's new manager. While the Mets contemplated the choice of a permanent GM, Weiss, who at the age of 73 was not yet prepared for a life of permanent retirement, indicated that he would give any assistance that management required. Don Grant, Chairman of the Board, however, indicated that Weiss's offer was appreciated but wasn't needed, and he quickly announced that Murphy would fill the GM post on a permanent basis.[10]

For the next few years, George and Hazel enjoyed their smaller home in Greenwich, where they had moved in 1966. Like their former 200-year-old colonial, it contained two rooms full of mementos from George's many years in baseball. From there, Weiss drove to Shea Stadium once or twice a week to answer letters and calls.[11] He made it a point to visit the team during spring training, but in 1968, Weiss again suffered an ulcer attack and was hospitalized in Mound Park Hospital in Tampa.[12]

The year 1969 was a momentous one for Weiss personally, as well as for the Mets and major league baseball. George Weiss, "74 and mentally as spry as ever," marked 50 years in organized baseball on May 14, 1969.[13] He quietly observed this milestone by watching the Mets play the Braves.[14] And as almost any baseball fan knows, 1969 was the year the Mets, cellar dwellers for five of their first seven seasons in existence, not only won the National League pennant, but became World Champions by defeating the heavily favored Baltimore Orioles four games to one in the World Series.[15]

Weiss could take special pride in the huge win for the previously unheralded team because sports pundits credited him with developing most of the players on the 1969 squad. Many of them had come up through the small farm system he created. His acquisitions included Tom Seaver, Jerry Koosman, Nolan Ryan, Tug McGraw, Cleon Jones, Ed Kranepool, and Bud Harrelson.[16]

For a man whose entire life had been tied to baseball, the highest accolade the game could pay was his election to Baseball's Hall of Fame. No players of the modern era received enough votes from the Baseball Writers' Association of America following the 1970 season, but on Sunday, January 31, 1971, the 12-member Veterans Committee unanimously elevated two men—legendary hurler Rube Marquard, who held the record of 19 consecutive victories in a single season, and legendary executive genius George M. Weiss.[17] Also named were Chick Hafey, Harry Hooper, Joe Kelley, Jake Beckley, and Dave Bancroft.[18]

Upon hearing of his selection, the elated Weiss called Hazel to inform her of the good news. "We're in! We're in!" he said excitedly to his wife. "In what?" she asked him. "More trouble?"[19]

While some baseball writers were lukewarm about endorsing the selections of the six former players, all were enthusiastic about Weiss deserving the recognition for his achievements and his contributions to the game. Sportswriter Ed Nichols wrote, "He's one of the most intelligent baseball men I've known. Our first acquaintance with him was back in the Eastern Shore League days when the New York Yankees operated a farm club in Easton."[20] Columnist Arthur Daley wrote, "No one has labeled the newly elected members of baseball's Hall of Fame as representing a vintage crop.... There is one, however, so good as to match the crop of any year. It is the naming of George Weiss, long the front office manipulator for the Yankees and later for the Mets. He pulls up the entire average and gives it a loftier rank than it deserves."[21]

Columnist Red Smith noted that Weiss had given 51 years to the game and he ought to feel at home in the Hall of Fame. "Practically everybody there is a friend of his, and not only Yankees. Ty Cobb, for example, who was always ready to play exhibitions for his friend in New Haven unless George had Cannonball Redding pitching for the other side. Walter Johnson? It was on a double date with his pal Walter that George met Hazel, the lady he married."[22]

Although he did not look forward to public speaking, Weiss was eagerly anticipating the ceremony on August 9, 1971, when he would take his place among so many whose careers he had touched during his long tenure in the game.

But in May, George Weiss suffered a paralyzing stroke and had to move into a nursing home in Greenwich, Connecticut. Art Richman, who worked with Weiss as Mets Director of Promotions and who had become a close friend, reminisced that he would often visit Weiss in the nursing home. "He was the kindest, most gracious man I ever worked for," Richman stated, a view shared by those who knew him best.[23]

It soon became clear that Weiss would not be able to travel to Cooperstown to attend the Hall of Fame induction in August. Nonetheless, he wrote his acceptance speech and, with great regret, asked his friend Ford Frick to represent him. Frick began his remarks with his own feelings that George Weiss "contributed as much to baseball as any man the game could ever know." Frick then read a message that Weiss had dictated to him. "Being inducted today is the pinnacle of my dreams, particularly for one who never possessed the ability on the field." Weiss's message went on to recognize his family, who "enjoyed and suffered with me, through a lifetime to this day, which is to me a holy moment in my religion of Baseball." Weiss's speech closed by stating, "It is probably the greatest disappointment of my life that I cannot be with you good people today who have demonstrated by your presence, your love for our great game."[24] Weiss became only the third general manager inducted into Baseball's Hall of Fame."[25]

George Martin Weiss declined slowly and died on August 13, 1972, at the age of 78, in the nursing home. His widow Hazel, her son, John Wood, and three grandsons who always referred to Weiss as "Grandpa George," survived him.[26] Hazel died seven years after George on July 27, 1979.[27]

Art Richman and Yankees sportscaster Mel Allen were among the few invited to Weiss's private funeral. Also at his funeral was the current owner of the New York Yankees, Mike Burke, who said, "George Weiss inherited a legacy of Yankee greatness from Mr. Barrow and sustained it throughout his own uniquely distinguished Yankee career. In recent years we have been striving to regain the level of excellence Weiss set. We could pay him no more appropriate homage than to do so."[28] Former manager Joe McCarthy praised Weiss as a great executive and stated, "He came up through baseball the hard way and through the minor leagues. He understood the game thoroughly."[29] Later on the Sunday that Weiss died, the sellout crowd at Yankee Stadium stood with heads bowed for a moment of silence in his memory.[30]

Weiss's employees also spoke about his kindness and how his shyness often made him seem cold and standoffish, especially with people he didn't know and the press. Nonetheless, his death drew comments from sports writers and baseball observers from all over. Because of his hard-nosed bargaining, particularly with Yankees players, his penny-pinching over small matters, and his insensitivity at times, some of his critics and enemies called him not only miserly but also mean and vindictive.[31]

Gabe Paul, who became a Yankees executive the year following Weiss's passing, recalled what he had said of Weiss back in 1959: "Here is a humble, self-effacing man, who keeps himself more or less in the background. But he runs one of the most efficient organizations that professional baseball ever has known. George Weiss will go down in baseball history as one of the truly great general managers."[32]

It was undoubtedly true that like most of his contemporaries, Weiss kept down players' salaries, pocketing under-budget amounts, and some players never forgave him for not paying them what they thought they deserved. Mickey Mantle related that in 1957 he hit .365, "and they tried to get me to take a $10k cut. They said I don't have as good a year as before because I only hit 34 homers. That Weiss, boy, mean."[33]

Others, even some who had tough fights with him over contracts, saw past the disagreements to the man. Bob Cerv expressed both points of view, recalling that at contract time, the team would have at the table everyone from an attorney to the team president. "And there you sat by yourself," he said. "But I always say the Yankees were a great team as long as George Weiss was there. He was one of the best, if not the best general managers ever." As far as the 1969 Mets, Cerv explained their success easily. "Hell, they were just good ball players. Weiss could always spot a good ball player."[34]

Bobby Brown, who played for the Yankees from 1946 to 1952, and again in 1954, stated that Weiss never felt it necessary to be friends with his players, and was not known as a man who "chatted" with them. "He was not the easiest person to deal with," admitted Brown, "and few on the team felt he was their good friend." But Brown was emphatic in crediting Weiss with the Yankees' success.[35]

Jerry Coleman, Brown's teammate for three years and a Yankees infielder for nine seasons, acknowledged that Weiss was known to be "cheap" when it came to paying his players. Coleman praised Weiss, though, for his ability to hire the right people and to run a first-class organization. He called Weiss a shrewd executive who realized that money and personnel were the keys to success. "But Weiss as general manager always had the final word," said Coleman.[36]

Yogi Berra, who played for Weiss from 1946 until Weiss left the Yankees, indicated that Weiss was "tough." "I don't think anyone liked negotiating with him. But he was a smart man who understood the value of good scouts. He always did his homework on players. He was a smart, shrewd baseball man who was very well organized and detailed."[37] Berra once admitted that he liked Weiss a lot and that Weiss and Hazel were both good friends of his. He added, "I doubt you'll find any public record of anyone else saying they personally liked George Weiss."[38]

The flip side of Weiss's contract strategy was to treat his players like family. He would make sure the best doctors were there for any player or his family member who was ill, and he arranged loans for those who needed them. Bob Fishel, Yankees VP and PR man, stated, "The list of wonderful things he did for people that nobody will ever hear about could fill a book."[39] His critics called this paternalistic system a way to keep players grateful despite their low pay, while his supporters maintained this demonstrated that he cared.[40]

But when it came to baseball acumen, Weiss was almost universally acknowledged and praised. Unable to find every talented player he could personally, Weiss developed excellent and extensive networks of scouts for both the Yankees and the Mets. Yogi Berra, a product of the farm system, admitted, "He built both the Yankees and the Mets farm system."[41] These farm systems developed hundreds of excellent players that supplied Yankees for years and that were now making the Mets more than respectable.

Of course, not every player was home-grown, and that was where George Weiss's extraordinary trading skill came in. He dealt with any organization that had players he could use and that would negotiate with him, often obtaining not only players he wanted, but also others he could use in future trades. Frank Lane, Milwaukee Brewers general manager, knew Weiss for most of his 50 years in baseball. Lane, known as one of the most active traders in the game, was asked how many deals he had made with Weiss over the years. "I never made a single deal with Weiss," Lane confessed. "He was too smart for me."[42]

Lane knew all too well that Weiss had the uncanny ability to acquire that last bit of extra help for the Yankees late in the season by buying National League stars like Johnny Sain, Johnny Hopp, Enos Slaughter, and Johnny Mize.[43]

Lane's refusal to deal with Weiss was the result of his respect for the Yankees' executive, but Bill Veeck's attitude towards Weiss was replete with acrimony. When Veeck learned that Weiss had retired from his position with the New York Mets, Veeck stated, "Happiness is not a thing called George. He was a good operator, but he could have been a front man for a string of mortuaries. He could have sold everyone in Vermont a tombstone. The great triumvirate of murder, manslaughter, and mayhem are all gone—Topping, Webb, and Weiss. I'll miss them like the seven-year itch."[44]

Interestingly, almost every analyst lauded a strategy move which had nothing to do with players. Weiss was praised for recognizing Stengel's value as a manager when he hired him for the Yankees and for his shrewdness in hiring him again for the Mets where he also acted as the face of the team, amusing the fans and diverting attention from the team's performance.[45]

Weiss's one great failing was his reluctance to bring black and Latino players to the Yankees. Although his great baseball record spoke for itself, many felt that this failure was the single stain that would fester and eventually cause the downfall of the reigning Yankees dynasty.[46] Weiss explained to his critics that he wanted only talented players who would represent the team in a positive way regardless of their color. The critics felt the reason was simpler than that—Weiss was a bigot. Baseball historians Mark Armour and Dan Levitt shrewdly noted that most teams signed black players because they wanted to win, and top black players were available for relatively low salaries. But for many years, the Yankees were able to win without signing many blacks.[47]

Things were different when Weiss became head of the Mets organization. The Mets needed all the talent they could get, and as a National League team, Weiss had to compete against many black players, including Willie McCovey, Ernie Banks, and Willie Mays. With the Mets, Weiss began selecting black players immediately from the meager draft choices while trading for others.[48]

As for how this so-called bigot treated his black players, Joe Christopher, one of the Mets' original draft picks, sent a letter to Weiss after he was traded to the Red Sox before the 1968 season. "Dear Mr. Weiss," Christopher, a native of the Virgin Islands, wrote, "My wife, my kids, and myself would like to thank you personally for all you have done for us.... I know, Mr. Weiss, that despite everything that has been said about you, that you are a kind, considerate and conscientious person.... The four years I did spend with the Mets organization were the four most glorious years I ever did spend in baseball. I also want to thank you, Mr. Weiss, for having confidence within myself.... P.S. It still hurts not to be a Met." Weiss, understandably touched, answered Christopher, hoping that "the change of clubs will have a favorable effect on your play and enable you to go on to bigger and better accomplishments in baseball."[49]

George Weiss may have had his share of detractors, but he also had many loyal friends and supporters. Weiss received a brief note from broadcaster Red Barber shortly after retiring from his stint with the Mets. "What I wish for you, George, is what deep down in your heart you wish for yourself—the rest is window-dressing. You are a fine man—you have a great record, George, and it is a clean record. Your word is worth more than you ever had to value, and you have many more things to do."[50]

A former classmate of Weiss at Roger Sherman School in New Haven, Bill Farnham, proposed placing a plaque at the location where Weiss worked in his father's shop. "George Weiss is one of the few men I have ever known who accomplished exactly what he wanted to do. When we were only 12, we called him Manager Weiss. He was an outstanding person. He was a New Haven native who accomplished a great deal. He became one of baseball's great executives and that reflects with favor on this city."[51]

Red Smith, writing shortly after Weiss's death, praised him and his accomplishments and called him "the ablest baseball executive who ever lived and probably the most self-effacing." Smith contended that not even giants such as Babe Ruth or Ty Cobb had a more profound and lasting influence on the game than George Weiss. "No one ever built, defying time to obliterate his work," Smith wrote, better than George Weiss, who "was so dedicated to excellence that to finish second was a disgrace, and that from the end of World War I, when Weiss entered organized baseball as operator of the New Haven franchise in the Eastern League until he created the Mets 'out of thin air' in 1962, he had only one second-division team, his first one in New Haven."[52]

15. Final Innings   187

Smith noted that to those who knew him only slightly, Weiss seemed aloof and chilly. "Actually," wrote Smith, "he loved companionship and reveled in conviviality, though in any gathering he was the quietist. He was so shy that it was difficult for him to speak in the first person, even among friends."[53]

In addition to his election to baseball's Hall of Fame, in 1982 Weiss was one of the first four individuals, along with Mrs. Joan Payson, Casey Stengel, and Gil Hodges, to be named to the New York Mets Hall of Fame.[54] Baseball historians and sports writers who rate players and executives still place George Weiss near the top of the list of general managers. Shale Briskin, a featured columnist, ranks Weiss among the ten greatest general managers of all time. "Weiss should receive credit," wrote Briskin, "for creating the inner core that the Mets were fortunate to have for many years."[55] And almost 100 years after his high school graduation, Weiss, who never played on the school's baseball team, would have been elated when he was named to the Hillhouse High School Athletic Hall of Fame.[56]

Mark Armour and Dan Levitt place Weiss #5 among the 25 best GMs in baseball history. They admit that they would have ranked him even higher except that during the 1950s, the Yankees had a financial edge over the other teams in the American League. They do note, however, that there is no denying Weiss's shrewdness and wisdom in running the Yankees. He was rewarded for his accomplishments by being named

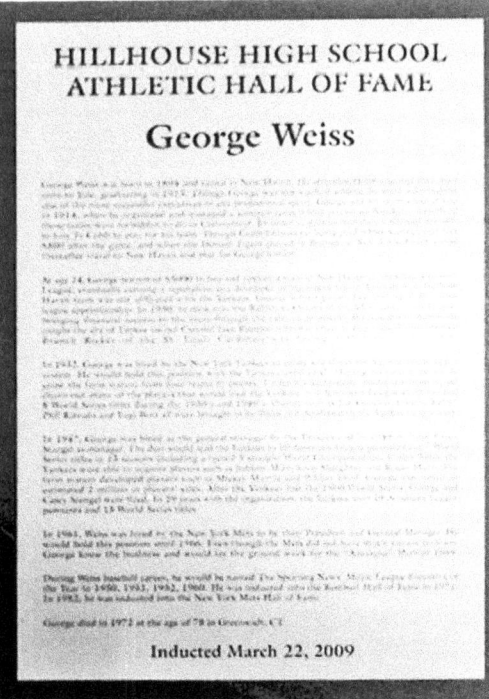

The James E. Hillhouse Athletic Hall of Fame is an educational institution dedicated to honoring the history and athletic achievements of former Hillhouse standouts as well as those who have made outstanding contributions to the school. George Weiss was inducted into the Hall in 1909, nearly 100 years after his graduation in 1911 (courtesy Jack Paulishen).

"Executive of the Year" four times by *The Sporting News,* more than anyone else in the history of the award.[57]

George Martin Weiss spoke from his heart about baseball in the very brief speech he wrote for his Hall of Fame induction. He thanked his wife and family, who had enjoyed and suffered with him for many years. He then paid homage to his friends and associates in the "front office" who labored with him and assisted him often without recognition. He quoted an unnamed figure who once made the statement that "Baseball is not a game, it is a religion," and he unashamedly called his entry into the Hall of Fame "a holy moment in my religion of Baseball."[58]

Chapter Notes

Preface

1. "George Weiss Induction Speech," Weiss Scrapbook, Volume 37, 1971, Baseball Hall of Fame.

Chapter 1

1. Joseph Durso, *Casey: The Life and Legend of Charles Dillon Stengel* (Englewood Cliffs, NJ: Prentice Hall, 1967), 155.
2. *New Haven Register*, September 16, 2012; Tim Cohane, *Bypaths of Glory: A Sportswriter Looks Back* (New York: Harper & Row, 1963), 16.
3. J. H. Beers, *Commemorative Biographical Record of New Haven County* (Chicago: J. H. Beers, 1902), 767.
4. Rollin G. Osterweis, *Three Centuries of New Haven, 1638–1938* (New Haven: Yale University Press, 1953), 369; Douglas W. Rae, *City: Urbanism and Its End* (New Haven: Yale University Press), 15.
5. Beers, *Commemorative Biographical Record for New Haven County*, 767.
6. Fourteenth Census of the United States, New Haven, Connecticut, June 2, 1920.
7. New Haven Bureau of Vital Statistics.
8. AHL.com/The American Hockey League Home Page.
9. www.sportsencyclopedia.com
10. Hillhouse Athletic Hall of Fame, www.hillhouseathletichalloffame.com.
11. Jacob Podoloff to Harold Rosenthal, December 1955, Volume 23, Weiss Scrapbook, Baseball Hall of Fame, Cooperstown, New York.
12. *Ibid.*
13. James E. Hillhouse High School History, Hillhouse Athletic Hall of Fame History.
14. *Biographical Directory of the United States Congress*; 2010 New Haven Magnet School Catalogue (New Haven Public Schools), 31.
15. Rae, *City: Urbanism and Its End*, 170.
16. Senior Class Book, New Haven High School, 1911.
17. Short biographical sketch of George Weiss, November 14, 1966; Weiss Scrapbook, Baseball Hall of Fame.
18. Harold Rosenthal, *Baseball is Their Business* (New York: Random House, 1951), 156; Daniel R. Levitt, *Ed Barrow: The Bulldog Who Built the Yankees' First Dynasty* (Lincoln: University of Nebraska Press, 2008), 277.
19. Sam Rubin, *Baseball in New Haven* (Mt. Pleasant, SC, 2003), 10–11.
20. *Ibid.*, 12.
21. "Minor League Baseball in New Haven, Connecticut," www.luckyshow.org; Rubin, *Baseball in New Haven*, 21.
22. *New Haven Register*, September 24, 1915.
23. *The Sporting News*, December 30, 1937.
24. World War I Draft Registration Card, June 5, 1917, copy at Yale Alumni Office.
25. *History of the Class of 1917, Yale College, Fifty Years*, 1967.
26. Steven Goldman, *Forging Genius: The Making of Casey Stengel* (Washington, D.C.: Potomac Books, Inc., 2005), 87; Page From George Weiss's Scrapbook, National Baseball Hall of Fame (online at www.enotes.com).
27. Harold Rosenthal, "Yankee Trader," *Collier's*, 44 (Undated, George Weiss Scrapbook, Vol. 20), 1952.
28. Robert Smith, *Baseball in the Afternoon: Tales From a Bygone Era* (New York: Simon & Schuster, 1993), 43.
29. Gary Gillette, and Peter Palmer, eds. *The ESPN Baseball Encyclopedia, Fifth Edition* (New York: Sterling, 2006), 339.
30. *New York Times*, August 14, 1972.
31. Rosenthal, *Baseball Is Their Business*, 156–157; Smith, *Baseball in the Afternoon*, 43.
32. Smith, *Baseball in the Afternoon*, 190.
33. Rubin, *Baseball in New Haven*, 26; Smith, *Baseball in the Afternoon*, 193; Historical Background On Weiss, George Weiss Scrapbooks, Baseball Hall of Fame; Cohane, *Bypaths of Glory*, 17; *The Sporting News*, February 13, 1933; Levitt, *Ed Barrow*: 277; *New York Times*, August 14, 1972.
34. George M. Weiss, with Robert Shaplen, "The Best Decision I Ever Made," *Sports Illustrated*, March 13, 1961, 29.
35. Smith, *Baseball in the Afternoon*, 191–192.
36. Frank, "Yankee Farmer," 6.
37. Rubin, *Baseball in New Haven*, 28.
38. Cohane, *Bypaths of Glory*, 17.
39. *The Sporting News*, December 30, 1937; Ronald A. Mayer, *The 1937 Newark Bears*, 20.

40. Weiss, "The Best Decision I Ever Made," 28.
41. Rubin, *Baseball in New Haven*, 28.
42. Tom Meany, *The Yankee Story* (New York: E. P. Dutton, 1960), 148; John Thorn, Phil Birnbaum, and Bill Deane, eds., *Total Baseball: The Ultimate Baseball Encyclopedia, 8th Edition* (Wilmington. DE: Sports Media Publishing, 2004), 346; *Boston Globe*, October 21, 1916; Daniel Levitt to Author, June 16, 2013.
43. Rosenthal, *Baseball Is Their Business*, 158; Goldman, *Forging Genius*, 87.
44. *New York Times*, August 14, 1972.
45. *New Haven Register*, August 30, 2012.
46. Baseball-reference.com; baseball-almanac.com.
47. *The Sporting News*, February 16, 1933.
48. Ibid.
49. Ibid.
50. *New York Times*, August 14, 1972; Durso, *Casey: The Life and Legend of Charles Dillon Stengel*, 156.

Chapter 2

1. *Biographical Dictionary of American Sports*, David L. Porter, ed. (online); *Boston Globe*, April 25, 1919; Robert Shaplen, "The Yankees' Real Boss," *Sports Illustrated*, September 20, 1954, 34; Allen Barra, *Yogi Berra: Eternal Yankee* (New York: W.W. Norton, 2009), 26.
2. *The Hartford Courant*, April 25, 1919.
3. *Bridgeport Standard and Tribune*, May 5, 1919.
4. Baseball-reference.com.
5. *New York Times*, May 15, 1969; *New Haven Criterion*, May 14, 1919.
6. Baseball-reference.com; Minor League Baseball in Connecticut, luckyshow.org/baseball.
7. *New York Times*, September 21, 1919.
8. Ibid., September 28, 1919.
9. Rubin, *Baseball in New Haven*, 29; Minor League Baseball in New Haven.
10. Copy of check for $5, 800 in George Weiss Scrapbook, Volume I, 1914–1919, George Weiss Collection, Baseball Hall of Fame, Cooperstown, NY; Stanley Frank, "Yankee Kingmaker," *Saturday Evening Post*, July 24, 1948, 110; Cohane, *Bypaths of Glory*, 18.
11. *Ironwood* (MI) *Daily Globe*, March 30, 1920.
12. *Bridgeport Telegraph*, December 11, 1920.
13. *Oshkosh* (WI) *Daily Northwestern*, December 20, 1920; *Waukesha* (WI) *Daily Freeman*, December 20, 1920; *Muscatine* (IA) *Journal and News Tribune*, December 21, 1920.
14. Gillette and Palmer, *The ESPN Baseball Encyclopedia*, 1156; baseball-reference.com.
15. *The Sporting News*, December 27, 1945.
16. Ibid., February 16, 1933.
17. Ibid., January 8, 1920.
18. *Bridgeport Telegram*, January 29, 1920.
19. Gillette and Palmer, *The ESPN Baseball Encyclopedia*, 1083; short biographical profile of Chief Bender, George Weiss Scrapbook Volume II, 1920, George Weiss Collection, Baseball Hall of Fame, Cooperstown, NY.
20. *Altoona Mirror*, January 8, 1920.
21. Lloyd Johnson, and Miles Wolff, eds., *The Encyclopedia of Minor League Baseball: The Official Record of Minor League Baseball*, (Durham, NC: Baseball America, 1997), 220, 223.
22. *Bridgeport Telegram*, January 29, 1920.
23. Henry W. Thomas, *Walter Johnson, Baseball's Big Train* (Washington, D.C.: Phenom Press, 1995), 174.
24. *Hartford Courant*, April 20, 1920.
25. *The Sporting News*, May 20, 1920.
26. Smith, *Baseball in the Afternoon*, 54–55.
27. Ibid., 55.
28. Ibid., 194–195.
29. *The Sporting News*, May 4, 1930.
30. Mark Armour, *Joe Cronin: A Life in Baseball* (Lincoln: University of Nebraska Press, 2010), 22–23.
31. Smith, *Baseball in the Afternoon*, 195.
32. *Atlanta Constitution*, February 10, 1921.
33. Weiss and Robert Shaplen, "The Best Decision I Ever Made," 28.
34. *Steubenville* (OH) *Herald-Star*, June 19, 1921.
35. Smith, *Baseball in the Afternoon*, 196.
36. Johnson and Wolff, *The Encyclopedia of Minor League Baseball*, 220; Baseball-reference.com.
37. *Lowell* (MA) *Sun*, August 11, 1920.
38. Baseball-reference.com.
39. *Oshkosh* (WI) *Daily Northwestern*, December 20, 1920; *Waukesha* (WI) *Daily Freeman*, December 20, 1920; *Evening Gazette* (Cedar Rapids, IA), December 20, 1920.
40. *Bridgeport Telegram*, December 30, 1920.
41. *The Sporting News*, November 21, 1921.
42. Ibid., November 24, 1921.
43. For a complete biographical sketch of Chief Bender, see Tom Swift's SABR Baseball Bio Project online.
44. *The Sporting News*, November 3, 1921.
45. Doug Skipper, "Bill Donovan," sabr.org./bioproj, 3.
46. *Boston Globe*, December 22, 1921.
47. Robert W. Creamer, *Stengel: His Life and Times* (New York: Simon & Schuster, 1984), 133.
48. Marty Appel, *Pinstripe Empire: The New York Yankees from Before the Babe to After the Boss* (New York: Bloomsbury, 2012), 85.
49. Skipper, "Bill Donovan," 1.
50. *The Sporting News*, February 16, April 20, 1922.
51. *Bridgeport Tribune*, March 10, 1922; Baseball-Reference.com.
52. luckyshow.org; *Sporting News*, October 5, 1922.
53. Smith, *Baseball in the Afternoon*, 196–201.
54. Cohane, *Bypaths of Glory*, 18.
55. *The Sporting News*, January 26, 1923; Smith, *Baseball in the Afternoon*, 200–201.
56. Baseball-reference.com.
57. *Bridgeport Telegram*, March 6, 1923.
58. *Hartford Courant*, March 31, 1923.
59. Meany, *The Yankee Story*, 149.
60. *New York Times*, June 25, 1923; Peter Golenbock, *Dynasty: The New York Yankees 1949–1964* (Englewood Cliffs, NJ: Prentice Hall), 270; Peter Golenbock, *Amazin': The Miraculous History of New York's Most Beloved Baseball Team* (New York: St. Martin's Press, 2002), 89; "Baseball Businessman," *Forbes*, August 1, 1951, 13.
61. Levitt, *Ed Barrow*, 278; *New York Herald*, February 13, 1957.
62. Goldman, *Forging Genius: The Making of Casey Stengel*, 87.
63. Johnson and Wolff, *The Encyclopedia of Minor League Baseball*, 231; 1923 Prof's Statistics, Baseball-Reference.com.
64. *The Sporting News*, October 25, 1923; *Bridgeport Telegram*, October 30, 1923.

65. Tom Meany, "George Weiss: The *Real* Yankee Clipper," *Sport*, 1947, 78.
66. *The Sporting News*, December 6, 1923.
67. Meany, "The Yankee Story," 142.
68. *Ibid.*, 143; Smith, *Baseball in the Afternoon*, 201.
69. Skipper, "Bill Donovan," 3; Rubin, "Baseball in New Haven," 30; "Wild Bill Donovan," New York Historical Society's Bill Shannon Dictionary of New York's Sports History, sports.nyhistory.org; Smith, "Baseball in the Afternoon," 201–202; Appel, "Pinstripe Empire," 85; The Ballplayers-Bill Donovan, BaseballLibrary.com.
70. *New York Times*, December 10, 1923.
71. Appel, "Pinstripe Empire," 86.
72. *Ibid.*, 85.
73. *New Haven Register*, December 10, 1923; *New Haven Journal Courier*, December 10, 1923.
74. *New York Times*, December 10, 1923; *Olean* (NY) *Evening Herald*, December 10, 1923.
75. *New Haven Journal Courier*, December 12, 1923; *The Bradford* (PA) *Era*, December 9, 1923; various newspaper clippings, George Weiss Scrapbook, Volume 4, 1923, Baseball Hall of Fame.
76. Connie Mack to George Weiss, January 3, 1924, George Weiss Files, Baseball Hall of Fame.
77. John Heydler to George Weiss, January 23, 1924, George Weiss Files, Baseball Hall of Fame.
78. Douglas Fairbanks, Jr., to George Weiss, February 21, 1924, Weiss Scrapbook, Volume 4, Baseball Hall of Fame.
79. *Bridgeport Telegram*, January 28, 1924; *The Sporting News*, January 31, 1924; *New Haven Journal Courier*, January 14, 1924.
80. Clyde Milan, findagrave.com.
81. *The Hartford Courant*, February 29, 1924; *The Sporting News*, April 17, 1924.
82. *Hartford Courant*, February 3, 1924; *The Sporting News*, February 7, 1924.
83. *The Sporting News*, February 21, 1924.
84. *The Hartford Courant*, April 2, 1924.
85. *Bridgeport Telegram*, September 17, 1924.
86. Johnson and Wolff, *The Encyclopedia of Minor League Baseball*, 235.
87. *Hartford Courant*, October 23, 1924; *Oakland Tribune*, October 27, 1924.
88. Thomas, *Walter Johnson: Baseball's Big Train*, 192, 255–257; undated newspaper clippings, George Weiss Scrapbook, Volume VII, 1917–1924, Baseball Hall of Fame.
89. *The Sporting News*, November 6, 1924.
90. Thomas, *Walter Johnson*, 258; *Hartford Courant*, November 18, 1924; *Edwardsville* (IL) *Intelligencer*, November 18, 1924; *Oakland Tribune*, November 18, 1924; *New York Times*, November 18, 1924.
91. The Ball Players—George Weiss. Baseballlibrary.com; *New York Times*, November 19, 1924; *Lethbridge* (Alberta, Canada) *Daily Herald*, November 20, 1924.
92. *The Sporting News*, November 20, 1924.
93. *New York Times*, November 24, 1924; *Logansport* (IN) *Pharos Tribune*, November 24, 1924; *The Sporting News*, November 27, 1924.
94. Thomas, *Walter Johnson*, 249–250; *Times Signal* (Zanesville, OH), January 4, 1925.
95. *Lowell* (MA) *Sun*, February 18, 1925; *New York Times*, February 19, 1925; *The Sporting News*, January 13, 1925.
96. *Bridgeport Telegram*, March 13, 1925; CNN/SI-Baseball-Neal Ball sportsillustrated.cnn.com; Neal Ball-BR Bullpen, baseball-reference.com; Neal Ball SABR sabr.org/bioproject.
97. *Bridgeport Telegram*, April 21, 1925.
98. Johnson and Wolff, *Encyclopedia of Minor League Baseball*, 239.
99. *Bridgeport Telegram*, February 23, 1926.
100. *The Sporting News*, March 4, 1926.
101. Baseball-almanac.com; baseball-reference.com.
102. *The Sporting News*, March 18, 1926.
103. *Hartford Courant*, July 11, 1926.
104. *Ibid.*
105. *The Sporting News*, August 12, 1926.
106. Armour, *Joe Cronin: A Life in Baseball*, 23–24; *Hartford Courant*, August 7, 1926; John Kieran, "Sports of the Times," *New York Times*, May 4, 1930.
107. 1926 New Haven Profs Stats-Minor League Baseball, baseball-reference.com.
108. *Hartford Courant*, March 3, 1927.
109. *Ibid.*, June 21, 1927.
110. *Bridgeport Telegram*, April 23, 1927.
111. *Ibid.*, September 18, 1926; April 23, 1927; *Hartford Courant*, April 24, 1927.
112. Minor League Baseball in New Haven, lucky show.org.
113. Albert W. Keane. "Calling 'Em Right," *Hartford Courant*, September 2, 1927.
114. *New York Times*, February 5, 1928.
115. "Eugene Martin Minor League Statistics & History," baseball-reference.com.
116. *New York Times*, March 11, 1928; *Hartford Courant*, March 22, 1928; Rubin, *Baseball in New Haven*, 33.
117. Johnson and Wolff, *The Encyclopedia of Minor League Baseball*, 253.
118. *Hartford Courant*, November 28, 1928.
119. Unidentified newspaper clipping, January 10, 1929, George Weiss files, Baseball Hall of Fame.
120. 1928 New Haven Profs Statistics, baseball-reference.com; unidentified newspaper article, January 10, 1928, George Weiss Files, Baseball Hall of Fame.
121. *New Haven Register*, February 14, 1929.
122. *Hartford Courant*, February 15, 1929.
123. *Ibid.*, January 27, 1929.

Chapter 3

1. *New Haven Register*, February 18, 1929; Golenbock, *Dynasty*, 270; Frederick G. Lieb, *The Baltimore Orioles: The History of a Colorful Team in Baltimore and St. Louis* (New York: G. P. Putnam's Sons, 1955), 161; Lowell Reidenbaugh, *Baseball's Hall of Fame: Cooperstown Where the Legends Live Forever* (New York: Gramercy Books, 1983), 330.
2. Levitt, *Ed Barrow*, 279; Lieb, *The Baltimore Orioles*, 161; Robert F. Burk, *Much More Than a Game: Owners, Players, and American Baseball Since 1921* (Chapel Hill: University of North Carolina Press, 2001), 51.
3. James H. Bready, *Baseball in Baltimore: The First Hundred Years* (Baltimore: Johns Hopkins University Press, 1998), 186.
4. *Hartford Courant*, February 15, 1929; *Hagerstown* (MD) *Morning Herald*, February 15, 1929; *New York Times*, February 15, 1929.
5. *New Haven Register*, February 18, 1929.

6. Bready, *Baseball in Baltimore*, 186.
7. Jimmy Keenan, Jack Dunn/SABR—mlb.org, 3.
8. *Ibid.*
9. *Ibid.*, 4.
10. "Major and Minor League Baseball in Baltimore," teachingamericanhistorymd.net.
11. "International League History," mlb.com.
12. Keenan, "Jack Dunn," 7.
13. Lieb, *The Baltimore Orioles*, 159.
14. Tom Flynn, *Baseball in Baltimore* (Charleston, SC: Arcadia, 2008), 55.
15. "Keenan," Jack Dunn, *6–7*.
16. *Catonsville* (MD) *Herald-Argus*, April 22, 1967.
17. Stanley Frank, "Yankee Farmer," 30; Robert Shaplen, "The Yankees' Real Boss," *Sports Illustrated*, September 20, 1954, *36*.
18. Weiss would later match that sale when he disposed of young outfielder Vince Barton. He sold him also for $40,000, to the Chicago Cubs (undated news clip, George Weiss Hall of Fame Files).
19. Lieb, *The Baltimore Orioles*, 162; Joseph Durso, *Casey: The Life and Legend of Charles Dillon Stengel*, 156. (Englewood Cliffs, NJ: Prentice-Hall, Inc.), 156.
20. Tom Meany, "The *Real* Yankee Trader," *Sport*, September 1947, 17.
21. Lieb, *The Baltimore Orioles*, 163.
22. Jimmy Powers, "Baseball's Master Architect," *New York Daily News*, Undated article in George Weiss Files, Baseball Hall of Fame.
23. Golenbock, *Dynasty*, 270; Peter Golenbock, *Amazin': The Miraculous History of New York's Most Beloved Baseball Team*, (New York: St. Martin's Press, 2002), 89.
24. *The Sporting News*, February 14, 1929.
25. *Hagerstown* (MD) *Morning Herald*, March 16, 1929.
26. *North Adams* (MA) *Evening Transcript*, March 22, 1929.
27. *The Sporting News*, April 18, 1929.
28. *Olean* (NY) *Evening News*, April 6, 1929.
29. Johnson and Wolff, *Encyclopedia of Minor League Baseball*, 257.
30. 1929 Baltimore Statistics, baseball-reference.com.
31. Lieb, *The Baltimore Orioles*, 163; Bready, *Baseball in Baltimore*, 187; Gillette and Palmer, *The ESPN Baseball Encyclopedia*, 782.
32. *Hartford Courant*, September 29, 1929.
33. *Frederick* (MD) *News Post*, July 19, 1930; John H. Kieran, "Sports of the Times," *New York Times*, July 20, 1930; *Oakland Tribune*, August 16, 1930.
34. *The Sporting News*, October 31, 1929.
35. *Ibid.*, November 14, 1929.
36. Gillette and Palmer, *The ESPN Baseball Encyclopedia*, 1250.
37. 1930 Baltimore Oriole Statistics, baseball-reference.com.
38. Bready, *Baseball in Baltimore*, 187; Gillette and Palmer, *The ESPN Baseball Encyclopedia*, 568; Lieb, The Baltimore Orioles, 162.
39. Lieb, *The Baltimore Orioles*, 164; Bready, *Baseball in Baltimore*, 187.
40. Johnson and Wolff, *The Encyclopedia of Minor League Baseball*, 264; Bready, *Baseball in Baltimore*, 187.
41. *San Antonio Express*, August 23, 1930; *Hagerstown* (MD) *Daily Mail*, August 30, 1930; *New York Times*, November 9, 1930.
42. Mayer, *The 1937 Newark Bears: A Baseball Legend* (New Brunswick, NJ: Rutgers University Press, 1994).
43. *Ibid.*
44. Albert W. Keane, "Calling 'Em Right," *Hartford Courant*, December 30, 1930.
45. Lieb, *The Baltimore Orioles*, 163; www.baseball-reference.com/players/s/sothede01-bat.shtml.
46. *Hagerstown* (MD) *Daily Mail*, January 26, 1931; *Frederick* (MD) *News Post*, January 26, 1931.
47. *The Sporting News*, May 14, 1931.
48. *Ibid.*, March 19, 1931.
49. *Hagerstown* (MD) *Daily Mail*, April 28, 1931.
50. *The Sporting News*, May 14, 1931.
51. *Ibid.*, July 16, 1931; Bready, *Baseball in Baltimore*, 187; 1931 Baltimore Orioles Statistics, baseball-reference.com.
52. Bready, *Baseball in Baltimore*, 187; 1931 Baltimore Orioles Statistics, baseball-reference.com.
53. *The Sporting News*, June 25, 1931.
54. Johnson and Wolff, *The Encyclopedia of Minor League Baseball*, 268.
55. Bready, *Baseball in Baltimore*, 188; 1931 Baltimore Orioles Statistic-baseball-reference.com.
56. *The Sporting News*, September 13, 1931.
57. *Ibid.*, December 17, 1931.
58. Lieb, *The Baltimore Orioles*, 162.
59. *The Sporting News*, February 13, 1933; New York Mets Press Release, November 14, 1966, Weiss Files, Baseball Hall of Fame.
60. Dan Daniel, "Weiss Brought Varied Talents Into General Management of the Yankees," *Baseball Magazine*, February 1948, 300.
61. *Ibid.*, 322.
62. *The Sporting News*, December 27, 1945.
63. Hazel H. Wood Weiss, findagrave.com.
64. Golenbock, "Amazin'," 93.
65. *Ibid.*, 93–94.
66. *Syracuse Herald*, February 12, 1932; James Charlton, ed., *The Baseball Chronology: The Complete History of the Most Important Events in the Game of Baseball* (New York: Macmillan, 1991), 266.
67. Meany, "George Weiss: The *Real* Yankee Clipper," 78.
68. *The Sportinng News*, December 17, 1931.
69. *Ibid.*

Chapter 4

1. Jacob Ruppert, Jr., findagrave.com; Jacob Ruppert, Jr., bioguide.congress; http://www.history.com/this-day-in-history/new-york-highlanders-join-american-league.
2. "Bill Shannon Biographical Dictionary of New York Sports," sports.nyhistory.org. Ed Barrow, findagrave.com; baseballlibrary.com.
3. *The Sporting News*, December 27, 1945; Dan Daniel, "Lary-Reese Deal Landed in Yankee Picture," undated newspaper clipping, George Weiss files, Baseball Hall of Fame; Marty Appel, Pinstripe Empire, 174.
4. Levitt, *Ed Barrow*, 278–279.
5. *The Sporting News*, December 27, 1945.
6. Golenbock, *Amazin'*: 90; Neil J. Sullivan, *Minors: The Struggles and the Triumph of Baseball's Poor Relation From 1876 to the Present* (New York: St. Martin's Press, 1990), 135.
7. Levitt, *Ed Barrow*, 277; Daniel, "Lary-Reese

Deal Landed Weiss in Yankee Picture"; Milton Gross, *Yankee Doodles* (Boston: House of Kent, 1948), 151.
  8. Levitt, *Ed Barrow*, 277; Jim Sandoval and Bill Nowlin, eds., *Can He Play? A Look at Baseball Scouts and Their Profession* (Phoenix: SABR, 2011), 27.
  9. Meany, "The *Real* Yankee Clipper." *Sport*, 1947, 78.
  10. Biographic sketch of George Weiss, Weiss Files, Baseball Hall of Fame.
  11. *Reno Evening Digest*, February 13, 1932.
  12. *Syracuse Herald*, February 12, 1932; *Corsicana* (TX) *Daily Sun*, February 13, 1932.
  13. *Ibid.*, November 2, 1939.
  14. *The Sporting News*, February 18, 1932.
  15. *Monitor Index and Democrat* (Moberly, MO), February 23, 1932.
  16. *The Sporting News*, February 18, 1932; David Voigt, *Baseball: An Illustrated History* (University Park: Pennsylvania State University Press, 1987), 191.
  17. Charles C. Alexander, *Breaking the Slump: Baseball in the Depression Era* (New York: Columbia University Press), 48; *The Sporting News*, February 24, 1932.
  18. *New York Times*, February 24, 1932; *Cumberland* (NC) *Evening Times*, February 24, 1932; *Waterloo* (IA) *Daily Sun*, February 25, 1932.
  19. *The Sporting News*, February 25, 1932.
  20. *Newcastle* (PA) *News*, April 19, 1932.
  21. *The Sandusky* (OH) *Register*, March 3, 1932.
  22. Frank, "Yankee Farmer," n.p.
  23. *Charleston* (WV) *Gazette*, July 24, 1932.
  24. *Florence* (SC) *Morning News*, November 9, 1932; *The Sporting News*, November 24, 1932.
  25. Appel, *Pinstripe Empire*, 174.
  26. *Salt Lake City Tribune*, June 19, 1933; *The Sporting News*, January 3, 1935.
  27. Appel, *Pinstripe Empire*, 174–175; Frank Graham, "Those Yankees!" *Liberty*, October 1, 1942, 14.
  28. *Charleston* (WV) *Gazette*, February 2, 1933.
  29. *Cumberland Evening Times*, February 24, 1933.
  30. *Ibid.*
  31. *Hagerstown* (MD) *Morning Herald*, February 24, 1933; *The Sporting News*, January 26, 1933.
  32. *The Sporting News*, January 3, 1935; Appel, *Pinstripe Empire*, 174.
  33. Baseball-reference.com.
  34. *The Sporting News*, July 22, 1937.
  35. *Ibid.*, November 11, 1937.
  36. *Ibid.*
  37. *Lowell* (MA) *Sun*, March 5, 1938.
  38. *The Sporting News*, December 30, 1937.
  39. *Wisconsin State Journal*, August 12, 1938.
  40. *The Sporting News*, November 2, 1939.
  41. Golenbock, *Dynasty*, 270–271.
  42. George M. Weiss with Robert Shaplen, "The Man of Silence Speaks," *Sports Illustrated*, March 6, 1961, 46.
  43. *Big Springs* (TX) *Daily-Herald*, August 12, 1958.
  44. Sullivan, *Minors*, 143.
  45. Mark Gallagher, *The Yankee Encyclopedia* (Champaign, IL: Sagamore, 1996).
  46. Jerry Coleman to authors, January 8, 2012.
  47. Bob Brown to authors, January 10, 2012.
  48. *Zanesville* (OH) *Times Recorder*, October 10, 1939.
  49. "The Unknown Yankee," *Newsweek*, July 15, 1957, 62.
  50. *The Sporting News*, January 11, 1940.
  51. W. C. Heinz, "I Scout for the Yankees," *Colliers*, July 11, 1953, 19; Jonathan Eig, *Luckiest Man: The Life and Death of Lou Gehrig* (New York: Simon & Schuster, 2005), 40.
  52. Appel, *Pinstripe Empire*, 110; Roger Kahn, *The Era 1947–1957: When the Yankees, the Giants, and the Dodgers Ruled the World* (New York: Ticknor & Fields, 1993), 249; Mayer, *The 1937 Newark Bears*, 24.
  53. "Scouting Story by Marty Appel," www.appelpr.com.
  54. Levitt, *Ed Barrow*, 341.
  55. *The Sporting News*, March 27, 1941.
  56. Sullivan, *Minors*, 143; "Paul Krichell," Find A Grave.com; Sandoval and Nowlin, 31–32, 62; *New York Times*, June 5, 1957.
  57. *New York Times*, April 27, 1943; www.baseball-reference.com.
  58. Sandoval and Nowlin, *Can He Play?*, 39.
  59. Baseball-reference.com; *New York Times*, October 13, 1951.
  60. *New York Times*, October 13, 1951.
  61. Baseball-reference.com; "Scouting Story" by Marty Appel, www.appelpr.com; Sandoval and Nowlin, *Can He Play?*, 33–39.
  62. *New York Times*, October 12, 1951.
  63. Weiss and Shaplen, "Man of Silence Speaks," 51; *Big Springs* (TX) *Daily Herald*, August 12, 1958.
  64. Armour, *Joe Cronin*, 255–256.
  65. "Scouting Story," by Marty Appel, appelpr.com; Sandoval and Nowlin, *Can He Play?*, 41; Levitt, *Ed Barrow*, 297–298; Richard Ben Cramer, *Joe DiMaggio: The Hero's Life* (New York: Simon & Schuster, 2000), 66.
  66. Sandoval and Nowlin, *Can He Play?*, 38.
  67. www.waswatching.com; Cramer, *Joe DiMaggio: The Hero's Life*, 66.
  68. Reprinted in *New York*, March 22, 1991, "Can Bo Follow Joe in Yank Order?"
  69. *Ibid.*
  70. Appel, *Pinstripe Empire*, 188; Cramer, *Joe DiMaggio: The Hero's Life*, 69; "Joe DiMaggio Statistics," baseball-reference.com; *New York Times*, March 22, 1991; www.waswatching.com; Gross, *Yankee Doodles*, 151–152; Mayer, *The 1937 Newark Bears*, 24–25; Sullivan, *Minors*, 143.
  71. Gross, *Yankee Doodles*, 151.
  72. Golenbock, *Amazin'*, 94.
  73. Joe Devine to George Weiss, August 11, 1950, George Weiss Scrapbook, Volume 16, 1950, Baseball Hall of Fame, Cooperstown, NY.
  74. Sandoval and Nowlin, *Can He Play?*, 42.
  75. Bill Madden, *Pride of October* (New York: Warner Books, 2003), 92.
  76. Sandoval and Nowlin, *Can He Play?*, 44; "Tom Greenwade—The Great Yankee Who Helped Nine World Series," www.bleacherreport.com.
  77. Richard C. Crepeau, *Baseball: America's Diamond Mind* (Orlando: University Presses of Florida, 1980), 109.
  78. Frank Graham, "Those Yankees," 15.
  79. Lance A. Berger and Dorothy R. Berger, *Management Wisdom From the New York Yankees Dynasty* (New York: John Wiley & Sons, 2005), 144.
  80. *The Sporting News*, August 8, 1937.
  81. Crepeau, *Baseball: America's Diamond Mind*, 110.

Chapter 5

1. *Frederick* (MD) *News*, February 13, 1932.
2. Sullivan, *The Minors*, 142.
3. Baseball-reference.com/bullpen /Newark Bears.
4. "Al Mamaux Minor League Statistics & History," baseball-reference.com.
5. Mayer, *The 1937 Newark Bears*, 13–17.
6. "Newark Bears—BR Bullpen," baseball-reference.com.
7. Appel, *Pinstripe Empire*, 175; *The Sporting News*, October 23, 1932.
8. Mayer, *The 1937 Newark Bears*, 27–30.
9. Bill O'Neal, *The International League* (Austin: Eakin Press, 1992), 112.
10. Mayer, *The 1937 Newark Bears*, 31.
11. *The Sporting News*, November 9, 1932.
12. Mayer, *The 1937 Newark Bears*, 36.
13. *The Sporting News*, December 7, 1932; *Titusville* (PA) *Herald*, December 7, 1932; *Morning Avalanche* (Lubbock, TX) December 7, 1932.
14. *The Sporting News*, January 12, 1933, October 26, 1933, November 2, 1933.
15. *Ibid.*, February 14, 1933; *New York Times*, February 10, 1933.
16. *Ibid.*, February 16, 1933.
17. "Frank Shaughnessy," SABR—sabr.org.bioproject.
18. *Ibid.*, 3.
19. *Ibid.*
20. *Ibid.*
21. O'Neal, *The International League*, 113–114.
22. "History—International League," mlb.com.
23. Mayer, *The 1937 Newark Bears*, 40.
24. *Ibid.*, 41.
25. "1933 Newark Bears Statistics & History" baseball-reference.com.
26. *Ibid.*, 41–42; "Newark Bears-BR Bullpen" baseball-reference.com.
27. Mayer, *The 1937 Newark Bears*, 46.
28. O'Neal, *The International League*, 115.
29. *The Sporting News*, September 28, 1933.
30. O'Neal, *The International League*, 115.
31. "Frank Shaughnessy," SABR, 4 sabr.org/bioproject.
32. O'Neal, *The International League*, 115; *The Sporting News*, September 28, 1933.
33. *The Sporting News*, November 8, 1933.
34. Mayer, *The 1937 Newark Bears*, 47; *The Sporting News*, November 24, 1933; *Winnipeg Free Press*, November 24, 1933; *Raleigh* (NC) *Register*, November 24, 1933.
35. *The Sporting News*, January 11, 1934.
36. Gillette and Palmer, *The ESPN Baseball Encyclopedia*, 1522.
37. *Ibid.*
38. Mayer, *The 1937 Newark Bears*, 48.
39. *The Sporting News*, December 14, 1933.
40. *Ibid.*, January 18, 1934.
41. *San Antonio Express*, January 25, 1934.
42. *The Sporting News*, January 18, 1934; Mayer, *The 1937 Newark Bears*, 49.
43. *Ibid.*
44. *New York Times*, January 8, 1934.
45. *The Sporting News*, November 21, 1934; December 20, 1934; O'Neal, *The International League*, 117.
46. *The Sporting News*, March 1, 1934.
47. *Ibid.*, February 8, 1934.
48. Mayer, *The 1937 Newark Bears*, 50.
49. Baseball-reference.com.
50. Mayer, *The 1937 Newark Bears*, 55; *The Sporting News*, October 11, 1934.
51. *The Sporting News*, October 11, 1934.
52. *Ibid.*, October 25, 1934; November 8, 1934.
53. *Ibid.*
54. *New York Times*, November 16, 1934; *The Sporting News*, November 15, 1934.
55. Gross, *Yankee Doodles*, 152.
56. *The Sporting News*, December 20, 1934.
57. *Ibid.*, January 3, 1935.
58. *Ibid.*, February 21, 1935, March 21, 1935.
59. Mayer, *The 1937 Newark Bears*, 59–62; O'Neal, *The International League*, 117.
60. Mayer, *The 1937 Newark Bears*, 62–63.
61. O'Neal, *The International League*, 117.
62. O'Neal, *The International League*, 117, 119; Mayer, *The 1937 New York Bears*, 64.
63. Mayer, *The 1937 Newark Bears*, 63.
64. *Ibid.*; *The New York Times*, November 11, 1935; *San Antonio Light*, November 11, 1935.
65. Gillette and Palmer, *The ESPN Baseball Encyclopedia*, 995.
66. "Oscar Vitt," oaklandoaks.tripod.com.
67. *The Sporting News*, November 28, 1935; *Oakland Sports Tribune*, November 20, 1935.
68. *The Sporting News*, February 6, 1936, May 28, 1936.
69. "Baseball Businessman," 15.
70. Appel, *Pinstripe Empire*, 175.
71. *The Sporting News*, September 17, 1936.
72. *Ibid*; O'Neal, *The International League*, 118; Mayer, *The 1937 Newark Bears*, 71.
73. *New York Times*, October 28, 1936; *Galveston* (TX) *Daily News*, October 28, 1936.
74. *The Sporting News*, October 28, 1936.
75. *Ibid.*, October 22, 1936; December 3, 1936.
76. Gross, *Yankee Doodles*, 156.
77. Peter C. Bjarkman, Ed., *Encyclopedia of Major League Baseball Team Histories: American League* (Westport, CT: Meckler, 1991), 263.
78. *Joplin* (MO) *Globe*, October 31, 1951; http://sabor.org./bioproj/ person; *Logansport* (IN) *Pharos Tribune*, August 9, 1937.
79. "Top 100 Teams," mlb.com; O'Neal, *The International League*, 120.
80. "Top 100 Teams." O'Neal, *The International League*, 121; Gross, *Yankee Doodles*, 157; Gillette and Palmer, *The ESPN Baseball Encyclopedia*, 534.
81. *Ibid.*, 581.
82. "Top 100 Teams," 5.
83. *Ibid.*
84. O'Neal, *The International League*, 120–121.
85. Tommy Henrich with Bill Gilbert, *Five O'Clock Lightning: Ruth, Gehrig, DiMaggio, Mantle and the Glory Years of the NY Yankees* (New York: Birch Lane Press, 1992), 71–72.
86. *The Sporting News*, June 24, 1937; O'Neal, *The International League*, 121; Sullivan, *The Minors*, 144.
87. Sullivan, *The Minors*, 144; O'Neal, *The International League*, 121–123.
88. *The Sporting News*, December 1, 1962.
89. *Ibid.*, October 14, 1937.
90. O'Neal, *The International League*, 125–126.
91. *Port Arthur* (TX) *News*, January 25, 1937.
92. Johnson and Wolff, *Encyclopedia of Minor*

League Baseball, 283, 287; "Top 100 Teams," mlb.com/mlb/history.
   93. *The Sporting News*, June 10, 1937, July 22, 1937.
   94. Circleville (OH) *Daily Herald*, July 26, 1937; *The Sporting News*, August 19, August 26, 1937.
   95. Johnson and Wolff, *The Encyclopedia of Minor League Baseball*, 292; *The Sporting News*, August 19, 1937, November 30, 1937; *Jefferson City* (MO) *Post-Tribune*, October 27, 1937.
   96. *New Haven Journal Courier*, June 14, 1937, June 16, 1937; *The Sporting News*, June 24, 1937, December 30, 1937.
   97. Golenbock, *Amazin'*, 93–94; "Memorial Article—Allen H. Wood," west-point.org/users/usma 1946.
   98. Lowell (MA) *Sun*, December 21, 1937; *New Haven Register*, December 22, 1937; *New Haven Journal-Courier*, December 22, 1937.
   99. *The Sporting News*, December 23, 1937; December 30, 1937.
   100. *Ibid.*
   101. *New York Times*, October 21, 1937.
   102. *Ibid.*, October 27, 1937.
   103. *Ibid.*, October 21, 1937.
   104. "Johnny Neun Minor League Statistics & History," baseball-reference.com /minors/player.
   105. *The Sporting News*, November 11, 1937.
   106. *Ibid.*, February 24, 1938.
   107. *Wisconsin* (Madison) *State Journal*, September 3, 1938.
   108. *New York Times*, April 4, 1938; *The Sporting News*, April 14, 1938.
   109. Gillette and Palmer, *The ESPN Baseball Encyclopedia*, 748, 626.
   110. Gross, *Yankee Doodles*, 154.
   111. *Montana* (Butte) *Standard*, May 29, 1938.
   112. O'Neal, *The International League*, 127.
   113. *Reno Evening Gazette*, August 26, 1938; *Big Springs* (TX) *Daily Herald*, August 16, 1938; *Hutchinson* (KS) *News*, August 28, 1936; *Bismarck* (ND) *Tribune*, August 26, 1938.
   114. *Ibid.*
   115. *Dunkirk* (NY) *Evening Observer*, October 1, 1938.
   116. Meany, "The *Real* Yankee Clipper," 78.
   117. *Sandusky* (OH) *Register*, October 4, 1938.
   118. Meany, The Yankee Story, 151.
   119. *The Sporting News*, November 24, 1938.
   120. *Ibid.*, December 8, 1938.
   121. *New York Times*, December 7, 1938; *Syracuse Herald*, December 7, 1938; *Wisconsin* (Madison) *State Journal*, December 10, 1938; *The Sporting News*, December 15, 1938.
   122. Gross, *Yankee Doodles*, 155.

Chapter 6

   1. *Williamsport* (PA) *Gazette and Bulletin*, January 14, 1939; Graham, *The New York Yankees*, 247–248; Levitt, *Ed Barrow*, 317; Appel, *Pinstripe Empire*, 201–202.
   2. *New York Times*, January 18, 1939; *Appleton* (WI) *Post-Crescent*, January 18, 1939; *Moberly* (MO) *Monitor Index*, January 18, 1939; *San Antonio Light*, January 18, 1939; *The Sporting News*, January 19, 1939.
   3. *Brainerd* (MN) *Daily Dispatch*, January 19, 1939; *Dunkirk* (NY) *Evening Observer*, January 19, 1939.
   4. *The Sporting News*, January 26, 1939.
   5. *Ibid.*, April 6, 1939.
   6. *El Paso Herald-Post*, August 1, 1939.
   7. *The Sporting News*, January 2, 1939, April 6, 1939.
   8. O'Neal, *The International League*, 127–128; baseball-reference.com/bullpen/Newark Bears; luckyshow.org/baseball/trunkmakers.
   9. Top 100 Teams mlb.com; I-70 Baseball.com./2011/07/22.
   10. *Olean* (NY) *Times Herald*, September 9, 1939; *Zanesville* (OH) *Signal*, August 26, 1939.
   11. Top 100 Teams, 3.
   12. Bill James, *New Bill James Historical Abstract* (New York: Free Press, 2011), 525.
   13. Gillette and Palmer, *The ESPN Baseball Encyclopedia*, 837, 863.
   14. *Ibid.*, 587–588.
   15. Gillette and Palmer, *The ESPN Baseball Encyclopedia*, 885.
   16. Top 100 Minor League Teams, 3; Gillette and Palmer, *The ESPN Baseball Encyclopedia*; Johnson and Wolff, *Encyclopedia of Minor League Baseball*, 885.
   17. Top 100 Minor League Teams, 3; Gillette and Palmer, *The ESPN Baseball Encyclopedia*, 860.
   18. Top 100 Teams, 4–5; Gillette and Palmer, *The ESPN Baseball Encyclopedia*, 1097.
   19. Vince DiMaggio—BR Bullpen, baseball-reference.com; Top 100 Teams, 3–4; Gillette and Palmer, *The ESPN Baseball Encyclopedia*, 451.170 baseball.com.
   20. Top 100 Teams, 1.
   21. *The Sporting News*, October 5, 1939.
   22. *Ibid.*, October 19, 1939; *Newark Eagle*, October 19, 1939.
   23. *Ibid.*, November 9, 1939.
   24. *Blytheville* (AR) December 9, 1939; *New York Times*, December 9, 1939.
   25. *New York Times*, January 10, 1940.
   26. *The Sporting News*, January 22, 1940.
   27. *Kingsport* (TN) *Times*, January 22, 1940.
   28. *Blytheville* (AR) *Courier News*, January 23, 1940; *The Sporting News*, January 22, 1940; *Sheboygan* (WI) *Journal*, January 23, 1940; *New York Times*, January 23, 1940; *Joplin Globe*, January 24, 1940.
   29. *Lowell* (MA) *Sun*, February 3, 1940; *Syracuse* (NY) *Herald Journal*, February 3, 1940.
   30. *The Sporting News*, June 17, 1940; John Simonson, *Kansas City 1940* (Charleston, SC: History Press, 2013), 118.
   31. O'Neal, *The International League*, 128–129; Johnson and Wolff, *Encyclopedia of Minor League Baseball*, 314; Newark Bears BR Bullpen, baseball reference.com.
   32. *The Sporting News*, January 11, 1940.
   33. *Ibid*; December 12, 1940; *New Haven Journal Courier*, January 27, 1941.
   34. *Lowell* (MA) *Sun*, January 28, 1941.
   35. *The Sporting News*, December 19, 1940.
   36. *Ibid.*, March 27, 1941.
   37. *Ibid.*, April 10, 1941.
   38. Johnson and Wolff, *Encyclopedia of Minor League Baseball*, 321.
   39. Newark Bears—BR Bullpen, baseball-reference.com; O'Neal, *The International League*, 130.
   40. *The Sporting News*, July 17, 1941.

41. The 1941 World Series by Baseball Almanac, baseball-almanac.com.
42. *The Sporting News*, September 18, 1941.
43. *Sandusky* (OH) *Register Star News*, September 13, 1941.
44. *New York Times*, May 4, 1941.
45. *The Sporting News*, December 11, 1940.
46. *Syracuse Herald Journal*, January 20, 1942.
47. *The Sporting News*, January 29, 1942.
48. Mark Gallagher, *Day by Day in New York Yankees History* (New York: Leisure Press, 1983), 134; Burton A. Boxerman and Benita W. Boxerman, *Ebbets to Veeck to Busch: Eight Owners Who Shaped Baseball* (Jefferson, NC: McFarland, 2003), 90.
49. Baseball History in 1942—The Home Grown Champions, www.thisgreatgame.com.
50. *Ibid.*
51. Gillette and Palmer, *The ESPN Baseball Encyclopedia*, 566; Lyle Spatz, *Yankees Coming, Yankees Going: New York Yankee Player Transactions, 1903 Through 1999* (Jefferson, NC: McFarland, 2000), 76–77. Glenn Stout, *Yankees Century: 100 Years of New York Yankees History* (Boston: Houghton Mifflin, 2002), 188–189.
52. *Ibid.*, 593; Gallagher, *Day by Day in New York Yankees History*, 134.
53. O'Neal, *The International League*, 130.
54. *Ogden* (UT) *Standard-Examiner*, August 5, 1941; *Galveston* (TX) *Daily News*, August 12, 1941; Johnson and Wolff, *Encyclopedia of Minor League Baseball*, 328.
55. *Zanesville* (OH) *Times Recorder*, February 17, 1942; *The Sporting News*, February 19, 1942; *Joplin* (MO) *News Herald*, *Brownsville* (TX) *Herald*, *Ogden* (UT) *Standard Examiner*, February 14, 1942.
56. Johnson and Wolff, *Encyclopedia of Minor League Baseball*, 332.
57. O'Neal, *The International League*, 130–131.
58. The 1942 World Series-baseball-reference.com; Bjarkman, *Encyclopedia of Major League Baseball Team Histories*, 266.
59. *Nevada* (Reno) *State Journal*, September 29, 1942; *Chester* (PA) *Times*, September 29, 1942; *New York Times*, September 18, 1942.
60. *Berkshire* (MA) *Evening Eagle*, October 17, 1942; *Altoona* (PA) *Mirror*, October 17, 1942.
61. William Willingham, Jr., en.cyclopedia.net.
62. *The Sporting News*, October 22, 1942.
63. *Ibid.*, October 29, 1942; unidentified newspaper clipping, George Weiss Scrapbook Volume 10, 1940–1942, Major League Baseball Hall of Fame.
64. *Kingston* (NY) *Daily Freeman*, October 24, 1942.
65. Gallagher, *Day by Day in New York Yankees History*, 137.
66. 1943 World Series by Baseball Almanac baseball-almanac.com.
67. *Burlington* (NC) *Daily Times News*, January 1, 1943.
68. Statistics, 1943 Newark Bears, baseball-reference.com.
69. Johnson and Wolff, *Encyclopedia of Minor League Baseball*, 337; 1943 Kansas City Blues Statistics-Minor Leagues, baseball-reference.com; *Laredo* (TX) *Times*, July 30, 1943; *Waterloo* (IA) *Daily Courier*, July 30, 1943.
70. Bjarkman, *Encyclopedia of Team Histories American League*, 266–67; 1943 World Series by Baseball Almanac, baseball-almanac.com; *New York Times*, August 19, 1947; *The Sporting News*, November 11, 1943.
71. *Zanesville* (OH) *Times-Recorder*, January 1, 1943.
72. Johnson and Wolff, *Encyclopedia of Minor League Ball*, 338, 341, 345; Stout, *Yankees Century*, 188; *Joplin* (MO) *Globe*, March 21, 1944.
73. *New Haven Journal Courier*, November 30, 1943.
74. *New York Times*, March 21, 1944.
75. *Titusville* (PA) *Herald*, March 21, 1944; *Twin Falls* (ID) *Times News*, March 21, 1944.
76. *New York Times*, April 7, 1944.
77. *Waterloo* (IA) *Daily Courier*, July 14, 1944; *Brainerd* (MN) *Daily Dispatch*, July 15, 1944; *Blytheville* (AR) *Courier*, July 15, 1944.
78. Johnson and Wolff, *Encyclopedia of Minor League Baseball*, 340; 1944 Kansas City Blues Statistics, baseball-reference.com.
79. Johnson and Wolff, *Encyclopedia of Minor League Baseball*, 340; Triple A Baseball.com.
80. Thorn et al., *Total Baseball*, 374.
81. The 1944 Baltimore Orioles, baltimoresun.com.
82. *The Sporting News*, November 9, 1944.

Chapter 7

1. *New York Times*, January 27, 1945.
2. Tommy Henrich with Bill Gilbert, *Five O'Clock Lightning: Ruth, Gehrig, DiMaggio, Mantle and the Glory Years of the New York Yankees* (New York: Carol Publishing Group, 1992), 197.
3. *Ibid.*
4. Kahn, *The Era*, 17.
5. *Ibid.*, 19; Larry MacPhail, baseball-fever.com.
6. *New York Times*, January 27, 1945, February 22, 1945.
7. *The Sporting News*, November 1, 1945; *New York Times*, February 22, 1945.
8. *The New York Times*, January 27, 1945.
9. *The Sporting News*, February 1, 1945.
10. *New York Times*, January 27, 1945; *The Sporting News*, February 1, 1945.
11. Donald Dewey and Nicholas Acocella, *The Baseball Clubs* (New York: Harper Perennial, 1993), 377.
12. *New York Times*, November 16, 1945; Dewey and Acocella, *The Baseball Clubs*, 377; Charles C. Alexander, *Our Game: An American Baseball History* (New York: Henry Holt, 1991), 168.
13. Johnson and Wolff, *Encyclopedia of Minor League Baseball*, 343.
14. Recap for 1945 New York Yankees Season, thebaseballpage.com.
15. *The Sporting News*, September 24, 1945.
16. Biographical Sketch, Allen H. Wood, westpoint.org.
17. *New York Times*, November 9, 1945; *The Sporting News*, November 15, 1945.
18. *The Sporting News*, November 22, 1945.
19. *New York Times*, November 15, 1945.
20. *The Sporting News*, November 22, 1945.
21. *Ibid.*, November 29, 1945, December 6, 1945.
22. *Joplin* (MO) *Globe*, January 9, 1946.
23. *The Sporting News*, January 31, 1946.

24. Frank Lane–BR Bullpen, baseball-reference.com; *Altoona* (PA) *Mirror*, January 10, 1946.
25. *The Sporting News*, March 7, 1946.
26. *Ibid.*, March 14, 1946.
27. Spatz, *Yankees Coming, Yankees Going*, 85.
28. Gillette and Palmer, *The ESPN Baseball Encyclopedia*, 451, 534, 577, 636; 1946 New York Yankees Season Recap, thebaseballpage.com.
29. The 1946 New York Yankees Season Recap.
30. *The Sporting News*, August 28, 1946.
31. Bjarkman, *Encyclopedia of Baseball Team Histories: American League*, 267. "Editorial Comment," *Baseball Magazine*, December 1947, 217.
32. Bjarkman, *Encyclopedia of Baseball Team Histories: American League*, 267; *The Sporting News*, September 18, 1946; Dewey and Acocella, *The Ball Clubs*, 377.
33. Bjarkman, *Encyclopedia of Baseball Team Histories*, 267.
34. *San Antonio* (TX) *Light*, October 15, 1946; *Galveston* (TX) *Daily News*, October 15, 1946.
35. *The Sporting News*, November 20, 1946.
36. *Greeley* (CO) *Daily Tribune*, February 4, 1955; *Mansfield* (OH) *News Journal*, February 4, 1955.
37. *The Sporting News*, June 11, 1947.
38. The 1947 New York Yankees Season Recap, thebaseballpage.com; baseball-reference.com./players plus.
39. Johnson and Wolff, *Encyclopedia of Minor League Baseball*, 365; *The Sporting News*, February 12, 1947.
40. *New York Times*, January 22, 1947.
41. *Syracuse Herald Journal*, May 8, 1947.
42. *Long Beach* (CA) *Independent*, April 14, 1947.
43. Gillette and Palmer, *The ESPN Baseball Encyclopedia*, 320.
44. *Kingsport* (TN) *News*, August 5, 1947; *The Sporting News*, August 27, 1947; *Anita* (IA) *Tribune*, September 18, 1947.
45. *The Sporting News*, September 24, 1947.
46. Baseball-reference.com.
47. The 1947 New York Yankees Season Recap, thebaseballpage.com.
48. Dewey and Acocella, *The Ball Clubs*, 377.
49. The 1947 New York Yankees Season Recap, thebaseballpage.com; Dewey and Acocella, *The Ball Clubs*, 377; Bjarkman, *Encyclopedia of Baseball Team Histories: American League*, 268; 1947 World Series at baseball-almanac.com; Gallagher, *Day by Day in New York Yankees History*, 158–159.
50. *Titusville* (PA) *Herald*, October 7, 1947; *Lowell* (MA) *Sun*, October 17, 1947; *Waukesha* (WI) *Daily Freeman*, October 7, 1947; "Baseball Businessman," *Forbes*, 16; Gross, *Yankee Doodles*, 149–150; Meany, "George Weiss: The *Real* Yankee Clipper," 7.
51. "Baseball Businessman," *Forbes*, August 1, 1951, 16; Gross. *Yankee Doodles*, 149; Golenbock, *Amazin'*, 91; Appel, *Pinstripe Empire*, 265.
52. Gallagher, *Day by Day in New York Yankees History*, 159; Stout, *Yankees History*, 222; Golenbock, *Amazin'*, 92–95; Appel, *Pinstripe Empire*, 265; Kahn, *The Era*, 142; Levitt, *Ed Barrow*, 370; Henrich, *Five O'Clock Lighting*, 196–197; "Baseball Businessman," *Forbes*, 16; Gross, *Yankee Doodles*, 149–150; Roger Kahn, *October Men: Reggie Jackson, George Steinbrenner, Billy Martin, and the Yankees' Miraculous Finish in 1978* (New York: Harcourt), 54–56.
53. Meany, George Weiss: The *Real* Yankee Clipper, 78; "Editorial Comment," *Baseball Magazine*, December 1947, 217; William Marshall, *Baseball's Pivotal Era 1945–1951* (Lexington: University Press of Kentucky, 1999), 164.

Chapter 8

1. Brief Biography of George Weiss, Hall of Fame Files, George Weiss.
2. Daniel, "Weiss Brought Varied Talents Into General Managership of Yankees," 299–300.
3. *Syracuse Herald Journal*, January 20, 1942; *The Sporting News*, January 29, 1942.
4. *New York World Telegram*, October 5, 1947; Volume 12, 1947 George Weiss Scrapbook; *The Sporting News*, October 15, 1947.
5. Stanley Frank, "Yankee Kingmaker," *Saturday Evening Post*, January 24, 1948, 23.
6. Daniel, "Weiss Brought Varied Talents Into General Managership of Yankees," 299.
7. Daniel Topping and Del Webb to George Weiss, October 7, 1947, Weiss Scrapbook Volume 12, 1947; Meany, *The Yankee Story*, 125; Appel, *Pinstripe Empire*, 267.
8. Appel, *Pinstripe Empire*, 267.
9. Will Harridge to George Weiss, Weiss Scrapbook, October 8, 1947, Volume 13, 1947–1948.
10. Tom Meany (and others), *The Magnificent Yankee* (New York: A. S. Barnes, 1952), 5.
11. Frank, *Yankee Kingmaker*, 23.
12. Unidentified newspaper clipping, George Weiss Scrapbook, Volume 12, October 8, 1947.
13. *Ibid.*
14. *The Sporting News*, October 15, 1947.
15. *Syracuse Herald Journal*, October 17, 1947.
16. *New York Journal American*, October 22, 1947; Kahn, *October Men*, 58.
17. Rosenthal, *Baseball Is Their Business*, 147–154.
18. *Hutchinson* (KS) *News Herald*, July 20, 1948.
19. *The Sporting News*, January 28, 1948.
20. *New York Times*, October 9, 22, 1947; *Hagerstown* (MD) *Morning Herald*, October 9, 1947; Appel, *Pinstripe Empire*, 268.
21. Daniel, "Weiss Brought Varied Talents Into General Managership of Yankees," 300.
22. *Lima* (OH) *News*, October 12, 1947; *Harrisburg* (IL) *Daily Register*, October 15, 1947; *Syracuse* (NY) *Herald Journal*, November 26, 1947.
23. *Freeport* (IL) *Journal Standard*, October 10, 1947; *New York Journal American*, October 22, 1947.
24. *Ibid*; *The Sporting News*, December 23, 1947; *Long Beach* (CA) *Independence*, December 24, 1947.
25. Gillette and Palmer, *The ESPN Baseball Encyclopedia*, 1198.
26. *The Sporting News*, December 10, 1947.
27. *Oakland Tribune*, January 6, 1948; *Waterloo* (IA) *Daily Courier*, January 6, 1948.
28. *Kingston* (NY) *Daily Freeman*, January 13, 1948.
29. *The Sporting News*, January 14, 21, 28, February 4, 1948; *New York Times*, January 14, 20, 22, 23, February 11, 1948; *Traverse City* (MI) *Record-Eagle*, February 24, 1948.
30. *Titusville* (PA) *Herald*, February 25, 1948; *Logansport* (IN) *Press*, February 25, 1948; *New York Times*, February 25, 1948; Appel, *Pinstripe Empire*, 268–269.

31. Spatz, *Yankees Coming and Going*, 92; Dewey and Acocella, *The Ball Clubs*, 378.
32. Golenbock, *Dynasty*, 88.
33. Gillette and Palmer, *The ESPN Baseball Encyclopedia*, 1356.
34. Ibid., 866.
35. Ibid., 1102.
36. Ibid., 1604.
37. *The Sporting News*, April 7, 1945.
38. David Halberstam, *Summer of '49* (New York: William Morrow, 1989), 76–77.
39. Ibid.
40. www.baseball-reference.com.
41. *The Sporting News*, August 11, 18, 1948.
42. Gillette and Palmer, *The ESPN Baseball Encyclopedia*, 1465.
43. Gallagher, *Day by Day in New York Yankees History*, 163; 1948-New York Yankees Season Recap–www.thebaseballpage.com.
44. Charleston (WV) *Mail*, Atlanta *Mirror*, Waterloo (IA) *Daily Courier*, September 15, 1948.
45. Tyrone (PA) *Daily Herald*, September 15, 1948.
46. *The Sporting News*, September 17, 1948.
47. Tucson *Daily Citizen*, Clovis (NM) *News Journal*, Kokomo (IN) *Tribune*, Nevada (Reno) *State Journal*, October 5, 1948; Dewey and Acocella, *The Ball Clubs*, 378; Bjarkman, *Encyclopedia of Major League Baseball Team Histories*, 268; Gallagher, *Day by Day in New York Yankees History*, 165.
48. Newcastle (PA) *News*, October 23, 1948.
49. Lowell (MA) *Sun*, October 23, 1948.
50. Jack Smiles, *Bucky Harris: A Biography of Baseball's Boy Wonder* (Jefferson, NC: McFarland, 2012), 231.
51. Henrich, *Five O'Clock Lightning*, 205.
52. Gallagher, *Day by Day in New York Yankees History*, 165; Harvey Frommer, *New York City Baseball: The Last Golden Age 1947–1957* (New York: Macmillan, 1980), 130; Dewey and Acocella, *The Ball Clubs*, 378; Golenbock, *Dynasty*, 1; Goldman, *Forging Genius*, 22; Gittleman, *Reynolds, Raschi and Lopat*, 38–39; Barra, *Yogi Berra*, 89.
53. Goldman, *Forging Changes*, 21.
54. David Kaiser, *Epic Season: The 1948 American League Pennant Race* (Amherst: University of Massachusetts Press, 1978), 187; Carlo De Vito, *Scooter: The Biography of Phil Rizzuto* (Chicago: Triumph Books, 2010), 134; Shaplen, "The Real Boss," 37; Charles Dexter, "New Reign of Terror," *Sport* 16, February 1954, 88; Ed Linn, *The Great Rivalry: The Yankees and the Red Sox 1901–1990* (New York: Ticknor & Fields, 1991), 191–192.
55. Reno (NV) *State Journal*, October 13, 1948; Robinson and Jennison, *Pennants & Pinstripes*, 95; Dexter, "New Reign of Terror," 28.
56. Goldman, *Forging Genius*, 88.
57. Creamer, *Stengel: His Life and Times*, 114; Golenbock, *Dynasty*, 2–3.
58. Jack Mann, *Fall of the New York Yankees* (New York: Simon & Schuster, 1967), 118.
59. Maury Allen, *You Could Look It Up: The Life of Casey Stengel* (New York: Times Books, 1979), 9.
60. *Hartford Courant*, June 21, 1927; Gallagher, *Day by Day in New York Yankees History*, 165; Dewey and Acocella, *The Ball Clubs*, 378; "Casey Stengel," *American National Biography Online*, webmaster@www.anb.org. 2.
61. Gittelman, *Raschi, Reynolds and Lopat*, 40.

62. "Casey Stengel," *American National Biography Online* 2–3.
63. Paul Dickson, *Bill Veeck: Baseball's Greatest Maverick* (New York: Walker, 1996), 99.
64. Meany, *The Magnificent Yankees*, 40; Allen, *You Could Look It Up*, 1335.
65. Creamer, *Stengel: His Life and Times*, 204.
66. Bill Bishop, "Casey Stengel," sabr.org/bio project, 4; Meany, *The Magnificent Yankees*, 40.
67. Allen, *You Could Look It Up*, 13.
68. Berger and Berger, *Management Wisdom From the New York Yankees' Dynasty*, 41.
69. John Tullis, *I'd Rather Be a Yankee: An Oral History of America's Most Loved and Most Hated Baseball Team* (New York: Macmillan, 1986), 182.
70. Creamer, *Stengel: His Life and Times*, 210.
71. Allen, *You Could Look It Up*, 6–7.
72. Creamer, *Stengel: His Life and Times*, 210.
73. Beckley (WV) *Post-Herald*, October 13, 1948.
74. Goldman, *Forging Genius*, 243.
75. Rader, *A History of America's Game*, 165.
76. Ed Linn, *The Great Rivalry* (New York: Tickner & Fields, 1991), 233.
77. Creamer, *Stengel: His Life and Times*, 212; Tom Meany, "Stengel: The Man Who Laughed Last," *Sport*, April 1950, 90.
78. *The Sporting News*, October 27, 1948; Portland (ME) *Press Herald*, Waterloo (IA) *Daily Courier*, October 28, 1948.
79. Bluefield (WV), *Daily Telegraph*, October 28, 1948.
80. Creamer, *Stengel: His Life and Times*, 223; *The Sporting News*, November 3, 1948.
81. Portland (ME) *Press Herald*, October 28, 1948.
82. Creamer, *Stengel: His Life and Times*, 223; Gillette and Palmer, *The ESPN Baseball Encyclopedia*, 1507; *The Sporting News*, December 22, 1948.
83. Ibid., November 10, 24, 1948.
84. Ibid., October 6, 1948.
85. www.baseball-almanac.com.
86. *New York Times*, June 4, 2001.
87. *New York Times*, Middleboro (KY) *Daily News*, January 7, 1959; *The Sporting News*, January 5, 1949.
88. Portland (ME) *Press Herald*, January 15, 1949; *The Sporting News*, February 2, 1949; Gallagher, *Day by Day in New York Yankees History*, 166; Dewey and Acocella, *The Ball Clubs*, 379.
89. Statesville (NC) *Daily Record*, March 4, 1949; Dewey and Acocella, *The Ball Clubs*, 379.
90. Marshall, *Baseball's Pivotal Era*, 274.
91. Durso, *Casey: The Life and Legend of Charles Dillon Stengel*, 116.
92. *The Sporting News*, August 31, 1949.
93. Creamer, *Stengel: His Life and Times*, 230.
94. Marshall, *Baseball's Pivotal Era*, 275.
95. Long Beach (CA) *Independent*, October 3, 1949; Gallagher, *Day by Day in New York Yankees History*, 171; "1949 New York Yankees Season Recap, The Baseball Page," thebaseballpage.com; Bjarkman, *Encyclopedia of Baseball Team Histories: American League*, 269; Dewey and Acocella, *The Ball Clubs*, 379; Goldman, *Forging Genius*, 259–261; Lubbock (TX) *Morning Avalanche*, October 3, 1949.
96. Thorn et al., *Total Baseball*, 379; Beckley (WV), *Herald*, *Wisconsin State Journal*, October 10, 1949.
97. Goldman, *Forging Genius*, 262.

Chapter 9

1. factmonster.com/ipka.
2. Branch Rickey to George Weiss, George Weiss files, October 14, 1949, Baseball Hall of Fame.
3. Baseball-reference. com/bullpen/Bonus_rule; *Racine Journal*, December 8, 1949.
4. *New York Times*, December 7, 1949.
5. *Ibid.*, December 21, 1949; *The Sporting News*, November 11, 1949.
6. Roy Terrell, "Yankee Secrets: The Answers to Five Questions About Baseball's Greatest Team," *Sports Illustrated*, July 22, 1957, 9; Milton Gross, "The Yankees: After Weiss and Stengel, What?" *Sport*, June 1958, 80–81; Henrich, *Five O'clock Lightning*, 231.
7. Golenbock, *Dynasty*, 274.
8. Halberstam, *Summer of '49*, 134.
9. Golenbock, *Dynasty*, 273.
10. *Ibid.*, 274.
11. Burk, *Much More Than a Game*, 111.
12. "World Series Flashbacks," *Sport*, October 1959, 8.
13. Halberstam, *Summer of '49*, 102.
14. Rosenthal, "Yankee Trader," 42.
15. Halberstam, *Summer of '49*, 181.
16. Golenbock, *Dynasty*, 271.
17. *The Sporting News*, December 14, 1949.
18. *The Sporting News*, November 9, 23, 1949; December 14, 1949; *New York Times*, December 16, 1949; *Burlington* (IA) *Hawkeye Gazette*, December 6, 1949.
19. *The Sporting News*, February 1, 1950; *Syracuse Herald Journal*, February 5, 1950.
20. *The Sporting News*, November 23, 1949; Gallagher, *Day by Day in New York Yankees History*, 166; *New York Times*, January 24, 1950; *Racine* (WI) *Journal*, January 25, 1950.
21. *Altoona* (PA) *Mirror*, January 19, 1950; *New York Times*, January 24, 31, 1950.
22. *New York Times*, February 17, 1950; *The Sporting News*, March 8, 1950.
23. *Statesville* (NC) *Daily Record*, March 8, 1950; *New York Times*, March 8, 1950.
24. David Nemec and Dave Zeman, *The Baseball Rookies Encyclopedia* (Dulles, VA: Potomac Books), 179.
25. *The Sporting News*, May 1, 1950.
26. *San Antonio Express*, May 12, 1950.
27. *The Sporting News*, April 5, 1950.
28. *Ibid.*, October 19, 1949; *Statesville* (NC) *Daily Record*, March 8, 1950; Durso, *Casey*, 156; Gallagher, *Day by Day in New York Yankees History*, 176–177; *Salt Lake Tribune*, June 19, 1950; *Frederick* (MO) *News Post*, June 17, 1950.
29. *Frederick* (MO) *News Post*, June 17, 1950; Lyle Spatz, *Yankees Coming, Yankees Going: New York Yankee Player Transactions, 1903 Through 1999* (Jefferson, NC: McFarland, 2000), 99; *The Sporting News*, June 21, 1950.
30. Baseball-reference.com., May 7, 1951; Howard Siner, *Sweet Seasons: Baseball's Top Teams Since 1920* (New York: Pharos Books, 1998), 169; Durso, *Casey*, 130.
31. www.baseball-almanac.com; baseball-reference.com; Gallagher, *Day by Day in New York Yankees History*, 177–178.
32. Durso, *Casey*, 130.
33. *New York Times*, September 6, 1950.
34. *Racine* (WI) *Journal Times*, September 8, 1950; *Beatrice* (NE) *Daily Sun*, September 10, 1950.
35. Gallagher, *Day by Day in New York Yankees History*, 180; *Terre Haute Star*, October 4, 1950; *Middleburg* (KY) *Daily News*, October 4, 1950.
36. Siner, *Sweet Seasons*, 171.
37. *Ironwood* (MI) *Daily Globe, Tucson Daily Citizen*, October 9, 1950.
38. Sinar, *Sweet Seasons*, 171.
39. *New York Times*, October 9, 1950; *Lowell* (MA) *Sun*, October 15, 1950.
40. *San Antonio Light*, December 30, 1950; *Wisconsin State Journal* (Madison), December 30, 1950.
41. *New York Times*, October 10, 1950; *Elyria* (OK) *Chronicle Telegram*, October 12, 1950; *Uniontown* (PA) *Morning Herald*, October 13, 1950.
42. *Jefferson City* (MO) *Post Tribune*, November 20, 1950; *Oakland* (CA) *Tribune*, November 21, 1950; *Titusville* (PA) *Herald*, November 21, 1950.
43. *The Sporting News*, November 22, 1950; *New York Times*, December 19, 1950, December 1, 2009.
44. DeVito, *Scooter*, 164.
45. *San Antonio Express*, December 1, 1950.
46. DeVito, *Scooter*, 164.
47. *The Sporting News*, December 13, 1950.
48. *Ibid.*, January 10, 1951.
49. *Long Beach* (CA) *Press Telegraph*, January 13, 1951.
50. *San Mateo* (CA) *Times*, January 6, 1951.
51. *Lowell* (MA) *Sun*, January 6, 1951.
52. *Syracuse* (NY) *Post Standard*, February 14, 1951; *Bradford* (PA) *Era*, February 16, 1951.
53. Golenbock, *Dynasty*, 29.
54. Marshall, *Baseball's Pivotal Era*, 299; Donald Honig, *Baseball Between the Lines: Baseball in the '40s and '50s as Told by the Men Who Played It* (New York: Coward, McCann, and Geoghegan, 1976), 179; Dom Forker, *The Men of Autumn: An Oral History of the 1949–1953 World Champion New York Yankees* (Dallas: Taylor, 1989), 21.
55. *Abilene* (TX) *Reporter News*, January 13, 1951; *Portland* (ME) *Press Herald*, February 28, 1951; *High Point* (NC) *Enterprise*, March 18, 1951.
56. Barra, *Yogi Berra*, 142; Ed Fitzgerald, "The Fabulous Yogi Berra," *Sport*, August 1951, 42.
57. *Bradford* (PA) *Era*, February 3, 1951; *The Sporting News*, February 7, 1951.
58. Gallagher, *Day by Day in New York Yankees History*, 181; Allen, *You Could Look It Up*, 151.
59. *Salt Lake* (UT) *Tribune*, October 17, 1950.
60. Gallagher, *Day by Day in New York Yankees History*, 181; *Tucson* (AZ) *Daily Citizen*, January 10, 1951; www.bbpage.com.
61. Gittleman, *Reynolds, Raschi and Lopat*, 93; www.mayoclinic.org./diseases-conditions/osteomyelitis.
62. Creamer, *Stengel: His Life and Times*, 243; *Ada* (OK) *Daily News*, July 16, 1951; Bjarkman, *Encyclopedia of Baseball Team Histories: American League*, 270; James Lincoln Ray, *Mickey Mantle* (SABR BioProject, 2); Golenbock, *Dynasty*, 55–56.
63. *Ada* (OK) *Daily News*, July 16, 1951; Bjarkman, *Encyclopedia of Major League Baseball Histories, American League*, 270.
64. *San Antonio Light*, January 14, 1951.
65. *The Sporting News*, January 31, 1951.
66. *Long Beach* (CA) *Independent*, April 15, 1951.
67. *The Sporting News*, May 23, 1951.
68. Marshall, *Baseball's Pivotal Era*, 407.
69. Spatz, *Yankees Coming, Yankees Going*, 102–

103; Rosenthal, "Yankee Trader," 43; *New York Times,* June 16, 1961.
70. Bjarkman, *Encyclopedia of Baseball Team Histories, American League,* 270.
71. Siner, *Sweet Seasons,* 167.
72. Bjarkman, *Encyclopedia of Baseball Team Histories: American League,* 270; Gallagher, *Day by Day in New York Yankees History,* 185; Dewey and Acocella, *The Ball Clubs,* 379; 1951 New York Yankees Season Recap, thebaseballpage.com; nytimes.com/2010/11/30sports/baseball; *The Sporting News,* January 2, 1952.
73. *The Sporting News,* October 17, 1951.
74. Siner, *Sweet Seasons,* 168; Gallagher, *Day by Day in New York Yankees History,* 185.
75. Gallagher, *Day by Day in New York Yankees History,* 185; Bjarkman, *Encyclopedia of Baseball Team Histories: American League,* 270; Cramer, *Joe DiMaggio: The Hero's Life,* 314; *New York Times,* December 11, 1951; *Salt Lake* (UT) *Tribune,* December 12, 1951.
76. Dewey and Acocella, *The Ball Clubs,* 379; Bjarkman, *Encyclopedia of Baseball Team Histories: American League,* 270.
77. *The Sporting News,* October 24, 1951.
78. www.baseball-reference./leagues/AL.1951; *New York Times,* November 25, 1951; *Burlington* (NC), *Daily Times News,* March 12, 1952; *Fitchburg* (MA) *Sentinel,* March 12, 1952.
79. *The Sporting News,* March 12, 1952.
80. *New York Times,* October 31, 1951; *Joplin* (MO) *Globe,* October 31, 1951; *The Sporting News,* November 11, 1951; *Ogden* (UT) *Standard-Examiner,* October 31, 1951.
81. *The Sporting News,* January 9, 30, 1952; *New York Times,* January 25, 1952.
82. "Ed Lopat" BR Bullpen-baseball-reference.com/bullpen/Ed_Lopat; *Big Spring* (TX) *Daily Herald,* January 17, 1952.
83. *The Sporting News,* January 23, 1932.
84. *Ibid.,* January 30, 1952.
85. "Classic Yankees: Allie Reynolds," bronxbaseballdaily.com.
86. *New York Times,* February 5, 1952, March 2, 1952; *Billings* (MT) *Gazette,* February 1, 1952; *The Sporting News,* February 6, 1952; *Charleston* (WV) *Daily Mail,* February 2, 1952; De Vito, *Scooter,* 175–176.
87. *The Sporting News,* April 2, 1952.
88. www.thebaseballpage.com/season/1952-new-york-yankees; *The Sporting News,* January 30, 1952.
89. Gillette and Palmer, *The ESPN Baseball Encyclopedia,* 616, 1522.
90. Gallagher, *Day by Day in New York Yankees History,* 186; *San Mateo* (CA) *Times,* May 2, 1952; *Anniston* (AL) *Star,* May 4, 1952; *The Sporting News,* May 14, 21, 1952.
91. *The Sporting News,* July 30, 1952, August 4, 1952; *Statesville* (NC) *Daily Record,* August 22, 1952; *Chester* (PA) *Times,* August 22, 1952.
92. *San Mateo* (CA) *Times,* August 28, 1952; *Oshkosh* (WI) *Daily Northwestern,* August 25, 1982; *Leavenworth* (KS) *Times,* August 28, 1952.
93. Bjarkman, *Encyclopedia of Baseball Team Histories: American League,* 270; "1952 New York Yankees Season Recap, The Baseball Page," thebaseballpage.com/season/1952-new-york-yankees.
94. Gallagher, *Day by Day in New York Yankees History,* 193; Thorn et al., *Total Baseball,* 382; "1952 Recap—The Baseball Page," the baseballpage.com/season/1952-new-york-yankees.
95. *The Sporting News,* October 15, 1952.
96. *Pacific Stars and Stripes* (Tokyo, Japan), January 5, 1953; *The Sporting News,* January 28, 1953; *New York Times,* January 18, 1953.
97. *Ibid.*
98. *The Sporting News,* June 11, 1952; *Syracuse* (NY) *Herald-American,* December 28, 1952; *Huntington* (PA) *Daily News,* October 10, 1952.
99. *The Sporting News,* October 22, 1952; *Cedar Rapids* (IA) *Gazette,* October 31, 1952; *Santa Fe New Mexican,* October 30, 1952; *New York Times,* October 31, 1952; *Winona* (MN) *Republican Herald,* October 31, 1952; *Mount Vernon* (IL) *Register News,* October 31, 1952.
100. *El Paso* (TX) *Herald Post,* October 31, 1952; *Coshocton* (OH) *Tribune,* November 1, 1952; *Elyria* (OH) *Chronicle-Tribune,* November 1, 1952.
101. Baseballlibrary.com/chronology/byyear.php; *The Sporting News,* November 12, 1952.
102. *The Sporting News,* December 24, 1952.
103. Baseball-reference.com/teams/NYY.
104. *The Sporting News,* January 20, July 30, November 28, and December 25, 1952; *Jefferson City* (MO) *Post Tribune,* October 30, 1952.
105. *Salt Lake Tribune,* October 13, 1952.
106. *Wisconsin State Journal,* October 13, 1952.
107. *The Sporting News,* December 31, 1952.
108. *Billings* (MT) *Gazette,* January 21, 1953; *Abilene* (TX) *Reporter-News,* January 21, 1953.
109. *The Sporting News,* January 22, 1953.
110. *Long Beach* (CA) *Press-Telegram,* February 5, 1953; *Athens* (OH) *Messenger,* February 26, 1953.
111. Baseball-reference.com./leagues/AL/1952 pitching-leaders.shtml; Gillette and Palmer, *ESPN Baseball Encyclopedia,* 1482; baseball-almance.com/players/php.
112. "Classic Yankees: Allie Reynolds" bronxbaseballdaily.com.
113. *Sheboygan* (WI) *Daily Press,* February 23, 1953; *Twins Falls* (ID) *Daily Press,* February 23, 1953.
114. *Athens* (OH) *Messenger,* February 26, 1953; *Lubbock* (TX) *Evening Journal,* February 27, 1953; *The Sporting News,* March 4, 1953.
115. *New York Times,* March 22, 1953; *The Sporting News,* June 10, 1953.
116. *Lima* (OH) *News,* June 17, 1953; *Elyria* (OH) *Chronicle Telegram,* June 17, 1953.
117. Gallagher, *Day by Day in New York Yankees History,* 196; *The Sporting News,* September 2, 23, 1953; *Syracuse* (NY) *Herald Journal,* September 18, 1953.
118. "1953 New York Yankees Season Recap," thebaseballpage.com/season 1953-new-york-yankees.
119. *Mitchell* (SD) *Daily Republic,* September 17, 1953; *Nevada* (Reno) *State Journal,* September 16, 1953.
120. Bjarkman, *Encyclopedia of Baseball Team Histories: American League,* 279.
121. Siner, *Sweet Seasons,* 145; "1953 New York Yankees Season Recap"; Gallagher, *Day by Day in New York Yankees History,* 196; *Tyner* (PA) *Daily Herald,* October 2, 1983.
122. Frommer, *New York City Baseball,* 137.
123. *Ibid.*
124. *San Antonio* (TX) *Express,* June 17, 1953; *Albuquerque Journal,* June 18, 1953; *Iola* (KS) *Register,* June 23, 1953; *Oakland Tribune,* October 20, 1953.

125. *Ames* (IA) *Daily Tribune*, September 16, 1953; *Holland* (MI) *Evening Star*, September 16, 1953.
126. *Pacific Stars and Stripes* (Tokyo, Japan) October 16, 1953; *Mansfield* (OH) *News*, October 7, 1953; *Ogden* (UT) *Standard*, October 16, 1953.
127. *Monessen* (PA) *Daily Independent*, September 19, 1953; *Idaho State Journal* (Pocatello), September 21, 1953.
128. *The Sporting News*, November 4, 25, 1953.
129. *Ibid.*, October 4, 1953.
130. *New York Times*, December 18, 1953; *The Sporting News*, December 23, 1953.
131. *The Sporting News*, November 4, 11, 1953; *Pacific Stars and Stripes* (Tokyo, Japan), January 11, 1954; *New York Times*, November 5, 1954; *Kerrville* (TX) *Daily Times*, January 19, 1954; *Blytheville* (AK) *Courier News*, January 19, 1954.
132. *The Sporting News*, January 27, February 10, 1954.
133. *New York Times*, January 6, 1954.
134. *Hamilton* (OH) *Daily News Journal*, January 23, 1954; *Kokomo* (IN) *Tribune*, January 23, 1954.
135. *The Sporting News*, February 24, 1954.
136. *Indiana* (PA) *Evening Gazette*, February 24, 1954.
137. Halberstam, *Summer of '49*, 268.
138. "Vic Raschi Baseball Stats," baseball-almanac.com/players/player.php.
139. Spatz, *Yankees Coming, Yankees Going*, 109–110.
140. Golenbock, *Dynasty*, 29.
141. Halberstam, *Summer of '49*, 268; Gittelman, *Reynolds, Raschi and Lopat*, 185; Lawrence Baldassaro, *Beyond DiMaggio: Italian Americans in Baseball* (Lincoln: University of Nebraska Press, 2011), 258; Gallagher, *Day by Day in New York Yankees History*, 198.
142. *Lima* (OH) *News*, February 24, 1954.
143. *Winona* (MN) *Republican-Herald*, February 24, 1954; *Racine* (WI) *Journal*, March 12, 1954; *Galveston* (TX) *News*, March 22, 1954.
144. *Indiana* (PA) *Evening Gazette*, February 24, 1954.
145. *Canandaigua* (NY) *Daily Messenger*, February 25, 1954.
146. Baseball-reference.com.
147. *The Sporting News*, March 31, 1954; *New York Times*, February 4, 1954; *Newport* (RI) *Daily News*, March 12, 1954; *Mansfield* (OH) *News Journal*, March 14, 1954; Gallagher, *Day by Day in New York Yankees History*, 197.
148. *The Sporting News*, February 17, 1954.
149. *Ibid.*, March 17, 1954.
150. *Walla Walla* (WA) *Union Bulletin*, April 2, 1954; *Reno* (NV) *Evening Gazette*, April 21, 1954.
151. *New York Times*, April 12, 1954.
152. *Ibid.*
153. *Lethbridge* (Alberta, Canada) *Herald*, April 12, 1954; *Long Beach* (CA) *Independent*, April 12, 1954.
154. *Hagerstown* (MD) *Daily Mail*, April 14, 1954; *Lake Charles* (LA) *American Press*, April 14, 1954; *The Sporting News*, April 21, 1954.
155. *New York Times*, April 28, 1954.
156. *San Antonio Express*, May 5, 1954.
157. *The Sporting News*, May 12, 1954.
158. *Lima* (OH) *News*, July 28, 1954; *Kingsport* (TN) *News*, July 28, 1954.
159. *The Sporting News*, August 4, 1954.
160. *Ibid*; Appel, *Pinstripe Empire*, 302.
161. *Ibid*; *Sporting News*, August 18, 1954.
162. Appel, *Pinstripe Empire*, 302.
163. *The Sporting News*, April 21, 1954.
164. *European Stars and Stripes* (Darmstadt, Hesse), May 1, 1954.
165. *The Sporting News*, June 9, 1954.
166. Forker, *Sweet Seasons*, 48.
167. Gillette and Palmer, *The ESPN Baseball Encyclopedia*, 115.
168. Baseball-reference.coms/teams/CLE/1954.
169. Thorn et al., *Total Baseball*, 384.
170. Golenbock, *Dynasty*, 271.
171. *The Sporting News*, September 29, 1954.
172. *Ibid*; *Hagerstown* (MD) *Morning Herald*, September 22, 1954.
173. *The Sporting News*, October 15, 1954, November 3, 1954.
174. *San Antonio* (TX) *Light*, November 4, 1954; *Ft. Pierce* (FL) *News*, November 4, 1954; *The Sporting News*, November 10, 1954.
175. *Connellsville* (PA) *Daily Courier*, November 18, 1954; *Hayward* (CA) *Daily Review*, November 18, 1954; *New York Times*, November 19, 1954.
176. Spatz, *Yankees Coming, Yankees Going*, 113.
177. *Ibid.*
178. *Newport* (CA) *Daily News*, November 22, 1954.
179. *The Sporting News*, December 1, 1954.
180. Gallagher, *Day by Day in New York Yankees History*, 197.
181. Jeff Katz, *The Kansas City A's and the Wrong Half of the Yankees* (Hingham, MA: Maple Street Press, 2007).
182. *Ibid.*
183. *Winnipeg Free Press*, November 9, 1954; *New York Times*, November 30, 1954.
184. *The Sporting News*, December 15, 1954.

Chapter 10

1. www.sports-management-degrees.com/1—first-african-american-players-in-major-league-baseball; John Thorn, ed., *The Glory Days: New York Baseball 1947–1957* (New York: Collins, 2008), 27; Sullivan, *Minors*, 205; David G. Surdam, *The Postwar Yankees: Baseball's Golden Age Revisited* (Lincoln: University of Nebraska Press, 2008), 190–191; Stout, *Yankees Century*, 210–211.
2. Kahn, *The Era*, 189; Golenbock, *Dynasty*, 140.
3. Surdam, *Postwar Yankees*, 190–191; David Halberstam, *October 1964* (New York: Villard, 1994), 54; Neil Lanctot, *Negro League Baseball: The Rise and Ruin of a Black Institution* (Philadelphia: University of Pennsylvania Press, 2004), 390.
4. Ray Robinson and Christopher Jennison, *Pennants and Pinstripes: The New York Yankees 1903–2002* (New York: Penguin Group, 2002), 121.
5. Halberstam, *October 1964*, 54–55.
6. Glenn Stout, ed., *Top of the Heat: A Yankee Collection* (Boston: Houghton Mifflin, 2003), 108–109.
7. *Ibid*; James S. Hirsch, *Willie Mays: The Life and Legend* (New York: Scribner's, 2010), 62–63; Kahn, *The Era*, 189–190; Julius Tygiel, *Baseball's Great Experiment: Jackie Robinson and His Legacy* (New York: Oxford University Press, 1983), 296–297.

8. *The Sporting News*, August 19, 1953; Golenbock, *Dynasty*, 139.
9. *Ibid.*, 294.
10. Arlene Howard with Ralph Wimbish, *Elston and Me: The Story of the First Black Yankee* (Columbia: University of Missouri Press, 2001), 27.
11. Frommer, *New York City Baseball*, 128.
12. Dean Chadwin, *Those Damn Yankees: The Secret Life of America's Greatest Franchise* (New York: Verso, 1999), 144; Halberstam, *October 1964*, 54, 231.
13. Lanctot, *Negro League Baseball*, 390.
14. Golenbock, *Dynasty*, 139.
15. Shapiro, *Bottom of the Ninth*, 67–69.
16. Frommer, *New York City Baseball*, 138.
17. Henrich, *Five O'clock Lightning*, 283.
18. Chadwin, *Those Damn Yankees*, 144.
19. Smith, *Baseball in the Afternoon*, 192–193.
20. Milton Gross, "Will the Yankees Hire a Negro Player," *Our Sports*, July 1953, 9.
21. "Bob Thurman Statistics and History," www.baseball-reference.com; "Luis Marquez Statistics and History," www.baseball-reference.com; Gillette and Palmer, *The ESPN Baseball Encyclopedia*, 706, 973.
22. *Sandusky* (OH) *Register Star News*, May 18, 1949.
23. Thorn, *The Glory Days*, 28; "The Boston Globe," www.boston.com/boston globe/obituaries; *Kingston* (NY) *Daily Freeman*, February 11, 1949; *Hagerstown* (MD) *Morning Herald*, February 11, 1949; *Gettysburg* (PA) *Times*, February 12, 1949; *New York Times*, February 12, 1949; *The Sporting News*, February 23, 1949; *Waukesha* (WI) *Daily Freeman*, May 14, 1949.
24. *Mason City* (IA) *Globe Gazette*, May 16, 1949.
25. Gross, "Will the Yankees Hire a Negro Player?" 58.
26. *The Sporting News*, July 26, 1950.
27. *Ibid.*; Golenbock, *Dynasty*, 140; Thorn, *Glory Days*, 28.
28. *Ibid.*
29. *Hammond* (IN) *Times*, April 20, 1952; *Lowell* (MA) *Sun*, April 20, 1952; Howard, *Elston and Me*, 27; Barra, *Yogi Berra*, 171.
30. Tygiel, *Baseball's Great Experiment*, 296.
31. *The Sporting News*, July 19, 1952, November 26, 1952; *Walla Walla* (WA) *Union Bulletin*, December 2, 1952.
32. *San Antonio* (TX) *Light*, December 1, 1952; *North Adams* (MS) *Transcript*, December 1, 1952.
33. *Lowell* (MA) *Sun*, December 1, 1952; *Cedar Rapids* (IA) *Gazette*, December 1, 1952.
34. *Danville* (VA) *Bee*, December 6, 1952; *Billings* (MT) *Gazette*, December 7, 1952.
35. Arnold Rampersad, *Jackie Robinson: A Biography* (New York: Alfred A. Knopf, 1997), 254.
36. *Ibid.*
37. *The Sporting News*, December 10, 1952.
38. "Strike Out Demonstration," leaflet, April 1953, George Weiss file, Baseball Hall of Fame.
39. Lanctot, *Negro League Baseball*, 391.
40. *Ibid.*; Gross, "Will the Yankees Hire a Negro Player?" 9–10, 58–59.
41. *The Sporting News*, August 12, 19, 1953.
42. Stout, *Yankee Century*, 245.
43. Bjarkman, *Encyclopedia of Major League Baseball Team Histories*, 248–249; *New York Times*, November 30, 2005; Halberstam, *October '64*, 232; Robert Letarte, "That One Glorious Season," found at baseballlibrary.com; Edward Linn and Hal Lebovitz, "Vic Power: Master at First Base," *Saturday Evening Post*, July 29, 1961, 30, 49–51.
44. *Hagerstown* (MD) *Daily Mail*, October 14, 1953; *Ada* (OK) *Evening News*, October 14, 1953.
45. *The Sporting News*, October 21, 1953.
46. *Pacific Stars and Stripes* (Tokyo), November 5, 1953; *Nevada State Journal* (Reno), November 6, 1953.
47. *The Sporting News*, December 23, 1953; Appel, *Pinstripe Empire*, 299; Surdam, *The Postwar Yankees*, 187.
48. Madden, *Pride of October*, 150.
49. Surdam, *The Postwar Yankees*, 187.
50. *The Sporting News*, December 23, 1953, January 6, 1954.
51. Henrich, *Five O'clock Lightning*, 283.
52. *New Haven Register* (Interview on March 13, 1961, *Sports Illustrated*, reprinted September 16, 2012).
53. *The Sporting News*, March 3, 1954.
54. Surdham, *Postwar Yankees*, 187.
55. *The Sporting News*, March 3, 1954.
56. *Ibid.*, April 7, 1954.
57. *Ibid.*, October 17, 1954.
58. *Ibid.*, May 19, 1954.
59. *Ibid.*, September 15, 1954; *Logansport* (IN) *Express*, October 16, 1954; *Billings* (MT) *Gazette*, October 16, 1954; *New York Times*, October 16, 1954.
60. *Ibid.*, December 8, 1954.
61. *Newport* (RI) *News*, November 22, 1954.
62. Barra, *Yogi Berra*, 195–196; Golenbock, *Dynasty*, 141.
63. *The Sporting News*, December 22, 1954.
64. Dewey and Acocella, *The Ball Clubs*, 380; Golenbock, *Dynasty*, 142–43; *The Sporting News*, August 3, 1955.
65. "Classic Yankees: Elston Howard," bronxbaseballdaily.com/2011/03classic-yankees-elston-howard.
66. Halberstam, *October 1964*, 231.
67. *Ibid.*, 231–232; Berger and Berger, *Management Wisdom From the New York Yankees' Dynasty*, 191.
68. William J. Ryczek, *The Yankees in the Early Sixties* (Jefferson, NC: McFarland, 2008), 146.
69. Howard, *Elston and Me*, 31.
70. Stout, *Yankees Century*, 254.
71. John Tulius, *I'd Rather Be a Yankee: An Oral History of America's Most Loved and Most Hated Team*, (New York: Macmillan, 1986), 277.
72. *New York Times*, April 7, 1955; December 28, 1994.
73. Golenbock, *Dynasty*, 137–138; *The Sporting News*, January 26, 1955; *New York Times*, February 4, 1955; *Brownsville* (TX) *Herald*, February 23, 1955; *Oxnard* (CA) *Press-Courier*, February 23, 1955.
74. *Abilene* (TX) *Reporter News*, January 29, 1955; *The Sporting News*, February 9, 1955, March 2, 1955; *Anderson* (IN) *Herald*, February 20, 1955.
75. *San Antonio* (TX) *Light*, November 4, 1954; *Fort Pierce* (FL) *News*, November 4, 1954.
76. *The Sporting News*, December 7, 1955.
77. *Ibid.*, February 1, 1955; Gallagher, *Day By Day in New York Yankees History*, 202.
78. *The New York Times*, June 19, 1955.
79. *The Sporting News*, May 18, 1955.
80. *Waukesha* (WI) *Daily Freeman*, June 18, 1955; *Waco* (TX) *Tribune*, June 18, 1955.
81. Barra, *Yogi Berra*, 233; Stout, *Yankees Century*, 264; "Arnold Johnson—BR Bullpen," www.baseball-

reference.com/bullpen/ArnoldJohnson; Chadwin, *Those Damn Yankees*, 86.

82. "1955 New York Yankees," www.baseball-reference.com./teamsNYY/1955; "1955 New York Yankees Season Recap," www.thebaseballpage/com/season/1955; Bjarkman, *Encyclopedia of Baseball Team Histories: American League*, 271.

83. Gallagher, *Day by Day in New York Yankees History*, 206; Bjarkman, *Encyclopedia of Baseball Team Histories: American League*, 270; www.thebaseballpage.com.

84. *The Sporting News*, June 15, October 12, November 2, 1955; *Oakland Tribune*, October 8, 1955.

85. *New York Times*, October 8, 1955; *The Sporting News*, November 9, 1955.

86. *New York Times*, October 8, 1955.

Chapter 11

1. *New York Times*, October 8, 1955; *The Sporting News*, October 12, 1955.
2. *The Sporting News*, Jan. 18, 1956, Feb. 2, 1956.
3. *New York Times*, October 8, 1955.
4. "Yankee Dollars," February 2, 1959, 53–54.
5. *The Sporting News*, January 4, 1956.
6. *Racine* (WI) *Journal Times*, January 11, 1956; *Petersburg* (IN) *Progress-Index*, January 11, 1956; *The Sporting News*, January 18, 1956.
7. *Las Vegas* (NV) *Daily Optic*, January 14, 1956.
8. *San Mateo* (CA) *Times*, January 25, 1956.
9. *Corpus Christi* (TX) *Times*, January 27, 1956.
10. *New York Times*, November 27, 1955; *The Sporting News*, December 7, 1955.
11. Gillette and Palmer, *The ESPN Baseball Encyclopedia*, 1382; *Racine* (WI) *Journal Times*, February 6, 1956; *The Sporting News*, February 15, 1956.
12. *The Sporting News*, November 30, December 28, 1955; *Pacific Stars and Stripes*, February 11, 1956; *The Sporting News*, April 25, 1956.
13. *Helena* (MT) *Independent Record*, March 11, 1956.
14. "1956 New York Yankees Batting, Pitching and Fielding Statistics," baseball-reference.com; *New York Times*, March 2, 2009.
15. Gillette and Palmer, *The ESPN Baseball Encyclopedia*, 704; http://www.baseball-almanac.com/players/.
16. Jane Leavy, *The Last Boy: Mickey Mantle and the End of America's Childhood* (New York: HarperCollins, 2010), 152–153.
17. *The Sporting News*, June 13, 1956; *Altoona* (PA) *Mirror*, June 13, 1956.
18. *New York Times*, August 1, 1956; Brent Kelley, *Baseball's Biggest Blunder: The Bonus Rule of 1953–1957* (Lanham: MD: Scarecrow Press, 1997), 96; Dewey and Acocella, *The Ball Clubs*, 180.
19. Creamer, *Stengel*, 275; Golenbock, *Dynasty*, 171–172; Baldassaro, *Beyond DiMaggio*, 241; Forker, *Men of Autumn*, 50–51; Mickey Mantle with Mickey Herskowitz, *All My Octobers: My Memories of Twelve World Series When the Yankees Ruled Baseball* (New York: HarperCollins, 1994), 63; Madden, *Pride of October*, 17–18.
20. *Kingsport* (TN) *Times*, August 27, 1956; *Zanesville* (OH) *Signal*, August 27, 1956; *Van Wert* (OH) *Times-Bulletin*, August 27, 1956; *The Sporting News*, September 5, 12, 1956; Gallagher, *Day by Day in New York Yankees History*, 210; Frommer, *New York City Baseball*, 136.

21. Whitey Ford with Phil Pepe, *Few and Chosen: Defining Yankee Greatness Across the Era* (Chicago: Triumph Books, 2001), 57–58.

22. Appel, *Pinstripe Empire*, 312; DeVito, *Scooter*, 199; Gallagher, *Day by Day in New York Yankees History*, 213; Curt Smith, *Voices in the Game: The First Full-Scale Overview of Baseball Broadcasting, 1921 to the Present* (South Bend, IN: Diamond Communications, 1987), 380.

23. Thorn et al., *Total Baseball*, 386.

24. Bjarkman, *Encyclopedia of Major League Baseball Team Histories*, 271.

25. *Newport* (RI) *Daily News*, September 17, 1956.

26. *The Sporting News*, September 12, 1956.

27. *Ibid.*, October 3, 1956.

28. *Winnipeg* (Manitoba) *Free Press*, October 3, 1956.

29. *The Sporting News*, October 3, 17, 1956.

30. *Ibid.*, August 22, October 3, 1956; *Wisconsin State Journal* (Madison), October 13, 1956; *Connellsville* (PA) *Daily Journal*, October 13, 1956.

31. *The Sporting News*, November 7, December 12 and December 19, 1956; *Bradford* (PA) *Era*, December 17, 1956.

32. *Chester* (PA) *Times*, December 21, 1956; *The Sporting News*, January 2, 1957.

33. *New York Times*, February 16, 1957; *Hammond* (IN) *Times*, January 15, 1957; *Corsicana* (TX) *Daily Sun*, January 15, 1957; *New York Times*, February 5, 1957; *Berkshire* (Pittsfield, MA) *Eagle*, February 15, 1957.

34. *The Sporting News*, January 30, 1957; *New York Times*, January 30, 1957.

35. *Joplin* (MO) *Globe*, March 20, 1956; *Ogden* (UT) *Standard Examiner*, March 18, 1956.

36. Spatz, *Yankees Coming, Yankees Going*, 120; *Salisbury* (MD) *Times*, February 20, 1927; *New York Times*, February 20, 1927; *Hammond* (IN) *Times*, February 17, 1957; http://www.baseball-reference.com/teams/NYY/1957.

37. "Art Ditmar Baseball Stats," baseball-almanac.com; *The Sporting News*, February 27, 1957.

38. Gillette and Palmer, *The ESPN Baseball Encyclopedia*, 1521.

39. Spatz, *Yankees Coming, Yankees Going*, 120.

40. *The Sporting News*, March 6, 1957.

41. *Ibid.*

42. Terrell, "Yankee Secrets?" 12.

43. Kahn, *The Era*, 167.

44. *The Sporting News*, March 27, 1957.

45. *Ibid.*

46. *Ibid.*, May 15 and 29, 1957.

47. Dewey and Acocella, *The Ball Clubs*, 380; Frommer, *New York City Baseball*, 140–141.

48. Golenbock, *Wild, High and Tight*, 113.

49. John Tullius, *I'd Rather Be a Yankee: An Oral History of America's Most Loved and Most Hated Baseball Team* (New York: Macmillan, 1986), 248–250.

50. Dewey and Acocella, *The Ball Clubs*, 380; Frommer, *New York City Baseball*, 140–141; *New York Times*, May 16, 1957; Gittleman, *Reynolds, Raschi and Lopat*, 197; Appel, *Pinstripe Empire*, 318–319; *Amarillo* (TX) *Globe*, June 3, 1957; *Alton* (IL) *Evening-Telegraph*), June 4, 1957.

51. Golenbock, *Wild, High and Tight*, 119; Barra, *Yogi Berra*, 239.

52. Mantle, *All My Octobers*, 77.

53. Stout, *Yankees Century*, 267.
54. Leavy, *The Last Boy*, 183–184.
55. Whitey Ford with Phil Pepe, *Slick: My Life in and Around Baseball* (New York: William Morrow, 1987), 139; Ford, *Few and Chosen*, 111.
56. Stout, *Yankees Century*, 267.
57. Creamer, *Stengel*, 270.
58. *Salisbury* (MD) *Times*, July 9, 1957; Golenbock, *Dynasty*, 126–127.
59. Spatz, *Yankees Coming, Yankees Going*, 121; *Long Beach* (CA) *Independent Press Telegram*, June 16, 1957; *Oxnard* (CA) *Press-Courier*, June 26, 1957; *The Sporting News*, June 26, 1957.
60. Stout, *Yankees Century*, 267.
61. *Sandusky* (OH) *Register*, June 29, 1957; *New York Times*, August 13, 1957; *The Sporting News*, June 26, 1957.
62. *Lebanon* (PA) *Daily News*, September 3, 1957; "The Unknown Yankee," *Newsweek*, July 15, 1957, 62–64; *Newport* (RI) *Daily News*, October 2, 1957.
63. Thorn et al., *Total Baseball*, 387; "1957 New York Yankees Seasons Recap," thebaseballpage.com; "World Series Winners, Stats and Results and Postseason Series," baseball-reference.com; *Stevens Point* (WI) *Daily Journal*, September 28, 1959.
64. Thorn et al., *Total Baseball*, 387.
65. *Mason City* (IA), *Globe-Gazette*, October 11, 1957; *Yuma* (AZ) *Daily Sun*, October 11, 1957; *Lawton* (OK) *Constitution*, October 11, 1957.
66. *The Sporting News*, December 4, 1957; Leavy, *The Last Boy*, 182–183.
67. Stout, *Yankees Century*, 271; *The Sporting News*, January 22, 1958; *New York Times*, May 3, 1958.
68. *Alton* (IL) *Telegram*, October 17, 1957.
69. *New York Times*, January 5, 1958; *Zanesville* (OH) *Times Recorder*, January 6, 1958; *Long Beach* (CA) *Independent*, May 26, 1958; *Salisbury* (MD) *Times*, May 30, 1958; Allen, *You Could Look It Up*.
70. *The Sporting News*, November 13, 1957; "You're Killing Me," *Newsweek*, February 4, 1958, 100; *New York Times*, January 23, 1958; *The Sporting News*, March 3, 1958.
71. *The Sporting News*, February 19, 1958.
72. Ibid., February 12 and 19, 1958; *San Mateo* (CA) *Times*, February 14, 1958.
73. *Long Beach* (CA) *Independent*, May 26, 1958; *The Salisbury* (MD) *Times*, May 30, 1958; *Lebanon* (PA) *Daily News*, May 22, 1958.
74. *The Sporting News*, August 5, 1958.
75. Allen, *You Could Look It Up*, 188–189; Golenbock, *Dynasty*, 229–230; Shapiro, *Bottom of the Ninth*, 17.
76. Thorn et al., *Total Baseball*, 388; Shapiro, *Bottom of the Ninth*, 17–20; Allen, *You Could Look It Up*, 198; Stout, *Yankees Century*, 271–272; Golenbock, *Dynasty*, 230; Gallagher, *Day by Day in New York Yankees History*, 223; *New York Times*, May 5, 1959.
77. Shapiro, *Bottom of the Ninth*, 17, 19–20; Gallagher, *Day by Day in New York Yankees History*, 223.
78. *The Sporting News*, November 12, 1958.
79. *New York Times*, October 11, 1958.
80. *The Sporting News*, October 22, November 19, December 17, 1958.
81. *Salisbury* (MD) *Times*, October 31, 1958; *The Sporting News*, November 12, 1958, January 21, 1959.
82. Mark Armour, *Joe Cronin: A Life in Baseball* (Lincoln: University of Nebraska Press, 2010), 260; *Berkshire Eagle* (Pittsfield, MA), December 5, 1958; *New York Times*, December 5, 1958; *The Sporting News*, December 10, 17, 1958.
83. *The Sporting News*, December 31, 1958; Gallagher, *Day by Day*, 223; *Cuero* (TX) *Record*, January 22, 1959; *Great Bend* (KS) *Daily Tribune*, January 21, 1959; *The Sporting News*, January 28, 1959; *Lethbridge Herald* (Alberta CA), January 27, 1959.
84. Ibid., January 8, 17, 1959; *Oakland* (CA) *Tribune*, January 21, 1959; *New York Times*, February 22, 1959; *The Sporting News*, March 4, 1959.
85. *Ada* (OK) *Evening News*, February 23, 1959; *Newport* (RI) *Daily News*, February 22, 1959.
86. *New York Times*, February 22, 1959.
87. Ibid., May 4, 1959; *The Sporting News*, June 3, 1959.
88. *New York Times*, May 5, 1959; *The Sporting News*, May 13, 1959.
89. *Hutchinson* (KS) *News*, May 24, 1959; *Butte* (MT) *News*, May 24, 1959.
90. *Corpus Christi* (TX) *Times*, May 19, 1959; *Salisbury* (MD) *Times*, July 29, 1959; *The Sporting News*, August 19, 1959.
91. *Idaho Falls* (ID) *Post Register*, June 3, 1959; *The Sporting News*, June 10, 1959; *The Sporting News*, July 15, 1959.
92. Ibid., June 17, 1959.
93. *Ogden* (UT) *Standard Examiner*, July 7, 1959; *The Sporting News*, August 19, 1959.
94. *The Sporting News*, September 23, 1959; Gillette and Palmer, *The ESPN Baseball Encyclopedia*, 105.
95. Surdam, *The Postwar Yankees*, 21.
96. *Lima* (OH) *Daily News*, May 24, 1959.
97. *Long Beach* (CA) *Press Telegram*, May 22, 1959.
98. *The Sporting News*, May 13, 27, 1959.
99. *Salt Lake City* (UT) *Tribune*, August 7, 1959; *The Sporting News*, June 3, 1959.
100. Leavy, *The Last Boy*, 190.
101. *The Sporting News*, May 13, September 23, 1959; *Corpus Christi* (TX) *Times*, May 19, 1959.
102. *The Sporting News*, June 3, 1959.
103. *Ogden* (UT) *Standard Examiner*, July 7, 1959; *Salisbury* (MD) *Times*, July 29, 1959; *The Sporting News*, August 19, 1959.
104. *The Sporting News*, August 12, 1959; *Jefferson City* (MO) *Post Tribune*, October 22, 1959; *Appleton* (WI) *Post-Crescent*, October 22, 1959.
105. *The Sporting News*, September 30, December 23, 1959.
106. Ibid., October 21, 28, December 18, 1959; *New York Times*, October 29, 1959.
107. *New York Times*, December 17, 1959; *The Sporting News*, December 30, 1959.
108. Spatz, *Yankees Coming, Yankees Going*, 127–128.
109. Bill Morales, *Farewell to the Last Golden Era: The Yankees, the Pirates and the 1960 Baseball Season* (Jefferson, NC: McFarland, 2011), 11–12; *The Sporting News*, December 23, 1959.
110. Henry D. Fetter, *Taking On the Yankees: Winning and Losing in the Business* (New York: W.W. Norton, 2003), 318.

Chapter 12

1. *The Sporting News*, January 27, 1960.
2. *Lima* (OH) *News*, January 28, 1960; *Pasadena* (CA) *Independent*, January 28, 1960.

3. *The Sporting News*, February 10, 1960.
4. *San Antonio* (TX) *Light*, March 5, 1960.
5. *Corpus Christi* (TX) *Times*, March 1, 1960; Shapiro, *Bottom of the Ninth*, 172.
6. *New York Times*, March 2, 1960.
7. *Cumberland* (MD) *Evening News*, March 4, 1960.
8. *Wisconsin State Journal* (Madison), March 8, 1960.
9. *The Sporting News*, March 9, 1960.
10. *Tucson* (AZ) *Daily Citizen*, March 11, 1960; *North Adams* (MA) *Transcript*, March 12, 1960; *Alton* (IL) *Daily Telegram*, March 12, 1960.
11. *The Sporting News*, April 20, 1960; *San Antonio* (TX) *Light*, February 5, 1960.
12. Gallagher, *Day by Day*, 230.
13. *Pacific Stars and Stripes* (Tokyo), May 11, 1960.
14. *Monessen* (PA) *Daily Independent*, April 5, 1960.
15. Gallagher, *Day by Day*, 230.
16. Morales, *Farewell to the Last Golden Era*, 90.
17. Barra, *Yogi Berra*, 267; Morales, *Farewell to the Last Golden Era*, 90.
18. *New Castle* (PA) *News*, July 23, 1960.
19. *The Sporting News*, August 31, 1960.
20. "1960 New York Yankees Season Recap" www.thebaseballpage.com.
21. "1960 World Series by Baseball Almanac," www.baseball-almanac.com., Morales, *Farewell to the Last Golden Era*, 167, 170–173.
22. Baseball-almanac.com.
23. Morales, *Farewell to the Last Golden Era*, 173–175.
24. Bill Bishop, "Casey Stengel," sabr.org/bioproject, 7.
25. Morales, *Farewell to the Last Golden Era*, 176–179.
26. Dewey and Acocella, *The Ball Clubs*, 380.
27. baseball–almanac.com; Gallagher, *Day by Day*, 234.
28. Morales, *Farewell to the Last Golden Era*, 179.
29. *New York Times*, September 16, 1960.
30. *Tyrone* (PA) *Daily Herald*, September 28, 1960.
31. *New York Times*, October 15, 1960; *The Sporting News*, October 15, 1960.
32. Bjarkman, *Encyclopedia of Team Histories: American League*, 272. Bishop, *Casey Stengel*, 7; Dewey and Acocella, *The Ball Clubs*, 381; Gallagher, *Day by Day*, 236; *New York Times*, October 19, 1960; Tullius, *I'd Rather Be a Yankee*, 259.
33. *New York Times*, October 21, 1960.
34. Allen, *You Could Look It Up*, 210.
35. *Iola* (KS) *Register*, November 2, 1960; *Helena* (MT) *Independent Record*, November 2, 1960; *New York Times*, November 3, 1960; Gallagher, *Day by Day*, 236; Robinson and Jennison, *Pennants and Pinstripes*, 143.
36. Charles C. Alexander, "Weiss, George Martin," *American National Biography online*, 3.
37. Ibid; *Lowell* (MA) *Sun*, November 3, 1960; *Mt. Vernon* (IL) *Register News*, November 3, 1960; *Cedar Rapids* (IA) *Gazette*, November 3, 1960; Rice, *The Yankees in the Early 1960s*, 45.
38. *New York Herald Tribune*, November 3, 1960; Gallagher, *Day by Day*, 236; Dewey and Acocella, *The Ball Clubs*, 378; Bjarkman, *Encyclopedia of Baseball Team Histories: American League*, 268.
39. Quoted in DeVito, *Scooter*, 212.
40. *Lowell* (MA) *Sun*, November 3, 1960.
41. *Fitchburg* (MA) *Sentinel*, November 5, 1960; *Long Beach* (CA) *Independent*, November 7, 1960; *New York Times*, November 9, 1960; *High Point* (NC) *Enterprise*, November 11, 1960; *Berkshire Eagle* (Pittsfield, MA), December 12, 1960.
42. *New York Times*, November 3, 1960; *The Sporting News*, November 16, 1960.
43. *The Sporting News*, November 16, 1960.
44. *Charleston* (WV) *Daily Mail*, November 16, 1960; *Lima* (OH) *News*, November 16, 1960.
45. *The Sporting News*, January 4, 1961.
46. Authors' telephone conversation with *Joplin Globe* archivist Mike Caldwell, February 2, 2015.
47. *Joplin* (MO) *Globe*, November 13, 1960.
48. *Pacific Stars and Stripes* (Tokyo), November 10, 1960; *New York Herald Tribune*, November 3, 1960.
49. Charles P. Korr, *The End of Baseball As We Knew It: The Players Union, 1960–81* (Urbana: University of Illinois Press, 2002), 174.
50. *Arizona* (Phoenix) *Republic*, March 10, 1961.
51. Gallagher, *Day by Day*, 236; "Executive of the Year Award by the Sporting News" www.baseball-almanac; Ryczek, *Yankees in the Early 1960s*, 45; *The Sporting News*, January 4, 1961; *Galveston Daily News*, January 9, 1961.
52. *Steubenville* (OH) *Herald Star*, April 20, 1961.
53. Gallagher, *Day by Day*, 236.
54. Golenbock, *Dynasty*, 271, 278.

Chapter 13

1. Meany, *The Yankee Story*, 145; Gross, *Yankee Doodles*, 160.
2. Golenbock, *Dynasty*, 275.
3. "Any Player/Any era: George Weiss," posted by Graham Womack on baseballpastandpresent.com. (posted May 5, 2011); Janet Paskin, *Tales From the 1982 Mets: A Collection of the Greatest Stories Ever Told*, (Champaign, IL: Sports Publishing, 2004), 10; Maury Allen, *The Incredible Mets*, (New York: Paperback Library, 1969), 26; Jack Mann, *Fall of the New York Yankees*, (New York: Simon & Schuster, 1967), 175; George Vescey, *Joy in Mudville: Being a Complete Account of the Unparalleled History of the New York Mets from Their Most Perturbed Beginnings to Their Amazing Rise to Glory and Renown*, (New York: McCall, 1970), 19.
4. Larry Fox, *Last to First: The Story of the New York Mets*, (New York: Harper & Row, 1970), 23.
5. Leonard Koppett, *Koppett's Concise History of Major League Baseball*, (Philadelphia: Temple University Press, 2004), 272–273; Allen, *The Incredible Mets*, 21; Dennis D'Agostino, *This Date in New York Mets History* (New York: Stein & Day, 1981), 129.
6. Ibid.
7. Koppett, *Koppett's Concise History of Major League Baseball*, 275.
8. Ibid.
9. *The Sporting News*, June 18, 1958; *Oakland* (CA) *Tribune*, August 14, 1958; *The Sporting News*, August 26, 1958.
10. Morales, *Farewell to the Last Golden Era*, 67–68.
11. *New York Times*, August 1, 1959; *Charleston* (WV) *Gazette*, August 1, 1959; *San Antonio* (TX) *Express*, August 1, 1959.
12. D'Agostino, *This Date in New York Mets History*,

129–130; Alexander, *Our Game*, 246; "Continental League—BR Bullpen," baseball-reference.com/bullpen/Continental League.
13. Allen, *The Incredible Mets*, 21; D'Agostino, *This Day In New York Mets History*, 129.
14. Kerry Keene, *1960: The Last Pure Season*, (Champaign: IL: Sports Publishing, 2000), 74.
15. D'Agostino, *This Date in New York Mets History*, 130.
16. Keene, *1960: The Last Pure Season*, 80.
17. Allen, *The Incredible Mets*, 22; Koppett, *Koppett's Concise History of Major League Baseball*, 277; Mann, *The Decline and Fall of the New York Yankees*, 79.
18. D'Agostino, *This Date in New York Mets History*, 130.
19. Paskin, *Tales From the 1962 New York Mets*, 11.
20. "Mets Timeline" newyorkmets.mlb.com/nym/history/timeline.
21. Allen, *The Incredible Mets*, 23–24; Golenbock, *Amazin'*, 87.
22. Allen, *The Incredible Mets*, 23; Jack Lang and Peter Simon, *The New York Mets: Twenty-Five Years of Baseball Magic* (New York: Henry Holt, 1986), 18; "Political Forkball," *Sports Illustrated*, March 27, 1961, 11.
23. Lang and Simon, *The New York Mets*, 16.
24. Allen, *Incredible Mets*, 24–26; Golenbock, *Dynasty*, 275; Fox, *The Story of the Mets*, 23.
25. Allen, *Incredible Mets*, 24–26; Fox, *Last to First*, 23; Golenbock, *Dynasty*, 275; *New York Times*, March 14, 1961; *Racine* (WI) *Times*, March 14, 1961; *Naugatuck*, (CT) *News*, March 13, 1961.
26. *New York Times*, March 15, 1961.
27. *Ibid.*, March 17, 1961.
28. Ralph Houk and Robert W. Creamer, *Season of Glory* (New York: G. P. Putnam's Sons, 1988), 88.
29. *Jefferson City* (MO) *Daily Capital News*, March 15, 1961; *Port Angeles* (WA) *Evening News*, March 15, 1961; *Fort Pierce* (FL) *News Tribune*, March 16, 1961.
30. *The Sporting News*, March 22, 1961.
31. Paskin, *Tales From the 1962 New York Mets*, 12; Golenbock, *Amazin'*, 88.
32. Houk and Creamer, *Season of Glory*, 87.
33. Vecsey, *Joy in Mudville*, 19.
34. *The Sporting News*, March 22, 1961.
35. *New York Times*, March 25, 1961.
36. Lang and Simon, *The New York Mets*, 21; *Galveston* (TX) *Daily News*, March 30, 1961; *New York Times*, October 26, 1961.
37. *Fitchburg* (MA) *Sentinel*, March 20, 1961; *Elyria* (OH) *Chronicle Telegram*, March 22, 1961; *New York Times*, October 29, 1961; D'Agostino, *This Date in New York Mets History*, 130; Lang and Smith, *The New York Mets*, 17.
38. Lang and Simon, *The New York Mets*, 17.
39. Vecsey, *Joy in Mudville*, 34–35; D'Agostino, *This Date in New York Mets History*, 131.
40. *Connelsville* (PA) *Daily Courier*, April 8, 1961; *The Sporting News*, April 3, 1961.
41. *Idaho Falls* (ID) *Register*, October 3, 1961; *New York Times*, October 3, 1961.
42. Lang and Simon, *The New York Mets*, 17–18.
43. *New York Times*, May 4, 1961; *Hammond* (IN) *Times*, May 4, 1961.
44. *Billings* (MT) *Gazette*, May 11, 1961.
45. *Mason City* (IA) *Globe Gazette*, September 20, 1961.
46. Allen, *Incredible Mets*, 26; Lang and Simon, *New York Mets*, 18.
47. *Helena* (MT) *Independent Record*, September 20, 1961.
48. *Long Beach* (CA) *Press Telegram*, July 11, 1961.
49. *Ogden* (UT) *Standard Examiner*, July 13, 1961.
50. Lang and Simon, *New York Mets*, 18; Fox, *Last to First*, 24; Shapiro, *Bottom of the Ninth*, 278; Allen, *You Could Look It Up*, 215; *Greeley* (CO) *Daily Tribune*, September 29, 1961; *New York Times*, September 30, 1961.
51. *Portsmouth* (NH) *Herald*, September 30, 1961; *Denton* (TX) *Record*, October 1, 1961.
52. *New York Times*, October 1, 1961.
53. Appel, *Pinstripe Empire*, 226; Fox, *Last to First*, 25; Allen, *You Could Look It Up*, 215; Golenbock, *Amazin'*, 161.
54. Vecsey, *Joy in Mudville*, 31–32; Honig, *The New York Mets*, 12; Fox, *The New York Mets*, 27–28.
55. *Racine* (WI) *Journal Times*, June 27, 1961; *New York Times*, June 27, 1961; *Pasadena* (CA) *Independent*, June 28, 1961; Donald Honig, *The New York Mets: The First Quarter Century* (New York: Crown, 1986), 12.
56. Lang and Simon, *The New York Mets*, 20.
57. George Vass, "A Long Tough Road Ahead for Two New Expansion Teams," *Baseball Digest*, August 1992, 32.
58. Vecsey, *Joy in Mudville*, 32; Fox, *Last to First*, 28.
59. Paskin, *Tales From the 1962 New York Mets*, 21; Honig, *The New York Mets*, 12; *New York Times*, October 11, 1961.
60. D'Agostino, *This Date in New York Mets History*, 131.
61. Honig, *New York Mets*, 12–13; *Eureka* (CA) *Humboldt Standard*, October 11, 1961.
62. Vecsey, *Joy in Mudville*, 32.
63. Honig, *The New York Mets*, 13.
64. *Ibid.*
65. *New York Times*, October 11, 1961.
66. *Hammond* (IN) *Times*, October 11, 1961.
67. *The Sporting News*, November 16, 1961.
68. Honig, *The New York Mets*, 13; Golenbock, *Amazin'*, 115; Fox, *Last to First*, 28–29; Vecsey, *Joy in Mudville*, 33–34; Paskin, *Tales From the 1962 New York Mets*, 33–36; *Racine* (WI) *Times*, October 17, 1961; *The Sporting News*, December 20, 27, 1961.
69. Vecsey, *Joy in Mudville*, 34.
70. Durso, *Casey*, 162–163.
71. *The New York Times*, November 17, 1961.

Chapter 14

1. *Logansport* (IN) *Pharos Tribune*, March 4, 1962.
2. Jimmy Breslin, "Worst Team in Baseball," *Sports Illustrated*, May 30, 1994.
3. *Milwaukee Journal*, February 24, 1962; *Titusville* (PA) *Herald*, April 3, 1962.
4. Koppett, *New York Mets: The Whole Story*, 43.
5. *Oxnard* (CA) *Press-Courier*, March 16, 1962.
6. *Lima* (OH) *News*, March 23, 1962; *Eureka* (CA) *Humboldt Standard*, March 23, 1962.
7. *New York Times*, April 9, 1962.
8. *Lima* (OH) *News*, March 23, 1966.
9. *New York Times*, April 8, 1962.
10. *Ibid.*, April 9, 1962.

11. Peter Bjarkman, ed., *Encyclopedia of Baseball Team Histories: National League* (Westport, CT: Meckler, 1991), 348.
12. *Mason City* (IA) April 23, 1962; *Bridgeport* (CT) *Telegram*, April 27, 1962; *The Sporting News*, May 2, 1962.
13. *The Sporting News*, May 2, 1962.
14. *Salt Lake City* (UT) *Tribune*, May 7, 1962; *Salisbury* (MD) *Times*, May 7, 1962.
15. *The Sporting News*, May 16, July 21, 1966.
16. *Lima* (OH) *News*, May 8, 1962.
17. *The Sporting News*, July 14, 1962.
18. Golenbock, *Amazin'*, 119.
19. D'Agostino, *This Date in New York Mets History*, 133; Koppett, *The New York Mets*, 63; Keith Olbermann, "The '62 Mets," *National Pastime*, 2006, 23; "Marvelous Marv," *Sports Illustrated*, July 4, 1994, 9.
20. *Gastonia* (NC) *Gazette*, August 21, 1962; *Pacific* (Tokyo) *Stars and Stripes*, August 23, 1962.
21. Roger Angell, *The Summer Game* (New York: Popular Library, 1972), 23.
22. Bjarkman, *Encyclopedia of Baseball Teams: National League*, 350; Creamer, *Stengel: His Life and Times*, 302.
23. Vecsey, *Joy in Mudville*, 57.
24. *Ibid.*, 57–58; Dewey and Acocella, *The Ball Clubs*, 394.
25. Gillette and Palmer, *The ESPN Baseball Encyclopedia*, 98.
26. William J. Ryczek, *The Amazin' Mets* (Jefferson, NC: McFarland, 2008), 33.
27. Bjarkman, *Encyclopedia of Baseball Team History: The National League*, 350; baseball-reference.com, 1962 New York Mets.
28. *Kingsport* (TN) *Times-News*, May 13, 1962; *Ogden* (UT) *Standard-Examiner*, June 8, 1962; *San Mateo* (CA) *Times*, June 16, 1962; *Racine* (WI) *Sunday Bulletin*, July 1, 1962.
29. *The Sporting News*, July 21, 1962.
30. *Hayward* (CA) *Daily Review*, September 24, 1962; *Indiana* (PA) *Evening Gazette*, September 24, 1962; *New York Times*, September 25, 1962.
31. *Bridgeport* (CT) *Post*, September 29, 1962; *The Sporting News*, October 27, 1962.
32. *The Sporting News*, December 15, 1962; http://www.baseball-reference.com/register/affiliate.cgi?id=NYM&year=1962.
33. Fox and Lang, *The New York Mets*, 35; *Big Springs* (TX) *Daily Herald*, December 12, 1962; *Brainerd* (MN) *Daily Dispatch*, December 12, 1962.
34. *The Sporting News*, November 10, 1962.
35. Lang and Simon, *The New York Mets*, 35; D'Agostino, *This Date in Mets History*, 33; *Florence* (SC) *Evening News*, December 12, 1962; *Kingsport* (TN) *News*, December 12, 1962.
36. *Uniontown* (PA) *Evening Standard*, December 11, 1962.
37. *The Sporting News*, October 20, November 10, December 1, 1962.
38. *Ibid.*, December 23, 1962.
39. *Ibid.*, January 5, 1963.
40. *Ibid.*, February 16, 1963.
41. *Bakersfield* (CA) *Californian*, March 1, 1963; *Southern Illinoisan* (Carbondale), March 1, 1963; *New York Times*, April 1, 1963.
42. Golenbock, *Amazin'*, 139.
43. *Long Beach* (CA) *Independent*, December 5, 1962; *Brownsville* (TX) *Herald*, December 5, 1962.

44. Vecsey, *Joy in Mudville*, 83.
45. Tom Clavin and Danny Peary, *Gil Hodges: The Brooklyn Bums, the Miracle Mets, and the Extraordinary Life of a Baseball Legend* (New York: New American Library, 2012), 270; *The Sporting News*, February 16, 1963; *Pasadena* (CA) *Independent*, April 2, 1963.
46. *Oxnard* (CA) *Press Courier*, April 6, 1963.
47. *The Sporting News*, May 4, 11, 1963.
48. *Lima* (OH) *News*, May 10, 1963; *The Sporting News*, May 11, 1963.
49. Bjarkman, *Encyclopedia of Baseball Team Histories: National League*, 250.
50. D'Agostino, *This Date in New York Mets History*, 133; Gillette and Palmer, *The ESPN Baseball Encyclopedia*, 1605.
51. Dewey and Acocella, *The Ball Clubs*, 394.
52. *Beckley* (WV) *Post Herald*, May 15, 1963.
53. *The Sporting News*, May 11, 1963.
54. *Shelby* (KY) *Press*, September 26, 1963.
55. *New York Times*, October 5, 1963.
56. *Kingsport* (TN) *Times*, October 11, 1963; *Oxnard* (CA) *Press-Courier*, October 11, 1963; Koppett, *New York Mets*, 84; Gillette and Palmer, *The ESPN Baseball Encyclopedia*, 1211; Ryczek, *The Amazin' Mets*, 109–111.
57. *Berkeley* (WV) *Post Herald*, October 11, 1963; *Long Beach* (CA) *Independent*, October 11, 1963; *The Sporting News*, October 19, 1963; Koppett, *The New York Mets*, 80.
58. *The Sporting News*, October 12, 1963.
59. *New York Times*, November 5, 1963; *Kingsport* (TN) *Times*, November 5, 1963; *Uniontown* (PA) *Morning Herald*, November 5, 1963.
60. *Cumberland* (MD) *Times*, December 29, 1963.
61. Koppett, *The New York Mets*, 76, 80–81, 85; *The Sporting News*, January 4, 25, 1964.
62. Golenbock, *Amazin'*, 154; Koppett, *The New York Mets*, 77; Vecsey, *Joy in Mudville*, 93.
63. Golenbock, *Amazin'*, 154; Koppett, *The New York Mets*, 77–78; Vecsey, *Joy in Mudville*, 95.
64. Lang and Simon, *The New York Mets*, 41.
65. Vecsey, *Joy in Mudville*, 96; "New York Mets," baseballlibrary.com; Bjarkman, *Encyclopedia of Team Histories: National League*, 352–353; Koppett, *The New York Mets*, 78; *The Sporting News*, January 18, 1964.
66. *The Sporting News*, November 18, February 1, 1964; *Salisbury* (MD) *Times*, January 21, 1964; "New York Mets," www.sportscyclopedia.com; Lang and Simon, *The New York Mets*, 41–42.
67. "The Story of Mr. Met," newyork.mets.mlb.com; "Don't Touch His Head," www.rollingstones.com.
68. Koppett, *The New York Mets*, 88–89; *New York Times*, June 1, 1964.
69. Vecsey, *Joy In Mudville*, 100.
70. *Ibid.*, 101; Koppett, *The New York Mets*, 97; Bjarkman, *Encyclopedia of Baseball Team Histories: National League*, 35; D'Agostino, *This Date in New York Mets History*, 134–135.
71. *Zanesville* (OH) *Times Recorder*, September 30, 1964; *El Paso* (TX) *Herald Post*, September 29, 1964; *Aiken* (SC) *Standard and Review*, September 29, 1964.
72. Rob Rains, *St. Louis Cardinals: The 100th Anniversary History* (New York: St. Martin's Press, 1992), 153.
73. Bjarkman, *Encyclopedia of Baseball Team Histories: National League*, 35; Dewey and Acocella, *The Ball Clubs*, 395; *The Sporting News*, October 3, 1964.

74. Koppett, *The New York Mets*, 99.
75. *Clovis* (NM) *News-Journal*, November 18, 1964; *Sheboygan* (WI) *Journal*, November 18, 1964; *New York Times*, November 17, 1964.
76. *Tucson* (AZ) *Citizen*, November 24, 1964; *Mansfield* (OH) *News Journal*, November 24, 1964; *New York Times*, November 24, 1964.
77. *Ibid.*, February 27, 1965.
78. Koppett, *The New York Mets*, 99–100.
79. *Ibid.*, 100.
80. Ryczek, *The Amazin' Mets*, 113.
81. Bjarkman, *Encyclopedia of Baseball Team Histories: National League*, 355; http://www.baseball-almanac.com/teamstats/schedule.php?y=1965&t=NYN.
82. *Hayward* (CA) *Daily Review*, April 27, 1965; *Cedar Rapids* (IA) *Gazette*, April 27, 1965.
83. Bjarkman, *Encyclopedia of Baseball Team Histories: National League*, 354–355; Ryczek, *The Amazin' Mets*, 126.
84. *Oakland Tribune*, July 6, 1965; *Bennington* (VT) *Banner*, July 7, 1965.
85. *San Antonio* (TX) *Express*, July 15, 1965; *Tucson* (AZ) *Daily Citizen*, July 14, 1965.
86. Gillette and Palmer, *The ESPN Baseball Encyclopedia*, 1539.
87. Vescey, *Joy in Mudville*, 120–121; *Ogden* (UT) *Standard Examiner*, July 26, 1965; *Albuquerque* (NM) *Journal*, July 26, 1965; *New York Times*, July 27, 1965; "The Lively One," *Newsweek*, August 9, 1965, 71–72; Creamer, *Stengel*, 310–311.
88. *Lebanon* (PA) *Daily News*, August 31, 1965; *Denton* (TX) *Record Chronicle*, August 31, 1965; *New York Times*, August 31, 1965; Golenbock, *Amazin'*, 175.
89. *Kingsport* (TN) *News*, September 1, 1965; *Salt Lake City* (UT) *Tribune*, October 5, 1965.
90. *San Antonio* (TX) *Press*, October 5, 1965; *Reno* (NV) *Evening Gazette*, October 5, 1965; *The Sporting News*, October 16, 1965.
91. *Eureka* (CA) *Humboldt Standard*, September 1, 1965; *The Sporting News*, September 11, 1965.
92. Gillette and Palmer, *The ESPN Baseball Encyclopedia*, 92.
93. Ryczek, *Amazin'*, 129; *New York Times*, November 18, December 1, 1965.
94. D'Agostino, *This Date in New York Mets History*, 135–136.
95. *Ibid.*, 136; Vecsey, *Joy in Mudville*, 128; *The Sporting News*, October 30, November 6, 1965; *Eau Claire* (WI) *Daily Telegram*, October 31, 1965.
96. *Arizona Republic* (Phoenix), January 20, 1966.
97. Golenbock, *Amazin'*, 180–185; Koppett, *The New York Mets*, 127.
98. *Altoona* (PA) *Mirror*, January 27, 1966.
99. Vecsey, *Joy in Mudville*, 128; Bjarkman, *Encyclopedia of Baseball Team Histories: National League*, 356.
100. Vecsey, *Joy in Mudville*, 130.
101. *San Mateo* (CA) *Times*, August 4, 1966.
102. Gillette and Palmer, *The ESPN Baseball Encyclopedia*, 90; Vecsey, *Joy in Mudville*, 130.
103. *New York Times*, September 7, 1966; *Appleton* (WI) *Post Crescent*, November 16, 1966; *Nashua* (NH) *Telegraph*, November 15, 1966.
104. Koppett, *The New York Mets*, 125.
105. *New York Times*, November 16, 1966; *Pacific Stars and Stripes* (Tokyo) November 19, 1966; *The Sporting News*, November 26, 1966.

Chapter 15

1. Statement by George Weiss, November 14, 1956, George Weiss Files, Baseball Hall of Fame.
2. *Ibid.*
3. Vecsey, *Joy in Mudville*, 131.
4. Golenbock, *Amazin'*, 180.
5. *Appleton* (WI) *Post Crescent*, November 15, 1966; *New York Times*, November 15, 1966; *Pacific Stars and Stripes* (Tokyo), November 19, 1966; *The Sporting News*, November 26, 1966; Ryczek, *The Amazin' Mets*, 176.
6. *The Sporting News*, April 15, 1967.
7. *Ibid.*, Ryczek, *The Amazin' Mets*, 176.
8. *New Haven* (CT) *Register*, August 1967; *Lowell* (MA) *Sun*, July 9, 1967; *The Sporting News*, April 15, May 27, June 10, July 22, 1967.
9. *New York Times*, December 6, 1967.
10. Ryczek, *The Amazin' Mets*, 177.
11. Mets PR Department statement, November 16, 1966; *New York Times*, November 19, 1966; *New Haven Register*, August 1967.
12. *Madison* (WI) *Capital Times*, March 20, 1968; *Albuquerque* (NM) *Journal*, March 20, 1968.
13. *Washington* (D.C.) *Evening Star*, July 22, 1969.
14. *New York Times*, May 15, 1969.
15. www.baseball-reference.com./1969; Thorn et al., *Total Baseball*, 401.
16. Golenbock, *Dynasty*, 275. Golenbock, *Amazin'*, 239; *American National Biography Online*, 2; Undated newspaper clipping by Tim Horgan, "Weiss Assembled Pennant-Winning Team Behind the Scenes," George Weiss Clippings File, Baseball Hall of Fame; Honig, *The New York Mets*, 42.
17. *Salisbury* (MD) *Daily Times*, February 1, 1971; *Gastonia* (NC) *Gazette*, February 1, 1971.
18. *Billings* (MT) *Gazette*, February 1, 1971; *Oneonta* (NY) *Star*, February 2, 1971; *The Sporting News*, February 13, 1971.
19. *Huntington* (PA) *Daily News*, August 14, 1972; *Sandusky* (OH) *Register*, August 14, 1972.
20. *Salisbury* (MD) *Daily-Times*, February 10, 1971.
21. *San Antonio* (TX) *Express*, February 9, 1971.
22. *Pacific Stars and Stripes* (Tokyo), February 10, 1971.
23. Golenbock, *Amazin',* 100; *Huntington* (PA) *Daily News*, August 14, 1972.
24. "George Weiss Induction Speech," Weiss Scrapbook, Volume 37, 1971, Baseball Hall of Fame.
25. Doug Pappas, "Only Four GM's in Hall of Fame," ESPN.com: MLB.
26. *New York Times*, August 14, 1972; *Chicago Tribune*, August 14, 1972; *Pasadena* (CA) *Star News*, August 14, 1972.
27. *New York Times*, July 29, 1979.
28. *Hagerstown* (MD) *Morning Herald*, August 14, 1972; *Pacific Stars and Stripes* (Tokyo) August 15, 1972.
29. *San Antonio* (TX) *Express*, August 15, 1972.
30. *New York Times*, August 14, 1972.
31. Fox, *Last to First*, 25.
32. *The Sporting News*, March 11, 1959.
33. Tullius, *I'd Rather Be a Yankee*, 173–174.
34. *Ibid.*, 174–175.
35. Bobby Brown phone interview with authors, January 10, 2012.
36. Jerry Coleman phone interview with authors, January 8, 2012.

Notes. Chapter 15

37. E-mail, Berra to authors, January 16, 2012.
38. Barra, *Yogi Berra*, 333.
39. *Raleigh Register*, August 14, 1972.
40. Golenbock, *Dynasty*, 275.
41. *Sandusky* (OH) *Register*, August 14, 1972.
42. *Huntington* (PA) *Daily News*, August 14, 1972.
43. *Charleston* (WV) *Gazette*, August 14, 1972.
44. Dickson, *Bill Veeck*, 263.
45. Vecsey, *Joy in Mudville*, 132; Fox, *Last to First*, 24; *Carbondale* (IL) *Southern Illinoisan*, October 14, 1969; William Leggett, "The Men Who Fire Managers," *Sports Illustrated*, September 13, 1966, 45.
46. Stout, *Yankees Century*, 278.
47. Mark Armour and Dan Levitt, "George Weiss—In Pursuit of Pennants," pursuitofpennants.wordpress.com, 3; Barra, *Yogi Berra*, 313.
48. Armour and Levitt, "In Pursuit of Pennants," 3; Barra, *Yogi Berra*, 278.
49. *The Sporting News*, March 5, 1966.
50. Letter, Red Barber to George Weiss, November 22, 1966, George Weiss Papers, Baseball Hall of Fame, Cooperstown, NY.
51. *New Haven Register*, October 31, 1978.
52. *New York Times*, August 8, 1972.
53. *Ibid*.
54. Mets press release June 11, 1982, Weiss Scrapbook, Baseball Hall of Fame, Cooperstown, New York; *National Cyclopedia of American Biography*, 85.
55. Shale Briskin, "10 Greatest Mets General Managers of All Time," March 23, 2011.
56. Program Book, James E. Hillhouse High School Fifth Annual Athletic Hall of Fame.
57. Armour and Levitt, *In Pursuit of Pennants*, 1; *National Cyclopedia of American Biography*, 85.
58. Weiss acceptance speech at Hall of Fame, August 9, 1971, Weiss Scrapbook Volume 37, 1971, Cooperstown, NY.

Bibliography

Books

Alexander, Charles C. *Breaking the Slump: Baseball in the Depression Era.* New York: Columbia University Press, 2002.
____. *Our Game.* New York: Henry Holt, 1991.
____. *Rogers Hornsby: A Biography.* New York: Henry Holt, 1995.
Allen, Maury. *The Incredible Mets.* New York: Paperback Library, 1969.
____. *You Could Look It Up: The Life of Casey Stengel.* New York: Times Books, 1979.
Angell, Roger. *The Summer Game.* New York: Popular Library, 1972.
Appel, Marty. *Pinstripe Empire: The New York Yankees Before the Babe and After the Boss.* New York: Bloomsbury, 2012.
Armour, Mark. *Joe Cronin: A Life in Baseball.* Lincoln: University of Nebraska Press, 2010.
Bak, Richard. *Casey Stengel: A Splendid Baseball Life.* Dallas: Taylor, 1997.
Baldassaro, Lawrence. *Beyond DiMaggio: Italian Americans in Baseball.* Lincoln: University of Nebraska Press, 2011.
Barber, Red. *Rhubarb in the Catbird Seat.* New York: Doubleday, 1968.
Barra, Allen. *Yogi Berra: Eternal Yankee.* New York: W.W. Norton, 2009.
Barrow, Edward Grant. *My Fifty Years in Baseball.* New York: Coward-McCann, 1951.
Beers, J. H. *Commemorative Biographical Record of New Haven County.* Chicago: J.H. Beers, 1902.
Berger, Lance A., and Dorothy R. Berger. *Management Wisdom from the New York Yankees' Dynasty: What Every Manager Can Learn from a Legendary Team's 80-Year Winning Streak.* New York: John Wiley & Sons, 2005.
Berra, Yogi. E-mail to authors, January 16, 2012.
Bjarkman, Peter C., ed. *Encyclopedia of Major League Baseball Team Histories.* Westport, CT: Meckler, 1991.
Bove, Vincent. *And on the Eighth Day God Created the Yankees.* Plainfield, NJ: Haven Books, 1981.
Boxerman, Burton A., and Benita W. Boxerman. *Ebbets to Veeck to Busch: Eight Owners Who Shaped Baseball.* Jefferson, NC: McFarland, 2003.
Bready, James H. *Baseball in Baltimore: The First 100 Years.* Baltimore: Johns Hopkins University Press, 1998.
Breslin, Jimmy. *Can Anybody Here Play This Game?* New York: Viking Press, 1963.
Brown, Bobby. Phone interview with authors, January 12, 2012.
Burk, Robert F. *Much More Than a Game: Players, Owners, and American Baseball Since 1921.* Chapel Hill: University of North Carolina Press, 2001.
____. *Never Just a Game.* Chapel Hill: University of North Carolina Press, 1994.
Caldwell, Mike, *Joplin Globe*. Phone interview with authors, February 2, 2015.
Chadwin, Dean. *Those Damn Yankees: The Secret Life of America's Greatest Franchise.* New York: Verso, 1999.
Charlton, James, ed. *The Baseball Chronology: The Complete History of the Most Important Events in the Game of Baseball.* New York: Macmillan, 1991.
Clavin, Tom, and Danny Peary. *Gil Hodges: The Brooklyn Bums, The Miracle Mets, and the Extraordinary Life of a Baseball Legend,* New York: New American Library, 2012.
____. *Roger Maris: Baseball's Reluctant Hero.* New York: Touchstone, 2010.
Cohane, Tim. *Bypaths of Glory: A Sportswriter Looks Back.* New York: Harper & Row, 1963.
Coleman, Jerry. Phone interview with authors, January 8, 2012.
Corcoran, Dennis. *Induction Day at Cooperstown: A History of the Baseball Hall of Fame Ceremony.* Jefferson NC: McFarland, 2011.
Cramer, Richard Ben. *Joe DiMaggio: The Hero's Life.* New York: Simon & Schuster, 2000.
Creamer, Robert W. *Babe: The Legend Comes to Life.* New York: Simon & Schuster, 1974.
____. *Baseball in '41: A Celebration of the Best Baseball Season Ever.* New York: Viking, 1991.
____. *Stengel—His Life and Times.* New York: Simon & Schuster, 1984.
Crepeau, Richard C. *Baseball: America's Diamond Mine 1919–1941.* Orlando: University of Central Florida, 1980.
D'Agostino, Dennis. *This Date in New York Mets History.* New York: Stein & Day, 1981.
Danzig, Alison, and Joe Reichler. *History of Baseball—Its Great Players, Teams, and Managers.* Englewood Cliffs, NJ: Prentice-Hall, 1959.

DeVito, Carlo. *Scooter: The Biography of Phil Rizzuto.* Chicago: Triumph Books, 2010.

____. *Yogi: The Life and Times of an American Original.* Chicago: Triumph Books, 2008.

Dewey, Donald, and Nicholas Acocella. *The Ball Clubs.* New York: Harper Perennial, 1996.

Dickson, Paul. *Bill Veeck: Baseball's Greatest Maverick.* New York: Walker, 2012.

Durso, Joseph. *Amazing—The Miracle of the Mets.* Boston: Houghton Mifflin, 1970.

____. *Casey: The Life and Legend of Charles Dillon Stengel.* Englewood Cliffs, NJ: Prentice-Hall, 1967.

Eig, Jonathan. *Luckiest Man: The Life and Death of Lou Gehrig.* New York: Simon & Schuster, 2005.

Eisenhammer, Fred, and Jim Binkley. *Baseball's Most Memorable Trades: Superstars Swapped, All-Stars Copped, and Megadeals That Flopped.* Jefferson, NC: McFarland, 1997.

Ercalono, Patrick. *Fungoes, Floaters, and Fork Balls: A Colorful Baseball Dictionary.* Englewood Cliffs, NJ: Prentice-Hall, 1987.

Fetter, Henry D. *Taking On the Yankees.* New York: W.W. Norton, 2003.

Flynn, Tom. *Baseball in Baltimore.* Charleston, SC: Arcadia, 2008.

Ford, Whitey, and Phil Pepe. *Few and Chosen: Defining Yankee Greatness Across the Eras.* Chicago: Triumph Books, 2001.

____. *Slick: My Life In and Around Baseball.* New York: William Morrow, 1987.

Forker, Dom. *The Men of Autumn: An Oral History of the 1949–1953 World Champion New York Yankees.* Dallas: Taylor, 1989.

____. *Sweet Seasons: Recollections of the 1955–1964 Yankees.* Dallas: Taylor, 1990.

Fox, Larry. *Last to First: The Story of the Mets.* New York: Harper & Row, 1970.

Frommer, Harvey. *New York City Baseball: The Last Golden Age 1947–1957.* New York: Macmillan, 1980.

Gallagher, Mark. *Day by Day in New York Yankees History.* New York: Leisure Press, 1983.

____. *The Yankee Encyclopedia.* Champaign, IL: Sagamore, 1996.

Gallagher, Mark, and Neil Gallagher. *Baseball's Greatest Dynasties—The Yankees.* New York: Gallery Books, 1990.

____. *Mickey Mantle.* New York: Chelsea House, 1991.

George Weiss Collection. Baseball Hall of Fame. Cooperstown, NY.

Gillette, Gary, and Pete Palmer, eds. *The ESPN Baseball Encyclopedia Fifth Edition.* New York: Sterling, 2008.

Gittleman, Sol. *Reynolds, Raschi, and Lopat: New York's Big Three and the Yankee Dynasty of 1949–1953.* Jefferson, NC: McFarland, 2007.

Goldman, Steven. *Forging Genius: The Making of Casey Stengel.* Washington, D.C.: Potomac Books, 2005.

Golenbock, Peter. *Amazin': the Miraculous History of New York's Most Beloved Baseball Team.* New York: St. Martin's Press, 2002.

____. *Dynasty: The New York Yankees 1949–1964.* Englewood Cliffs, NJ: Prentice-Hall, 1975.

____. *Wild, High, and Tight: The Life and Death of Billy Martin.* New York: St. Martin's Press, 1994.

Graham, Frank. *The New York Yankees: An Informal History.* Carbondale: Southern Illinois University Press, 1943.

Gross, Milton. *Yankee Doodles.* Boston: House of Kent, 1948.

Halberstam, David. *October 1964.* New York: Villard Books, 1994.

____. *Summer of '49.* New York: William Morrow, 1989.

Helyar, John. *Lords of the Realm: The Real History of Baseball.* New York: Villard Books, 1994.

Heminway, J. Callendar, ed. *History of the Class of 1917 Yale College,* Vol. III. New Haven: Yale University Press, 1928.

____. *History of the Class of 1917 of Yale College,* Vol. V, New Haven: Yale University Press, 1942.

____. *Yale University Class of 1917 Twenty Years After,* New Haven: Yale University Press, 1938.

Henrich, Tommy, with Bill Gilbert. *Five O'Clock Lightning: Ruth, Gehrig, DiMaggio, Mantle, and the Glory Years of the New York Yankees.* New York: Carol Publishing Group, 1992.

Hirsch, James S. *Willie Mays: The Life and Legend.* New York: Scribner's, 2010.

History of the Class of 1917 Yale College, Fifty Years. New Haven, CT, 1967.

Honig, Donald. *Baseball Between the Lines—Baseball in the '40s and '50s as Told by the Men Who Played It.* New York: Coward, McCann, and Geoghegan, 1976.

____. *The New York Mets: The First Quarter Century.* New York: Crown, 1986.

Houk, Ralph, and Robert Creamer. *Season of Glory.* New York: G. P. Putnam's Sons, 1988.

Howard, Arlene, with Ralph Wimbish. *Elston and Me: The Story of the First Black Yankee.* Columbia: University of Missouri Press, 2001.

Jacobson, Steve. *Carrying Jackie's Torch: The Players Who Integrated Baseball and America.* Chicago: Lawrence Hill Books, 2007.

James, Bill. *The New Bill James Historical Abstract.* New York: Free Press, 2011.

Jennison, Christopher. *Wait 'Til Next Year.* New York: Norton, 1974.

Johnson, Lloyd, and Miles Wolff, eds. *The Encyclopedia of Minor League Baseball, Third Edition.* Durham, NC: Baseball America, 2007.

Kahn, Roger. *October Men: Reggie Jackson, George Steinbrenner, Billy Martin, and the Yankees Miraculous Finish in 1978.* New York: Harcourt, 2003.

____. *The Era 1947–1957: When the Yankees, the Giants, and the Dodgers Ruled the World.* New York: Tickner & Fields, 1993.

Kaiser, David. *Epic Season: The 1948 American League Pennant Race.* Amherst: University of Massachusetts Press, 1998.

Katz, Jeff. *The Kansas City A's and the Wrong Half of the Yankees.* Hingham, MA: Maple Street Press, 2007.

Keene, Kerry. *1960: The Last Pure Season.* Champaign, IL: Sports Publishing, 2000.

Kelley, Brent. *Baseball's Biggest Blunder: The Bonus Rule of 1953–1957.* Lanham, MD: Scarecrow Press, 1997.

Koppett, Leonard. *Koppett's Concise History of Major League Baseball.* Philadelphia: Temple University Press, 2004.

____. *The New York Mets: The Whole Story.* New York: Macmillan, 1969.

Korr, Charles P. *The End of Baseball As We Knew It: The Players' Union, 1960–1981.* Urbana: University of Illinois Press, 2002.

Kubek, Tony, and Terry Pluto. *Sixty-One. The Team, the Record, the Men.* New York: Macmillan, 1987.
Lanctot, Neil. *Negro League Baseball: The Rise and Ruin of a Black Institution.* Philadelphia: University of Pennsylvania Press, 2004.
Lang, Jack, and Peter Simon. *The New York Mets: Twenty-Five Years of Baseball Magic.* New York: Henry Holt, 1986.
Leavengood, Ted. *Ted Williams and the 1969 Washington Senators: The Last Winning Season.* Jefferson, NC: McFarland, 2009.
Leavy, Jane. *The Last Boy: Mickey Mantle and the End of America's Childhood.* New York: HarperCollins, 2010.
Levitt, Daniel R. *Ed Barrow: The Bulldog Who Built the Yankees' First Dynasty.* Lincoln: University of Nebraska Press, 1987.
Lieb, Frederick G. *The Baltimore Orioles: The History of a Colorful Team in Baltimore and St. Louis.* New York: G. P. Putnam's Sons, 1955.
Linn, Ed. *The Great Rivalry: The Yankees and the Red Sox 1901–1990.* New York: Tickner & Fields, 1991.
Lowenfish, Lee. *Branch Rickey: Baseball's Ferocious Gentleman.* Lincoln: University of Nebraska Press, 2007.
Macht, Norman L. *Connie Mack: The Turbulent and Triumphant Years, 1915–1931.* Lincoln: University of Nebraska Press, 2012.
Madden, Bill. *Pride of October: What It Was to Be Young and a Yankee.* New York: Warner Books, 2003.
Mann, Jack. *The Decline and Fall of the New York Yankees.* New York: Simon & Schuster, 1967.
Mantle, Mickey, with Mickey Herskowitz. *All My Octobers: My Memories of Twelve World Series When the Yankees Ruled Baseball.* New York: HarperCollins, 1994.
Marshall, William. *Baseball's Pivotal Era 1945–1951.* Lexington: University Press of Kentucky, 1999.
Mayer, Ronald A. *The 1937 Newark Bears: A Baseball Legend.* New Brunswick, NJ: Rutgers University Press, 1994.
McKelvey, G. Richard. *The MacPhails: Baseball's First Family of the Front Office.* Jefferson, NC: McFarland, 2000.
Meany, Tom. *The Magnificent Yankees.* New York: A.S. Barnes, 1952.
_____. *The Yankee Story.* New York: E. P. Dutton, 1960.
Miller, James Edward. *The Baseball Business: Pursuing Pennants and Profits in Baltimore.* Chapel Hill: University of North Carolina, 1990.
Mitchell, Jerry. *The Amazing Mets.* New York: Grossett & Dunlap, 1970.
Montville, Leigh. *The Big Bam: Life and Times of Babe Ruth.* New York: Doubleday, 2006.
Morales, Bill. *Farewell to the Last Golden Era: The Yankees, the Pirates, and the 1960 Baseball Season.* Jefferson, NC: McFarland, 2011.
Murray, George M., ed. *History of the Class of MCMXVII,* Vol. I. New Haven: Yale University Press, 1917.
Nemec, David, and Dave Zeman. *The Baseball Rookies' Encyclopedia.* Dulles, VA: Potomac Books, 2004.
Neyer, Rob, and Eddie Epstein. *Baseball Dynasties: The Greatest Teams of All Time.* New York: W.W. Norton, 2000.
O'Neal, Bill. *The International League—A Baseball History 1884–1991.* Austin: Eakin Press, 1992.

Orodenker, Richard. *Phillies Reader.* Philadelphia: Temple University Press, 1946.
Osterweis, Rollin G. *Three Centuries of New Haven, 1638–1938.* New Haven: Yale University Press, 1953.
Paskin, Janet. *Tales from the 1982 New York Mets: A Collection of the Greatest Stories Ever Told.* Champaign, IL: Sports Publishing, 2004.
Pepe, Phil. *The Yankees: The Authorized History of the New York Yankees.* Dallas: Taylor, 1995.
Peterson, John E. *The Kansas City Athletics: A Baseball History 1954–1967.* Jefferson, NC: McFarland, 2003.
Pietrusza, David. *Major Leagues: The Formation, Sometimes Absorption and Mostly Inevitable Demise of 18 Professional Baseball Organizations, 1871 to Present.* Jefferson, NC: McFarland, 1991.
Pietrusza, David, Matthew Silverman, and Michael Gershman, eds. *The Biographical Encyclopedia.* Kingston, NY: Sports Illustrated, 2000.
Rader, Benjamin G. *Baseball: A History of America's Game.* Urbana: University of Illinois Press, 1992.
Rae, Douglas W. *City: Urbanism and Its Ends.* New Haven: Yale University Press, 2003.
Rains, Rob. *The St. Louis Cardinals: The 100th Anniversary Issue.* New York: St. Martin's, 1992.
Rampersad, Arnold. *Jackie Robinson A Biography.* New York: Alfred A. Knopf, 1997.
Reidenbaugh, Lowell. *Cooperstown: Where the Legends Live Forever.* New York: Gramercy Books, 2001.
Riess, Steven. *City Games: The Evolution of American Urban Society and the Rise of Sports.* Champaign: University of Illinois Press, 1989.
Robinson, Ray, and Christopher Jennison. *Pennants and Pinstripes: The New York Yankees 1903–2002.* New York: Penguin Group, 2002.
Rosenthal, Harold, ed. *Baseball Is Their Business.* New York: Random House, 1952.
Rossi, John P. *The National Game: Baseball and American Culture.* Chicago: Ivan R. Dee, 2000.
_____. *A Whole New Game: Off the Field Changes in Baseball, 1946–1960.* Jefferson, NC: McFarland, 1999.
Rubin, Sam. *Baseball in New Haven.* New York: Arcadia Press, 2000.
Ryczek, William. *The Amazin' Mets 1962–1969.* Jefferson, NC: McFarland, 2008.
_____. *The Yankees in the Early 1960s.* Jefferson, NC: McFarland, 2008.
Sandoval, Jim, and Bill Nowlin, eds. *Can He Play? A Look at Baseball Scouts and Their Profession.* Phoenix: SABR, 2011.
Shapiro, Michael. *Bottom of the Ninth: Branch Rickey, Casey Stengel, and the Daring Scheme to Save Baseball From Itself.* New York: Times Books, 2009.
Silverman, Al. *Yankee Colors: The Glory Days of the Mantle Era.* New York: Harry N. Abrams, 2009.
Simonson, John. *Kansas City 1940.* Charleston, SC: History Press, 2013.
Siner, Howard. *Sweet Seasons: Baseball's Top Teams Since 1920.* New York: Pharos, 1998.
Smiles, Jack. *Bucky Harris: A Biography of Baseball's Boy Wonder.* Jefferson, NC: McFarland, 2012.
Smith, Curt. *Voices of the Game.* South Bend, IN: Diamond Communications, 1987.
Smith, Robert. *Baseball in the Afternoon: Tales from a Bygone Era.* New York: Simon & Schuster, 1993.
Spatz, Lyle. *Yankees Coming, Yankees Going.* Jefferson, NC: McFarland, 2000.

Stout, Glenn, ed. *Top of the Heap: A Yankee Collection*. Boston: Houghton Mifflin, 2003.

_____. *Yankees Century: 100 Years of New York Yankee Baseball*. New York: Houghton Mifflin, 2002.

Sullivan, Neil J. *The Minors: The Struggles and the Triumph of Baseball's Poor Relation from 1876 to the Present*. New York: St. Martin's Press, 1990.

Surdam, David G. *Postwar Yankees, Baseball's Golden Age Revisited*. Lincoln: University of Nebraska Press, 2008.

Thomas, Henry W. *Walter Johnson: Baseball's Big Train*. Washington, DC: Phenom Press, 1995.

Thorn, John, ed. *The Glory Days: New York Baseball 1947–1957*. New York: Collins, 2008.

Thorn, John, Phil Birnbaum, and Bill Deane. *Total Baseball: The Ultimate Baseball Encyclopedia 8th Edition*. Wilmington, DE: Sport Media, 2004.

Tofel, Richard J. *A Legend in the Making*. Chicago: Ivan R. Dee, 2002.

Tullius, John. *I'd Rather Be a Yankee: An Oral History of America's Most Loved and Most Hated Baseball Team*. New York: Macmillan, 1986.

Tygiel, Jules. *Baseball's Great Experiment: Jackie Robinson and His Legacy*. New York: Oxford University Press, 1983.

_____. *Past Time: Baseball as History*. New York: Oxford University Press, 2000.

Vecsey, George. *Joy in Mudville: Being a Complete Account of the Unparalleled History of the New York Mets from Their Most Perturbed Beginnings to Their Amazing Rise to Glory and Renown*. New York: McCall, 1970.

Veeck, Bill, and Ed Linn. *Veeck—as in Wreck*. New York: G. P. Putnam's Sons, 1962.

Voigt, David. *Baseball: An Illustrated History*. University Park: Pennsylvania State University Press, 1987.

Warfield, Don. *The Roaring Redhead: Larry MacPhail, Baseball's Great Innovator*. South Bend, IN: Diamond Communications, 1987.

White, G. Edward. *Creating the National Pastime: Baseball Transforms Itself 1903–1953*, Princeton: Princeton University Press, 1956.

Wiggins, Robert Peyton. *The Federal League of Base Ball Clubs: The History of an Outlaw Major League*. Jefferson, NC: McFarland, 2008.

Wright, Marshall D. *The International League: Year-by-Year Statistics, 1884–1953*. Jefferson, NC: McFarland, 1998.

Magazine Articles

Angell, Roger. "Baseball—The Perfect Game." *Holiday*. May 1954.

"Baseball Businessman." *Forbes*. August 1, 1951.

"Baseball—1967." *Newsweek*. December 16, 1967.

"Baseball TV." *Broadcasting*. December 1, 1952.

"Baseball: Weiss at the Plate." *Newsweek*. October 20, 1947.

Bisher, Furman. "The Yankees Second-Hand Pitching." *Baseball Digest*. January 1959.

Breslin, Jimmy. "Worst Baseball Team Ever." *Sports Illustrated*. May 30, 1994.

Connery, Thomas J. "An Analysis of the Chain System." *Baseball Magazine*. February 1946.

Crusinberry, James. "General Managers." *Baseball Magazine*. June 1950.

Daniel, Dan. "DiMaggio, Lazzeri, Moore Deals Stand Out in Barrow's Recollection." *Baseball Magazine*. May 1940.

_____. "Is This a Bad Yankee Club?" *Sport*. February 1959.

_____. "Those Yankees Carry On." *Baseball Magazine*. March 1939.

_____. "Weiss Brought Varied Talents Into General Management of Yankees." *Baseball Magazine*. February 1948.

Dexter, Charles. "New Reign of Terror." *Sport*. February 1954.

Drebinger, John. "Were They Worth the Money?" *Baseball Magazine*. March 1956.

"Editorial Comment." *Baseball Magazine*. December 1947.

"Erratic Superstar." *Time*. June 27, 1960.

Fitzgerald, Ed. "The Fabulous Yogi Berra." *Sport*. August 1951.

Frank, Stanley. "Boss of the Yankees." *Saturday Evening Post*. April 16, 1960.

_____. "The National League Comes Back." *Saturday Evening Post*. July 5, 1952.

_____. "Yankee Farmer." *Elks Magazine*. August 1944.

_____. "Yankee Kingmaker." *Saturday Evening Post*. July 24, 1948.

Freed, Frederick. "The Yankees Mean Business." *Pageant*. October 1948.

Graham, Frank. "Those Yankees." *Liberty*. October 1, 1942.

Gross, Milton. "The Yankees: After Weiss and Stengel, What?" *Sport*. June 1958.

_____. "Will the Yankees Hire a Negro Player?" *Our Sports*. July 1953.

"He Just Keeps Rolling Alone." *Newsweek*. October 20, 1958.

Heinz, W. C. "I Scout for the Yankees." *Collier's*. July 11, 1953.

Henrich, Tommy. "How to Beat the Yankees." *Sport*. April 1954.

"How Much Will It Hurt?" *Baseball Digest*. May 1954.

Kaese, Harold. "Can Martin Play Shortstop?" *Baseball Digest*. February 1958.

Lane, Frank. "Casey Stengel is Wise—But Weiss is Wiser." *Colliers*. May 14, 1954.

_____. "I'm Here to Win a Pennant." *Saturday Evening Post*. June 23, 1956.

Leather, Tom. "The Day Mickey Came to Town." *The Squire*. July 2005.

Leggett, William. "The Men Who Fire Managers." *Sports Illustrated*. September 12, 1966.

Linn, Edward, and Hal Lebovitz. "Vic Power: Master at First." *Saturday Evening Post*. July 29, 1961.

"The Lively One." *Newsweek*. August 9, 1965.

"Lucky to Be a Yankee." *Sport*. October 1959.

"Marvelous Marv." *Sports Illustrated*. July 4, 1994.

Meany, Tom. "George Weiss—The Real Yankee Clipper." *Sport*. December 1947.

_____. "Stengel: The Man Who Laughed Last." *Sport*. April 1950.

"No Harm to Yanks." *Broadcasting*. April 21, 1952.

Olbermann, Keith. "The '62 Mets: Blame Weiss and Stengel." *National Pastime: Review of Baseball History*. May 2006.

"Organizational Men of Baseball." *Life*. September 29, 1958.

Parker, Dan. "Will Television Wreck Sports?" *American Legion Magazine*. August 1949.

"Paul Richards Says—Yanks Need Five Pitchers." *Baseball Digest*. January 1960.
Paxton, Harry T. "Have the Bonus Boys Paid Off for Baseball?" *Saturday Evening Post*. June 21, 1952.
"Pickets March at Yankee Stadium—Charge Jim Crow." *Jet*. May 1, 1952.
"Political Football." *Sports Illustrated*. March 27, 1961.
Rosenthal, Harold. "When the Yankees Won Five Straight World Series." *Baseball Digest*. October 1987.
____. "Yankee Trader." *Collier's* (Undated).
Shaplen, Robert. "How to Build a Ballclub." *Sports Illustrated*. March 5, 1962.
____. "The Yankees Real Boss." *Sports Illustrated*. September 20, 1954.
Smith, Wendell. "The Most Prejudiced Team in Baseball." *Ebony*. May 1953.
"Sports." *The Nutmegger*. June 1971.
Stann, Francis. "General Managers Often Are Unsung When They Win." *Baseball Digest*. February 1967.
"Still No Help From the Front Office." *Sports Illustrated*. April 8, 1963.
Terrell, Roy. "Yankee Secrets?" *Sports Illustrated*. July 22, 1957.
Treder, Steve. "Baseball's New Frontier." *Nine*. Spring 2004.
"The Unknown Yankee." *Newsweek*. July 15, 1967.
Vass, George. "A Long Tough Road Ahead For Two New Expansion Teams." *Baseball Digest*. August 22, 1992.
Veeck, Bill. "I Believe in Fireworks." *Sport*. April 1950.
"Weiss at the Plate." *Newsweek*. October 20, 1947.
Weiss, George. "The Best Decision I Ever Made, Part II." *Sports Illustrated*. March 13, 1961.
____, and Robert Shaplen. "The Man of Silence Speaks, Part I." *Saturday Evening Post*. March 6, 1961.
____, and Robert Shaplen. "The Man of Silence Speaks, Part II." *Saturday Evening Post*. March 13, 1961.
"Why Yanks Second-Hand Pitching Wins." *Baseball Digest*. April 1959.
"World Series Flashbacks." *Sport*. October 1959.
"WPIX Signs to Telecast Yankee Games." *Broadcasting*. February 26, 1951.
"Yankee Dollars." *Newsweek*. February 2, 1959.
"You're Killing Me." *Newsweek*. February 24, 1958.
Young, Dick. "The Man Who Handles Maris and Mantle." *Sport*. May 1962.

Newspapers

Abilene (TX) *Reporter News*
Ada (OK) *Daily News*
Aiken (SC) *Standard and Review*
Albuquerque *Journal*
Alton (IL) *Evening Telegraph*
Altoona (PA) *Mirror*
Amarillo (TX) *Globe*
Ames (IA) *Daily Tribune*
Anderson (IN) *Herald*
Anita (IA) *Tribune*
Anniston (AL) *Star*
Appleton (WI) *Post Crescent*
Arizona Republic (Phoenix)
Athens (OH) *Messenger*
Atlanta *Constitution*
Atlanta *Mirror*
Bakersfield *Californian*
Beatrice (NE) *Daily Sun*
Beckley (WV) *Post Herald*
Bennington (VT) *Banner*
Berkshire (MA) *Evening Eagle*
Big Springs (TX) *Daily Herald*
Billings (MT) *Daily Gazette*
Bismarck (ND) *Tribune*
Bluefield (WV) *Daily Telegraph*
Blytheville (AR) *Courier News*
Boston *Globe*
Bradford (PA) *Era*
Brainerd (MN) *Daily Dispatch*
Bridgeport (CT) *Post*
Bridgeport (CT) *Standard and Tribune*
Bridgeport (CT) *Telegram*
Brownsville (TX) *Herald*
Burlington (IA) *Hawkeye Gazette*
Burlington (NC) *Daily Times News*
Butte (MT) *News*
Canandaigua (NY) *Daily Messenger*
Catonsville (MD) *Herald Argus*
Cedar Rapids (IA) *Gazette*
Charleston (WV) *Daily Mail*
Charleston (WV) *Gazette*
Chester (PA) *Times*
Circleville (OH) *Daily Herald*
Clovis (NM) *News Journal*
Connellsville (PA) *Daily Courier*
Corpus Christi (TX) *Times*
Corsicana (TX) *Daily Sun*
Coshocton (OH) *Tribune*
Cuero (TX) *Record*
Cumberland (NC) *Evening Times*
Danville (VA) *Bee*
Denton (TX) *Record Chronicle*
Dunkirk (NY) *Evening Observer*
Eau Claire (WI) *Daily Telegram*
Edwardsville (IL) *Intelligencer*
El Paso (TX) *Herald Post*
Elyria (OK) *Chronicle Telegram*
Eureka (CA) *Humboldt Standard*
Fitchburg (MA) *Sentinel*
Florence (SC) *Morning News*
Fort Pierce (FL) *News*
Frederick (MD) *News Post*
Freeport (IL) *Journal Standard*
Galveston *Daily News*
Gastonia (NC) *Gazette*
Gettysburg (PA) *Times*
Great Bend (KS) *Daily Tribune*
Greeley (CO) *Daily Tribune*
Hagerstown (MD) *Daily Mail*
Hagerstown (MD) *Morning Herald*
Hamilton (OH) *Daily News*
Hammond (IN) *Times*
Harrisburg (IL) *Daily Register*
Hartford (CT) *Courant*
Hayward (CA) *Daily News*
Helena (MT) *Independent Record*
High Point (NC) *Enterprise*
Holland (MI) *Evening Star*
Huntington (PA) *Daily News*
Hutchinson (KS) *News*
Idaho Falls (ID) *Post Register*
Idaho State Journal (Pocatello)
Indiana (PA) *Evening Gazette*
Iola (KS) *Register*

Ironwood (MI) *Daily Globe*
Jefferson City (MO) *Post Tribune*
Joplin (MO) *Globe*
Kerrville (TX) *Daily Times*
Kingsport (TN) *News*
Kingsport (TN) *Times*
Kingston (NY) *Daily Freeman*
Kokomo (IN) *Tribune*
Lake Charles (LA) *American Press*
Las Vegas Daily Optic
Lawton (OK) *Constitution*
Leavenworth (KS) *Times*
Lebanon (PA) *Daily News*
Lethbridge Daily Herald (Alberta, Canada)
Lima (OH) *News*
Logansport (IN) *Pharos Tribune*
Long Beach (CA) *Independent*
Laredo (TX) *Times News*
Lowell (MA) *Sun*
Lubbock (TX) *Evening Journal*
Madison (WI) *Capital Times*
Mansfield (OH) *News Journal*
Mason City (IA) *Globe Gazette*
Middleburg (KY) *Daily News*
Mitchell (SD) *Daily Republic*
Moberly (MO) *Monitor*
Monessen (PA) *Daily Independent*
Montana Standard (Butte)
Morning Avalanche (Lubbock, TX)
Mount Vernon (IL) *Register News*
Muscatine (IA) *Journal and News Tribune*
Nashua (NH) *Telegraph*
Naugatuck (CT) *News*
New Haven Register
New York Journal American
New York Times
New York World Telegram
Newark Eagle
Newcastle (PA) *News*
Newport (RI) *Daily News*
North Adams (MA) *Evening Transcript*
Oakland Tribune
Ogden (UT) *Standard Examiner*
Olean (NY) *Evening Herald*
Oneonta (NY) *Star*
Oshkosh (WI) *Daily Northwestern*
Oxnard (CA) *Press Courier*
Pacific Stars and Stripes (Tokyo)
Pasadena (CA) *Independent*
Petersburg (IN) *Progress Index*
Port Angeles (WA) *Evening News*
Port Arthur (TX) *News*
Portland (ME) *Press Herald*
Racine (WI) *Journal*
Racine (WI) *Sunday Bulletin*
Raleigh Register
Reno Evening Digest
Salisbury (MD) *Times*
Salt Lake City Tribune
San Antonio Express
San Antonio Light
San Mateo (CA) *Times*
Sandusky (OH) *Register*
Santa Fe New Mexican
Sheboygan (WI) *Daily Press*
Sheboygan (WI) *Journal*
Shelby (KY) *Press*
The Sporting News
Southern Illinoisan (Carbondale, IL)
Statesville (NC) *Daily Record*
Steubenville (OH) *Herald Star*
Stevens Point (WI) *Daily Journal*
Syracuse Herald
Terre Haute (IN) *Star*
Titusville (PA) *Herald*
Traverse City (MI) *Eagle*
Tucson Daily Citizen
Twin Falls (ID) *Times News*
Tyrone (PA) *Daily Herald*
Uniontown (PA) *Evening Standard*
Uniontown (PA) *Morning Herald*
Van Wert (OH) *Times Bulletin*
Waco (TX) *Tribune*
Walla Walla (WA) *Union Bulletin*
Washington, D.C. Evening Star
Waterloo Daily Sun
Waukesha (WI) *Daily Freeman*
Winnipeg Free Press (Manitoba, Canada)
Winona (MN) *Republican Herald*
Wisconsin State Journal (Madison)
Yuma (AZ) *Daily Sun*
Zanesville (OH) *Times Signal*

Online Resources

AHL.com (American Hockey League home page)
anb.org
baltimoresun.com
BaseballAlmanac.com
baseballlibrary.com
baseballpastandpresent.com
baseballreference.com
baseball-fever.com
"Bill Donovan." SABR.org/bioproject
bioguide.congress
bleacherreport.com
bronxbaseballdaily.com
"Casey Stengel." SABR.org/bioproject
en.cyclopedia.net
espn.com
factmonster.com
findagrave.com
"Frank Shaughnessy." SABR.org/bioproject
hillhouseathletichalloffame.com
"Jack Dunn." SABR.org.bioproj
luckyshow.org (Minor League in New Haven, CT)
mayoclinic.org
"Mickey Mantle." SABR.org/bioproject
mlb.com
nymets.mlb.com
oaklandoaks.tripod.com
rollingstones.com
sports.nyhistory.org
sportsillustrated.cnn.com
teachingamericanhistorymd.net
thebaseballpage.com
thisgreatgame.com
waswatching.com
west-point.org

Other Sources

14th Census of the United States, 1920
2010 New Haven Magnet School Catalog

Berra, Yogi, e-mail Interview, January 16, 2012
Brown, Bobby, e-mail Interview, January 10, 2012
Caldwell, Mike (Joplin *Gazette*)—Phone Interview, February 2, 2015
Coleman, Jerry, e-mail Interview, January 8, 2012
George Weiss Files, Baseball Hall of Fame, Cooperstown NY
George Weiss Scrapbook, Baseball Hall of Fame, Cooperstown NY
New Haven Bureau of Vital Statistics
Program Book, James E. Hillhouse High School Fifth Annual Athletic Hall of Fame, March 26, 2011
Senior Class Book, New Haven High School, 1911

Index

Page numbers in **_bold italics_** indicate photographs

Allen, Mel 100, 135, 184
Alou, Jay 177
Altman, George 176
American Association 5, 30, 37, 46, 52, 55, 56, 59, 62, 65, 70, 74, 79, 90
American Association All-Star Game 64
American Labor Party 124
American League 3, 8, 21, 38, 44, 66, 70, 81, 84, 104, 113, 120, 127, 133, 136, 145, 146, 149, 163
Anderson, Craig 166, 170
Appel, Marty 117
Armour, Mark 186, 187
Ashburn, Richie 167
Associated Press 49, 50, 60
Auburn Mets 174

Baker, Bill 53
Ball, Neal 21, 23
Ballentine Beer 135
Baltimore Orioles (American League) 118, 138, 143, 182
Baltimore Orioles (International League) 24, 25–32, 51, 92, 128
Baltimore Sun 51
Baltimore Terrapins 26
Bancroft, Dave 183
Banks, Ernie 186
Barber, Red 72, 135, 186
Barnes, Fred 124
Barney, Rex 43
Barrow, Ed 17, 33, **36**, 42, 58, 59, 60, **63**, 66, 67, 69, 70, 72, 83, 84, 95, 113, 154, 184
Barry, Jack 9
Bartell, Dick 85
Barton, Vince 29, 48, 51
Baseball Hall of Fame 1971 182
Baseball Writers' Association of America 80
Basketball Association of America 4

Bauer, Hank 1, 43, 92, 97, 104, 110, 111, 113, 129, 139, **140**, 146
Beckley, Jake 183
Beggs, Joe 38, 55
Belardi, Wayne 137
Bell, Gus 165, 167, 170
Bender, Charles Albert "Chief" 8, 13, 15, 22
Berra, Yogi 1, 78, 79, **80**, 87, 89, 92, 93, 98, 103, 106, 107, 110, 115, 122, 130, 131, 133, 134, 137, 139, 142, 144, 146, 149, 178, 179, 182, 184
Bevens, Bill 74
Birmingham Barons 123
Blackwell, Ewell 108, 109, 110, 114
Blue Ridge League 28
Blume, Clint 157
Bolen, Stew 29
Bollweg, Don 126
Bonham, Ernie "Tiny" 37, 62
Bonus Rule (1947) 95
Bool, Al 28
Borowy, Hank 65
Boston Bees 62, 90
Boston Braves 12, 29, 65, 67, 170
Boston Red Sox 9, 17, 28, 33, 52, 53, 81, 86, 87, 89, 126, 131, 134, 147, 175
Bouchee, Ed 166
Boyer, Clete 137
Boyer, Ken 179
Boyle, Ralph 31
Bradley, Fred 87
Bramham, Judge William 78
Breadon, Sam 38, 68
Bressoud, Ed 179
Brickley, Charley 7
Bridewiser, Jim 125
Briskin, Shale 187
Brooklyn Dodgers 23, 26, 68, 69, 72, 79, 81, 90, 109, 120, 123, 132, 135, 141, 143, 157, 158, 168
Brooklyn Robins 8, 16
Brown, Bobby 39, 76, 87, 93, 104, 117, 184
Brown, Warren 138
Brown, Willard 120
Buffalo Bisons 48, 61, 79
Buffalo Courier Express 78
Bunning, Jim 177
Burdette, Lew 104, 141
Burke, Mike 184
Burwell, Charles 56
Busch, Gussie 178
Bush, George H.W. 8
Bush, Joe 17
Bush, Prescott 8
Byrd, Harry 114, 126
Byrne, Tommy 68, 69, 94, 104, 131, 133, 142

Camilli, Dolph 146
Candee Rubber Factory 3
Candini, Milo 69
Cannizzero, Chris 166, 178
Cannon, Jimmy 90, 97, 143
Carey, Andy 41, 117, 129, 133, 149
Carey, Max 90
Carlston, Rolf "Swede" 31
Carrasquel, Chico 118
Carter, Leon "Buddy" 127
Cassell, Randall 35
Cereghino, Ed 127
Cerv, Bob 116, 125, 145, 149, 151, 184
Chacon, Elio 167, 170
"chain-store system" 34
Chandler, Happy (Baseball Commissioner) 98, 124
Chandler, Spud 37, 58, 65, 69, 74, 87, 95
Chartak, Mike 65

219

Chicago American 138
Chicago Cubs 12, 56, 61, 67, 95, 170, 175
Chicago White Sox 9, 22, 98, 118, 131, 143, 145, 146, 149
Chiti, Harry 170
Christopher, Joe 167, 178, 179, 186
Cincinnati Reds 55, 72, 76, 85, 108, 123, 158, 170
Cisco, Galen 174, 177
Citi Field 177
Clark, Allie 79, 86
Cleveland Indians 12, 15, 17, 58, 78, 86, 112, 120, 123, 131, 134, 145, 146, 170, 176
Coates, Jim 151
Cobb, Ty 8, 9, 12, 13, 15, 23, 123, 186
Cochrane, Mickey 23
Cohen, Andy 46, 142
Coleman, Clarence "Choo Choo" 166, 169
Coleman, Jerry 39, 41, 86, 107, 108, 111, 113, 116, 134, 141, 142, 184–185
Coleman, Rip 137, 138
Collins, Eddie 9, 23
Collins, Joe 86, 104, *105*, 107, 111, 126, 130, 142
Collins, Kevin 178
Colonial League 5
Columbia School of Journalism 6
Columbus Red Birds 55, 74
Connecticut Sports Writers Alliance 64
Connecticut State League (1899) 5
Connery, Bob 34
Consodine, Bob 66
Continental League 158–160
Cook, Cliff 170
Cooke, Dusty 48
Cooney, Johnny 16
Copa Affair 139–141
Corum, Bill 68–69, 88
Cottrell, John 106
Courtney, Clint 106
Craig, Roger 165, 166, 170, 175, 176
Crandall, Del 177
Creamer, Robert 152
Crelin, Wilbur 50
Cronin, Joe 14, 35, 41, 144
Cronin, Pat 28
Crosetti, Frank 92, 95

Dahlgren, Babe 54, 58
Daley, Arthur 154, 164
Damn Yankees 1
Daniel, Dan 79, 110, 126, 135, 152
Danning, Ike 31
Davenport, Jim 177
Daviaut, Ray 166
Davis, Dwight, Jr. 160
Davis, Harry 170

Davis, Piper 121
Davis, Sammy, Jr. 139
Delsing, Jim 99
DeMaestri, Joe 146
Demerit, Johnny 167
Denver Bears 119, 142, 143
Derry, Russ 76
DeShong, Jimmie 48
Detroit Tigers 12, 28, 53, 61, 74, 98, 99, 126, 138
Devens, Charlie 48
Devine, Bill 41–43
Devine, Bing 178, 181–182
Devine, Joe 106
DeWitt, William O. 116, 117, 118, 133, 137
Dickey, Bill 78, 79, 92, 127, 149
DiGregorio, Joseph 179
DiMaggio, Joe 1, 38, *41*, 42–43, 51, 65, 68–70, 74, *75*, 76, 79, 80, 81, 86, 92, 93, 97, 99, 102, 103, 104, *105*, 107–108, 116, 122, 129, 135, 144, 148, 149, 157, 182
DiMaggio, Vince 62
Dismukes, Dizzy 125
Ditmar, Art 137–138, 151
Doby, Larry 117, 120, 125
Donald, Atley 38, 55
Donovan, William E. "Wild Bill" 16, 17, 18, *19*; *see also* Train Wreck
Down, Fred 113
Downing, Al 129
Drake, Sammy 169
Drebinger, John 102
Dressen, Charlie 92
Drews, Karl 79
Dugan, Edward J. 11
Dugan, "Jumping" Joe 7, 17
Dunn, John Joseph "Jack" 26, *27*, 31
Duren, Ryne 140, 142, 143, 145, 148
Durocher, Leo 64
Dyck, Jim 86

Earnshaw, George 26
Easter, Luke 124
Eastern League 7, 8, 9, 11, 12, 13, 18, 21, 22, 23, 24, 28, 33, 34, 35, 94
Ebbets, Charles 16
Ebbets Field 74, 81, 109, 113
Eckert, William (Baseball Commissioner) 180
Embree, Charlie "Red" 86
Essick, Bill 39–40, 42, 61, 65
Etten, Nick 74

Face, Elroy 151
Fairbanks, Douglas, Jr. 19–20
Farley, James 157
Farnham, Bill 186
Farrell, Doc 50
Federal League 8, 26, 158
Ferrick, Tom 99, 104, 114
Fishel, Bob 117

Fisher, Jack 176
Flynn, John 22
Forbes Field 151
Ford, Whitey 1, 94, **99**, 100, 104, 108, 111, 112, 115, 130, 131, 133, 137, 139–141, 142, 143, 144, 148, 149, 151
Foxx, Jimmy 23
Frank, Stanley 83
Frick, Ford (baseball commissioner) 106, 110, 117, 125, 132, 162, 183

Gabler, John 149
Garrett, Adrian 177
Gehrig, Lou 53, 55, 58, 97
Gibbs, C.M. 51
Gibson, Bob 50
Giles, Warren 54, 175
Gill, John 29
Gimbel, Bernard 157
Ginsburg, Joe 170
Gittel, Allen 65
Gleason, Billy 22, 23
Gleeson, Jimmy 55, 58
Gomez, Lefty 86, 87
Gomez, Ruben 124
Gooch, Johnny 30
Gordon, Joe "Flash" 37, 38, 54, 58, 65, 66, 74, 76, 78–79
Gotto, Ray 168
Goudy, Hank 12
Gould, Alan 35
Graff, Milt 137
Grant, Donald 159–161, *160*, 172, 182
Gray, John 126
Grayson, Harry 154
Green, "Pumpsie" 174, 175
Greenberg, Hank 74, 108, 109, 110, 112, 131
Greenwade, Tom 43, 121
Griffith, Clark 12, 20, 21, 30, 63, 66
Grimes, Burleigh 86, 95
Grimm, Bob 116
Gross, Milton 125, 169
Grote, Jerry 177
Grove, Lefty 23, 26
Gumbert, Harry 29

Haas, Bill 175–176
Hadley, Kent 146, 148
Hafey, Chick 183
Hagerstown Hubs 28
Halberstamm, David 122
Hamey, Roy 56, 69, 101–102, 106–108, 111, 114, 116, 117, 126, 143, 144, 148, 152
Harder, Mel 176
Hargrave, Pinky 35
Harrelson, Derrell "Bud" 176, 177, 182
Harridge, Will 84, *101*
Harris, Bucky 78, 79, 81–82, 85, 88–89
Hassett, Buddy 38, 53, 67
Hauser, Joe 29, 30–31

Hawkins, Jack 50
Heffner, Don 31
Held, Woodie 140
Hemus, Solly 163, 173, 176
Hendley, Bob 177
Henrich, Tommy 39, 66, 69, 74, *75*, 76, 79, 80, 87, 89, 92, 93, 97, 99, 100, 101–102, 107, 122, 129, 182
Herman, Babe 163
Hershberger, Willard 51, 53, 55
Heydler, John A. 17, 19, 30
Hickman, Jim 167, 178
Hill, Gov. David B. 33
Hillhouse High School (New Haven) 1, 4, 5; Hillhouse Athletic Hall of Fame 4, *187*
Hitchcock, Billy 61
Hoag, Myril 48
Hodges, Gil 43, 165–166, 170, *171*, 179, 182, 187
Holmes, Tommy 65
Hook, Jay 170, 177
Hooper, Harry 12, 22, 183
Hopp, Johnny 100, 104, 109, 114, 185
Hornsby, Rogers 163, 170
Houk, Ralph 79, 87, 142, 152
Houston Astros 179
Houston Colt .45s 164–166, 172
Howard, Elston 43, 124, 126–130, *128*, 132, 133, 144, 169
Huggins, Miller, death of 49
Hunt, Ron 175
Hunter, Billy 118, 133, 134, 137, 138
Hurth, Charlie 162
Huston, Cap 16
Hyman, Sammy 14

Intercollegiate Baseball Association (1880) 5
International League 30, 37, 46, 49, 51, 52, 54, 59, 68, 79, 127, 128, 143
International League Hall of Fame 26
Irvin, Monte 120

Jackson, Al 166, 169, 170, 178, 179
Jacobson, Baby Doll 12
James, Bill 61
Japan's Tokyo Dome 177
Jensen, Jackie 94, 108, 145
Jensen, Woody 47
Jersey City Skeeters 49
Johnson, Arnold 118, 138
Johnson, Ban 8
Johnson, Billy 69, 80, 87, 106
Johnson, Don 79, 99
Johnson, Lew 141
Johnson, Walter 8, 12, 13, 21, 32, 183
Jones, Cleon 176, 180, 182
Jones, Sherman 167, 169
Joost, Eddie 58
Joplin Globe 154

Junior World Series 1933 48
Junior World Series 1934 50
Junior World Series 1937 55
Junior World Series 1939 59, 61
Junior World Series 1940 64–65
Junior World Series 1941 65–66
Junior World Series 1942 68

Kahn, Roger 122
Kanehl, Rod 172
Kansas City Athletics 43, 134, 137, 138, 145, 146, 148, 149
Kansas City Blues 56–59, 118–119, 124, 126, 131
Kansas City Monarchs 74, 123, 124
Kansas-Oklahoma-Missouri League 94
Kapitzke, August 4
Kefauver, Sen. Estes 158–159
Kell, George 43
Kelleher, Frank 54, 65
Keller, Charlie *41*, 55, 58, 59, 66, 69, 74, 76, 80, 81, 87, 92, 93, 97
Kelley, Joe 183
Kelly, Billy 78
Kelly, Mike 49
Kennedy, Ray L. 50, 74
Kies, Norman 53
Killiam, Mrs. Dorothy 160
Kiner, Ralph 163
King, Betty 177
Kling, Johnny 56
Knapp, Charles H. 25, 32
Koenig, Mark 34
Konstanty, Jim 131
Koosman, Jerry 178, 182
Koppett, Leonard 129
Kraly, Bill 125
Kranepool, Ed 171, 176, 182
Krichell, Paul 39–40, 53, 65, 83, 106, 128
Kryhoski, Dick 93
Kubek, Tony 129, 134, 137, 141, 151
Kucks, John 130, 139, 145, 149
Kuhel, Joe 30, 95
Kuzava, Bob 104, 109, 114

Labine, Clem 170
Landis, Judge Kenesaw (baseball commissioner) 16, 17, 26, *27*, 30, 56, 63, 64, 66
Landrith, Hobie 165–166, *166*, 172
Lane, Frank 76, 96, 98, 108, 118, 185
Lang, Don 65
Larry, Frank 177
Larry, Lyn 33
Larsen, Don 118, 130, 131, 132, 135, 137, 141, 143, 145, 146
Lavagetto, Cookie 163, 173, 176
Law, Vernon 151
Lazzeri, Tony 38, 55
Leishman, Eddie 83
Lemon, Bob 117

Levitt, Dan 186, 187
Levy, Ed 70
Lewis, Johnny 178
Lieb, Fred 94
Lighthouse Point 8
Lighthouse Point Park 7, 9, 11
Lima News 171
Lindell, Johnny 65, 69, 70, 87, 92, 93
Linton, Bob 31
Little World Series 1922 16
Little World Series 1932 46
Loepp, George 28, 29
Loes, Billy 167
Lollar, Sherman 93
Lombardi, Ernie 55
"Lonesome George" 90
Lopat, Ed 1, 87–88, 94, 100, 104, *105*, 106, *107*, 108, 110, 111, 114, 122, 143
Lopez, Hector 129, 145, 149
Louisville Colonels 62
Lumpe, Jerry 134, 145, 149
Lyle, Sparky 147

Mack, Connie 12, 19, 23, 49, 118, 131
MacKenzie, Ken 167
MacPhail, Larry 63–64, 68, 69, 72, 73–74, 75–76, *77*, 79, 81–83, 84, 85, 91, 106
MacPhail, Lee 83, 106, 120, 137, 143
Maglie, Sal 135, 141
Mahan, Eddie 7
Maisel, Fritz 26
Majeski, Hank 65, 68, 69
Major League Baseball Players Association 142
Malone, Louis 16
Maloney, Jim 178
Mamaux, Al 45, 47, 49
Mantilla, Felix 174
Mantle, Mickey 1, 43, 92, 94, 103–104, 106, 108–109, 111, 116, 117, 120, 122, 129, 130, 131, 133, 134, 135, 139, 141, 142, 143, 144, 145, 146, 148, 149, *150*, 151, 163, 184
Mapes, Cliff 87
Maranville, Rabbit 9, 12
Marichal, Juan 177
Maris, Roger 43, 145, 146, 147, 149, *150*, 151, 164
Marquard, Rube 183
Marquez, Luis 123–124
Marshall, Cuddles 87
Marshall, Jim 170
Martin, Billy 94, 98, *103*, 108, 111, 113, 124, 129, 132, 133, 134, 139–141, 145, 149
Martin, Gene 83
Martyn, Bob 140
Mascot Hall of Fame 177
Mathes, Joe 68
Mauch, Gene 162
May, Merrill 58, 59
Mayo Clinic 142

Index

Mays, Willie 121, 123, 159, 177, 186
Mazeroski, Bill 151
McCann, Gene 39–40
McCarthy, Joe 49, 53, 55, 58, *63*, 65, 68, 69, 70, 73, *77*, 78, 85, 95, 184
McCorry, Bill 121
McCovey, Willie 186
McCullough, Clyde 61–62
McDermott, Mickey 134, 137
McDonald, Jim 106
McDonald, Joe 178
McDonald, John 81
McDougald, Gil 41, 103, 104, *105*, 107, 111, 113, 133, 134, 144, 163
McGowan, Frank 31
McGraw, John *27*, 90
McGraw, "Tug" 178, 182
McHale, John 138
McKechnie, Bill 55
McMahon, Jack 137
McMillan, Roy 177
McQuinn, George 51, 54, 58, 79, 80
Meany, Tom 162
Mercer, Bobby 43, 46
Metheny, Bud 70
Meyer, Bill 50, 58, 62, 64, 66, 68, 74, 78, 85
Meyers, John "Chief" 11, 13
Milan, Clyde 20, 22
Miller, Bill 111, 125
Miller, Bob 166
Miller, Bob J. 170
Miller, Bob "Lefty" 170
Miller, Eddie 58
Milwaukee Braves 141, 143, 175
Milwaukee Brewers (minor league) 90
Minneapolis Millers 46, 62
Miranda, Willy 138
Mishkin, Sollie 51
Mr. Met 177
Mize, Johnny *93*, 97, 100, 102, 104, 106, 109, 110, 114, 185
Mizell, Vinegar Bend 170
Montreal Royals 47, 54
Moore, Gene 67
Moore, Wiley "Cy" 50
Moran, Al 174, 175
Morgan, Tom 104, 108, 137
Muehlebach Field 56
Murphy, Bob 163
Murphy, Johnny 38, 50, 65, 174, 182
Murray, Jim 177
Musial, Stan 182

National Association of Professional Baseball Leagues 70
National Basketball League 4
National League 8, 29, 69, 114, 116, 157, 158, 163, 173, 175
Neal, Charlie 167
Nelson, Lindsey 163
Nettles, Gregg 147

Neun, Johnny 28, 50, 58, 59, 62, 65, 66, 69, 70, 85, 92, 95
New Haven, CT 3
New Haven Colonials 1, *6*, 7, 9, 13, 17
New Haven Indians 16
New Haven Max Feds 5
New Haven Murlins 5, 8, 11
New Haven Profs 17, 20, 22, 23, 24, 25, 28
New Haven Weissmen 11, 12, 13, 15
New Haven White Wings 8
New York Baseball Writers' Association 109
New York Daily News 61
New York Giants 9, 11, 17, 72, 93, 103, 110, 113, 117, 141, 157, 158, 162
New York Herald Tribune 4, 84
New York Journal American 68–69
New York Metropolitan Baseball Club, Inc. (NY Mets) 160–168
New York Mets Hall of Fame 187
New York Mirror 66
New York Post 129
New York Times 116, 126, 154
New York World Telegram 154
New York World Tribune & Sun 126
New York Yankees 1, 2, 3, 14, 16, 17, 18, 28, 31, 34, 38, 44, 45, 54, 56–59, 64, 66, 69, 72, 76, 78–79, 81, 95, 98, 108, 118, 120, 126, 130, 137, 146, 158, 177, 180
Newark Bears (International League) 35, 39, 45–59, 95, 123
Newark Evening News 49
Newhouser, Hal 87
Newkirk, Floyd 51
Newsom, Bobo 79
Newspaper Enterprise Association 154
Newsweek 141
Niarhos, Gus 86, 87
Niehoff, Bert 86
Niss, Lou 169
Noren, Irv 108, 114, 126, 133, 138
Norfolk Tars 38, 58

Oakland Oaks 21, 53, 55, 57–58, 90–92, 98
"Old Perfesser" 90
Olsen, Joe 50
Orange Street School (New Haven) 4
Ostrowski, Joe 99
Overmire, Stubby 104
Owen, Marvin 46
Owens, Jesse 53

Pacific Coast League 21, 30, 33, 37, 92

Page, Joe 74, 80, 81, 89, 95, 98, 107
Parker, Dan 37
Parsons, Tom 177
Patterson, Arthur "Red" 84, 117
Paul, Gabe 184
Payson, Joan Whitney *159*, 159–161, 181, 187
Pennock, Herb 9, 49
Perry, Gaylord 177
Philadelphia Athletics 7, 9, 12, 19, 20, 23, 26, 49, 118, 126, 131
Philadelphia Phillies 30, 116, 126, 141, 158
Phillips, Jack 70
Pilarcik, Hal 138
Pillette, Dwayne 99
Pisoni, Jim 140
Pittsburgh Pirates 14, 29, 41, 48, 85, 101, 141, 151, 158, 170
Pittsfield Hillies 28
Podoloff, Abraham 4
Podoloff, Jacob 4
Podoloff, Maurice 4
Podres, Johnny 132
Polo Grounds 7, 8, 160, 162, 163, 168, 172, 175
Porterfield, Bob 88–89, 97, 104
Povich, Shirley 116
Power, Vic 124, 126
Powers, Francis J. 43
Powers, Jimmy 61
Priddy, Gerry 61, 65
Puccinelli, George 48, 52

Queen, Mel 65
Quincy Jets 174

Raschi, Vic 78, 80, 87–88, 94, 100, 102, *103*, 104, 110, 111, 112, 115, 130, 148
Redding, Cannonball Dick 123, 183
Reese, Jimmy 33
Reese, Pee Wee 43, 61
Regan, Bill 31
Renna, Bill 126
Reynolds, Allie 78, 79, 80, 87–88, 94, 97, 100, 104, *107*–108, 110, 111, 112, 114, 115, 118, 130, 182
Rice, Grantland 84, 91
Richards, Paul 118, 129, 138, 175
Richardson, Bobby 140, 141
Richman, Art 183, 184
Richmond, Beryl 31
Richmond Virginians 143
Rickey, Branch 34, 37, 45, 51, 56, 68, 69, 72, 79, 81, 95, 158, 160
Riddle, Johnny 62
Rizzuto, Phil 61, 65, 69, 97, 99, 101, 102, 107–108, 110, 111, 118, 129, 130, 133, 134–135, *136*
Roberts, Curt 137
Robertson, Bill 126
Robinson, Aaron 69, 87

Index

Robinson, Bill 53
Robinson, Eddie 80, 114, 126
Robinson, Jackie 79, 120, 122, 125
Robinson, Wilbert "Uncle Robbie" 30
Rochester Red Wings 48, 53–54, 61–62
Rodgers, Frank 30
Roger Sherman School (New Haven) 186
Rolfe, Red 38, 46, 48, 50, 69
Roosevelt, Franklin W. 66, 157
Rosar, Buddy 54, 59
Rose, Pete 175
Rosen, Al 113, 117
Rosenthal, Harold 4
Roy, Luther 29
Ruffing, Red 69, 70, 74, 78, 163
Runyon, Damon 3
Ruppert, Colonel Jacob 7, 8, 16, 17, 19, 31–32, 33–35, *36*, 37–38, *42*, 43–44, 45, 46, 47, 51, 58, 72, 129; death 60
Ruppert Stadium (Kansas City) 56, 64
Ruppert Stadium (Newark) 45, 53
Ruth, Babe 8, 17, 26, 34, 134, 164, 186
Ryan, Nolan 182

Saigh, Fred 106
Sain, Johnny 104, 109, 111, 112, 114, 130, 131, 185
St. Louis Browns 26, 66, 70, 92, 106, 117, 120
St. Louis Cardinals 34, 45, 51, 55, 68, 106, 115, 116, 141, 176, 178, 179, 182
Salisbury Braves 174
Saltzgaver, Jack 48, 50, 70, 74
San Diego Padres (Pacific Coast League) 124
San Francisco Giants 167
San Francisco Seals 51, 53, 62, 92
Sand, Heinie 31
Sanford, Fred 92, 104
Santa Barbara Rancheros 174
Saturday Evening Post 139
Savin Rock (Ball Park) 24
Sawyer, Eddie 100
Scarborough, Ray 110
Scarsella, Les 58, 59
Schacht, Al 85
Schalk, Roy 50, 51
Schmitz, Johnny 108
Seaver, Tom 179–180, 182
Seeds, Bob 55, 58
Selkirk, George 38, 48, 50, 86
Selma, Dick 178
Sewell, Joe 49
Shantz, Bobby 137–138, 151
Shaughnessy, Frank "Shag" 47, 54
Shaughnessy Playoffs (Plan) 47, 49

Shaw, Bob 180
Shawkey, Bob 49, 52
Shea, Frank "Spec" 79, 80, 87, 89, 108, 182
Shea, William 157–159, *158*
Shea Stadium 160, 168, 176, 177, 178, 179
Sheehan, Joseph F. 116
Sherry, Norman 174
Shinault, Enoch "Ginger" 14
Shore, Ernie 9
Siebern, Norm 142, 144, 146
Silvera, Charlie 86
Simmons, Al 23
Simpson, Harry "Suitcase" 140, 141
Simpson, William 160
Sisler, George 12
Skiff, Bill 38, 50
Skowron, Bill 125, 129, 131, 134, 142, 144, 146, 149
Slaughter, Enos 116, 131, 134, 145, 185
Slocum Award 109
Smith, Bobby Jean 170
Smith, Charlie 179
Smith, Hal 138
Smith, Mayo 96
Smith, Red 135, 154, 157, 183, 186–187
Smith, Wendell 125
Smythe, Harry 31
Snider, Duke 174, 176
Sothern, Denny 30
Souchock, Steve 87
Spahn, Warren 178, 179
Speaker, Tris 12, 45
The Sporting News 13, 20, 35, 37, 38, 53, 54, 60, 62, 66, 100, 105, 109, 117, 118, 125, 126, 129, 130, 132, 135, 143, 145, 154, 162, 168, 170, 171, 177, 188
spring training 17, 18, 22, 23, 28, 50, 53, 58, 61, 65, 67, 76, 85–87, 89, 92, 95, 97–98, 103–104, 108, 111, 115–116, 124, 126–130, 134, 137, 142–143, 148–149, 161, 168–170, 176, 178, 180, 182
Stafford, Bill 151
Stainback, Tuck 76
Stallard, Tracy 174, 175
Stanky, Eddie 178, 179
Stengel, Casey 74, 89–94, 101, 103–104, 110, 111, *112*, 116, 117, 118, 119, 129, 130, 132, 134, 135, 139, 141, 142, 143, 145, 146, 148, 149, 151–152, 154, 157, 164–168, *165*, 176–180, 186
Stengel, Edna (wife) 132
Stevens, Dr. Mal 81
Stewart, Ed 86, 87
Stirnweiss, George "Snuffy" 68, 69, 74, 76, 97, 99
Stoneham, Horace 103, 110
Stroner, Jim 31, 38

Sturdivant, Tom 43, 127, 134, 145
Sturm, Johnny 65, 67
Sundra, Steve 53, 55, 58
Swoboda, Ron 176
Syracuse Chiefs 52
Syracuse Herald Journal 66

Tamulis, Vito 53, 55, 58
Taylor, Sammy 170
Terry, Bill 140
Terry, Ralph 43, 145, 149, 151
Thomas, Frank 167, 170, 177
Thomson, "Big Jim" 162
Thomson, Bobby 104, 168
Three-I League 30
Throneberry, Marv 142, 146, 172, *173*, 174
Thurman, Bob 123
Tillinghast, Huston L'Hommedieu 33
Tolson, Charles "Slug" 30–31
Toporcer, Specs 48
Topping, Dan 72, *73*, 81–83, 84, 86, 88, 91, 94, 97, 100, 102, 106, 111, 116, 121, 122, 126, 131, 133, 142, 143, 134, 146, 151–152, 154, 155, 158, 161, 185
Toronto Maple Leafs 46, 50–51
"Trader George " 96
Train Wreck 1923 18–20; *see also* Donovan, William
Trautman, George 52
Triandos, Gus 125, 127, 138
Tucson Lizards 62
Turley, Bob 118, 131, 142, 143, 144, 145, 151
Turner, Jim 92, 95
"Ty Cobb All Stars" 90

*United Press{en}*113
Upton, Tommy 108
Urban, Jack 137

Valo, Elmer 149
Vaughn, Arky 41
Veeck, Bill 78, 88, 90, 117, 124, 146, 185
Virdon, Bill 43, 116, 126, 127, 151
Vitt, Oscar 52, 54, 58

Wagner, Mayor Robert 157, 160
Wakabayashi, Harry, Tadashi 132
Wakefield, Bill 176
Wakefield, Dick 98
Walker, Dixie 46, 47–48, 52
Walker, Herbert G. 160
Wallop, Douglass 1
Walls, Lee 166
Walsingham, William, Jr. 68
Waner, Lloyd 41
Waner, Paul 41
Washington Senators 12, 20, 23, 29, 78, 95, 98, 104, 134, 182
Weaver, Jim 48

Weaver, Monte 31
Webb, Del 72, *73*, 81–83, 84, 94, 97, 103, 121, 122, 126, 132, 143, 145, 158, 185
Weiss, Anna Kapitzke (mother) 3, 4, 56; death 57
Weiss, Conrad (father) 3, 4
Weiss, Edwin (brother) 4, 57
Weiss, Florence (sister) 4, 57
Weiss, George *52*, *63*, *77*, *85*, *101*, *153*, *155*, *161*, *187*
Weiss, Hazel H. Wood (wife) 32, *57*, 57, 66, 74, 96, 117–118, 132, 157, 182, 183, 185
Weiss, Jeorge (grandfather) 3
Weiss, Mary Koppman (grandmother) 3
Weiss Park 13, 15, 17
Western Association 51
Western International League 79
Westrum, Wes 176, 179, 180
Wheat, Zach 23, 97
White, Ernie 176
"Whiz Kids" (Philadelphia Phillies, 1950) 100

Wicker, Kemp 55
Wight, Bill 87
Willey, Carl 175
Williams, Joe 126, 154
Williams, Ted 80, 86, 87, 141, 154
Wilson, Artie 121, 123
Wilson, Jimmy 16, 35
Wittich, Porter 154
Wood, Allen 57, 74
Wood, "Smoky" Joe 12, 17
Woodling, Gene 92, 111, 113
Woods, Jim 135
WOR-TV (Channel 9 New York) 163
World Series 1923 17
World Series 1942 68
World Series 1947 81
World Series 1949 94
World Series 1950 100
World Series 1951 104–105
World Series 1952 108–109
World Series 1953 113–114
World Series 1955 132
World Series 1956 135

World Series 1957 141
World Series 1958 143
World Series 1960 151
World Series 1964 178
World Series 1969 182
World War I 72
World War II 67, 69, 72, 74, 76
Wright, Mel 127
Wrigley Field 67
Wynn, Early 117

Yale Elis 8, 9
Yale University 4, 5, 7, 17
Yankee Stadium 85, 96, 110, 118, 124–125, 129, 131, 142, 151
Yawkey, Tom 81, 87
The Year the Yankees Lost the Pennant 1
Young, Buddy 121
Young, Dick *155*

Zaharias, Babe Didrikson 85
Zimmer, Don 165–166
Zuber, Bill 70
Zwilling, Dutch 56, 58

www.ingramcontent.com/pod-product-compliance
Ingram Content Group UK Ltd.
Pitfield, Milton Keynes, MK11 3LW, UK
UKHW050702160426
5217IPUK00038B/1876